Toward a Humanist Justice

Toward a Humanist Justice

The Political Philosophy of Susan Moller Okin

Edited by

Debra Satz

Rob Reich

OXFORD
UNIVERSITY PRESS
2009

Oxford University Press, Inc., publishes works that further
Oxford University's objective of excellence
in research, scholarship, and education.

Oxford   New York
Auckland   Cape Town   Dar es Salaam   Hong Kong   Karachi
Kuala Lumpur   Madrid   Melbourne   Mexico City   Nairobi
New Delhi   Shanghai   Taipei   Toronto

With offices in
Argentina   Austria   Brazil   Chile   Czech Republic   France   Greece
Guatemala   Hungary   Italy   Japan   Poland   Portugal   Singapore
South Korea   Switzerland   Thailand   Turkey   Ukraine   Vietnam

Copyright © 2009 by Oxford University Press, Inc.

Published by Oxford University Press, Inc.
198 Madison Avenue, New York, New York 10016

www.oup.com

Oxford is a registered trademark of Oxford University Press

Library of Congress Cataloging-in Publication Data
Toward a humanist justice : the political philosophy of Susan Moller Okin/
edited by Debra Satz, Rob Reich
    p.   cm.
Articles previously presented at a conference.
Includes bibliograghical references.
ISBN 978-0-19-533739-6
1. Feminism—Congresses.   2. Women's rights—Congresses.   3. Equality—Congresses.
4. Justice—Congresses.   5. Liberalism—Congresses.   6. Okin, Susan Moller—Political and social views
—Congresses.   I. Satz, Debra.   II. Reich, Rob.

HQ1106.T68 2008
301.92—dc22   2008012284

9   8   7   6   5   4   3   2   1

Printed in the United States of America
on acid-free paper

Acknowledgements

We are indebted to many people for helping this book get to press. In particular, we would like to thank Joan Berry for her handling the upfront logistics of the conference that resulted in this volume, for her scanning the volume's chapters, for corresponding with authors, and for always working with good humor. Alexander Berger did a magnificent job indexing the volume and also managed to catch a number of errors in the text. We are also grateful to our Oxford University Press editor Peter Ohlin and production editors Christi Stanforth and Jessica Ryan, and to a resourceful Stanford undergraduate, Meredith Ely, who undertook formatting revisions and updates of the chapters as they came in. The Barbara and Buzz McCoy Program in Ethics in Society and the Dean's Office of the School of Humanities and Sciences at Stanford University provided support for the original conference that we gratefully acknowledge here. Finally, we wish to thank the many authors whose works appear here, as well as their thoughtful commentators and the many other conference participants, including Susan Moller Okin's former students, who traveled far and wide to attend.

The proceeds of this book are donated to the Global Fund for Women, an international organization committed to "a world of equality and social justice," whose work Susan supported.

Contents

Toward a Humanist Justice

Introduction

Toward a Humanist Justice

A Critical Introduction to the Work of Susan Moller Okin

Debra Satz and Rob Reich

Susan Moller Okin (1946–2004) was a liberal theorist whose feminist perspective challenged the complacency or total inattention of political philosophers to questions about gender and the family. She insisted that liberalism, properly understood as a theory opposed to social hierarchies and supportive of individual freedom and equality, provided the tools for criticizing the substantial inequalities between men and women.

The feminist perspective that informed and guided all of Okin's work is not difficult to identify. For Okin, feminism represented the view that women, as well as men, are full human beings to which a theory of justice must apply.[1] Despite the simplicity and seemingly unobjectionable nature of the claim, Okin's work showed that most political theories, both past and present, have failed to view women as full human beings. Okin assumed nothing more complicated than the moral and political equality of men and women. She sought then to rehabilitate political theories, particularly the political theory of liberal egalitarianism, in such a way as to accommodate the equality of the sexes. And she did so with an eye toward improving the actual condition of women and families in the existing world of massive gender inequalities.

The differences in the lives of men and women are systematic and pervasive. In every society in the world, to varying degrees, women have fewer opportunities than men, must contend with stereotypes about what they can do and be, and have less earning power than men even when they perform equivalent work. Women are disproportionately victims of sexual violence, including rape, incest, and battery, and are frequently subject to sexual harassment. In some societies, they lack equal rights under the law. In the United States, women are more likely than men to be poor and are more likely to be marginalized from the important political and economic positions of authority and power. There has never been a female U.S. president, only a handful of women lead Fortune 500 companies, and in 2006 there were only 14 women out of 100 senators. Globally, one-fourth of all households in the world are headed by women, and

---

1. The title for this introduction is taken from the concluding chapter of Okin's *Justice, Gender, and the Family* (hereafter *JGF*). For a statement of Okin's perspective, see *WWPT*, 274; *JGF*, 23.

female-headed households are among the world's poorest. In many cultures, "women and girls tend to get less to eat and less health care than men and boys in the same household."[2] If more political theorists now acknowledge the centrality of these facts to questions of social justice, this is in large part due to the contributions of Susan Moller Okin.

From the outset, Okin's work was guided by the desire to contribute to the end of gender inequality—indeed, to the abolition of gender itself—and to the creation of a more just society. While her work is unmistakably aimed at an audience of scholars, and while she wrote in the meter of academic political theory, the practical consequences of her scholarship are impossible to miss. At a ceremony to mark her installation as the Marta Sutton Weeks Professor of Ethics in Society at Stanford University, she remarked, "Having some influence on the world outside as well as inside the university has always been of great importance to me." She described her scholarship as driven by an interest in "positive change—in changes that will both make ours a more just society and will help it to exert influence toward greater global justice."[3]

She did this by showing how the traditional family, with its unequal division of domestic labor and with the different societal roles and expectations that attach to men and women as a result of their sex, interacts with the employment structure to render women vulnerable and unequal. She argues that the inequalities in the workplace and at home "reinforce and exacerbate each other,"[4] so that one cannot dismantle gender inequality without also attending to the differences between men and women in families. Women spend far more time doing household labor and parenting children than their male counterparts. In the words of one scholar, women employed in the labor market work a "second shift" at home, while women who work only in the home perform unpaid and unrecognized labor.

Okin points out the existence of a "cycle of vulnerability," which is established in the mutually reinforcing structures of work and family that condition the lives and choices of men and women. Women who assume primary responsibilities for parenting and the household cannot generally pursue high-paid and rewarding careers. Such careers reward investment in human capital, not in raising children, and are structured on the assumption that the worker has a wife at home who can devote herself to the household. At the same time, the discrimination and stereotyping that lead to women's lower pay for work equivalent to men's reinforces the allocation of domestic work in the family to women. It makes sense to withdraw women and not men from the workforce to assume parenting duties if women's pay prospects are lower than men's. After women leave the labor force, they are increasingly economically dependent on their husbands. Women's standard of living typically declines after divorce, while men's remains at least the same.

In 2005, a year after her premature death, scholars assembled to take stock of Okin's contributions to our understanding of political theory and the implications of her

---

2. Okin, "Poverty, Well-Being and Gender: What Counts, Who's Heard?" 284.
3. Okin's remarks on her appointment as the first Marta Sutton Weeks Professor of Ethics in Society, Stanford University, April 27, 1993.
4. *JGF*, 146.

work for political philosophy. In what follows, we provide an introduction to certain crucial ideas that structure her work and thought. Our aim is not to provide a comprehensive overview of her vast scholarly output, but to emphasize those ideas that will aid the reader in understanding Okin's work and the contributions to this volume.

THE FAMILY AND POLITICAL THEORY

What would it mean for political theory to include women as the equals of men? Okin's answer is that we must direct our attention to the family. "There is no way," she writes, "in which we can include women, formerly minor characters, as major ones within the political drama without challenging basic and age-old assumptions about the family, its traditional sex roles, and its relation to the wider world of political society."[5] The vulnerability of women and the transmission of gender inequality across generations begins, Okin argues, in the family.

In her first book, *Women in Western Political Thought* (1979b), Okin examines the great historical traditions in political theory through the works of Plato, Aristotle, Rousseau, and John Stuart Mill. Her thesis is that the ideology of the "natural" family, in which women are assumed to have primary responsibility for home and children, has been taken to justify the exclusion of women from public political life. Mothers are held to naturally desire to raise children, and so accept this role willingly. Fathers represent the interests of their families in the public political realm and work to support them. Women have been regarded as "by nature" unsuited to the public realm and rightly focused on the family. Even Mill, an early philosophical advocate of women's equality, assigns primary parenting responsibilities to women. Only Plato's radical abolition of the family in *The Republic* frees women to participate on equal terms with men.

Okin argues that most of the existing traditions of political philosophy cannot "sustain the inclusion of women" in their subject matter. These traditions, she argues, are deeply committed to the differentiation of the functions of men and women. The assumption of the natural inequality of men and women is not simply an oversight, or a passing bias, but the fundamental and enduring premise of earlier political theories. When we view these traditions from the perspective of women's freedom and equality, we find them to be deeply inadequate.

And what of contemporary political philosophy, produced by theorists who presumably have shed antiquated assumptions about the natural differences between men and women and who accept as given the equal citizenship of men and women? In *Justice, Gender, and the Family* (1989a), Okin continues to use gender as a lens through which to evaluate the most influential of current political theories. For the most part, she finds them similarly wanting.

Okin first analyzes the situation of women in the family structure of modern society. Okin argues that the interactions of the unequal domestic division of labor and the gendered work environment produce a cycle of vulnerability for women. Women clock long hours of housework in the family, without pay, and consequently have less time

5. *WWPT*, 286.

and energy to commit to wage work. Because of their lower levels of workforce commitment and their tendency to work part time at jobs that accommodate the family's needs, women's wages tend to become lower in relation to men's as they get older. This renders women more dependent on their husbands and more vulnerable through marriage and parenting. At the same time, differences in earning power between husbands and wives lead families to prioritize husbands' careers and wages. Inequalities in the workplace and the family thus are mutually reinforcing.

Yet, Okin argues, contemporary political theories fail to address inequalities in the home, inequalities that reverberate outward into unequal life chances for men and women. Even John Rawls, whose magisterial *A Theory of Justice* (1999c) makes a striking case for greater equality in society, simply assumes that families can be represented by "heads of households" (whom he assumes to be male). Okin argues that this approach ignores both the existence of conflicts within the family and the fact that members of families are differentially situated with respect to benefits and burdens. Rawls simply assumes the existence of the gendered family. And he ignores the ways that this gendered family and other social institutions interact.

While its neglect of the family and gender has led some feminist philosophers to completely reject liberal political theory, Okin argues that liberalism has emancipatory potential for women. In her essay "Reason and Feeling in Thinking about Justice" (1989b), Okin contends that a reformed liberal theory can accommodate the basic feminist premise about the moral and political equality of men and women. Against those feminist theorists who argue that social contract theories abstract away from all relevant differences between people and are inherently individualistic, Okin argues that Rawls' "original position" is not a useless abstraction but a way of capturing respect for human differences. The point of the Rawlsian original position is to set limits on how certain morally arbitrary differences—differences due to race, class, or gender—lead to social inequality and oppression. On Okin's view, the original position is actually a device for modeling empathy for others. The tensions between feminism and liberal political theory are, on her view, not inevitable. Indeed, liberalism's emphasis on ethical individualism and the equal liberty of all persons contains, Okin believes, a conceptual toolbox that not merely accommodates but actually requires the basic feminist premise to which she is committed. However, to demonstrate the compatibility of liberalism and feminism requires a recasting of the traditional distinction between public and private and requires viewing the family as, at least in part, a political institution.

THE PERSONAL IS POLITICAL

Okin recognizes that reconciling feminism and liberalism would require significant revisions to the latter. In particular, traditional liberalism's view of the family as part of a separate, private sphere altogether protected from state intervention is mistaken. Justice cannot stop at the household's doorstep if the liberty and equality of men and women are to be secured.

Indeed, the picture of the family as part of a sealed-off realm of privacy does not even match the reality of families. Existing laws govern much of the behavior of the family, defining who has the right to form a family, the tax benefits and burdens of having a family, and the terms of divorce. Further, family structure is itself shaped by other social institutions. The organization of work, the availability of parental leave and day care, and the rate of remuneration for men's and women's work all affect the ways of becoming and organizing a family. Okin proposes redesigning these institutions to make it easier for men and women to play equal parenting roles within the family and to have equal access to careers and meaningful work. For example, she advocates splitting paychecks between adult family members, the publicly subsidized provision of high-quality day care, and the greater availability of rewarding part-time work.

As a liberal theorist, however, Okin recognizes the need for privacy. Privacy allows for the development of intimate relations with others, offers a safe space for experimentation with social roles and identities, and simply allows for time alone. Okin is critical of those feminists who wish to abolish the private sphere; as several of the chapters in this volume discuss, Okin seeks to transform it.

Okin's liberalism also embraces the importance of respect for individual choices. If men and women make different choices when faced with equal opportunities and life chances, then liberals will have to accept such choices. But she argues forcefully that men and women do not now face equal opportunities and life chances. If we look at the family and the distribution between husbands and wives of such important social goods as work, self-esteem, physical and economic security, and opportunities for self-development, "we find socially constructed inequalities between them right down the list."[6] Girls are socialized from a very young age to plan their lives around marriage and childbearing; many occupations tend to be sex segregated and sex typed. Following John Stuart Mill's lead in *The Subjection of Women*, Okin argues that we simply do not know what choices men and women would make if they were socialized differently and had equal opportunities.

MULTICULTURAL TENSIONS

Okin's work takes as central the fact that women are disadvantaged not only by laws and social structures but also by norms and expectations. In all of the world's cultures, different expectations attach to men and women simply on the basis of their sex. Gender, for Okin, is the deeply entrenched institutionalization of sexual differences,[7] a phenomenon at work not only in laws but also in sociocultural norms. To put the matter most plainly, girls and boys grow up with very different ideas of what they can be and do. Additionally, there are often strong sanctions applied when individuals try to break out of their traditional gender roles. For this reason, feminism is a countercultural movement, challenging the universal cultural division of men and women into distinct and unequal groups.

This critical position of feminists with regard to cultures puts feminists in some tension with those multicultural theorists who argue that liberal states ought to issue collective rights to make accommodations to the practices of different cultural

6. *JGF*, 136.
7. *JGF*, 6.

groups. A central aspiration of multicultural political theory is to make more just the relationship between minority ethnocultural groups and the majority group in any society by making it easier for the minority group to maintain its distinctive way of life. While sympathetic to this general aspiration, Okin is nevertheless sharply critical of the means by which multicultural defenders seek to improve the conditions of minority cultural groups. Her concern, like those of other critics, is that multiculturalism at one and the same time can have salutary consequences for intergroup equality but deleterious consequences for intragroup equality. When the state seeks through collective rights or accommodations to improve the status of minority groups and their members with respect to the larger society, it can also undermine the status of the weaker members within minority groups.

The primary reason has to do with the culturally sanctioned subordination of women. Okin argues that group rights often reinforce the subordination of women within groups. Because many traditional minority groups have cultural or religious norms that subordinate women to men, when the state confers rights to groups, it also tends to sanction and strengthen the patriarchy within those groups, and thereby makes less likely any attempts by women to alter their traditions from within.

The inattention of multicultural theorists to inequalities between men and women within cultural groups is especially striking since so many of the contested claims of minority groups concern questions related to gender, including the forced marriage of underage daughters to strangers, cultural defenses of clitoridectomy and polygamy, and the enforcement or sanction of traditional dress codes for girls. Practices such as these mean that feminism cannot issue a blanket defense of minority group rights. Indeed, Okin provoked a still ongoing controversy with her suggestion that, in the case of a more patriarchal minority culture operating in the context of a less patriarchal majority culture, women "*might* be much better off if the culture into which they were born were either to become extinct…or, preferably, to be encouraged to alter itself so as to reinforce the equality of women—at least to the degree to which this value is upheld in the majority culture."[8]

Her short essay "Is Multiculturalism Bad for Women?" (1997) throws down the gauntlet to defenders of differential rights for minority cultures and argues that, without consideration of the freedoms and interests of women, multiculturalism may become part of the problem of women's oppression. Feminists should not support group rights that permit the oppression of women. Those feminists who support multicultural policies must look critically at the relationship between existing cultural practices and gender inequalities if they are truly to diminish the extent of social injustice.

THE ROLE OF WOMEN IN ECONOMIC DEVELOPMENT

Throughout her career, Okin's work moved increasingly outward to an engagement with global concerns. While she is sensitive to the varying situations of women who differ by class, culture, race and ethnicity, religion and citizenship, she defends feminism as

---

8. IMBFW, 22–23.

a universal political movement, respecting no state or cultural boundaries. She believes that feminism and liberalism are both rooted in a moral universalism that makes them "weapons of the weak" everywhere. She argues that liberalism needs to focus greater attention on the plight of the world's poor, a majority of whom are women. Her last project, which resulted in several important essays but was unfinished as a book at her untimely death, concerned the role of gender in economic development.

Okin points out that, until quite recently, most economists ignored the role of gender in economic development. Yet not only are female-headed households among the world's poorest families, but also within the household women and girls tend to receive a lesser share of family resources. Compared to poor boys and men, poor girls and women in many societies eat less and have less access to health care. They have higher mortality rates. They have fewer social and political rights. Too often, however, gender has been invisible to development specialists. For example, girls working inside the home, who are often unable to attend school, are not registered as child laborers in most national statistics. If the burden inside the household increases, perhaps because hospitals or public day care centers are closed, this also does not show up in any economic measures. When economic aid has been given to fathers, it has been simply assumed that this aid would be used to support the man's household, that is, his wife and children. This assumption is not borne out by the evidence. Men are less likely than women to use their resources for the support of their children; they are more likely to spend scarce monies on cigarettes, alcohol, and other women. Including gender, then, alters our understanding of poverty and the paths out of it.

Not only has the plight of women been ignored by most economists in their characterizations of different economies, but also they have ignored gender's importance for development. Drawing on the work of Nobel Prize–winning economist and philosopher Amartya Sen, Okin defends a broad idea of development, beyond mere per capita gross domestic product (GDP), which looks at what individuals in a country are able to be and do. GDP measures aggregate incomes into a sum; and per capita GDP tells us nothing about how resources are distributed across the population. Analyses of GDP also are silent on such issues as the nature of rights and liberties in a society, the extent of democracy, and the extent of corruption. Okin's humanist liberalism insists that we attend to the circumstances of every individual in a given society, especially the most disadvantaged. Further, in her writing on development, as in her writing on the family and liberalism, Okin emphasizes that, in evaluating the circumstances of individuals, what matters is not the extent of their formal freedom, but rather, their substantive freedoms. What freedoms are actually available to the worst-off individuals? To what can they realistically aspire? What are the impediments to their living their lives in accordance with their individual priorities? How can we ensure that the lives of the least advantaged—often, poor girls and women—are improved?

CONTRIBUTIONS TO THIS VOLUME

Proceeding roughly in parallel with the chronology of her scholarship, Okin's writings can be organized around a set of themes. First, her writings challenged the view of political philosophy, and especially the political philosophy of liberalism, of the family and of the place of women within it. She aimed to show that liberalism's unthinking assumption of a natural division of labor based on sex rendered it complicit in the subordination of women. She sought to extend the promise of liberal egalitarian theories to liberate individuals from oppression, applying liberal principles to the family and to gender.

Second, she insisted that liberalism's way of drawing the private-public distinction needed reformulation. The family is not natural but is part of the public sphere, a school for justice, and the state is already implicated in the formation and functioning of families. The question for liberals is how the state should treat the family in order to render it more just—not whether it should consider the family as roped off in a zone of privacy.

Third, she insisted that the proper concern of liberalism is with the well-being and freedom of each individual. This led her to be suspicious of group rights that do not attend to the position of individuals within groups and of aggregate measures of well-being. Theories that ignore gender tend to keep women vulnerable and powerless. For this reason, liberalism cannot be silent in the face of views and practices that question or undermine women's equality to men.

SUMMARIES OF THE VOLUME'S CHAPTERS

The chapters in this book focus on Okin's contributions to liberal theory, to our understanding of gender and the family, to our understanding of the relationship between feminism and cultural differences, and to issues of global justice. Many of the chapters in this volume are critical of Okin's work, but they also reveal the continuing importance for contemporary political philosophy of engaging with Okin's thought.

Several important questions cluster around the relationship between Okin's feminism and political philosophy. Nancy Rosenblum's contribution to this volume argues that Okin's liberal feminism represents a continuation of the radical nature of liberal theory more generally. By showing that the contemporary family is in fact a mechanism for the perpetuation of women as an inferior caste, Okin reveals liberalism's potential as an emancipatory theory, its capacity to up-end conventional social arrangements. Joshua Cohen's chapter questions whether or not what he calls Okin's "elementary feminist premise"—that women and men are full human beings to which a theory of justice must apply—is really quite as devastating to the history of political thought as Okin herself believed it to be. For example, Cohen finds Okin to be accepting of, or at least ambivalent about, the traditional liberal divide between public and private and determines that Okin's arguments do not completely annul the idea that the family is "beyond justice." In short, not all theories are undermined by the inclusion of women. In a more personal essay, Elizabeth Wingrove argues that Okin's use of empirical evidence to evaluate forms of the family represents a welcome departure from the more abstract modes of analysis that typically characterize analytic philosophy. She also worries that Okin failed to use this approach—deployed to devastating effect in *Justice, Gender, and the Family*—in her writings on multiculturalism and feminism. Finally, John Tomasi unearths a history of feminist criticism in the nineteenth century to show that feminism need not rely on what he calls "governmentalism," or the view that the state is the proper agent to right or fight sexual inequalities. Okin, Tomasi argues, was a pioneer in exposing and showing the injustice of these inequalities but was too ready to deploy the state and a collectivist approach as the remedy.

Other chapters concentrate on the tensions between gender and liberal egalitarianism. David Miller examines the ways that families reproduce inequalities across generations. He notes that certain unequal paths for children must be morally tolerated if we are to give weight to important parental interests in shaping their children's personalities. This may include tolerating parents' inculcation of certain gender roles. Mary Lyndon Shanley's chapter examines Okin's views about the relationship between injustice and the perpetuation of gender. She argues that Okin sought not only to eliminate the unjust effects of gendered roles and expectations but to abolish gender itself as a form of human identity. Shanley finds this latter project—the abolition of gender—especially compelling and seeks to describe what it might actually mean. In a chapter exploring the relationship between religious liberty and sexual equality, Cass Sunstein argues that Okin's views form the basis for applying antidiscrimination law—just as we now apply ordinary civil and criminal law—directly to religious organizations. There is no reason for a just society to tolerate discrimination on the basis of sex, even if such discrimination flows out of sincere religious convictions.

The third section of the book focuses on Okin's work on the tensions between feminism and multiculturalism. Ayelet Shachar identifies three variants of a feminist critique of multiculturalism: liberal feminism, postcolonial feminism, and multicultural feminism, and she locates Okin as the most visible and persuasive of the liberal feminists. Through a detailed critique of Okin's work and a consideration of the creation of a shari'a law tribunal for Muslims in Canada, Shachar argues for the superiority of the multicultural feminist approach. Alison Jaggar's chapter argues that Okin failed to appreciate—from a theoretical standpoint—the significance of criticisms of her work as "essentialist." Nevertheless, Jaggar finds that Okin was able to blunt the force of this criticism practically—as she increasingly called attention to the diversity of women's global experiences. Chandran Kukathas contributes a chapter largely devoted to the compelling story of a young Javanese woman of noble birth whose life exhibited many of the very tensions discussed by Okin: the reconciliation of loyalty to tradition and the desire for independence, the extension of group rights, and the further subordination of women. Kukathas uses the history of Kartini to examine questions about the right to exit from a minority culture and the claims of cultural groups over their members.

Finally, a pair of essays takes up Okin's last phase of scholarly work on gender and global development. Robert Keohane asks whether the institutions and organizations that contribute to globalization can be structured in such a way as to promote gender equality in developing countries. He accepts Okin's arguments that deeply entrenched patterns of gender inequality are unjust and concludes that, under current institutional arrangements, multilateral organizations and especially the World Bank, rather than the flotilla of smaller nongovernmental organizations, must be the centerpiece of a gender equality strategy. Iris Marion Young's chapter concludes the volume by showing that the gendered cycle of vulnerability that Okin identified at work in North America and Europe is equally at work in less developed countries. Despite the large differences between developed and developing countries, Young argues that Okin's identification of a cycle of vulnerability has equal force in developing countries, and Young develops some suggestions about how to combat this cycle within this very different context.

Iris Young died soon after completing this chapter. Sadly, like Okin, she died at an early age. But also like Okin, Young's voice and writings have helped to shape a generation of scholars interested in issues of gender and justice. We hope that this volume reflects and carries forward some of what we have learned from these two thinkers, including their sense that political philosophy has something to contribute to our understanding of what we might do to create a world with less misery.

PART I

RETHINKING POLITICAL THEORY

1

Okin's Liberal Feminism as a Radical Political Theory

Nancy Rosenblum

Whoever suffers from the malady of being unable to endure any injustice, must never look out of the window, but stay in his room with the door shut. He would also do well, perhaps, to throw away his mirror.

—*W. H. Auden, "Justice," in* A Certain World: A Commonplace Book

RADICAL POLITICAL THOUGHT

This entry for "Justice" in W. H. Auden's *Commonplace Book* comes to mind when I read Susan Okin's work. Okin suffered the malady of being unable to endure injustice, but she rejected the poet's advice. She opened the window and looked in the mirror; her writings reflect the torment of injustice and an acute awareness that her position of privilege and good fortune made the work she did a personal moral imperative. The motivation for Okin's work was this roiling sense of injustice. The temper of her work was set by her political sensitivity to the consequences of powerlessness and by her unflagging attention to the events of our world. These were bedrock for her. Only the arguments of her work were shaped by systematic debates in academic political theory.[1]

I will make my way through key elements of Okin's work to drive home a simple point: liberal political thought was and remains a radical political theory. I won't put too much weight on the concept "radical," nor on historical varieties of liberalism with their varied philosophic foundations. My object is not conceptual analysis but the perennial critical potential of liberal ideas plain in Okin's work, and plainly recognized by her. I say "critical potential" as a concession to the host of critics who point to the failings of liberal thinkers in practice: a propensity (hardly unique) to ignore the distance between theory and practice; unfaithfulness to the moral and logical import of liberal ideas; complacency amounting on occasion to conservatism. "Liberalism's past is deeply, and, for the most part, unambiguously patriarchal," Okin acknowledged, and she spoke of "the liberal tradition's failure to perceive the family as a political institution."[2] She committed her professional life to redeeming liberalism from its own failings;

---

1. I say "only the arguments" knowing that, for political theorists, that may seem like the whole cloth. Okin did not use arguments strategically, by any means, but she was not committed to a systematic position, as I explain below.

2. Okin, "Humanist Liberalism," in Nancy L. Rosenblum, ed., *Liberalism and the Moral Life* (Cambridge, MA: Harvard University Press, 1998), 47.

her unrelenting challenge to John Rawls and her revision of his "original position" are perhaps the best-known elements of her answer to the question of whether patriarchal liberalism can be replaced "with a political theory of humanist liberalism."[3]

Okin was a liberal or, as she sometimes put it, a "humanist" feminist. Her work was motivated by the classic liberal concern for individual freedom within a political framework of rights and constitutional protections against the abuse of power. Her foundational text was J. S. Mill's *The Subjection of Women*, which she edited in 1988. She opposed humanist liberalism to traditionalist, communitarian, and "essentialist" visions of gender and family, of course. Less fruitfully, she was forced to spend much energy countering feminist theorists who rejected liberal values wholesale as conservative at home and as instruments of a culturally imperial mission abroad. For these antiliberals, rights are an arid and masculinist way of thinking and relating; individualism signals by definition egoism and, what is worse, separation from and conflict with others; it "feeds a privatizing, withdrawalist conception of citizenship";[4] the whole apparatus of liberalism is at best a distraction from preferred understandings of the condition of women, which give priority to language or bodies or, more specifically, eroticism and the sexual domination and objectification of women.

I need a baseline for bringing out the radicalism of Okin's liberal feminism, and J. S. Mill provides one. He was an avowed philosophic radical, whose demands on behalf of women (and men) were unthinkable to most Victorians. In her editor's introduction, Okin cites the virulent reactions of James Fitzjames Stephen and Sigmund Freud and Mill's own awareness of the "enormous weight of popular opinion and feeling against the position he is to argue."[5] Mill was also a moralist—a universalist and perfectionist, who nonetheless applied his vision differentially, stopping if not at Britain's shores, then at the borders of British settlements abroad. Okin's affinity for Mill and her one signal point of divergence as well (which I discuss toward the end of this chapter) help to identify the ways in which her feminism was liberal and, as such, radical.

Is "radical" a term of praise? In political theory at least, it has a positive valence built in. After all, if radical means "unearthing a root problem or argument," then anything less is a failing of political theory. Similarly, if radical means "at a distance from conventional understandings in a given context," political theory is not doing its business if it simply mirrors popular opinion at a higher level of abstraction. That is, political theorists must have an iota of utopianism to do their work. Finally, and this is the last I will say about radicalism, political theory is distinguished from philosophy by attention to the fact that dangerous ideas, first cooked in the heads of philosophers, "find a welcome among the masses and acquire the driving force of a political passion."[6] Karl Mannheim brought Tocqueville's point home to scholars when he observed that "philosophers have

---

3. "Humanist Liberalism," 40.

4. See the responses in Joshua Cohen, Matthew Howard, and Martha Nussbaum, eds., *Is Multiculturalism Bad for Women? Susan Moller Okin with Respondents* (Princeton, NJ: Princeton University Press, 1999); the quote is from Bonnie Honig, "My Culture Made Me Do It," 39.

5. Okin, "Editor's Introduction," to Mill, *The Subjection of Women* (Indianapolis, IN: Hackett, 1988), v, vii, x.

6. Alexis de Tocqueville, *The Old Regime and the French Revolution* (New York: Anchor, 1955), 139.

too long concerned themselves with their own thinking."[7] Okin grapples with philosophers' theories of justice, of course, but she is motivated less by philosophic questions than by an interest in the force of ideas in the world. Her concern is how certain ideas uphold or upset social arrangements, and who is posed to exploit these ideas (the family as "beyond justice," for example) in their own interests or who is in a position to effectively wield ideas in the general interest. All political theory is done with half an eye to politics, radical political thought more so. Like Mill, Okin was a keen analyst of the political forces opposed to feminism, and like him, she did not admit a line between political theory and advocacy. When others drew the line, she trespassed over it. She advised: "Feminism is a political stance more than a systematic theory."[8]

Consider the liberal elements of *The Subjection of Women* and why Okin adopted them for her radical purposes.

LIBERAL FEMINISM AS POLITICAL EMANCIPATION

"In every chapter of the essay, Mill calls up the image of slavery," Okin noted.[9] The affinity Mill held for her is captured by his title: *The Subjection of Women*. The heart of Mill's essay is less an analysis of the condition of women, though he certainly ventured social and historical explanations. Rather, the heart of his essay, and of liberalism, is an itemization of subjection and a summary of the repulsiveness of unconstrained power. Mill's language of subjection—his political language—is crucial. It recognizes the cruel pleasure of despotism and the acute vulnerability of subjection. Women are in a "subordinate state" and require liberation. Neither Mill nor Okin were oblivious to other subjections, including the domination of some women over others, but the case of women was spectacular for its scope, its myriad forms, its implacability, its sheer waste.[10] The case of women, for Mill, "was the case of humanity in extremis. It was women who experienced, in its most fatal form, the social tyranny described in *On Liberty*"—and legal despotism as well.[11] When Mill wrote, arguments against political despotism were familiar and effective; he surveyed the progress of liberty. A widely held commitment to resisting the sway of the absolute arbitrary will of another had been institutionalized in constitutionalism, religious tolerance, and civil and political rights for men regardless of class. In this context, the condition of women was anomalous. Mill did not have to ground the principles of liberty nor proselytize for consent to obligations; it was enough to demonstrate unfaithfulness to familiar standards, a blatant moral inconsistency. "One monstrous contradiction" would become Okin's touchstone as well.[12]

---

7. Karl Mannheim, *Ideology and Utopia* (London: Routledge and Kegan Paul, 1940), 1.

8. Jane Mansbridge and Susan Okin, "Feminism," in Robert E. Goodin and Philip Pettit, eds., *The Blackwell Companion to Contemporary Political Philosophy* (Oxford: Basil Blackwell, 1993), 269.

9. "Editor's Introduction," xi.

10. Okin reiterates her interest in other oppressions and other inequalities, for example, in *Is Multiculturalism Bad for Women?* 118.

11. Gertrude Himmelfarb, *On Liberty and Liberalism: The Case of John Stuart Mill* (New York: Knopf, 1974), 127.

12. John Stuart Mill, *The Subjection of Women* (Cambridge, MA: MIT Press, 1970), 79 (hereafter *Subjection*).

The title *The Subjection of Women* carried a load of meaning, then. Not just that the condition of women is analogous to subjection to absolute and arbitrary political power, but that subjection accurately describes the fact that women are legally controlled in every aspect of their lives by the unrestrained power of men. Women are without political rights. They do not consent to their government in either realm. The marriage contract is not one whose terms they design with a view to their interests; they consent only to the status of wife, and then frequently from necessity. Mill spoke of the subjection of women, because it was the legal subordination of one sex to the other, legally enforced. The husband has a lifelong lawful entitlement to command and to be obeyed.

> The sufferings, immoralities, evils of all sorts produced in innumerable cases by the subjection of individual women to individual men are far too terrible to be overlooked....And it is perfectly obvious that the abuse of power cannot be very much checked while the power remains. It is a power given, or offered, not to good men, or to decently respectable men, but to all men; the most brutal, and the most criminal.[13]

The arbitrary exercise of power by men over women is unjust even if it is not abused. And like any unconstrained power, it is bound to be cruelly used. Women are subject to the basest and most ferocious, the "vilest malefactor," "absolute monsters," "absolute fiends,"[14] and have no regular possibility of exit (Okin's subject too): "no amount of ill usage, without adultery superadded, will in England free a wife from her tormenter,"[15] Mill warned. He stood in the House of Commons to say: "I should like to have a return laid before this House of the number of women who are annually beaten to death, kicked to death, or trampled to death by their male protectors."[16]

The legal structures of male dominance "have begun to be eroded in the past century, and more rapidly in the last twenty years," Okin wrote of the United States, though she was alert to differences (the situation of some poor women in poor countries is more like the situation of Western women in the nineteenth century, she wrote in an early comparative effort).[17] In the United States, male dominance has not been erased, and the weight of both tradition and socialization remain powerful.[18] In other parts of the world, she wrote, cold-eyed, "most cultures have as one of their principal aims the control of women by men."[19] Despite significant reforms, the political terminology of subjection held for Okin. It was plain in the "lived reality" of marriage and domestic life as relations of power and dependence. She captured it in the phrase "vulnerability by marriage."[20] The term "vulnerable," which she uses everywhere, is worth

---

13. *Subjection*, 79.

14. *Subjection*, 35–36.

15. *Subjection*, 33.

16. On-Line Library of Liberty: John Stuart Mill, *The Collected Works of John Stuart Mill*, vol. 28, *Public and Parliamentary Speeches*, Part I, November 1850–November 1868, 55: The Admission of Women to the Electoral Franchise, May 20, 1867, paragraph 552. http://oll.libertyfund.org.

17. Okin, "Gender Inequality and Cultural Differences," *Political Theory* 22.1 (February 1994): 15.

18. Susan Moller Okin, *Justice, Gender, and the Family* (New York: Basic, 1989), 6 (hereafter *JGF*).

19. *Is Multiculturalism Bad for Women?* 13.

20. This was consistent with her work on interhousehold inequalities and with her recognition that perhaps the most vulnerable women were female heads of households and widows in poor countries; see "Poverty, Well-Being and Gender."

examining. Even without a subordinate clause, it suggests a susceptibility to physical danger (bodily harm, inadequate food and shelter), humiliation, and fear. Like Mill, she was always alert to brutality. Okin's essays are rife with reminders of "power in its crassest form, physical violence" against women and children generally and within the family in particular—where despite advocacy, new laws, and campaigns to make it unacceptable, domestic violence continues unabated.[21] "Vulnerability by marriage" bridges countries and classes.[22] Mill's "subjection" and "slavery" were resonant for Okin; "Uncle Tom" under his first master had his own life in his "cabin...but it cannot be so with the wife."[23] She employed the rhetoric, perhaps most tellingly, in the title "'Forty Acres and a Mule' for Women" (2005); after legal emancipation, what is necessary for freedom to be a lived reality?

Mill's basic themes had still not been incorporated into social and political theory when Okin wrote, and it was necessary for her to repeat that the state has not only regulated and controlled the family in innumerable ways, reinforcing male dominance, but that marriage and family are creations of law.[24] "Public" and "private" spheres are standard feminist terminology, and Okin employed them as Mill had to insist that the formation and functioning of the family were creations of law and politics, including what counts as a family under law, who is recognized as a parent, and so on. The correlation typically drawn between public and private and political and nonpolitical was unwarranted: public decisions create domestic inequalities of power.[25] The breakdown of this misleading distinction has remained a radical aspiration. The question is not whether, but how, government intervenes, and Okin insisted that her proposals do not amount to an "unwarranted invasion of privacy or any more state intervention into the life of families than currently exists."[26]

Similarly, it was still necessary for Okin, as for Mill, to use liberal individualism to pry open the nut of the family as integral, as a unity, much less as harmony. It was there in Mill's rejection of the Victorian notion of home as haven. Okin continued to battle those who saw the family as a whole: economists who focused on households and assumed the black box of rational "heads of households"; theorists of justice for whom the family was a harmonious and altruistic sphere "beyond justice"; judges whose decisions asserted "the rights of families to make decisions regulating their members," without recognizing conflicting claims to privacy within the family (the rights of wives or minors to seek abortion, for example).[27] Okin argued for individual rights that might constitute "rights against families."[28]

---

21. *JGF*, 128–129, 152.

22. Again, with frequent caveats from Okin that single women, single parents especially, may be among the worst off.

23. *Subjection*, 32.

24. "Humanist Liberalism," 42.

25. Mansbridge and Okin, "Feminism," 13.

26. *JGF*, 182.

27. "Humanist Liberalism," 45.

28. "Humanist Liberalism," 45. She would make the same argument against the unity, organic or legal, of cultural groups claiming group rights and protections from generally valid laws—disaggregating groups into their individual members—in *Is Multiculturalism Bad for Women?* This is not to say that her prescriptions for families and minority groups in liberal societies are identical.

There is another affinity here. Mill drives home the point that, if women are victims of despotism, men are despots. Their subjection has nothing to do with social expedience. It is rooted in the worst part of human nature and runs deep. In one passage, Mill sees subjection as a residue of an original, primitive brutality of the strong over the weak. Other social relations have been modified by laws, softened by civilization and manners; this one is stuck in the primate. In *The Subjection of Women*, Mill did not explore this developmental curiosity.[29] Nor did he attribute domination and subjection anonymously, to "society," as he would with his focus on conformity in *On Liberty*. He did not think that implacable enmity was rife between men and women, and he held out the ideal of "perfect friendship,"[30] but in the meantime, he pointed to the despotism of men personally and individually. Simply, he showed that arbitrary power is to men's pleasure and advantage. The gratification of pride in possessing power and a personal interest in exercising it extends to the entire male sex. It is not limited to one class. Most will not experience the exercise of political power, but the subjection of women "comes home to the person and hearth of every male head of a family, and of everyone who looks forward to being so. The clodhopper exercises his share of power equally with the highest nobleman."[31]

Feminists are divided on the causes of the subjection of women, Okin conceded, whether male domination is biologically based, and if it is "socially constructed," as she thought, whether that entails deliberate agency.[32] But the picture of male pleasure and advantage in the domination of women is plain enough, and Okin sharpened it. In her introduction to *The Subjection of Women*, she quoted from Harriet Taylor's tract, *The Enfranchisement of Women*: there is nothing better to be said of the traditional role of wives but "that men like it. It is agreeable to them that men should live for their own sake, women for the sake of men."[33] Translated into law and policy, this was enraging. It accounts for the tenor of Okin's radicalism, her barely submerged fury, as in this passage: "How, until recently, have men managed with a semblance of legitimacy to exclude women from formal politics in almost every tribe, state and civilization on the globe?"[34] Or this: "the major reason that husbands and other heterosexual men living with wage-working women are not doing more housework is that *they do not want to, and are able, to a very large extent, to enforce their wills*."[35] Okin's substantive arguments were propelled by a tide of moral emotion. Hers was a liberal moral ferocity, meaning, it was profoundly connected to the intolerability of absolute and arbitrary power, of willfulness given political sway and comfortably and familiarly wedded to classic liberal terms and methods of restraint. Everyone knows that most people are unfit to govern unless they are constitutionally constrained, Mill wrote, and the same is true for domestic power. Marriage corresponds to *the* liberal evil: absolute, arbitrary power.

29. The allusions are brief at *Subjection*, 6–7.
30. This goes against Himmelfarb's reading in *On Liberty and Liberalism*, 178.
31. *Subjection*, 12.
32. Mansbridge and Okin, "Feminism," 36.
33. "Editor's Introduction," x.
34. Mansbridge and Okin, "Feminism," 6.
35. *JGF*, 153.

Mill and Okin also modeled the characteristic liberal advisory: profound, cease-less, mistrust. "Eternal vigilance" is radical: it alerts us to the endless possibilities for subjection, its ceaseless recurrence and innumerable variations, hence the need to con-tinuously scrutinize women's roles and responsibilities for the marks of despotism: "Manifestations of power…appear in the bed, in the home or streets, where women are raped and battered, and in the halls of Parliament."[36] They are found in the abortion of female fetuses, higher female mortality rates in some cultures, and undernourish-ment. Okin insisted, in response to critics, that emphasizing the commonalities among women in terms of subjection is politically defensible. Mill, and Okin after him, were among those few theorists obsessed with the sheer cruelty of those with power, of the suffering of the powerless. Neither underestimated physical pain. Mill calls being sub-ject to the will of another "atrocious." That is what despotism, domestic and social, is: arbitrariness and unrestrained power.

This, then, is the great affinity Okin had with Mill: a classic liberal opposition to absolutism and arbitrariness and a sense of the despicableness of despots, political or domestic. Opposition did not require sophisticated philosophy, only a modicum of history and keeping one's eyes open: "The despotism of Louis XVI was not the des-potism of Caligula…but it was bad enough to justify the French Revolution, and to palliate even its horrors."[37] What would a French Revolution at home look like?

JUSTICE, GENDER, AND THE FAMILY

Okin's edition of Mill's *The Subjection of Women* was published in 1988; *Justice, Gender, and the Family* was published in 1988. Mill's essay was in her mind as she wrote, and it remained a touchstone for her work. At its most basic, the affinity Mill had for Okin was a shared negative: a resistance to unconstrained power. Her remarks on gender and equality were chiefly aimed at eliminating subjection. Her aim was personal liberty for women. In Mill's words, "[t]he peculiar character of the modern world" is that "human beings are no longer born to their place in life, and chained down by an inexorable bond to the place they are born to, but are free to employ their faculties, and such favourable chances as offer, to achieve the lot which may appear to them most desirable."[38] In a phrase she was to repeat: "Liberalism's central aim, in my view, should be to ensure that every human being has a reasonably equal chance of living a good life according to his or her unfolding views about what such a life consists in."[39] Toward that end, she excoriated certain inequalities. Mill was prone to pronouncements of "one very simple principle," among them "the principle of perfect equality admitting no privilege on the one side or disability on the other." Okin did not subscribe to the "principle of per-fect equality," nor any other determinate principle. Nonetheless, she is susceptible to interpretation as an egalitarian. Here and in the next section, I reject that reading and

36. Mansbridge and Okin, "Feminism," 21.

37. *Subjection,* 34.

38. Wendell Robert Carr, "Introduction," in John Stuart Mill, *The Subjection of Women* (Cam-bridge, MA: MIT Press, 1970), xv.

39. *Is Multiculturalism Bad for Women?* 119.

suggest why what has been called her "egalitarian liberalism" was loose, unsystematic, open to diverse interpretations, and frustrating to stern analytic philosophers.[40] She wrote critically about the limitations of many accounts of equality and adopted disparate elements from a variety of theories. Okin spoke of equality often, clearly, but it is difficult to locate her on the map of egalitarian liberalism. What may seem like vagueness or unwillingness to commit to the grounds of equality is explained in part by the fact that equality was not her chief concern; she focused on inequalities of the sort that reflect and entrench women's status as a caste, i.e., inherited dependence and civil disabilities that confine many women to domesticity and service to men and children.[41]

Mill was her touchstone in all of this. He argued for the enfranchisement of women and for the admission of women by law to "equality in all rights, political, civil, and social with male members of the community." By themselves, these prescriptions (sometimes thoughtlessly diminished by antiliberals as merely "formal rights") were radical when he wrote. But they were not as unsettling as the connection he drew to domestic life—the connection between the status of women in the family and their rights and status in the world of paid work and the professions, property, and civil and political rights. It hardly bears repeating that, in Mill's day and continuing still, advocates of women's civil and political rights did not necessarily see an inconsistency between political and civil equality, on the one hand, and domestic patriarchy, on the other.[42] Mill made the inconsistency plain: domestic patriarchy was a political relation—instituted and enforced by law. The bulk of his essay, Okin noted, is focused on the institution of marriage.[43] She appreciated the fact that he gave marriage arrangements equal standing, if not priority, over the two major issues of radical politics of the time—the right to vote and trade unionism—just as she focused more on the family than on political mobilization or the labor market. She adopted his motto: "as long as the citadel of the enemy is not attacked," all other attempts at respect and justice are futile.[44]

Mill's argument had two parts. Until the law offers protection to women in marriage, they will be abused. And by denying them the independence to earn, the law prevents women from protecting themselves. Hence, his insistence that equal education and what follows from it, the "power of earning," are essential to women's dignity. They earn husbands' respect. They ensure an end to subjection and a modicum of equity in marriage.

---

40. Amy R. Baehr, "Toward a New Feminist Liberalism: Okin, Rawls, Habermas," *Hypatia* 11.1 (Winter 1996): 49–66, points out that Okin proposes to apply Rawls' principles of justice directly to the family, but that her own writing on family relations is closer to a flat principle of equality than the difference principle (60). Also see J. S. Russell, "Okin's Rawlsian Feminism? Justice in the Family and Another Liberalism," *Social Theory and Practice* 21.3 (Fall 1995): 397–427; and Joshua Cohen, "Okin on Justice, Gender, and Family," *Canadian Journal of Philosophy* 22.2 (June 1992): 263–286.

41. *Is Multiculturalism Bad for Women?* 17.

42. Only recently has what I have called the "logic of congruence" penetrated every sphere. For my objections, see Nancy L. Rosenblum, *Membership and Morals: The Personal Uses of Pluralism in America* (Princeton, NJ: Princeton University Press, 1998).

43. "Editor's Introduction," xiii.

44. *JGF*, 20.

Mill's distance from contemporary liberal feminists derives mainly from his speculation that, under appropriate conditions, most women—at least those whose husband's
earnings or other income could support the family (and those who, he observed unchiv-
alrously, are "sufficiently attractive to be chosen by any man as his companion" in the
first place)[45]—would freely choose marriage and a division of labor in which the man
earns the income and the wife superintends the domestic expenditures. Mill predicted
that this division would continue after emancipation, and he judged it reasonable:

> In an otherwise just state of things, it is not, I think, a desirable custom, that the
> wife should contribute by her labour to the income of the family. The *power* of
> earning is essential to the dignity of a woman, if she has not independent property.
> But if marriage were an equal contract, not implying the obligation of obedience;
> if the connexion were no longer enforced to the oppression of those to whom it
> is purely a mischief, but a separation, on just terms...could be obtained by any
> woman who was morally entitled to it; and if she would then find all honourable
> employments as freely open to her as to men; *it would not be necessary for her pro-
> tection*, that during marriage she should make this particular use of her faculties.[46]

Mill describes marriage over career as if being a wife (and mother) were equivalent
to a profession:

> Like a man when he chooses a profession, so when a woman marries, it may in
> general be understood that she makes choice of the management of a household,
> and the bringing up of a family, as the first call upon her exertions, during as many
> years of her life as may be required for the purpose; and that she renounces, not all
> other objects and occupations, but all which are not consistent with the require-
> ments of this.[47]

"Each is absolute in the executive branch of their own department," on his representation, as if this were a recipe for a sort of constitutional balance of power, and not
subordination.

Is this sheer conventionalism? Not exactly, as I will show below. In any case, it is
based in part on Mill's unconventional recognition that other arrangements were likely
to burden and exploit women even more. Mill was famously unattuned to parenting, at least mothering, but he was sensitive to domestic drudgery. *Subjection* contains
pages describing women's work, in particular the obligations of middle-class women,
and the toll that housework takes on leisure, energy, and freedom of mind. He could
only imagine work outside the home as added to domestic labor, and domestic labor
as exclusively women's. On this point, he is histrionic: "The care, which she is herself
disabled from taking of the children and the household, nobody else takes; those of
the children who do not die, grow up the best they can, and the management of the
household is likely to be so bad, as even in point of economy to be a great drawback
from the value of the wife's earnings."[48]

---

45. *Subjection*, 30.
46. *Subjection*, 48. My italics.
47. *Subjection*, 48.
48. *Subjection*, 51.

Still, although unwilling or insufficiently imaginative to conjure different arrangements, Mill is a consistent defender of women's personal liberty:

> But the utmost latitude ought to exist for the adaptation of general rules to individual suitabilities; and there ought to be nothing to prevent faculties exceptionally adapted to any other pursuit, from obeying their vocation, notwithstanding marriage; due provision being made for supplying otherwise any falling-short which might become inevitable in her full performance of the ordinary functions of mistress of a family.[49]

Even if the division of labor were traditional, it should not be established by law and should "depend on individual capacities and suitabilities," apportioned by agreement between the partners themselves.[50]

Okin conceded that "contemporary feminists are unlikely to agree with Mill that justice in the family can readily coexist with the traditional division of labor between the sexes."[51] Nonetheless, she insisted that *The Subjection of Women* has continuing significance for feminist arguments.[52] Its radicalism owed to the priority that Mill gave to marriage and the family in his account of subjection. Before the 1960s, she noted, few feminists focused on women's role in the family. Not only did Mill lead the way in this, but he identified what would become a key element in Okin's analysis: women's inordinate share of unpaid domestic labor. In affluent countries and for affluent women, this meant housekeeping, childrearing, and caretaking of the elderly and unwell; in poorer countries and for poorer women, it included subsistence farming, tending to animals, domestic crafts, and arduous daily chores. In all cases, "women's work" is unpaid and rarely considered productive and underscores their economic dependence on men.[53] Mill's appreciation of women's labor in the home was not without precedent,[54] but it was powerful, and the accuracy of his prediction about women's double workload was striking. The value to women of suffrage and civil rights, antidiscrimination laws in education and employment, was diminished by inescapable domestic roles and responsibilities: "the gendered structure of marriage *makes* women vulnerable."[55]

Okin often pointed to the reciprocity and mutual reinforcement between economic and political opportunities and domestic constraints. Among her formulations: "underlying and intertwined with all these inequalities is the unequal distribution

---

49. *Subjection*, 49.
50. *Subjection*, 40–41.
51. "Editor's Introduction," xiv.
52. "Editor's Introduction," vi.
53. Okin, "Gender Inequality and Cultural Differences," 11, 13.
54. "Editor's Introduction," vi.
55. *JGF*, 5.

> They are rendered vulnerable by the actual division of labor within almost all current marriages. They are disadvantaged at work by the fact that the world of wage work, including the professions, is still largely structured around the assumption that "workers" have wives at home. They are rendered far more vulnerable if they become the primary caretakers of children, and their vulnerability peaks if their marriages dissolve and they become single parents. (*JGF*, 138)

of unpaid labor in the family"; "a cycle of power relations and decisions pervades both family and workplace, each reinforcing the inequalities between the sexes that already exist within the other";[56] "the causal arrow runs in both directions";[57] "a cycle of vulnerability...results from women's having far greater responsibility than men for domestic work...then being further disadvantaged in the (male-centered) paid workplace by direct discrimination and the indirect discrimination that results from greater domestic responsibilities."[58] In other places, the argument changed, and Okin made family arrangements and the expectations they generate the key to the system of subjection. The family, rather than the gendered structure of the labor market or formal education, say, plays the pivotal part in shaping expectations and restricting opportunities ("vulnerability by anticipation of marriage" refers to investment in "human capital").[59] The family "constitute[s] the pivot of a societal system of gender that renders women vulnerable to dependency, exploitation, and abuse."[60] "Pivot" will not satisfy rigorous social theorists requiring empirical evidence and an account of causality. "Pivot" also invites criticism for what it implies about the priority of reforms—with domestic reforms in the forefront.[61] I'm not certain that Okin would want to be held to severe standards of social explanation here; her point (and the political point for her is always central) is the inescapability of this set of constraints: "The division of labor that prevails between the sexes...often leads to the economic, psychological, or even physical vulnerability of women and children. It contributes much to women's inequality of opportunity and actual inequality of power and influence in society at large."[62]

Okin's policy prescriptions applied to the workplace but mostly to the family, and her interventions were designed to check the power of husbands and fathers, to encourage a sharing of burdens, and to offer protections and safety nets for dependent women, particularly in cases of divorce. She advocated shared earnings (legal entitlement of the non-wage-earning spouse to wages), earning power as a legally recognized "marital asset," guaranteed income to single parents, child care subsidies, and alimony and child support to ensure similar standards of living after divorce "for at least as long as the traditional division of labor in the marriage did...until the youngest child enters first grade and the custodial parent has a real chance of making his or her own living."[63]

---

56. *JGF*, 4.

57. Mansbridge and Okin, "Feminism," 13.

58. Mansbridge and Okin, "Feminism," 35.

59. *JGF*, 142. See her discussion on 146–147 about women's (and couples') decisions about education and work, and her critique of human capital theory, which takes the family as a unit.

60. *JGF*, 136.

61. Joshua Cohen, "Okin on Justice, Gender, and Family," *Canadian Journal of Philosophy* 22.2 (June 1992): 263–286.

62. "Sexual Orientation and Gender," in David Estlund and Martha Nussbaum, eds., *Sex, Preference, and Family* (New York: Oxford University Press, 1997), 56.

63. Okin did not ignore disparities among families, races, or classes; there is a lot of back and forth in feminist writing on this point. Her point was that the disparities are exacerbated for women and girls, and "if all these disparities were somehow eliminated, we would still not attain equal opportunity for all"; *JGF*, 16, 134. I discuss this further below.

For the workplace she advocated flexible work time, parental leaves, and other adjust-ments in the workplace for caretakers. She prescribed two sets of policies, then. One provides incentives (not legal requirements) to end women's dependence by enabling them to work and to earn more or less on a par with men; these focus on couples' paid and unpaid work. The other set of policies provides protection for "those [perhaps mostly, but not exclusively, women] who chose to undertake the bulk of unpaid family work."[64] Of course, Okin was an advocate of the more stable and gratifying protection that comes with earning and of the alleviation of the egregious inequalities of domes-tic obligations: "An equal sharing between the sexes of family responsibilities is 'the great revolution that has not happened.'"[65]

It would be misleading, however, to take "equal sharing" too seriously as an ideal or imperative. Equality per se is not Okin's "French Revolution." Her well-known recast-ing of Rawls' original position extends the veil of ignorance to sex, assigns the thought experiment to all adults, not just "heads of households"—assuring that principles of justice will be acceptable to women as well as men—and unambiguously estab-lishes the family as part of the basic structure of society, to which principles of justice apply. Tellingly, Okin herself never said how Rawlsian principles would apply to the family—what the difference principle would mean, for example—assuming that women were the "worst off." Her detailed critique of theories of justice that do not do justice to women, her insistence on corrections to ensure rights and opportunities for women, were not matched by her adoption of one exclusive set of standards for gender equality. Her prescriptions cannot be consistently deduced from any single principle: not the difference principle nor simple equality nor equal opportunity nor a capa-bilities approach. Each makes an appearance in her work. Okin recommended shared domestic and public roles between husband and wife, but she was not as adamant about equal partition, would not legally mandate it, and did not stigmatize couples who deviated from it. "Equal sharing" is best understood as shorthand or as a slogan for challenging the entrenched inequalities that amount to subjection. She was less fixed on egalitarian relations than on the fair assignment of roles and responsibilities, where "fair" entails reciprocity. (Modeling some sort of reciprocal decision making is also why Okin favored two-parent families.) It is at least as faithful to her work overall to say that Okin would realize liberty in and through the family—"the terms and con-ditions within families are genuinely set by the choices of different men and women moved by diverse values and understandings"—as to say, as one reader has, that "fami-lies would embody ideals of equality."[66]

I want to pursue this claim. The unifying feature of Okin's prescriptions is that "the unit of analysis both for studies and for much policy making must be the individual, not the household."[67] (In the same spirit, Mill abhorred the expression "the woman question," referring always to women, plural and individual.)[68] Again, Okin's standard

64. Okin, "Forty Acres," 14.
65. *JGF*, 4.
66. Cohen, "Okin on Justice, Gender, and Family," 285.
67. Okin, "Gender Inequality and Cultural Differences," 17.
68. Himmelfarb, *On Liberty and Liberalism*, 170.

was to ensure "that every human being has a reasonably equal chance of living a good life according to his or her unfolding views about what such a life consists in."[69] The concept to which she appeals most consistently is Rawls' "fair equality of opportunity," not surprisingly since, more than other standards, it is closely tied to personal liberty. "The interconnections between the domestic and the nondomestic aspects of our lives are deep and pervasive,"[70] she wrote, and "public life is far less distinct from personal and domestic life for women than for men....The claim that the two spheres are separate is premised upon, but does not recognize, both a material and a psychological division of labor between the sexes."[71] Men are able to transition back and forth from domestic to public life with relative ease "largely because of the functions performed by women in the family."[72] A humanist liberalism "must focus heavily on private as well as public life"[73] with the aim of enabling women as well as men to move from one sphere to the other and back, as "liberal individuals are supposed to do." This point is important. It echoes Mill's insistence that, even if women exercise power at home ("the power of the scold, or the shrewish sanction"), power is no "compensation for the loss of freedom."[74]

Like feminists of many stripes, Okin rejected the constraining assumptions that lie behind "separate spheres," but she did not claim that the distinction between public and private is meaningless or dissoluble. There are reasonable distinctions to be made.[75] She certainly rejected the thought that every aspect of the family is properly subject to coercive regulation,[76] writing firmly, "Advocating justice within families is not equivalent to saying that such justice should be directly enforced by law."[77] She did not insist on forcing shared responsibility (no household spies or "kitchen police") nor on fines for unequal parenting. Government "cannot allow gendered practices that make women and children vulnerable," but neither can government "simply dictate and enforce the abolition of gender."[78] The "cannot allow" prescribes protections and rejects wholly unregulated, libertarian, contractual marital and family arrangements. The "cannot simply dictate" prohibits most regulation of internal family life.[79] "In face of these difficulties— balancing freedom and the effects of past choices against the needs of justice—I do not

69. *Is Multiculturalism Bad for Women?* 119.

70. *JGF*, 126.

71. "Humanist Liberalism," 43.

72. *JGF*, 8.

73. "Humanist Liberalism," 53.

74. *Subjection*, 37–38.

75. *JGF*, 127. See 127ff. for her summary of the flaws of the dichotomy between public and private as it is conventionally understood.

76. Mansbridge and Okin, "Feminism," 12.

77. Okin, "Forty Acres," 24.

78. "Humanist Liberalism," 53.

79. Does Okin's analysis of subjection and her prescriptions for a more just family add up, as some have said, to a "comprehensive liberalism"? And if so, does this incline her to a more interventionist interest in the family than my liberal characterization allows? In challenging Rawls' account of the family as it appears in *Political Liberalism*, Okin argues that justice cannot be sustained without full-blown education for justice in the family. Rawls' proposal to class certain social spheres, including the family and religious organizations, as nonpolitical—meaning the principles of justice do not apply there

pretend to have arrived at any complete or fully satisfactory answers."[80] It is not clear that balancing is what Okin does, in fact, and if so the weight she puts in the balance against "freedom" is not equality but opposition to caste or to specific institutionalized inequalities.[81] A better reading than a balancing approach is that she prioritized liberty and the privacy of family life, and that interference (in contrast to protections and incentives) must be justified. I do not think she would agree that "there is no such thing as a private space that simply exists independent of and immune from the need to justify its existence."[82] She assumed both the nuclear family in some form and privacy there. She did not justify either. Serving as a "school of justice," for example, may be an important good that the well-ordered family provides, but it is not a justification for this institution or for mandating a form of family organization.[83]

Why this requirement that regulation must be justified? Here, too, it is hard to isolate the grounds for liberty and family privacy in Okin's work: autonomy, respect, the circumstances of reasonable pluralism—all make appearances. All of them are compatible with recognition that certain forms and uses of personal liberty are possible only in intimate and familial relations. Within a legal framework of protections and

---

directly—and his inclusion of certain doctrines that are antifeminist within his notion of reasonableness fall afoul of her notion of what justice requires. But what follows from this judgment? As for her quarrel with Rawls' category of "reasonable doctrine," it is unclear what follows from this, since Rawls did not (and she did not) intend to legally prohibit unreasonable speech, including doctrines that are repressive or degrading on ethnic, racial, or gender grounds. Rawls appears to mean that unreasonable comprehensive doctrines should not (again, without legal censure) be used in public arenas to support public reasons for political proposals. Does Okin intend to outlaw unreasonable legislative proposals regarding women and the family? There is insufficient evidence for Martha Nussbaum's conclusion:

> At bottom, Okin is, I think, basically a comprehensive liberal who finds it insufficient that the state should confine itself to pronouncing on doctrines concerning citizenship without pronouncing on all aspects of the various comprehensive doctrines. It seems to her half-hearted for the state to endorse equal citizenship and not to construct, and vigorously support, the rest of a comprehensive way of life that protects it by teaching comprehensive doctrines of sex equality. ("Rawls and Feminism," in Samuel Freeman, ed., *The Cambridge Companion to Rawls* [Cambridge: Cambridge University Press, 2003], 511)

80. *JGF*, 172.
81. Joshua Cohen reads Okin to say that the fundamental value of liberty "must be 'balanced' against the fundamental value of domestic equality"; the passage he cites balances liberty against justice. "Okin on Justice, Gender, and Family," 269.
82. The phrase is Corey Brettschneider's; I am not convinced of his argument as it applies to Okin's work in "Publicly Justifiable Privacy and Rawls' *Political Liberalism*: An Analysis of the Rawls/Okin Exchange," unpublished paper in possession of author (Rosenblum), 2.
83. Cultural minority groups in liberal societies concern Okin because their demands for public policies that would exempt them from general laws and for other forms of accommodation that center on women and the family are not in the identical position as families per se. There is no space to discuss this here. Again, there is a distance between what Okin argues that justice requires and what should be legally mandated, but there is more latitude for denying exemptions for religious groups than for kitchen police. Her discussion of religious accommodation, following Cass Sunstein, is in First Amendment terms, in *Is Multiculturalism Bad for Women?* 127ff. She is most adamant about public control of aspects of children's education; that arena is where she would presumably advocate government regulation; see 129ff.

incentives, "public policy must respect people's views and choices," she cautioned. This argues absolutely against women's vulnerability to absolute and arbitrary power and against caste-like ascriptive roles. It also says that liberty allows traditional gendered domesticity when it is not a matter of caste, a point to which I will return. For now, personal liberty is her aim for everyone, including unreconstructed women:

> In our society at present, gender is a hotly disputed issue. There are those, at one extreme, for whom the different roles of the two sexes, especially as parents, are deeply held tenets of religious belief. At the other end of the spectrum are those of us for whom the sooner all social differentiation between the sexes vanishes, the better it will be for all of us. And there are a thousand varieties of view in between.[84]

Recall her definition of liberalism's central aim: "every human being has a reasonably equal chance of living a good life according to his or her *unfolding views* about what such a life consists in."[85] Okin erected—at least, her liberal feminism, even to the extent that it was egalitarian, did not dismantle—a liberal seawall that holds back the unrestricted exercise of public power, even for good. Her position has been disparaged as "the sort of liberalism...in which public policy is guided by basic principles of justice, but individuals are left to choose their own conception of the good."[86] Precisely.

I have argued so far that Okin's feminist touchstone is subjection, that her liberal aim is personal liberty of a Millian sort (with an important caveat I will discuss shortly). I have said that she did not subscribe consistently to any of the philosophical variations of egalitarian liberalism. She did not propose a systematic standard for government regulation of family life. Similarly, Okin cannot be profitably fit in a typology of liberalism, comprehensive or political. (She said she "subscribed to a position in between.")[87] I do not think this is the result of philosophic carelessness or a matter of the shifting grounds of case-by-case advocacy given her attention to specific entrenched inequalities in a variety of contexts. I think that, to her mind, "humanist liberalism" is the best that liberalism can and ought to offer, and I want to explore what direction humanist liberalism provides, without the support of a firmly grounded account of equality or liberty. What work does "humanist" do, beyond simply restating her preoccupation with subjection and vulnerability?

WHAT IS "HUMANIST" IN HUMANIST LIBERALISM?

The answer to this question begins with Okin's assertion that women are "full human beings to whom a theory of justice must apply."[88] Which is not to say that "human" is defined by being an object of justice (Okin may have thought that justice extended to

---

84. *JGF*, 172. Institutions and practices, she submits, must be acceptable to all views, with social protections for the vulnerable (*JGF*, 180).

85. *Is Multiculturalism Bad for Women?* 119.

86. Nussbaum, "A Feminist Theory of Justice," *New York Review of Books* 39.16 (October 8, 1992): 46. Nussbaum's assimilation of Okin to Rawls on the matter of basic resources is unwarranted.

87. *Is Multiculturalism Bad for Women?* 129.

88. *JGF*, 23.

other species), only that women are "full human beings." "Women matter…and their well-being matters at least as much as that of men"[89] (a red flag for a strict egalitarian interpretation). Mill cast the same idea in these terms: a woman has the right to be "a human being like any other, entitled to choose her pursuits, urged or invited by the same inducements as anyone else to interest herself in whatever is interesting to human beings."[90] Okin spoke of the capacity "to live as freely chosen lives as they can."[91]

Okin was agnostic about woman's nature—"I do not say anything about what defines woman," she insisted,[92] or human nature either. Reflecting this agnosticism, humanist liberalism brings her into conflict with those who rationalize constraints on women's freedom on the grounds of their presumed nature, not least "difference feminists," who insist on the distinctive epistemological and ethical outlooks of women and view them as outgrowths of instincts of care and connection. "Humanist" also brings her into conflict with various strands of antiessentialism—she was, recall, agnostic—and at the same time it brings her into conflict with most forms of anti-antiessentialism.

In her thought, "humanist" serves three identifiable purposes that contribute to her radical liberalism. They are all connected to a minimalist, noncomprehensive view of "human." And they are all bound up with agnosticism about women's nature and human nature. First, humanist accentuates the anticaste position that guided her work. At the extreme, in Okin's terms, she was concerned with women whose "lives are to be confined to domesticity and service to men."[93] In Mill's terms, again a touchstone, "in the more improved countries, the disabilities of women are the only case, save one [royalty], in which laws and institutions take persons at their birth, and ordain that they shall never in all their lives be allowed to compete for certain things."[94] "We live in a society that has over the years regarded the innate characteristic of sex as one of the clearest legitimizers of different rights and restrictions, both formal and informal," Okin wrote, and humanist rejects that.[95] Humanist also challenges "the deeply entrenched institutionalization of sexual difference,"[96] where "deeply entrenched" means the practically inescapable and severe limits on most women's liberty. Whatever the elements of a human life (I argue that Okin is agnostic and appropriately minimalist), women should not be systematically denied them because they are women. And vice versa: "nothing in our natures dictates that men should not be equal participants in the raising of children."[97] Her aim was less equal

---

89. "Gender Inequality and Cultural Differences," 11. Okin speaks of "human dignity equal to that of men and boys" in *Is Multiculturalism Bad for Women?* 11.

90. *Subjection*, 84.

91. *Is Multiculturalism Bad for Women?* 12.

92. "Response to Jane Flax," *Political Theory* 23.3 (August 1995): 511.

93. *Is Multiculturalism Bad for Women?* 17.

94. *Subjection*, 20.

95. *JGF*, 5. When she wrote, "If principles of justice are to be adopted unanimously by representative human beings ignorant of their particular characteristics and positions in society, they must be persons whose psychological and moral development is in all essentials identical," it was restricted to the thought experiment of the original position, which isolates a certain moral aspect of the person (*JGF*, 107).

96. *JGF*, 6.

97. *JGF*, 5.

parenting per se than challenging the sheer irrationality of a society where "no experience of raising children would be the practical prerequisite for attaining positions of the greatest influence."[98]

Mill's famous agnosticism about women's nature provides a window onto all this.[99] Recall that Mill's argument for civil and political equality for women is indirect: subjection is justifiable only if they are inherently inferior to men. Granted that there was never "any domination which did not appear natural to those who possessed it," in this case the evidence against natural inferiority is plain.[100] At a minimum, Mill could say that women are sufficiently equal to the worst men in those respects deemed relevant for civil and political rights. His refrain was that it would be ludicrous to think that we know what women are, since they have suffered "forced repression in some directions, unnatural stimulation in others."[101] He focused on women (at least in the first instance) because his concern was not cultural construction or socialization in general but specific dispositions and distortions produced by civil and domestic subjection. (Okin singled out a quote from Mill in her introduction: "the only thing that could advance knowledge of the natures of the two sexes meanwhile is the development of that branch of psychology now in a backward state—the study of the influence of circumstances on character.")[102]

It is worth noting that there are two catalogs of difference in *The Subjection of Women*. One set consists of the attributes that Mill himself ascribes to women, which he thinks may or may not be inherently characteristic of the sex and which in his account complement male attributes: better practical reasoning, more attention to details, insight into present facts rather than grasp of general principles ("a woman seldom runs wild after an abstraction");[103] intuition, and better insight into character. The other set consists of characteristics that Mill is confident can be attributed to circumstance: women as they appear are ignorant and disinterested in the world; as a rule they neither know nor care what is the right side in politics; they (middle-class women) are preoccupied only with money and invitations, comfort and public opinion. Women's aversion to war and "addiction to philanthropy" are no cause for

---

98. *JGF*, 171. Again, her concern is to undercut the dominant, institutionalized experiences that perpetuate coercive gender norms for women (and men). This is why she questioned any presumptive universal, "excluding or discriminating against individuals whose experiences are not encompassed by that norm," including unexamined impartiality or universality that "will not accept or accommodate difference." Mansbridge and Okin, "Feminism," 24.

99. See Okin's discussion of this in "John Stuart Mill, Liberal Feminist," in *Women in Western Political Thought* (Princeton, NJ: Princeton University Press, 1979).

100. *Subjection*, 13.

> It is not sufficient to maintain that women on the average are less gifted than men on the average, with certain of the higher mental faculties, or that a smaller number of women than of men are fit for occupations and functions of the highest intellectual character. It is necessary to maintain that no women at all are fit for them, and that the most eminent women are inferior in mental faculties to the most mediocre of the men on whom those functions at present devolve. (*Subjection*, 51)

101. *Subjection*, 22.
102. *Subjection*, 13.
103. *Subjection*, 58–59.

celebration.[104] Philanthropy is often attached to religious proselytizing, or directed toward friends not strangers, and in any event these sentiments are shaped by subjection: "all moralities tell them that it is the duty of women, and all current sentimentalities that it is their nature, to live for others."[105] Neither category gives prime place to the qualities that difference feminists valorize: mothering, nurturing capacities, "connection." Perhaps Mill had no sense of these things; he was childless, perceived his own mother as distant, and was notoriously skewed in his view of his wife. In any case, Mill had a cold-eyed view of the hypocrisy that lay behind valorizations of selflessness: "we are perpetually told that women are better than men, by those who are totally opposed to treating them as if they were as good."[106]

If women's nature does conform to how it appears under conditions of subjection, Mill concluded, allowing inclinations and vocations free play will not alter women's propensity to willingly become wives and mothers: "The anxiety of men to intercede on behalf of nature is altogether unnecessary solicitude."[107] If, however, emancipated women turn out to be more like men, then giving them free play will produce lively and general social progress. It would double the mass of mental faculties available for the higher service of humanity. It would add fresh social power, the stimulus of competition would be good for male intellects, and freedom of choice in occupations would be a boon to meritocracy and efficiency.

Despite his agnosticism, Mill imagined that ending subjection, especially under the conditions of social liberty and experiments in styles of life he envisioned in *On Liberty*, would produce a range of women's characters that mirrors men's. He set aside his speculation that women's and men's minds are positively complementary. Rather, "[a]ll women are brought up from the very earliest years in the belief that their ideal of character is the very opposite to that of men; not self-will and government by self-control, but submission, and yielding to the control of others."[108] Emancipated, women would no longer be brought up to be the opposite of men. He objected to the praise of Madame Roland "that she was almost more a man than a woman." Was there really, he asked, any distinction between the "highest masculine and the highest feminine character"?[109] Liberty would double the existing range of characters and talents rather than bring wholly different talents to work and to citizenship. He imagined, as Okin would, that liberty and opportunity for women would produce talents and characters, including what are now seen as gendered characteristics, in various combinations in both men and women. In her words: "In such a society, no assumptions would be made about 'male' and 'female' roles, and men and women would participate in more or less equal numbers in every sphere of life, from infant care to different kinds of paid work to high-level politics."[110]

104. *Subjection*, 87.
105. *Subjection*, 16.
106. *Subjection*, 42.
107. *Subjection*, 27.
108. *Subjection*, 16.
109. Himmelfarb, *On Liberty and Liberalism*, 197.
110. "Sexual Orientation and Gender," 45.

Against this background, I want to look again at gender and the family. *The Subjection of Women* is rife with the metaphor of the family as school. Mill wrote of the "perverting influence" of the typical English family and called it a "school of despotism," "a school of wilfullness, overbearingness, unbounded selfish indulgence, and a double-dyed and idealized selfishness." Ideally, it would be transformed into a "school of the virtues of freedom."[111] For Okin, too, the family was a carrier of caste, and perhaps her best-known notion is the family as a "school of justice." What does this mean for gender?

At present, typical family arrangements reflect and perpetuate entrenched gender roles and responsibilities that inhibit women's freedom. When Okin wrote that "gender can be done away with" and that difference in biological sex should have "no more social relevance than one's eye color or the length of one's toes,"[112] I don't think she should be read literally. "Gender-free" is ambiguous and liable to overinterpretation. Okin did not insist that all gendered attributes or roles should be eliminated. Her concern, once again, was that gendered roles and attributes assumed by individuals should not be the result of submission to coercive norms or institutionalized restrictions. There is no evidence that she would go further and erase the roles and responsibilities that are the product of historically gendered relations. David Estlund's conclusion that Okin advocated avoiding genders in their traditional roles, and avoiding traditional roles, regardless of which genders occupy them, makes her more systematic and emphatic than she was. She did not imagine the obliteration of familial practices and obligations (more on this in a moment). In this respect only, hers was a "rather cautious analysis."[113] The roles defined as "male" and "female" would remain; they might even be occupied by men and women, respectively. Gender-free means, modestly, that individuals are not born to nor bound by those roles and that law and public policy do not support them by regulations or incentives.[114]

Consider same-sex couples, which Okin invoked in several contexts: in discussions of equality, gender roles, and gender per se. She first commended same-sex relationships as more egalitarian, more likely to share paid and unpaid labor and to share equally than heterosexual couples. She also commended them, and this is a different point, as models of domestic relations devoid of traditional gender roles. Yet, she did not offer empirical evidence for this. She was unable to reasonably claim that same-sex couples do not assume gender roles traditionally defined, only that the participants are not the traditional gendered occupants of those roles.[115] Here, Estlund is half correct:

111. Cited in "Gender Inequality and Cultural Differences," 12; *Subjection*, 37, 44.

112. David Estlund's argument, citing Okin, in "Shaping and Sex," in Estlund and Nussbaum, eds., *Sex, Preference, and Family*, 155.

113. Nussbaum, "A Feminist Theory of Justice," 46.

114. There is little evidence for Estlund's conclusion that Okin advocates avoiding genders in their traditional roles and avoiding traditional roles, regardless of which genders occupy them; "Shaping and Sex," 158.

115. "Sexual Orientation and Gender," 55. Okin takes the argument for congruence too far—not in terms of legal enforceability but in terms of moral psychology; see Nancy L. Rosenblum, "Democratic Families: The 'Logic of Congruence' and Political Identity," *Hofstra Law Review* 32.1 (Fall 2003): 145–170. On whether Okin's concern is to avoid forced roles, unfair distributions of labor, or traditional gender roles, see Estlund, "Shaping and Sex," 158–159.

"Okin's main point is not to praise gay couples for avoiding traditional roles, but rather to argue that, insofar as they happen to avoid those roles, they are worthy models for heterosexual families."[116] I say "half correct" because Okin did not spend time imagining wholly new roles, responsibilities, or marital and family arrangements. The idea is not to avoid the roles, per se, but to avoid ascriptive roles. In earlier work, she insisted that altered heterosexual parenting would help to break down rigid gender roles and gendered notions of character and capabilities: "Only children who are equally mothered and fathered can develop fully the psychological and moral capacities that currently seem to be unequally distributed between the sexes."[117] In later pieces, she proposed that the same lesson is taught by same-sex parenting.[118] Given Okin's agnosticism about women's nature and human nature, it would be surprising if "humanist" entailed a severe and thoroughgoing gender-free ideal. Humanist does work positively to reinforce her anticaste standard and to underscore personal liberty. It is permanently radical because the forces and incarnations of ascriptive positions are innumerable and unending.

The second purpose that humanist serves in Okin's work is also tied to her agnosticism about women's nature. Humanist pushes sexuality away from center-stage, indeed off-stage almost entirely. She sometimes suggested that sexual difference should carry no social significance,[119] but qualified this elsewhere as "reducing the salience of sexual difference to a minimum," and she also said that "there are some socially relevant physical differences between women and men."[120] The work done by the term humanist is to discount sexual difference as the basis of feminism. One critic chides Okin for not having "a richer psychological and historical inquiry into the nature of human desire," adding that she was too "fond of making simple and unambiguous statements about matters that are deeply ambiguous and mysterious."[121] Okin did not delve into desire, and she would doubtless have conceded that sex and intimacy are "ambiguous and mysterious." Humanist is not antierotic or antisexual any more than it is antigender. Okin did suggest, however, that the consequences of certain institutionalized sexual differences for liberal rights and opportunities are unambiguous. The cases in which men, supported by cultural laws or norms, control women's sexuality and reproductive capabilities, rendering them servile to men, "shout out to us."[122]

---

116. Estlund, "Shaping and Sex," 159.

117. *JGF*, 107.

118. The lesson works both ways: "if a person's sex were of greatly diminished social and legal significance, then it would also be seen as of little matter whether a child who had two parents had two parents of the same sex or of different sexes." "Sexual Orientation and Gender," 46.

Oddly, Okin has been said to endorse a version of comprehensive liberalism with a perfectionist strain. In challenging Rawls' account of the family as it appears in *Political Liberalism*, she argues that justice cannot be sustained without full-blown education in the family of the sort that Rawls' notion of reasonableness does not endorse. I believe this is, if not a misreading, than an overreading of Okin's position. See note 77 above.

119. *JGF*, 12.

120. "Sexual Orientation and Gender," 45; *JGF*, 10.

121. Nussbaum, "A Feminist Theory of Justice," 46.

122. *Is Multiculturalism Bad for Women?* 17.

Humanist is a deliberate orientation away from the physical and presumptive sexual differences between men and women that is the core of much feminist philosophy, in particular work like Catharine MacKinnon's, which makes sexuality the dynamic of domination. In this approach, "the sexuality of dominance and submission" is crucial, on some level definitive of gender inequality.[123] Femininity is what male desire requires for arousal and satisfaction. It is not just that women's sexuality is shaped under conditions of gender inequality so that women cannot negotiate sexual encounters on equal terms. It is that sexuality itself is the dynamic of subjection. There is a noticeable vacuum at the heart of MacKinnon's work, a sort of "uncaused cause." Why is dominance erotic, and why does male eroticism center on force, hostility, contempt, and the enjoyment of violation epitomized in sadomasochism? In any case, Okin would have none of this. The dynamic of subjection is not erotic, and humanist is a way of denying sexuality's central place in feminism.

HUMANIST BUT "NOT FULLY HUMAN"

Humanism did a third piece of work for Okin, which I think of as evidence of philosophical humility. It has to do, once again, with her agnosticism about human nature, which reinforced her unwillingness to build ideals of human character or relationship into radical liberalism. Put simply, Okin insisted that women are "full human beings," but she did not speculate about what it is to be "fully human." She declined to speculate for good reason. "Subjection" and "vulnerability" were enough to motivate and direct liberal political theory; perfectionism was not necessary and could be harmful. Humanist as anti-idealist is counterintuitive, of course, since the historical associations of the idea are bound up with *bildung*. In Okin's case, agnosticism combined with a mature acceptance of men and women as they are, as improvable perhaps but not progressive or perfectible, to define liberal humanism. Again, Mill was the touchstone, only this time Okin diverged from him.

Mill saw liberty as the condition for the development of each individual's powers. Maximizing individual development is also crucial to the dynamic of social progress (indeed, "every step in improvement has been...invariably accompanied by a step made in raising the social position of women").[124] Happiness rightly understood (higher happiness) is the ultimate value, the only desirable end, in Mill's philosophy. He did not conflate the desirable with what is generally desired; he moved away from preference-based utilitarianism, and therefore did not insist that the emancipation of women would make everyone happier on their own terms.[125] Most men would not think themselves happier for losing absolute and arbitrary power over women.

123. Catharine MacKinnon, "Sexuality, Pornography and Method," in Cass R. Sunstein, ed., *Feminism and Political Theory* (Chicago: University of Chicago Press, 1982), 209.

124. *Subjection*, 22; "Editor's Introduction," iv. Okin wrote about Mill's progressivism in her chapter on Mill, "John Stuart Mill, Liberal Feminist," in *Women in Western Political Thought* (Princeton, NJ: Princeton University Press, 1979).

125. John Gray, "Introduction," in John Stuart Mill, *On Liberty and Other Essays* (New York: Oxford University Press, 1991), xi.

But an end to subjection would make men better. That is the thrust of these familiar passages: wives are a "dead weight" on husbands' ambitions so that "[w]hoever has a wife and children has given hostages to Mrs. Grundy," and, "[i]t is not with impunity that the superior in intellect shuts himself up with an inferior and elects that inferior for his chosen and sole completely intimate associate."[126] Unconstrained power nourishes self-worship, unjust self-preference; despotism makes men into moral brutes. If women were free, men would no longer be depriving themselves of the intimacy and moral uplift of the companionship of equals. On Mill's terms, then, men would be happier.

Writing about Harriet Taylor, Mill rhapsodizes about "the highest realizable ideal of human life." Presumably, he intended the "highest realizable ideal" to be consistent with his view that there is no determinate set of higher pleasures, no one ideal of human life. Individuality implies a possibly infinite variety of complex human natures, presumably embracing different elements of higher happiness. Individuality means uniqueness, every person his or her own "complete and harmonious whole." The counterpart of perfectionism in individuals is Mill's ideal of "perfect friendship," "marital friendship."[127] His description (a self-description and the opposite of what he saw as his father's "ill assorted marriage")[128] runs on for pages and invokes true affection, genuine moral sentiment, sympathy, "living together in love," an "unspeakable gain in private happiness," constant partaking in the same things, "complete unity and unanimity as to the great objects of life," and "alternately the pleasure of leading and being led in the path of development."[129]

Okin subscribed to Mill's notion of individuality: innumerable, complex human natures. But there is no hint in her writing of Mill's perfectionism or eudaimonism. Clearly, she did not countenance Millian arguments for despotism as potentially civilizing. Nor did she harbor ideals of friendship or family. This is worth noting. Like Mill, she never contemplated eliminating marriage or the family. Rawls simply "assumed" that the family was a just institution; Okin subjected it to principles of justice and was latitudinarian about its form (gay couples and parents, single-parent families, and other nontraditional shapes), but she was adamant: we "refuse to give up on the institution of the family, and refuse to accept the division of labor between the sexes as natural and unchangeable."[130] The nuclear family with one or more parents and children goes unquestioned. This is important evidence of her anti-utopianism. For utopian thought and utopian communities in practice have always revolved around the organization of work and sex (Mill was enthralled by Owenite and Fourierist schemes).[131] There is no whisper of the erasure of private family life in Okin's work, nor of the novel intimate relations and child-raising arrangements we find in every ideal community. She did not promote an ideal of marriage, family, or social order; her prescriptions were

---

126. *Subjection*, 90, 94.
127. "Editor's Introduction," xiii.
128. Himmelfarb, *On Liberty and Liberalism*, 190.
129. *Subjection*, 24–25, 43–45, 93–95.
130. *JGF*, 125.
131. Nancy L. Rosenblum, "Democratic Sex," in Estlund and Nussbaum, eds., *Sex, Preference, and Family*.

corrective, modestly improving, tolerant not perfecting. She did not indulge Mill's "dream of an enthusiast."[132]

Okin has been criticized on these grounds, for challenging those who refused to acknowledge the family as a scene of justice, without allowing that it could also be an attractive ideal beyond justice. "An unnecessary dismissal is preferable to an unreflective embrace," Joshua Cohen conceded. "Still, I think that Okin's view would have been strengthened if she had captured what is plausible in the view that ideal families lie beyond justice while rejecting the offending construals of it."[133] Okin wrote, plainly, "asserting that families should be organized justly or fairly does not mean that this is the best behavior we can or should expect of them."[134] But she did not belabor "the best" nor propose "a reasonable and attractive ideal." Not from "inside," examining personal experiences, nor from outside as a critic, did she think Mill's "perfect friendship" was a useful ideal, nor did she search for any other. Her liberalism and her agnosticism combined to make her resolutely anti-idealist.[135] In this respect, Okin's humanist liberalism is anti-antiessentialism; antiessentialism is seldom content with modest prohibitions, incentives, and improvements, and it often explicitly assumes that social construction entails limitless malleability, playful self-design constrained only by imagination.

We can learn more about the term humanist and Okin's spurning of perfectionism from her response to contemporary accounts of the good life and well-being. Martha Nussbaum took Okin to task for failing to adequately ground her liberalism and proposed a capabilities approach with an exhaustive catalog of desirable "functionings." By speaking more of capabilities than functionings, Nussbaum held strong perfectionism at bay, but what she referred to as a "full human life" includes at least ten capabilities; using one's imagination to produce self-expressive and self-chosen works and events (literary and religious) or to relate to animals, plants, and the world of nature are listed along with having a normal lifespan, bodily security, and the social basis of self-respect. Certain capabilities, Nussbaum argued, "exert a moral claim that they should be developed."[136] She spoke of the "tragic aspect" of being below the threshold in any of them;[137] of a complete human life; of planning "for one's own life without being able to do so in complex forms of discourse, concern, and reciprocity with other human beings [which] is…to behave in an incompletely human way";[138] of anything

132. *Subjection*, 95.

133. Cohen, "Okin on Justice, Gender, and Family," 277.

134. Okin, "Forty Acres," 24.

135. One argument for Okin as a would-be theorist of congruence is that her liberalism was "comprehensive," since on Rawls' definition a comprehensive moral conception includes what is of value in human life, ideals of personal character, and ideals of friendship and of familial and associational relationships. I argue below that Okin eschews every one of these.

136. Cited in Susan Okin, "Poverty, Well-Being and Gender: What Counts, Who's Heard?" *Philosophy and Public Affairs* 31.3 (2003): 294. Nussbaum speaks of "the thick vague conception of the good" in "Aristotelian Social Democracy," in R. B. Douglas et al., eds., *Liberalism and the Good* (New York: Routledge, 1990), 217.

137. Cited in Okin, "Poverty, Well-Being and Gender," 294.

138. Cited in Okin, "Poverty, Well-Being and Gender," 296.

less as a life that is "not fully human, in the sense of their not being worthy of the dignity of the human being."[139]

Okin did not accept the challenge of grounding her humanist liberalism, it should
now be clear. But she did challenge Nussbaum's perfectionism. The lives of Third
World women on which Nussbaum reports in *Women and Human Development* raised
questions in Okin's mind about her "rigid view" of human capabilities and an enu-
meration in which they appear equally important and central. Okin did not propose
an alternative account of capabilities nor an alternative ordering. Her point was that
Nussbaum's "professed sensitivity to what poor women actually say about their lives
and concerns is in some tension with her own preformed view of human capabilities."[140] Disputes about listening to women's voices and its perils (a mentality of "small
mercies"; women who come to terms with very little)[141] or about the critical stance of
insiders/outsiders[142] pale in this context next to Okin's main concern, which is as usual
more political than philosophical. She resisted both Nussbaum's set of capabilities and
the moral imperative of development as perfectionist. Nussbaum's view is incompatible with Okin's own modest agnosticism about women's nature and human nature.
This set of capabilities was *set*, rigid, presumptuous.

Given Okin's agnosticism and corresponding humility, her humanist compass was
oriented toward the known evil of subjection and vulnerability, with its allusion to fear
and physical insecurity.[143] That is why Okin thought Nussbaum's expansive catalog
of capacities verged on the promiscuous. It does not prioritize. Nussbaum's narrative contradicts her perfectionist philosophy, Okin observed: on women's own reports,
there is "no sign that they would consider such capabilities just as central in their lives
as being able to eat adequately or not to be beaten."[144] Other than this spare but vital
orientation, humanist has no core, positive content. But it suffices to provide another
reason for Okin's anti-antiessentialism: her insistence on commonalities and patterns
in the subjection of women, despite its variable forms. This accusation that antiessentialists willfully turn a blind eye to the vulnerabilities faced by women in general is
pure Okin:

> While this debate continues, women are being beaten by their husbands and are
> dying needlessly from botched illegal abortions, girls go undernourished and
> uneducated, and development policy is decided and executed. This is a critical
> juncture for feminist issues in a global context.[145]

---

139. Martha Nussbaum, "On Hearing Women's Voices: A Reply to Susan Okin," *Philosophy and
Public Affairs* 32.2 (2004): 197.

140. "Response to Martha Nussbaum," unpublished letter in possession of the author (Rosenblum).

141. "Gender Inequality and Cultural Differences," 19.

142. See her brief statement on standing outside a specific context in order to leverage critical force
for theorizing relations of domination in "Response to Jane Flax," 514.

143. She sides with Sen over Nussbaum when discussing "basic social minimum[s]" or "certain
very general values" in "Poverty, Well-Being and Gender," 297.

144. Okin, "Poverty, Well-Being and Gender," 296. See Nussbaum's response, "On Hearing Wom-
en's Voices."

145. "Response to Jane Flax," 514.

She did not say, with Mill, that "after the primary necessities of food and raiment, freedom is the first and strongest want of human nature."[146] But she could have cited Mill against feminists who see liberalism as parochial: "He who would rightly appreciate the worth of personal independence as an element of happiness, should consider the value he himself puts upon it as an ingredient of his own."[147] Her minimalist humanism should have been unexceptionable for reasons Joshua Cohen has put well: "she is not principally concerned to characterize general features of 'women's *experience* of the world,' but rather to indicate certain patterns of constraint, opportunity, and expectation faced by women generally."[148] The patterns are what Mill called subjection, and humanist liberalism is permanently radical because the "critical areas of concern" are contingent and ever-changing: "As an ideology, a way of seeing and making sense of things, we expect feminism, as it spreads across the globe, to take forms not easily predictable from western experience."[149]

It is not reductionist to say that humanism is compatible with lower happiness and does not require a notion of human nature, or capabilities, or a fully human or complete human life. In saying that women are "full human beings," she did not mean to invoke a notion of what is fully human. Okin demonstrated the sufficiency of spare humanism for radical liberalism. Her humanist rises above the bare minimalism of human as mortal. But Okin's focus on vulnerability is closer to minimalism than to perfectionism.

CONCLUSION: AN IOTA OF UTOPIANISM?

The Subjection of Women remains an inspiring book. Only a superficial reading or a complacency about the novelty and significance of contemporary feminist insights would find it conventional, conservative, or irrelevant to present conditions. Nonetheless, Mill himself was despairing. He held off publication to give the tract strategic punch. When the book was published in 1869, it was received with hostility even by his friends, and his practical political proposals went nowhere. The weight of received opinion was a formidable obstacle to undoing the subjection of women. Nothing in Mill's parliamentary experience when he proposed amending the suffrage bill to include women gave him much hope. He rued the fact that Britain lacked the conventions and organized parties that agitated for the rights of women in the United States.[150] Popular opinion was reinforced by the fact that so many men benefited from it. Nothing in Mill's grim analysis suggested why men *would* grant equality to women. The prospect of ideal friendship was no compensation for the pleasures of power. His despair emerged here and there: "the generality of the male sex cannot yet tolerate the idea of living with an equal." Rational argument could not change

---

146. *Subjection*, 95.
147. *Subjection*, 96.
148. Cohen, "Okin on Justice, Gender, and Family," 266–267.
149. Mansbridge and Okin, "Feminism," 38.
150. *Subjection*, 15.

things. We feel Mill's sympathetic despair in his description of the lives of women: "the feeling of a wasted life," the "weariness, disappointment, and profound dissatisfaction with life."[151]

What did change, and what gives Okin's feminism a more sanguine cast, was the moral outrage and political organization of women. When Mill wrote, he had to explain the passivity of subjection: "it is a political law of nature that those under any power of ancient origin, never begin by complaining of the power itself, but only of its oppressive exercise."[152] For Okin's generation, not only was women's liberation written into antidiscrimination laws and a host of public policies, but the political work was done by women, in political alliance with some men. Of course, Okin was troubled by the feebleness and incompleteness of the policies aimed at reducing "vulnerability by marriage." But on the matter of practical reforms and everyday feminism, she had an iota of utopianism. Her despair came from other sources: the persistent inattention of political philosophers and the writings of many academic feminists who were more preoccupied with elaborate theory than with the reality of subjection. She had a single object in view: using the most accessible, historically effective apparatus of political thought—rights and institutional constraints on power—to argue for the protection of and liberty for the vulnerable. In the tradition of great liberals, she gave us political theory as advocacy, liberalism as radical political thought.

151. *Subjection*, 100.
152. *Subjection*.

2

A Matter of Demolition?

Susan Okin on Justice and Gender

Joshua Cohen

Susan Moller Okin and I last spoke in December 2003. We had an electronic conversation, and it ended badly. Susan was angry with me, as I was with her. She thought I was abusing power; I thought she was past stubborn. Faced with rapidly diminishing returns to further communication, I suggested that we renew our discussion when we could get back on a more constructive footing. Susan did not respond. I interpreted the absence of response as an endorsement of the hopeful prospect of constructive future discussion. But that was it. A friendship of more than 15 years ended in a disturbing silence.

I take some consolation and comfort, then, from the fact that Susan Okin left us with a substantial body of writing. Her writing makes it possible to continue a conversation with her, at least in an attenuated sense of conversation, and at least about some common intellectual interests. Susan's voice—I am thinking of "voice" in that capacious sense that comprises both written and spoken words, both substance and intonation—remains vivid for me, sufficiently vivid that I am able to continue to learn from her, trying in imagination to occupy her sensibility, to see things as she might have seen them, and to let those ways of seeing exercise the kind of intellectual pressure on me that they did during the course of her life.

In that spirit, I would like to pick up a conversation that Susan Okin and I had in the early 1990s. I had just published a long review of *Justice, Gender, and the Family*.[1] The review, while generally very favorable, also made some criticisms. After it appeared, I received a letter from Susan.[2] She was appreciative of the extended discussion, grateful for the praise, and prepared to acknowledge the force of one criticism. I had argued that two parts of her view were in some tension. The first, expressed in her analysis of "vulnerability by marriage,"[3] focused on the ways that gender inequalities in labor markets and families are mutually reinforcing parts of a single system. Simplifying a

I presented earlier drafts of this chapter at the February 2005 Stanford conference in memory of Susan Okin and at Stanford Law School. I am grateful for comments and suggestions from Corey Brettschneider, Barbara Fried, Joseph Grundfest, Rob Reich, Deborah Rhode, and Debra Satz.

1. See Joshua Cohen, "Okin on Justice, Gender, and Family," *Canadian Journal of Philosophy* 22.2 (June 1992): 263–286.

2. I am reconstructing the letter from memory, but I am pretty confident that I have it more or less right.

3. *Justice, Gender, and the Family* (New York: Basic, 1989), ch. 7 (hereafter *JGF*).

complicated terrain, the dual-system idea was that labor market inequalities make it rational for women to spend more time on family concerns, while gendered expectations about domesticity make it rational for women to devote less time and effort to the labor market. The second, a central theme running through *JGF*, as well as through Okin's first book, *Women in Western Political Thought*,[4] identified domestic inequality as the "linchpin" in the gender system.[5] The dual-system analysis of mutual reinforcement, however, undermined the force of identifying domestic inequality as the linchpin—not because labor market inequality was really the linchpin, but because the system of mutually reinforcing disadvantage did not have or need a linchpin. In response, Okin agreed that the linchpin thesis may not have been doing any work.

But several of my criticisms struck her as misguided. She sketched some reasons; I was not convinced. But we never really explored the issues. That is what I would like to do here—with reduced confidence in my earlier convictions, but also with a little less preoccupation about who was right and who was wrong. Okin's central theme was that women and men are moral equals and that our normative political thought has not taken this point on board. My main concern is to appreciate more fully the ways in which that central theme shifts the terrain of political argument.

I will discuss the three points on which Okin expressed disquiet or disagreement with what I had written. Each point concerns an issue that loomed large in Susan Okin's work: the feminist method, the relationship between family and polity, and the public-private distinction.

FEMINIST METHOD

Susan Okin was not much interested in "method" (I share her limited enthusiasm for the subject). If she had a method, it was pretty straightforward. The idea was to consider a political-philosophical outlook, add to it the elementary feminist thesis—that women are "full human beings to whom a theory of social justice must apply"[6]—and then see whether the resulting combination combusts.

Okin believed that this method had some striking results. She thought that the elementary feminist thesis created troubles for an easy reconciliation of feminist and multiculturalist commitments by undermining a range of otherwise plausible-seeming proposals for group rights.[7] In *Justice, Gender, and the Family*, she argued that some contemporary conceptions of justice—including libertarianism and some forms of communitarian theory—are "completely demolished"[8] when confronted with the moral equality of men and women expressed in the elementary feminist thesis. Now, if a conception of justice simply denied that women and men were moral equals, then the demolition born of that confrontation would be straightforward. But Okin had

4. *Women in Western Political Thought* (Princeton, NJ: Princeton University Press, 1979).

5. See, for example, *JGF*, 6.

6. *JGF*, 23.

7. Joshua Cohen, Matthew Howard, and Martha Nussbaum, eds., *Is Multiculturalism Bad for Women?* (Princeton, NJ: Princeton University Press, 1999).

8. *JGF*, 23.

something else in mind, something deeper, more complicated, and addressed to views that do not reject the abstract principle that men and women are moral equals. Her reflections on libertarianism illustrate the point.

Okin's criticisms of libertarianism focus on Robert Nozick's possessive libertarianism.[9] I call it "possessive" because it assigned the notion of ownership a fundamental role in political argument, and it was founded in particular on the premise that persons are full proprietors of themselves: self-owners.[10] This view has been subjected to wide-ranging criticism, but Okin's objection was original. She claimed that, if one adds the elementary feminist thesis—that women are "full human beings to whom a theory of social justice must apply"—to possessive libertarianism, then possessive libertarianism degenerates into matriarchy and incoherence. To see how, consider a reconstruction of Okin's argument against Nozick:[11]

1. Each person fully owns him- or herself (libertarian premise 1).
2. A person's making something from materials that the person fully owns confers full ownership of the thing on the person who made it (libertarian premise 2).
3. I am a person (assumption).
4. I fully own myself (from 1, 3).
5. My mother is a person, within the meaning of premises 1 and 2 (applying the elementary feminist thesis).
6. My mother made me from materials that she fully owned (assumption).
7. My mother fully owns me (from 2, 5, 6).
8. But two people cannot fully own the same thing (definition of full ownership).
9. My mother does not own me (from 4, 8).
10. I do not own myself (from 7, 8).

Three points about this argument. First, to make it valid, a few details would need to be cleaned up, but it is close enough. Second, arguing over (6), though legitimate, will not help anyone.[12] Third, the argument does not, as Okin claims, give us "a bizarre combination of matriarchy and slavery": while (7) is matriarchy, we also have (9),

---

9. Robert Nozick, *Anarchy, State, and Utopia* (New York: Basic, 1974). Okin mentions that libertarianism "takes to extremes" the classical liberal ideas of Locke and Constant (*JGF*, 74); moreover, within the libertarian family, she distinguishes varieties that focus on property rights (Nozick and Ayn Rand) from other forms of libertarianism (*JGF*, 87–88). It is not clear, then, how and to what extent her criticisms of Nozick's possessive libertarianism were meant to generalize. For a forceful and, I think, convincing discussion of the sharp distinction between classical liberalism and libertarianism, see Samuel Freeman, "Illiberal Libertarians: Why Libertarianism Is Not a Liberal View," *Philosophy and Public Affairs* 30.2 (Spring 2001): 105–151.

10. See Nozick, *Anarchy, State, and Utopia*, 171–172. I believe that G. A. Cohen was the first to identify the idea of self-ownership as the root idea in Nozick's libertarianism. See his *Self-Ownership, Freedom, and Equality* (Cambridge: Cambridge University Press, 1995), esp. chs. 3, 6.

11. Here, I expand on the discussion in Cohen, "Okin on Justice, Gender, and Family," 274–275.

12. As Barbara Fried has reminded me, the assumption that birth mothers own genetic material is both obscure and highly controversial.

which denies matriarchy. But never mind matriarchy. The view does look pretty incoherent, in fact, flatly inconsistent. Moreover, the inconsistency does not arise because possessive libertarianism denies the elementary feminist thesis, but because possessive libertarianism accepts it.

The crucial idea in the argument is that possessive libertarianism is committed to (1) and (2). Accepting those moral premises, the only way to avoid inconsistency is to overlook (5). I say "overlook," because a possessive libertarian would not want to deny (5). Nozick in particular was simply not thinking about it: not thinking, in particular, that premises (1) and (2) apply to women, some of whom bear children. So we have a more or less perfect rendering of Okin's point: some theories are completely demolished —deriving an inconsistency from basic premises is a demolition job—once we attend to the commonly unattended but elementary feminist thesis.

The example is striking, but the obvious possessive libertarian reply is that the argument simply shows the need to restrict premise (2), which I will call the "modified pottery barn principle." The pottery barn principle says "you break it, you own it"; the modified pottery barn principle expressed in (2) says "you make it, you own it." The possessive libertarian, then, can call on a restricted version of the modified pottery barn principle, which says "you make it, you own it, except if you have made a person." Moreover, that restriction is well-motivated. After all, the possessive libertarian story is that people own what they make *because* they own themselves: whatever the force of that "because," that is the theory. Self-ownership—expressed in the first libertarian premise—is the core idea: the modified pottery barn principle is not an independent principle, but derived from the core idea. So we need to restrict the modified pottery barn principle so that it does not yield the ownership of other people; but that restriction is motivated by the basic self-ownership axiom. Put otherwise and more simply: only the restricted form of the modified pottery barn principle plausibly follows from the principle that people own themselves.

That's a slightly more elaborate version of what I said in my review, and it still strikes me as correct. I do not see that we have a demolition. So what might have bothered Susan Okin?

Two possibilities.

Okin might have thought, first, that the possessive libertarian response almost facetiously exemplifies the very problem that she had labored so hard to expose. After all, doesn't it essentially say that the modified pottery barn principle applies to everyone, except women? Haven't we landed in the world of *Geduldig v. Aiello*, which denied that there was sex discrimination in a regulation that covered lots of medical disabilities but excluded pregnancy from its coverage?[13]

Not really. The response simply says that persons cannot be owned unless they are sold by themselves: that is the basic moral idea. Self-ownership supports the modified pottery barn principle only when it is thus qualified. Women and men own everything else that they make with what they own. But it is misguided to claim to own someone else, who has the *very same claim to self-ownership that provides the basis of your claim*

13. *Geduldig v. Aiello*, 417 US 484 (1974).

to own that person, unless the person has sold him- or herself to you (a sale that Nozick takes to be morally acceptable).

But a second and more forceful response is waiting in the wings. This second response does not rest everything on alleged troubles for the self-ownership principle generated by the childbearing experience of some women, but treats that experience as the opening wedge in a broader argument about the moral significance of human relationships and the difficulty of using the category of ownership to capture the moral importance of those relationships. Consider me at age three. I was a person—a little person, but a person all the same. Still, I guess that I did not yet fully own myself. I could not make binding contracts, for example, or sell myself or parts of me. But my mother did not fully own me either: some sorts of treatment of me, even by her, were ruled out by my moral status. So, for example, on Nozick's view, it would have been fine for my mother, as full proprietor of her own person, to sell her eyes (fine, as in, had she contracted to do so, the contract would have been morally binding and the state ought to have enforced it). But it would have been wrong, impermissible, for her to sell my eyes. And that would have been wrong not because I owned myself and grabbing my eyes would have been a theft predicated on a trespass: as I said, at age three, I did not own myself, and no one else owned me either. So we need to say something about the moral relations between persons that cannot be fully explained by reference to the idea of self-ownership and the exercise of moral powers founded on self-ownership.[14]

And let's not stop here: it is not only that my mother should not have been peddling my eyes, or any other parts of me. She also owed me something more positive, say, appropriate care and concern, with attention to my health and, perhaps, as Locke supposed, some education.[15] Then, too, we might suppose that I owed something to my mother (and still do): some duty of respect, perhaps gratitude, maybe concern and support. But suppose I do owe something, in virtue of the concern and benefit conferred on me, the continuity of care over a long period, and not simply in virtue of the conferral of life (so the point applies to adopted children as well). Then we have a wider family of nonconsensual obligations, of nurturance and education, that cannot be explained in terms of self-ownership.

So we seem to have some kinds of moral relations, and it seems right to say that the relations bear on what we owe to one another (not only on what the humanly attractive qualities are). If one accepts that, then one agrees that we cannot fully account

14. Of course, there are lots of powers that parents have over children: not to extract their eyes, but to require a safe medical procedure on their eyes. And there are large areas of reasonable controversy about the range of those powers. Moreover, some of the powers of parents will of course coincide with the powers that an owner would have (as some powers of an employer coincide with the much more expansive powers of a slaveowner). But the powers will not be as extensive as those that a Nozickian self-owner has over him- or herself. And once we agree that the powers will be less extensive, we will make no headway in thinking about the proper range by using the idea of ownership as a basis for our reflections. On this last point, see Barbara Fried, "Left-Libertarianism: A Review Essay," *Philosophy and Public Affairs* 32.1 (Winter 2004): 70–84.

15. John Locke, *Second Treatise*, edited by Peter Laslett (Cambridge: Cambridge University Press, 1988), para. 56.

for the moral relations between and among persons by reference to considerations of self-ownership and the exercise of rights associated therewith. John Locke knew that. His natural law framework is founded on an overarching obligation to preserve humankind and provides a basis for obligations between parents and at least their biological offspring that cannot be accounted for in terms of the moral facts about equal freedom and consent that explain the obligations—in particular, the political obligations—owed to one another by free and equal adults.

The easy libertarian response is that these observations do not give us a demolition, but only show the need for an extension, that is, for supplementing the possessive libertarian's moral notions with an additional set of moral principles suited to the terrain of childbearing and childrearing. So the libertarian might say: "OK, I need to add something. I will get to that later. But what you say bears only on what I have not discussed. It has no bearing on my principal subject, which is the political morality of relations between and among adults." But maybe that response is not quite right. Maybe it is too quick.

To see why it might be too quick, consider two nonconsensual theories that are sometimes used to account for a range of social and political obligations: a theory based on the duty of fair play and a theory of "associative obligations." The first says, roughly, that when other people constrain their conduct to contribute to a cooperative activity, and that cooperative activity confers essential benefits on me (not simply any benefits at all, but those that are crucial to my having a minimally decent life), I have a duty to reciprocate by accepting corresponding constraints on my activity, even if I have not requested that the benefits be conferred nor volunteered to do a share of the work of providing them.

The second theory says, very roughly, that when I am a member of an association, and the other members of the association treat me with appropriate concern and respect, then I have an obligation to comply with the norms associated with my position or role in the association.[16] Ronald Dworkin advances this associative theory to account for a range of obligations, including—but not limited to—political obligations.

My concern here is not to argue the merits of these theories, understood in particular as accounts of political obligation. Suffice to say that they share the idea that political obligation is not founded on consent—more broadly, not voluntarily undertaken. The essential point here is that the plausibility of these views, as accounts of political obligation, depends on there being *some* relatively uncontroversial cases of nonvoluntary obligations that apply differently to different people. In particular, the plausibility of each theory—especially the associative—is enhanced by the case of familial obligations. But with these nonvoluntarist theories of obligation available—supported by, inter alia, the familial case and then extended to the political—the possessive libertarian now needs a more complicated story. Either the possessive libertarian needs to explain familial obligations—including the more positive obligations of nurturance and education—in terms of self-ownership (or the potential for such), or to explain why the fairness theory or the associative theory, which plausibly account for *some*

---

16. See Ronald Dworkin, *Law's Empire* (Cambridge, MA: Harvard University Press, 1986), 195–202.

obligations (namely, the familial), do not extend to the wider range of social and political obligations as well. The easy argument that familial obligations are simply a separate concern is too quick: there is a need to address the issue more directly.

The possessive libertarian may have a good answer; he or she will certainly have something to say, and that something will likely include a crisp distinction between family and polity, an emphasis on the distinctiveness of political obligations, and an effort to cabin the nonconsensual. So we do not have a demolition: that was a mistake.

But philosophy does not work by demolition, and positions that can be dispatched so completely and so quickly were not worth the attention in the first place. Philosophy works in part by drawing attention to phenomena that people are overlooking and thereby shifting burdens of argument. But on this point about shifting burdens, I now think that Okin had an important point. I now see in retrospect that my proposed libertarian qualification of the modified pottery barn principle—that it does not apply to persons—was correct but superficial. The possessive libertarian can respond exactly as I suggested, but the libertarian cannot stop there: he or she now owes an account of nonconsensual familial obligations and then also an account of how to restrict the moral notions used to account for nonconsensual, particularistic, familial obligations so that they do not spread to a wider terrain of social and political obligations.

Whether that can be done is another matter; I will leave it to clever libertarians. But when one overlooks the elementary feminist thesis, one is less likely even to see the need to take this task on. And that is at least a version of Susan Okin's point.

BEYOND JUSTICE

A second point of disagreement that emerged in our communication after my review appeared is more complex, both as to its substance and as to the nature of the disagreement. But like the first, it began with my skepticism about a proposed demolition.

Susan Okin criticized a variety of views—Michael Sandel's in particular—for putting the family "beyond justice." It is not at all clear what it means to say (or therefore to deny) that the family is an arena beyond justice, any more than it was clear what Marx meant when he said that communist society lay beyond the "narrow horizon of bourgeois right."[17] It seemed clear to me (and still does) that there are interpretations of the idea of the family as an arena beyond justice that give romantic cover to abuse and privilege, but also that there are interpretations that express something important about forms of human connection. And I supposed (as I still do) that some of the disagreement could be dispelled by fixing the interpretation.

Sandel seemed to think that if we say that principles of justice apply to the family then we are supposing something about, so to speak, the culture of family: that the members would openly and expressly aim to resolve their disagreements by explicit reference to, for example, Rawls' principles of justice. To say that the principles apply is to say that they are to enter in a fully explicit way into the domestic ethos. Thus the

---

17. Karl Marx, "Critique of the Gotha Program," in Robert Tucker, ed., *Marx-Engels Reader*, 2nd ed. (New York: Norton, 1978), 531.

relevance of Sandel's claim that this appeal to abstract principles would only happen in a far-from-ideal family, ridden by conflict, whose members were not acting out of affection for one another but would only "dutifully if sullenly abide by the two principles of justice."[18] While Sandel's point focused on Rawlsian principles, the force of the observation (like Marx's) seems to apply to other conceptions of justice as well: the point is about the (alleged) deficiencies of a social world in which people find it natural to make explicit appeals to abstract principles, to ideas about rights and about what we owe to each other. The point is about the form of justice and not only its content.

Okin, in contrast, seemed to be saying that, if one puts the family beyond justice, one is not making a point about how families are to make decisions about their own organization and allocation of resources, but is instead denying that principles of justice have any bearing at all on our thought about the family. One is claiming that those principles do not, for example, provide appropriate standards for the framework of law and public policy within which families are set.

But if this interpretation is right, then they are talking past each other, and Okin is unnecessarily exaggerating the disagreement between the "beyond justice" view and her own emphasis on the priority of justice. I thought her view could be strengthened by accommodating what was plausible in the beyond-justice conception. My strategy of accommodation was to distinguish two deliberative standpoints, each associated with distinct norms, attitudes, and understandings: the standpoint of a citizen reflecting on the implications of domestic arrangements for issues of justice, and the standpoint of a person as a member of a family, who is thinking about and discussing issues with other members. Reasoning from the citizen's standpoint, we deny that families are beyond justice, and in explanation of the content of that denial we say two things: (1) families are part of society's basic structure and need to be consistent with and supportive of a just scheme; (2) in justifying family law, public policy, and surrounding institutions that structure the opportunities of men and women, we proceed from the premise that the adult members of families are equal and independent and that children are so in prospect. We take as a premise that subordination on the basis of sex is wrong, that sexual difference ought not to predict social advantage, and that marriage does not fuse two citizens into a single person. When we adopt the citizen's standpoint, we are puzzled when Milton Friedman—who says that a country is "the collection of individuals who compose it"—then also says: "As liberals, we take the freedom of the individual, or perhaps the family, as our ultimate goal in judging social arrangements."[19] What's this "or perhaps the family"? What's the source of hesitation? And what would it mean to be concerned about the freedom of the family, but not principally about the freedom of its members?

But now, when we take the standpoint of the member of a family, these same considerations of justice need not (they may, but need not) provide the basis of deliberation and choice. Decisions might be informed by the view that members of a single

---

18. Michael Sandel, *Liberalism and the Limits of Justice* (Cambridge: Cambridge University Press, 1982), 33.

19. Milton Friedman, *Capitalism and Freedom* (Chicago: University of Chicago Press, 1962), 1, 12.

household have special responsibilities for one another, by feelings of love and attachment, by a conception of one another as partners in a common life, and by the intimate knowledge that comes from close association, but not by the thought "We ought to treat one another as equals, since we are all equal and independent moral agents." To borrow Bernard Williams' famous line: that's one thought too many.

Okin's initial response to the proposed reconciliation was that I was simply repeating what she had said in *Justice, Gender, and the Family*: namely, that we may expect more than justice from the family, but that is not the same as exempting it from the requirements of justice. I disagreed. I thought that my proposed division of deliberative standpoints was not simply a matter of supplementing the demands of justice with further conditions and that it provided a more compelling way of making sense of the claim that the family is beyond justice—a way to interpret and accommodate it, not demolish it. And Okin apparently came around to the view that the two-standpoints idea was not simply a restatement of her view. In a paper published in the *Fordham Law Review* in 2004, she mentions that Rawls endorses the two-standpoints idea (which he attributes to my review of her book).[20] She criticizes Rawls on this point and goes on to suggest that family decisions should be governed by Rawls' difference principle.[21]

Though I am not sure what it would mean to govern the family by the difference principle, I am inclined to think that some elements of this recent skepticism may be well-placed and that my relaxed reconciliation—with its assumed division of deliberative labor—may be too easy. To be sure, it may be attractive to imagine families conducting their lives without explicit reference to norms of political justice, while those norms operate in the background as the basis of law, public policy, and the structuring of social opportunities. But there may be great difficulties in achieving this division of deliberative labor in a just society, parallel to the difficulties that G. A. Cohen has explored in his writings on incentive inequalities.[22]

Cohen intends his point to generalize the feminist thesis that the personal is political. Suppose, then, that we have designed law and policy to ensure the maximum expected well-being of the least advantaged social group. It does not follow that the expected well-being of the least advantaged *is* maximized, because citizens

20. Susan Moller Okin, "Justice and Gender," *Fordham Law Review* 72.5 (April 2004): 1564–1565; John Rawls, "The Idea of Public Reason Revisited," in *The Law of Peoples* (Cambridge, MA: Harvard University Press, 1999), 159n63.

21. Okin, "Justice and Gender," 1564. Okin seemed to identify the claim that principles of justice apply to the family with the claim that Rawlsian principles apply: thus her claim about the difference principle applying to the allocation of resources among members of the family. An alternative view (also consistent with much that she says) is that there are standards of justice for families, which state what the members of a family owe to one another in virtue of the special relationships that obtain between and among them, but those standards are different from those that apply to relations among free and equal adults in a well-ordered society. A view of this kind—like the two-standpoints view discussed in the text—would then need to explain the relationship between standards of family justice and standards of justice for the wider society. I am indebted to David Miller for pressing this point.

22. For a statement of the central ideas, see G. A. Cohen, *If You're an Egalitarian, How Come You're So Rich?* (Cambridge, MA: Harvard University Press, 2001).

with scarce talents may demand incentives—perhaps large incentives—for deploying those talents in socially productive ways. Cohen argues that, if these citizens were guided in their market behavior by the demands of egalitarian justice, then they would not demand (such large) incentives. And if they did not demand incentives, then the marginal tax rates could be increased with no substantial labor supply response, and the less advantaged could then be made better off. The problem is that the incentive seekers divide their deliberative labor: they use completely different standards to guide their market and political conduct. Egalitarian citizens in the state, they remain self-interested maximizers in the market. And that problem could be quite large. If we confine egalitarian standards of justice to our institutions, while treating the market ethos as part of the fixed background for justice, then we might end up in a society with profound economic inequalities, with islands of great wealth surrounded by vast seas of misery and destitution. So the division of deliberative labor could have troubling implications.

Consider how a parallel concern might arise in the domestic arena. The Rawlsian standard of fair equality of opportunity says that people who are equally motivated and equally able ought to have equal chances to attain social desirable positions. But if, as a consequence of domestic circumstances and upbringing, men and women are very differently motivated, then fair equality permits a deeply gendered society, with substantial differences in life chances for men and women. And if we accept the division of deliberative labor, and the associated idea that norms of political justice do not have a role in the internal life of the family, aren't we inviting that result, even if we assume that Rawlsian egalitarianism is the right theory of justice?

Simply making the principle of fair equality part of the domestic ethos may not address the concern. Even if it were part of the domestic ethos, still—as I have just explained—it would permit differences of motivation to translate into differences of opportunity. So making the principle of fair equality part of the domestic ethos could leave substantial gender inequality: it is possible to endorse that principle while encouraging differences in motivation and aspiration between boys and girls. What might also need to be part of the ethos is the underlying idea that men and women are moral equals, that differences between men and women are morally contingent, and that those differences ought not to lead to differences in life prospects.

I say "might" because an alternative possibility is also worth considering. Start again with the incentive inequality issue. I said that a society might have vast inequalities and even destitution, consistent with meeting the principle of maximizing the advantage of the least advantaged, if we hold the social ethos—the ethics of the market, so to speak—fixed.[23] That is a logical possibility, but political philosophy is not about logical possibilities, and how plausible that result is depends both on the dispersion of human capital in a society with the investments in education and training required to ensure fair equality of opportunity and on the motivations that people can be expected to have in a democratic society. As Rawls put it, "the character and interests of individu-

---

23. The discussion that follows draws on Joshua Cohen, "Taking People as They Are?" *Philosophy and Public Affairs* 30.4 (2002): 363–386.

als themselves…are not fixed or given. A theory of justice must take into account how the aims and aspirations of people are formed; and doing this belongs to the wider framework of thought in the light of which a conception of justice is to be explained." Rawls continues:

> [A]n economic regime…is not only an institutional scheme for satisfying exist-ing desires and aspirations but a way of fashioning desires and aspirations in the future. More generally, the basic structure shapes the way the social system pro-duces and reproduces over time a certain form of culture shared by persons with certain conceptions of their good.[24]

So maybe a genuinely just society, with political equality and fair equality of opportu-nity, would dampen incentive demands because members would pervasively see one another as equals. Maybe the hypothetical concern about great dispersion and destitu-tion is not a real concern: perhaps it is located in the space of the logically possible, not the humanly and socially plausible. And if it is not, then the division of deliberative labor—between market and state—is perfectly sensible.

By analogy (an analogy that is in many ways imperfect), in the gender case, it may be that motivations and life aspirations are shaped as much by public norms of equality—in the arenas of education, employment, and politics—as by their domestic asser-tion or rejection. And if that is right, if parental norms and instruction have as little significance as children claim and as parents fear, then the concern about the repro-duction of gender as a consequence of the division of deliberative labor will be at least muted. The issue intersects with the topic I mentioned earlier, about whether the fam-ily is the linchpin in the gender system. The less conviction we have that the family is the linchpin, the less worry we have that the division of deliberative labor provides yet another cover for privilege.

Where, then, do things stand with the assertion that the domestic arena is "beyond justice"? Does the elementary feminist thesis demolish that idea? In my review of Okin, I suggested a way to interpret that idea, consistent with acknowledging the priority of justice. I think that that interpretation has much to be said for it and that a society that achieved the division of deliberative labor that I described would have much to recom-mend it. But its attractions are, of course, no assurance that deliberative labor can be divided along the proposed lines. And while Okin's initial response to me—that I was reasserting her view, in the guise of a criticism—was mistaken, her later suspicion was well-taken. Let's face it: we do not know whether we can achieve an acceptably gender-equal society with a division of deliberative labor any more than we know whether we can achieve an acceptably distributively fair society consistent with a division of delib-erative labor between state and market. Moreover, I do not think we have a good grasp of what to do if we cannot. The elementary feminist thesis does not demolish views that suppose that such achievements are possible. But it presents a forceful challenge to the relaxed reconciliation I proposed.

24. John Rawls, *A Theory of Justice*, rev. ed. (Cambridge, MA: Harvard University Press, 1999), 229, and *Political Liberalism*, 2nd ed. (New York: Columbia University Press, 1996), 269–271.

PUBLIC AND PRIVATE

The third issue that emerged in Okin's reply to my review concerned the public-private distinction: the issues I have just now been exploring have already put me in these precincts. In reading *Justice, Gender, and the Family*, I was struck by Okin's ambivalence about the public-private distinction: she said nothing like Catharine MacKinnon's trenchant remark that "the right of privacy is an injury got up as a gift."[25] Okin did express considerable disquiet about the distinction, and she said that it needed to be subjected to a "thorough examination and critique."[26] But she also seemed to embrace it very substantially. At the same time, she balked at my suggestion about the extent of her embrace.

Generally speaking, Okin said that "[b]oth the concept of privacy and the existence of a personal sphere of life in which the state's authority is very limited are essential."[27] And her embrace grew even tighter when she shifted from abstract principle to law and policy. Let me explain.

Suppose one thinks that the public-private distinction has as little to recommend it when it comes to domestic life as when it comes to economic ordering, as little to recommend it when we are thinking about regulating families as when we are thinking about regulating firms. Suppose, too, that one believes that the unequal domestic division of labor is the linchpin in the system of gender inequality—or even if not the linchpin, at least a big part of that system. Then one might well be attracted to—or at least would want to consider—a range of policies for ensuring gender equality, which Okin did not explore and many of which she would, I think, have found repugnant. So, for example, why not make the failure to share in domestic responsibilities an actionable form of sex discrimination, with married partners empowered to bring civil suits against spouses? Or make such sharing a clause—at least a default clause—in marriage contracts? Or why not have a regulatory agency that is responsible for ensuring a reasonable sharing of domestic responsibilities? Or, if you like market solutions, why not have tradable reduced-domestic-chores permits, which one could buy to get reduced responsibilities?[28] Or let children sue a parent for neglect or have him or her arrested for abuse if that parent is not sharing in the responsibilities? If the family is the linchpin, and if one thinks there's nothing—or even not too much—to the public-private distinction, then why not?

---

25. Catharine A. MacKinnon, *Feminism Unmodified* (Cambridge, MA: Harvard University Press, 1987), 100.

26. *JGF*, 111.

27. *JGF*, 128.

28. In discussion, Joseph Grundfest suggested that some kinds of prenuptial agreements could be interpreted as, in effect, agreements to provide financial compensation for reduced domestic responsibilities. I suspect that Okin would have been unhappy with such agreements for at least three reasons. First, class inequalities would restrict the general availability of the prenuptial solution. Second, the agreements would bring up privacy concerns of the sort noted in the text. Third, and most fundamentally, the agreements might reduce women's vulnerability at the cost of undermining the equal sharing of domestic responsibilities, which is important for the moral education of the next generation. On Okin's story about the family as a school of justice (borrowed substantially from Nancy Chodorow), the crucial point is that domestic responsibilities be shared in ways that are manifest to children. So, a sharply gendered division of domestic labor, even if freely agreed to, would limit the morally educative effects of the family.

But these were not the kind of solutions that Okin considered. She was troubled by what she described as vulnerability by marriage and troubled, too, by the effects of deep inequalities in the division of domestic labor on the moral development of children. But her proposals for reducing that vulnerability and changing that division were almost all more indirect, more focused on changing the background conditions to reduce imbalances of power and to create possibilities of choice and exit, and focused in particular on the labor market or on income support: flex time, child care support, parental leaves, a framework of divorce law designed to equalize living standards for postdivorce households, and, most directly, an equal splitting of wages between partners.[29]

My diagnosis for this policy focus—rather than a focus on more direct regulatory strategies—was that Okin endorsed a liberal conception of justice, including a public-private distinction, and an associated idea that people ought to be able to form the kinds of families they want and think appropriate, in light of their ethical and religious convictions and personal sensibilities, which sometimes will assign the principal domestic responsibility to women. Okin said, more or less, precisely that.[30] But then why wasn't she worried that lots of people would choose to form traditional families, with highly gendered divisions of labor? And worried, too, that if they did, then those choices would serve—through the socialization of children raised in families with gendered divisions of labor—to sustain gender norms and expectations within lots of families and thus a gendered division of labor in the wider society? And that, if such choices reproduced a gendered culture in the wider society, then the gendered culture would make an equality-sustaining division of domestic labor less likely, which in turn would serve to sustain gender inequality in the economy and polity? Because of her liberalism, Okin did not want to regulate these choices; because her views about vulnerability by marriage and about the moral education of children emphasized the importance of greater equality in the division of domestic labor—expressed in her conviction about the greater justness of "families in which roles and responsibilities are equally shared regardless of sex"[31]—Okin needed to be concerned about those choices.

The answer to the concern, I believe, is that Okin could not believe that, in a world with genuinely fair chances, large numbers of women would choose positions of domestic subordination. The historical prevalence of such subordination was not a product of choices made under fair conditions, but of social constraint: understandable accommodations to unjustly restricted opportunities. Okin's acceptance of a public-private distinction, I thought, was part of her more general hopeful moral-political outlook: we could have our liberty and our equality, too; these political values are not at war; and what underwrites the prospect of their reconciliation is a conception of the kinds of choices that people would make under free and fair conditions of a kind that has not thus far obtained. We do not know what those choices are, because we have never lived in those conditions. But we can hope, with reason, that diverse choices about work and family made under fair conditions will not lead to a gendered society.

29. I am grateful to Deborah Rhode for pressing the importance of Okin's support for income division.

30. See, for example, *JGF*, 180.

31. *JGF*, 183.

I found that picture very compelling and could not understand why Okin would feel the disquiet she expressed in her response to my review at my suggestion that she, to a larger extent than she sometimes suggested, endorsed a public-private distinction. Here, I can only speculate about the answer. My speculation is that she felt the fragility of the hope I just described. She was deeply uncertain about how much pressure on personal decisions would be needed to sustain a gender-free society and how much domestic diversity would really be possible in such a society. So Okin was prepared to say that "the concept of privacy and the existence of a personal sphere of life in which the state's authority is very limited are essential." But she also worried about how that conviction fit with others of comparable importance.

It is worth remembering that Plato was the great hero of Okin's *Women in Western Political Thought*. The most brilliant argument in that book was that Plato was able to take women seriously as human beings—and to consider the possibility of women guardians—only when, in the name of achieving the profound common allegiance required of a just polity, he contemplated the abolition of separate families and private property and considered a world in which feelings of pleasure and pain would be common, and everyone would say "mine" and "not mine" about the same things. To be sure, Plato contemplated dismantling the family to ensure unity in the ideal republic, not to achieve gender equality. But this dismantling in turn required that Plato suspend the conventional treatment of women by reference to their role in the family:[32] what Okin called the "functional" view of women as wives and mothers, which otherwise dominated the representation of women in Western political thought. "Book V of the *Republic*," Okin says, "contains a more remarkable discussion of the socially and politically relevant differences between the sexes than was to appear for more than two thousand years thereafter."[33] The account of women "in the *Republic* is clearly unparalleled in the history of Western thought."[34] True, but it is also true that Plato would not have said that "the concept of privacy and the existence of a personal sphere of life in which the state's authority is very limited are essential." Nor did his proposals in the *Republic* about regulating the fine details of the public culture—from literature to architecture—suggest any confidence in the choices that people would make under reasonable conditions.

I suggest, then, that Okin was ambivalent about the public-private distinction—she strongly embraced it and yet kept it at a distance—because she was deeply committed to the idea that justice requires a gender-free society; deeply committed to a world of vibrant, diverse, and emotionally committed families; and profoundly uncertain about the prospect of reconciling those fundamental commitments. Her uneasy relationship with the public-private distinction, then, was not a matter of intellectual inconsistency or evasiveness, but may instead have been a way to express the compelling force of these competing convictions and an unwillingness to make an impossible choice between them.

---

32. Here, Okin follows Rousseau's discussion of Plato in *Emile*. See *WWPT*, 37–38.
33. *WWPT*, 234.
34. *WWPT*, 234.

3

Of Linchpins and Other Interpretive Tools

Reconsidering Okin's Method

Elizabeth Wingrove

The following reflections on Susan Okin's contributions to political and feminist theory take up a dimension of her work that I believe has not been well recognized or, where it has been recognized, has not been well understood. I refer to how her approach to theory combined an analytic orientation with an empirical sensibility. Another way to put this, in terms that would surely cut against the grain of her self-understanding, is that I intend to discuss Okin's method. The question of method in political theory is not readily legible *as* a question, for reasons that date to the era of the postbehavioralist revolution in political science, when she was trained, and that continue today in the ubiquity of a "quantitative versus qualitative" divide that is taken to exhaust the methodological options. But the question of method lurks behind a recurrent malaise if not crisis in political theory, which Jeffrey Isaac diagnosed some years back in the field's apparent disinterest in the world historical events of 1989: its "strange silence," Isaac suggested, revealed political theory's failure to "illuminate" or "improve" the contemporary political world.[1] Seen in this light, Okin's approach warrants closer consideration inasmuch as her work was *always* "problem-driven," and the "problems" driving it were those of injustice. A current preoccupation with making the scholarly practice of political theory more relevant, timely, and engaged is thus a commitment that consistently informed Okin's research. One goal of this chapter is to consider how her modes of analysis reflected that commitment and, in so doing, contributed to the strength and the impact of her work.

But the will to timeliness also brings with it some perils, and thus there is a second goal of this reflection to consider some of the tensions to which Okin's work, in particular, her work on multiculturalism and feminist analyses in a global context, gave rise. My interest is not in her political conclusions per se, but in how she reached those conclusions. And while my assessment on this score draws from Okin's own exacting standards of argumentation and claims making, I do not make appeal to something *she* identified as "method." As intimated above, Okin's approach was so thoroughly naturalized as to be almost

An earlier version of this chapter was presented at the 2005 conference at Stanford University in honor of Susan Okin. I am grateful for feedback from the conference audience, as well as for extremely helpful comments on subsequent incarnations of this essay from Elizabeth Cole, Peggy McCracken, Yopie Prins, and Rob Reich.

1. Jeffrey Isaac, "The Strange Silence of Political Theory," *Political Theory* (1995): 646.

unrecognizable by that name. I mean to pursue the implications of this unrecognizability in part because I believe that they extend to problem-driven theory in general, where method fetishism—understood either as a tendency to let preferred methods dictate the criteria for problem selection or as a myopic preoccupation with technique—is regularly indicted as a central impediment to empirically relevant work, which is to say, work that resists the "flight from reality."[2] I worry that this effective foreclosure on method as a proper object of theoretical solicitude allows the demand for timeliness to circumscribe the tasks of interpretation such that simplification appears an acceptable, even inevitable, cost of clarity. I suggest that such a foreclosure occurs in some of Okin's later work, where her otherwise entwined conceptual analytic and empirical modes of inquiry threaten to unravel under the pressure of an imperative to judge. A potential consequence of such an unraveling, I conclude, is the failure of one's categories and terms to specify and comprehend sufficiently the "problem" that drives the analysis.

My discussion of the underspecification of Okin's analytic categories is largely in response to her third book, *Is Multiculturalism Bad for Women?* and to the dissatisfactions that it engendered, including for many of us who knew firsthand the profundity of her commitment to justice. A better understanding of those dissatisfactions propels me to revisit and retrieve crucial contributions from her earlier analyses whose reception I have likewise found frustrating, but in this instance, because they have been underappreciated. The linchpin metaphor is one such contribution, which Okin used to conceptualize and convey her claims about gender injustice: "the family," she wrote in *Justice, Gender, and the Family,* "is the linchpin of gender, reproducing it from one generation to the next."[3] By revisiting this metaphor—indeed, by citing it in my title— I mean to underscore the importance of looking anew at *how* Okin pursued feminist political theory, throughout her career, even or especially when this entails reading her against the grain. Such a practice does not aim to memorialize or, even less, to recuperate her foundational position in the field; it aims to complicate and advance an inquiry we held in common, and about which she continues to have much to say.

What I refer to as the twinned analytic and empirical modes of inquiry that characterize Okin's work can also be represented in terms of the multiple levels of analysis through which it unfolds. Consider, for example, her approach to familial relations and, in particular, to marital relations in *Justice, Gender, and the Family.* Okin introduces her argument as a critical intervention in a tradition of theorizing about justice. She thus takes up the categories and concerns characteristic of this tradition—equality, opportunity, dignity, human flourishing, and the like—and she shows how assumptions about sex difference up-end or violate principles of justice in that tradition; or alternatively, she reveals the unacknowledged work that gender assumptions do for many authors in that tradition. Here, she develops her arguments in large part by interrogating how central figures in and around liberal democratic theory have

2. See Ian Shapiro, *The Flight from Reality in the Human Sciences* (Princeton, NJ: Princeton University Press, 2005).

3. Okin, *Justice, Gender, and the Family* (New York: Basic, 1989), 170 (hereafter *JGF*).

conceptualized a just society, and how they've considered, or ignored, the fit between that conceptualization and familial roles and relations. Of central importance throughout her inquiry are the obfuscations that arise when theorists rely on static and typically ahistorical categories of public and private. At this level of analysis, inquiry proceeds through an interrogation of conceptual sufficiency and coherence, and more often than not, her textual interlocutors—e.g., Rawls, Walzer, Nozick—end up hoisted by their own petards.

But Okin's argument in *Justice, Gender, and the Family* is also rooted in a wide range of social scientific literature on contemporary marriage practices in the United States. She does not use this literature merely to illustrate, or even to substantiate, some broader and otherwise abstract set of theoretical and normative claims. Rather, her insights and claims take shape as she takes stock of the varied dimensions of the empirical phenomena represented in social scientific research. I am thinking in particular of chapter 7 ("Vulnerability by Marriage") in which Okin surveys the institution of marriage as it is lived *and* as it is imagined—as it is "anticipated," to use her term—by men and women. The picture she paints is conceptually and structurally complex. First, it depends on an analysis of the distribution of labor—both paid and unpaid—in American families and on an exploration of the effects of that distribution on men and women, in terms of both interpersonal and political resources. This comparative assessment of work and resources is in turn linked to an analysis of larger institutional formations—for example, the educational system, the professional and service labor markets—which reinforce, and sometimes amplify, the differential consequences of a gendered division of labor. Likewise, she explores how those institutions are themselves structured in ways that presume a gendered division of labor and that benefit from such a division, in terms of both externalities (e.g., the unpaid work of social reproduction) and normative justifications (e.g., the "family wage").

On this level of analysis, Okin's account of gender (in)justice emerges through a social structural analysis that embeds "choosing individuals" in patterned relations that afford them more or less power and opportunity and affect their very status as choosing individuals. At the same time, her account directs our attention to the systems of ideas, values, and beliefs—what I would call "ideologies"—that shore up the predominant division of labor by shaping and sustaining individual decision making, personality, and even symbolic attachments. From this perspective, the individual whose life choices and flourishing are central to Okin's account of justice is simultaneously (1) making calculations based on her knowledge of likely outcomes, (2) internalizing values and expectations about how her life decisions can and ought to be made, and (3) imagining other ways of being and acting in a present and future world.

The result of an inquiry that moves through these different levels—the social structural (which I would also characterize as the material institutional) and the ideological—is a closely drawn account of how the institution of marriage *as a set of structured relations, practices, and identities* systematically reproduces women's vulnerability. And this account in turn depends on a multifaceted psychological and social portrait of women (and men) that bears little resemblance either to the abstract individualism typically associated with liberal theorizing or to the minimalist notion of gender typically associated with liberal feminism. Otherwise put: the idiom of analytic philosophy in which Okin works can lull readers into not noticing the extent to which she deploys a richly sociological and psychologically nuanced account of gender, and how she challenges not only the substantive conclusions but the methodological commitments of much liberal theory.

Like any immanent critique—one that takes its bearings from within the conceptual framework it seeks to scrutinize—Okin's engagement with justice theory aims to reveal the contradictions between its premises and its conclusions; but her engagement also elaborates and extends its repertoire of interpretive resources. So it's not just that she draws on a range of literatures in developing her own approach to questions of justice and gender, although that's certainly true. It's also that she necessarily challenges the sufficiency of any analytic approach that does not attend to what its key terms look like on the ground, so to say. Shuttling between the concepts (equality, choice) and the facts of social scientific research (earning capacity, divorce rates), Okin's approach tethers justice theory to the actual circumstances of its intended subjects.

One could talk about this point in terms of evidence: trained as a political scientist, Okin was part of a knowledge community in which claims about the world must typically be substantiated with detailed empirical information, also known as data. But despite Okin's periodic appeals to the disciplinary dimensions of her theoretical enterprise, I am reluctant to wholeheartedly adopt the terms of evidence and proof when talking about her methodological contributions, for two reasons.[4] First, because that language suggests a priority relationship between theorizing, which comes first, and paying attention to the world—which comes later, *after* the theoretical claims have been developed and stand ready to be confirmed or disconfirmed. Such a priority relationship is typically associated with hypothesis-driven research, where inquiry consists in subjecting provisional propositions to factual verification or refutation. But it also haunts political theory, whose location within the discipline gives it limited (and dubious) warrant to undertake "non-empirical" research and so to pursue research unconstrained by facts.[5] Okin's work, by contrast, more regularly refused such a temporal (and experiential and political) ordering of theoretical and empirical processes; likewise, she strenuously refused the idealism bequeathed to the political theory subfield.

Second, I want to be careful with terms like evidence and proof because they risk invoking a narrow empiricism that not only misrepresents Okin's use of social scientific literature, but in addition, obscures how her more exclusively textual exegetical work—in particular, her engagements with the great books of the Western philosophical tradition—also incorporated a multilevel approach. Consider Okin's first book,

4. See note 16, below. I address the issue of Okin's own reliance on the logic of factual verification in a final section of this chapter.

5. For an analysis of this disciplinary division of labor as it organizes political science, see Sophia Mihic, Stephen Engelmann, and Elizabeth Wingrove, "Facts, Values, and 'Real' Numbers: Making Sense in and of Political Science," in George Steinmetz, ed., *The Politics of Method in the Human Sciences: Positivism and Its Epistemological Others* (Durham, NC: Duke University Press, 2005).

Women in Western Political Thought (1979b), whose overarching theme is the functionalist approach to women that threads through most canonical works. She argues there that what women *do*—procreatively and sensually—for, with, and to men is key to understanding how theorists have situated women in relation to a political world of rulers and citizens. Pitched at a general level, her conclusion is that women's privatization and domestication are dictated by the utility of the patriarchal family. In the texts she reads, those depoliticizing processes (1) secure reproductive labor, (2) calm otherwise disruptive worries about paternity, and (3) establish a public space emptied of potentially disruptive (hetero)sexual desire. And as she does later in interrogating contemporary justice theorists, Okin highlights the insufficiency and incoherence that so often characterize appeals to gender difference in the great books.

That project cannot, however, be reduced to the conclusion that "canonical authors are inconsistent, and often hatefully so, where women are concerned." Okin's inquiry into the (il)logic of sexism certainly includes retracing its contradictions. But she also pursues that (il)logic as it took shape through the social practices of men and women, even, as in this case, when those practices were located in the texts themselves. For example, in her analysis of Rousseau, Okin pursues the worldly counterparts to his muddled political concepts in his stories of romantic love, marital domesticity, and natural individualism. Her conclusions apropos the unsustainability of his political project emerge as she shuttles between these two levels of analysis: on the one hand, his principle-driven account of a just polity and, on the other, his thickly narrated accounts of how men and women live in his imagined societies, both those based on "facts" (e.g., the social world of Clarens in *Julie; ou, La Nouvelle Héloïse*) and those represented as wholly fictional (e.g., the state of nature in *Discourse on Inequality*). That in this case the conceptual analysis *and* the analysis of social fact take place on the shared turf of textual and literary depiction should not keep us from recognizing the same interpretive commitment that guides *Justice, Gender, and the Family*: in both studies, conceptual contradictions must be parsed at the level of ideological, institutional, and other social structural relations.

This interpretive commitment became central to my own reading of Rousseau, in which I trace the simultaneously conceptual, literary, and bodily construction of a "consensual nonconsensuality" that I have argued organizes his version of democratic and (hetero)sexual relations.[6] My analysis found, if not a reconciliation of the conceptual muddles Okin identified, then an embodied and eroticized enactment of their contradictions in the everyday lives of Rousseau's republicans. The apparent differences between her approach and the interpretive idioms that (also) inform my own—e.g., literary formalism, phenomenology, queer theory, poststructuralism—might serve to conceal this continuity. Okin taught me that, whatever else it does, political theoretical analysis always concerns the sufficiency of the representational forms—e.g., concepts, texts—through which we seek to apprehend political life. Likewise, any assessment of that sufficiency obliges the researcher to attend to the specific ways in which living a contradiction between principles and practices takes shape.

---

6. Elizabeth Wingrove, *Rousseau's Republican Romance* (Princeton, NJ: Princeton University Press, 2000).

In this sense, Okin's approach to canonical interpretation reveals a similar sensitivity to the multiple levels of analysis to which I've pointed in her work on contemporary justice theory, and what I consider to be the best sensibilities of the social scientist consistently inform and strengthen her more literary analyses. More boldly still: her analytic procedure concerning the (non)sense of gender contains within it a critical orientation that I want to call (even as I can imagine Susan's eyebrow arching high as I say it) ontological and phenomenological; which is to say, her analytic approach does not and could not proceed absent an acute attention to what and how social reality *is*, what the condition or situation of existing as a man or a woman encompasses. In her analytic practice, this means nothing more (nor less) than persistently attending to the local, social, particular contexts and forms in which any putatively universal or general principle is rendered meaningful. This is not to suggest that Okin was some sort of closeted Hegelian; it is to draw attention to how her interpretive commitments share as much or more with a social theoretical liberalism à la Montesquieu—even (again I imagine that arching brow) à la Judith Shklar—as they do with a predictably abstracting deontological liberalism à la Rawls.

The social theoretical undercurrent in Okin's work informs what I mean to insist is her nonreductionistic, nondeterministic framing of a sex/gender system, represented through the metaphor of the linchpin. The metaphor had been used earlier by Catharine MacKinnon in her 1983 article on feminist method and the state, when she represented sexuality as the "linchpin of gender inequality."[7] In a published review that touches briefly on MacKinnon's essay, Okin expresses concern about the "reductionism" of such a formulation, which she suggests was mitigated only by an overly broad definition of "sexuality," which made it difficult to know precisely to what MacKinnon referred.[8] Okin's subsequent redeployment of the metaphor in *Justice, Gender, and the Family* would thus seem to suggest a willingness on her part to "reduce" gender inequality to the relations, practices, and identities of the marriage-structured family. Likewise, Josh Cohen's account in this volume appears to suggest that she ultimately agreed with his criticism that her linchpin thesis gave unjustified priority to the role of domestic inequality (rather than to labor market inequality) in reproducing women's vulnerability.[9]

But the spatial model conjured by the linchpin metaphor denies precisely the relations of priority—causal, logical, or temporal—on which an accusation of reductionism depends. On the contrary, the linchpin invokes relations of connectivity rather than causality: it suggests that what is being identified—e.g., sexuality, the family—is not a source or origin, but a securing mechanism that sustains the functionality of a sex/gender system by enabling its various parts to hold together in a system-sustaining fashion. So to say that "the family is the linchpin of gender" is to say that the asymmetries of

7. See Catharine MacKinnon, "Feminism, Marxism, Method and the State: An Agenda for Theory," *SIGNS: Journal of Women in Culture and Society* 515 (1983): 7; reprinted in *Feminist Theory: A Critique of Ideology*, edited by Nannerl Keohane, Michelle Rosaldo, and Barbara Gelpi (Chicago: University of Chicago Press, 1982), 1–30.

8. See Okin's review of *Feminist Theory: A Critique of Ideology*, in *Ethics* 94 (1984): 723–724.

9. See Joshua Cohen's chapter in this volume.

power characteristic of familial relations and the ideologies of domesticity and natural complementarity that sustain those relations secure—connect and fix together—the constituent parts of a perforce multidimensional structure.

No doubt, Okin's identification of the family as the linchpin of gender prioritizes social reproduction, organized through heterosexual marriage, as critical to linking together the multiple relations and sites of power—the workplace, labor markets, educational institutions, etc.—that mutually reinforce a contemporary sex/gender system. Were that securing mechanism to be removed, the argument goes, the system would no longer cohere. There is ample room to debate and push on this conclusion, but a richer appreciation of the *kind* of analytic claim it represents might helpfully interrupt the eternal return to reductionism as *the* dilemma or danger against which feminist analyses of the social construction of gender must contend. Such an interruption might make it more readily apparent that a potential contribution of this model might be precisely that it does *not* force us to choose between what is primarily or essentially about gender—about making and sustaining differences between masculinity and femininity—on the one hand, and what is secondary or epiphenomenal to those basic processes, on the other.

In this sense, Okin's deployment of the linchpin metaphor captures an interpretive commitment that remains central to a diverse range of feminist analysis: that we will misunderstand gender if we try to read through it, to determine the "real" functions it performs, to identify the more primary needs or fears or desires for which it serves as cover or sign. What I referred to above as the ontological dimension of Okin's analytic procedure pertains here to an ontology of gender: implicit in her approach is the insight that, as a lived experience, gender *really is* the functions that it performs, the fears and desires that it organizes, the power asymmetries it enacts. So we ought not to assume that gender stands for something else; it is nothing more, nor less, than these social, symbolic, and interpersonal relations and "truths."[10] Perhaps this is one reason that Okin could conclude with such apparent confidence in *Justice, Gender, and the Family* that gender itself violated the terms of justice and that a truly just world entailed gender's abolition.[11] For many feminist theorists, the world-constituting dimensions of a sex/gender system make that claim akin to insisting that justice turns on the abolition of language, identity, and every (other) social formation the world has ever known. But inasmuch as Okin's method locates gender's truths in the worldly conditions of injustice, the claim that we must work to abolish those conditions leads logically to the conclusion that in so doing we will be working to end gender.

My comments thus far reflect an interest in "getting Okin right," if by that one means accurately representing her analytic processes and accomplishments. I acknowledge that I am doing so in a manner that risks cutting against the grain of her own self-presentation. My gestures toward ontology, the social facts of literary representation, and even or perhaps especially method, for example, admittedly do not resonate with

---

10. This interpretation differs markedly from what I thought and wrote in "Interpellating Sex," *SIGNS* (1999).

11. E.g., "A just future would be one without gender" (*JGF*, 171).

the terms in which Okin pursued political theoretical inquiry or in which her work is typically received. One of my goals in transposing her work is to invite readers—critics and enthusiasts alike—to consider anew what she can teach us about how we might practice, but also and as importantly, how we should read political and feminist theory. As indicated above, a better understanding of Okin's method on this score might usefully disrupt the tired assumptions that liberal feminism inescapably makes appeals to disembodied selves, abstract universalisms, strictly formal proceduralisms, and mini-, maxi-, or mediumly thick conceptions of the good. These representations strike me as, at best, a sadly partial and, at worst, a wholly caricatured version of what so many theorists, feminist and otherwise, working under the rubric of liberalism are actually doing. Among other things, such representations eclipse the richness of the historical and textual insights on offer in such work. Likewise, the cultural and sociological complexity that informs the analysis of polities and persons in much of this literature is simply erased.

But I am also insisting on a dissonant interpretation of Okin's humanist feminist enterprise and what I've sketched as its multiple levels of analysis because such a reading provides the grounds for an immanent critique of her work. As suggested in my introduction, such a critique might help those of us who learned so much from her as a teacher to understand better the frustrations produced by some of her later work on feminism and multiculturalism. But, in addition, I maintain that teasing out the connection between those frustrations and matters of method can help to clarify the risks that accompany the refusal to interrogate one's interpretive protocols, or perhaps, the failure to incorporate such interrogations into politically engaged, problem-driven scholarship. Put pointedly, my contention is that Okin's disinterest in matters of method led to a desensitization concerning her approach that makes it difficult to undertake a critical (re)assessment of its sufficiency.

In a 1994 article in *Political Theory* entitled "Gender Inequality and Cultural Differences," Okin responds to the accusation of essentialism being leveled against feminist theorists by those emphasizing race and class differences between women and/or by those more pervasively skeptical about the ability to sustain generalizable claims of any sort.[12] She presents her analysis as "taking up the gauntlet" thrown down by philosopher Elizabeth Spelman, who had proposed that feminist researchers "investigate different women's lives and see what they have in common" rather than assume the existence of commonalities.[13] What I referred to above as Okin's multilevel approach to theoretical analysis here takes the form of "put[ting] some Western feminist ideas about justice and inequality to the test by seeing how well these theories work when used to look at the very different situations of some of the poorest women in poor countries."[14] In conducting this test, she constructed a composite picture of Third World women's situation in the family and the labor force, drawing from what she refers to as "a sampling of the development literature"; with an acknowledged awareness of the offense it

    12. Okin, "Gender Inequality and Cultural Differences," *Political Theory* 22.1 (1994): 5–24.
    13. "Gender Inequality and Cultural Differences," 8–9 (quote from Elizabeth Spelman, *Inessential Woman: Problems of Exclusion in Feminist Thought* [Boston: Beacon, 1988], 137).
    14. Okin, "Gender Inequality and Cultural Differences," 9.

might give, she concludes that the problems of non-Western women are indeed "similar to ours but more so."[15]

The reply that this article elicited from feminist political theorist Jane Flax and Okin's subsequent response to that reply make for difficult, even painful, reading. At least they do for those of us who take Okin and Flax to be speaking past each other. I do not mean to deny the important differences—intellectual and political— contained within or perhaps signaled by their respective idioms of inquiry. But rather than catalog those differences, I want to revisit this dialogic impasse by considering Okin's self-positioning there as a feminist theorist trained in political science.[16] As I've already indicated, for her, this positioning indicated a need to shuttle between the levels of conceptual analysis and empirical inquiry. From this perspective, Okin's (to Flax, offensive) suggestion that "committed outsiders" might be better positioned to analyze social injustice than those who live within the "relevant culture" is perhaps best seen as a paradoxical warning about how that shuttling practice can be compromised.[17] On the one hand, Okin's suggestion calls to mind her typically fearless insistence that one take seriously the claim that oppression is damaging. We might call this the Beauvoir dilemma: while the sometimes shockingly nasty things that Simone de Beauvoir wrote about women—about their capacity for narcissism, for example, or their clinging dependency, suffocating jealousy, and obsessive investment in their appearance and their children—are regularly attributed to a masculinist existentialism she failed to interrogate, it is also plausible that these descriptions reflect what she took to be actual consequences of women's oppression. Is it so improbable that one would encounter, or so untenable that one would want to name, such stunted and stunting characteristics in circumstances where the dignity, respect, and recognition necessary to human growth (never mind flourishing) have been withheld?

These are, of course, notoriously complicated and difficult matters, provoking among other things the epistemological and political challenges that the notion of "false consciousness" inevitably introduces. And this is no small part of why I refer to Okin's willingness to acknowledge them as fearless. But, on the other hand, a sufficient—and sufficiently multifaceted—understanding of the implications of oppressive practices requires sustained investigation into the circumstances in which they take place. In other words, understanding the vulnerability—including the internalization of destructive norms—that any particular practice or institution inculcates in women requires an immersive study of those practices and institutions, akin to the immersion in various social scientific and feminist literatures that is evident in *Justice, Gender, and the Family* and to the textual immersion evident in *Women in Western Political Thought*.

15. "Gender Inequality and Cultural Differences," 8; see also Susan Okin, "Response to Jane Flax," *Political Theory* 23.3 (1995): 512.

16. "Trained as a philosopher, [Spelman] does not seem to consider it appropriate to take up the challenge of actually looking at some of this empirical evidence.... [T]rained as a political scientist, I shall attempt to look at some comparative evidence." Okin, "Gender Inequality and Cultural Differences," 9.

17. "Gender Inequality and Cultural Differences," 19; see also Jane Flax, "Race/Gender and the Ethics of Difference: A Reply to Okin's 'Gender Inequality and Cultural Differences,'" *Political Theory* 23.3 (1995): 507.

What constitutes sufficient immersion, what constitutes adequate historical knowledge, and what constitutes properly representative literatures and authors when the
practices and institutions to be investigated belong to a history and culture vastly different from the investigator's? While Okin insists that only "empirical evidence" (rather
than, say, theoretical deductions or philosophical fiats) allows us to reach conclusions
about the singularity or commonality of the oppression experienced by different
women, the range of materials on which she draws is extremely limited and, as Flax
points out, is an amalgam drawn from distinctly different Third World contexts. These
representational and evidentiary problems intensify in Okin's 1997 article "Is Multiculturalism Bad for Women?" where her multilevel approach aims to put to the empirical
test theoretical claims concerning the meaning of cultural differences for women. With
few exceptions, her factual information is drawn from newspaper accounts (e.g., the
New York Times, the *International Herald Tribune*) while the text presented as exem-
plary of the concept of culture is Will Kymlicka's *Multicultural Citizenship: A Liberal
Theory of Minority Rights*.[18]

The contrast between what and who counts as sufficiently representative—both
of the theory and of the actually existing circumstances of its intended subjects—in
Okin's later and earlier work is striking to me. Likewise, she seems increasingly to
have relied on precisely the priority relationship between theorizing and worldly
investigation that I suggested above is not typical in her work. In these later pieces, a
hypothesis is provided—e.g., "Western feminist ideas…[w]ork when used to look at
[poor women in poor countries],"[19] or "there is a considerable likelihood of tension
between…[f]eminism and a multiculturalist commitment to group rights"[20]—which
she then confirms through appeals to accumulated data concerning Third World women
and Third World cultural practices. This approach leaves untouched any interrogation or (re)consideration of the sufficiency of the representational forms upon which
the analysis relies, e.g., the concept of "culture," the identity category of "Third World
women," the social scientific and journalistic resources used to illustrate and document
both. The narrowed range of evidentiary materials reflects a narrowing of the analytic
procedure: her twofold attention to conceptual and empirical registers has been com-
pressed telescopically, resulting in a procedure better suited to isolating and amplifying
than to maintaining a mutually illuminating connection between the two registers.

I believe that this shift in—or, more strongly, diminution of—Okin's interpretive
sensibilities was produced in part by an intensification of her commitment to keep
Western feminist theorizing relevant, timely, and engaged. "While this debate continues," she concludes in her reply to Jane Flax, "women are being beaten by their
husbands…[g]irls go undernourished and uneducated, and development policy is
decided and executed."[21] A felt urgency concerning the need to respond to the suffering

---

18. Will Kymlicka, *Multicultural Citizenship: A Liberal Theory of Minority Rights* (Oxford: Oxford
University Press, 1995).

19. "Gender Inequality and Cultural Differences," 9.

20. Joshua Cohen, Matthew Howard, and Martha Nussbaum, eds., *Is Multiculturalism Bad for
Women?* (Princeton, NJ: Princeton University Press, 1999), 10.

21. Okin, "Response to Jane Flax," 514.

of women and children is palpable in her response. So too is her sense that feminist scholars can and must play a critical role in affecting the policy-making and policy-implementation processes. But with a passionate awareness of the timeliness of these issues, it can become too easy to overlook how time-consuming, interpretively demanding, and linguistically and historically complex the comprehension of the issues can be. The desire to alleviate suffering and to respond to injustice can appear immediate, in a way that an understanding of the problems underlying these needs never is. "This is not the time for self-analysis or abstruse theorizing," Okin implores.[22] But neither, I want to say to her, is it the time for interpretive shortcuts, for refusing—in the name of human suffering—the hard work of description and analysis.

The exacting demands of interpretive work do not arise from or reduce to the issues of identity and difference that Okin sometimes insisted were motivating her critics. The claim that "differences among women make it impossible for us to speak about anyone but ourselves," for example, or that "outsiders" (read: white, Western women) are prima facie improperly situated to do cross-cultural analyses of gender injustice[23]—these are insufficient renderings of what constitutes, to some large extent, concerns about method. The problem is not *who* is doing the analysis, but rather, in what consists the *doing*? The failure to identify methodology as a concern, and the complacency about the quotidian research practices that often result, can facilitate a collapse of the one issue into the other.

My insistence on this point is not intended to deny that there are important connections between the *who* and the *what* of research processes. Indeed, in some of her last writings, Okin seems increasingly attentive to how gender analyses in cross-cultural and global contexts require attending to "the silent and silenced voices of the oppressed,"[24] as she wrote in a 2003 article. In that review of books by Brooke Ackerly, Martha Nussbaum, and Amartya Sen, Okin explicitly links what Ackerly calls "listening to the silent voices" both to the conceptual sufficiency of scholarly analyses and to evidence that human meanings and needs vary significantly "from culture to culture, from context to contex[t]."[25] How her most recent travel, dialogues, and research would have transformed her political conclusions or policy preferences remains painfully unknowable. More significant than these issues, however, are the indications that she recognized and endorsed the demand for a richer, more variegated empirical basis to theorizing about gender and justice in a global context.

The irony of focusing on Okin's method to gain purchase on the insights and shortcomings of her problem-driven theory extends beyond the ill-fitting terminology. Also implicated is the conclusion that a more timely, relevant, and politically responsive theory requires stepping back from the immediate demands of action to the intensively mediated consideration of what our scholarly process is and should be. Now

---

22. Okin, "Response to Jane Flax," 515.
23. See Okin, "Response to Jane Flax," 513, 515.
24. Okin, "Poverty, Well-Being and Gender," 280.
25. Okin, "Poverty, Well-Being and Gender," 280, 297. Likewise, her January 2004 trip to India with the Global Fund for Women appears to have had a powerful effect on her understanding of poverty and human flourishing. See her comments at http://www.globalfundforwomen.org.

more than ever, we need to heed Hannah Arendt's exhortation to "think what we are doing."[26] Likewise, her example might help us to avoid countering the call for interpretive caution with an appeal to the world's urgent demands: precisely the very dark times through which Arendt lived propelled her toward interpretive prudence and conceptual innovation. Thinking what we are doing need not reduce to navel gazing or abstruse theorizing or hand wringing about authentic self-positioning or who has the legitimacy to speak. But it might entail something as simple (and, for many political theorists, as odd) as interrogating our methods. Reading and studying Okin's work—carefully, with good faith, a critical attention to her process, and perhaps against the grain of her own self-understanding—can continue to provide us with rich resources for learning how to do it well.

26. Hannah Arendt, *The Human Condition* (Chicago: University of Chicago Press, 1958), 5.

4

Can Feminism Be Liberated from Governmentalism?

John Tomasi

One fall day, I stood in the main quad at Stanford University while Susan Okin and a philosophy graduate student had a heated debate about feminism. The student, who described herself as an antiliberal feminist separatist, argued that freedom for women was impossible under any capitalist liberal regime. Okin insisted that liberalism, at least in its contemporary "high liberal" formulation, could be interpreted in such a way that equality for women could be realized under the constitutional principles of the United States.[1] In particular, Okin defended her proposal that the government require that paychecks be split and sent separately to marriage partners. Their debate ended without resolution. As Okin sailed across the quad and disappeared between the arches, the student shook her head and jokingly muttered: "Lapdog of the patriarchal establishment."

That student's remark, made in the early 1990s, is one instance of a continuing error that I mean in this chapter to correct. The error lies in accepting the conceptual divisions that contemporary academic feminists treat as foundational as, in fact, being foundational, or even near-foundational, for people concerned with the realization of gender equality.

In the 1980s and early 1990s, the most heavily signposted fissure within academic feminism was that dividing liberal feminists, such as Susan Okin, from their antiliberal, "post-Marxist" feminist critics, such as Catharine MacKinnon. Anyone concerned to promote gender equality had to choose one side or the other, it was said, and the choice was thought to matter deeply. The topography of academic feminism has become more complex in recent years. Indeed, we have seen a wild flowering of new feminisms—postmodern, poststructuralist, dual-system theoretic, and more. This efflorescence has complicated, and sometimes confounded, the simple liberal versus antiliberal division of old. But many of these new forms of feminism are directed at academic questions,

I presented early versions of this paper at workshops at the University of Toronto, Brown University, and Stanford University. I am indebted to Corey Brettschneider, Joseph Carens, Joshua Cohen, David Estlund, Jennifer Nedelsky, Clifford Orwin, Carmen Pavel, Rob Reich, Debra Satz, and Melissa Williams. I particularly thank Wendy McElroy, who first encouraged me to think of gender issues in what I call "indirect-governmentalist" terms.

1. On "High Liberal," see Samuel Freeman "Illiberal Libertarians: Why Libertarianism Is Not a Liberal View" (*Philosophy and Public Affairs* 30, no. 2 [2001]: 105–151).

and their expositors frequently do not see themselves as committed to producing clear public policy recommendations.

This chapter, written in commemoration of the life and work of Susan Okin, focuses on public policy issues regarding gender freedom. These are the issues about real women, men, children, families, and real relationships that Okin herself always treated as central to feminist scholarship. My essay proceeds by way of one main claim and one closely attendant suggestion. The main claim is a prickly assertion that I pressed upon Susan Okin many times when she and I discussed the state of contemporary feminist scholarship. The claim is this: when it comes to substantive public policy prescriptions, the most remarkable feature about contemporary academic feminism—whether in "liberal versus post-Marxist" or in "new wave" form—is not the diversity of contemporary feminism but its uniformity. Indeed, the uniformity of contemporary feminist scholarship with respect to public policy orientation is so complete that the issue that most elementally divides forms of feminism has barely been noticed by contemporary feminists. That issue concerns the respective roles of legislatively enacted and constitutionally entrenched rules in the process of social construction. The elemental distinction that has been lost within contemporary feminist scholarship is one dividing what I shall *direct-governmental* and *indirect-governmental* approaches to feminist public policy.

As we shall see, Susan Okin and others in her contemporary liberal camp take a direct-governmentalist approach to feminism. But post-Marxist and new wave scholars—at least those who make public policy recommendations—take a direct-governmentalist approach to feminism, too. The possibility for a truly radical division within feminist approaches to law and public policy rests on the powerful but forgotten indirect-governmental feminist ideal. Only by reviving that lost approach to feminist public policy could we generate distinctions among forms of feminism that matter deeply.

The suggestion I wish to make attendant to that main claim is gentler. This suggestion is that feminists who want to freshen their thinking about law and public policy, or who wish to broaden the horizons of contemporary scholarly debates, would do well to attend to a neglected group of American feminist thinkers from the late nineteenth century: Sarah Grimké, Angela Fiducia Tilton Heywood, Ezra Haywood, Lillian Harman, Voltairine de Cleyre, and Gertrude Kelly. These thinkers developed a potent indirect-governmentalist approach to feminism, an approach that demonstrates the narrowness of the public policy horizons under which contemporary feminist scholarship labors.

Wendy McElroy, a brilliant independent writer and scholar from Canada, has done wonderful work to exhume and make public the work of these neglected thinkers.[2] Following the path that McElroy has blazed, I shall first report and systematize the view of these thinkers. I then bring the work of these thinkers into direct contrast with Susan

2. See particularly her *Individualist Feminism of the Nineteenth Century: Collected Writings and Biographical Profiles* (Jefferson, NC: McFarland & Co., 2001) and *Freedom, Feminism, and the State* (New York: The Independent Institute, 1991).

Okin's humanist feminism. I shall use the distinction between direct and indirect-governmentalism to elucidate my own critique of Okin's main policy recommendations. The warm friendship that Susan Okin and I enjoyed was regularly punctuated by intensely heated debates regarding the claim I am making in this essay. Those debates taught me that, clichés to the contrary, heat often does throw light. Most important, therefore, in setting down my side of this debate with Susan, I hope to illuminate what I take to be the enduring legacy of Susan Okin's feminist scholarship.

TWO CONCEPTS OF GOVERNMENTALISM

I shall use the term "direct-governmentalism" to mark a general public policy orientation. That tendency is one of looking to legislatively enacted programs and rules as primary means of social construction. When direct-governmentalists identify a social concern—whether it be gender equality, environmental protection, or educational opportunity—they ask what law or statute might be crafted specifically to address that concern. Indirect-governmentalists, by simplest contrast, tend to look first to constitutionally entrenched rights and liberties as the main platform of social construction. They say the main role of government should be to enforce laws of general applicability, laws that provide a framework within respect to which individuals and groups can coordinate their activities in pursuit of projects they pursue for their own diverse purposes. By defining and securing those liberties, the state allows nongovernmental institutions—systems of market exchange, associational networks, and the creative power of individual human wills—to develop and strengthen in response to the challenges of social life.

Direct-governmentalists are optimistic about the moral appropriateness and practical efficacy of targeted regulations and statutes to bring about desired changes within complex social orders. Indirect-governmentalists are more skeptical of such regulatory ambitions, on both moral and practical grounds. On its democratic variants, the first reaction of direct-governmentalism to a social challenge is to ask what might be done by means of a politically channeled public will. Indirect-governmentalists are not anti-democratic. But indirect-governmentalists tend to look first to institutions through which the desires of human wills for change can be expressed without those wills being politically channeled.

Indirect-governmentalism does not imply a commitment to anarchism any more than direct-governmentalism implies a sympathy to totalitarianism. Indirect-governmentalists are not "anti-governmental" in their approach, just as direct-governmentalists are not "all-governmental" in theirs. The two sides simply conceive of the socially constructive role of the state in different ways. If direct-governmentalists think of coercively backed laws as society's main beams and supporting walls, for indirect-governmentalists such laws play a no less vital role as rivets. Strong rivets are just as essential to social construction as sound beams and well-crafted walls: indirect-governmentalists typically are not anarchists. Similarly, direct-governmentalists, like indirect-governmentalists, typically reject the ideal of totalitarianism. Even people who assign to government architects the ambitious goal of erecting social walls can recognize the importance of open spaces in which individuals can be free. (At the very least, people need to be able to rearrange the psychological furniture of the rooms in which they are themselves to live.)[3]

The difference between direct and indirect-governmentalism is one not of kind but of strategy. And yet this difference in strategy reflects an absolutely foundational difference of understanding about the relation of government power to social order.

To elucidate this difference, consider Friedrich Hayek's distinction between two different forms of social order: taxis and cosmos.[4] Hayek, following Michael Polanyi, defined a social order in terms of system theory.[5] A social order is a complex network characterized by regularities of human behavior such that understandings gained about behavioral patterns in any one part of the network are helpful in understanding or predicting patterns of behavior in other parts. Taxis and cosmos refer to two fundamentally different ways by which people's behaviors within social orders might acquire their regularities.

Hayek offers a corporation or firm as a paradigmatic example of a taxis. A corporation is a form of order with a definite purpose: here, that of producing goods or services for a profit. The patterns of relations among the various elements of a corporation are a product of explicit human design. Managers place employees in certain roles and assign them certain tasks such that the overall behavioral regularities of the system will tend toward the satisfaction of that order's (profit-making) purpose.

A cosmos, like a taxis, is an order in the systemic sense of being a complex network the elements of which exhibit regularized behavior. But with a cosmos, the overall design of the order, defined by the particular roles and tasks undertaken by the various elements, is not the result of anyone's conscious plan. Consider a market system for any type of good—footwear, for example. Given some basic rules, such as those defining and securing some conception of property rights, the actions of many individuals over time may produce a complex systemic order with respect to the design, production, and distribution of footwear. However, the overall pattern of goods produced by that system—say, what proportion of those products will be sandals, dress shoes, sneakers, or boots—just like the various roles and tasks undertaken by the many persons involved in that productive order, is not itself the result of anyone's conscious design. Rather, given some basic rules, people's behavior within a cosmos acquires its regularities endogenously, through self-organization or, as Hayek says, *spontaneously*.

Like my distinction between indirect and direct-governmentalism, Hayek's distinction between cosmos and taxis might be read ontologically. Understood that way, each term refers to mutually exclusive conceptions of social order itself: anarcho-capitalism

---

3. On this idea of rights as socially constructive rivets, see John Tomasi, *Liberalism Beyond Justice: Citizens, Society, and the Boundaries of Political Theory* (Princeton: Princeton University Press, 2001), and John Tomasi, "Individual Rights and Community Virtues," *Ethics* (April 1991).

4. F. A. Hayek. *Law, Legislation, and Liberty, Volume 2: Rules and Order* (Chicago: University of Chicago Press, 1973). See particularly chap. 2, "Cosmos and Taxis."

5. Michael Polanyi, *The Logic of Liberty* (London: Routledge & Kegan Paul, 1951).

on one side, perhaps; totalitarian socialism on the other.[6] However, I believe that Hayek's cosmos-taxis distinction has its greatest conceptual force (and, indeed, may well only acquire conceptual coherence) when considered not ontologically but at the level of social policy. By social policy, I mean the level of argument at which people decide whether the role of government in social construction should be the limited one of providing rivets, or the more ambitious one of setting beams and erecting walls.

Hayek's taxis-cosmos distinction—like my direct-indirect governmentalist one—marks a difference in understanding about the relation of governmental power to social order. On this direct-governmentalist approach to social policy, one looks mainly to legislative bodies to produce fine-grained laws or statutes crafted with the intention of affecting some desired change in the social order. Such laws assign relatively specific places and roles to members of society. The laws tell people precisely what they must do so that the social order will come to have the desired properties. Governmental agencies typically are created to monitor the rate of social change with respect to the desired outcome, and to ensure compliance with all regulations so far enacted.

On what I am calling the indirect-governmentalist approach, by contrast, one looks to the state mainly in its role of defining and enforcing constitutionally entrenched norms of general applicability. Such norms apply equally to all citizens and have the form of general rules of living-together, rather than being crafted toward any particular policy objectives. I call this the indirect approach because, while the governmental laws play a crucial supporting role, the interactions of the citizens are the primary or direct cause of social change. The public enforcement of law by government is a necessary condition for social change, but the role of government with respect to change is only indirect. Social change, we might say, is the product of self-organization. Such outcomes remain very much an order in the systems theory sense. But the specific patterns of regularized behavior that emerge in a social system of this type are far less predictable in advance. Change within the social order with respect to any identifiable topic—say, gender relations—tends to be incremental, with many different approaches being tried simultaneously. People's diverse reactions to the results determine which approaches will be tried again and which will be allowed to die out. The rationality of a social order based on direct-governmentalism, we might say, is constructivist; that of a social order based on indirect-governmentalism, evolutionary.

Direct and indirect-governmentalists differ about how human intentionality properly gets traction in the social world. The former think human intentions for social change regarding many issues of basic justice—gender equality, environmental protection, educational opportunity—should be gathered together and channeled into the social world through the coercive edicts of a democratic will. The latter also see a crucial role for democratically enacted coercive law. But these indirect-governmentalists see law as providing mainly a framework that enables

---

6. Because Hayek was a severe critic of socialism, he is sometimes read as treating the cosmos/taxis distinction in this ontological either/or way. In my view, this is a significant misreading of Hayek. See my manuscript "Social Justicitis."

humans to coordinate their behavior in pursuit of whatever goals they may have and on the basis of the often unique sets of information available to each. The direction of social change regarding any particular social issue, on this latter approach, is *emergent*. The moral shape of the social order is determined more by the social interactions people experience as individuals rather than by any collective deliberations they might engage in as citizens. Socially constructive citizens, we might say, are searchers rather than planners.

This difference between direct and indirect-governmentalism cuts across many policy issues, but has particular power when applied to debates among feminists. For, despite what some of today's feminists themselves think, the most foundational distinction between forms of feminism is the one dividing direct and indirect-governmental forms of feminism.

To support this claim, I wish now to examine the work of a group of indirect-governmental feminists from the late nineteenth century: Sarah Grimké, Angela Fiducia Tilton Heywood, Lillian Harman, Voltairine de Cleyre, and Gertrude B. Kelly. Wendy McElroy has done wonderful work to exhume and make public the work of these neglected writers. Some of these thinkers were political theorists in the traditional disciplinary sense; others were primarily activists. Together, they share the distinction of being nearly forgotten in contemporary debates about feminism. The neglect of these women is interesting in itself, and I mean to diagnose the cause of this neglect before the end of this chapter. In the next section, though, I simply follow the path that McElroy has blazed and report these thinkers' views. Next, I reconstruct and systematize the indirect-governmentalist feminist viewpoint they share, using the reconstruction to reveal the common—and worrying—assumptions of direct-governmental feminism. This before us, I then bring the viewpoint of these neglected thinkers into direct contrast with Susan Okin's egalitarian liberal or "humanist" feminism. I shall use the distinction between direct and indirect-governmentalism to elucidate my own critique of Okin's main policy recommendations. More important, though, I shall use that distinction to highlight what I take to be the enduring legacy of Okin's ideal of gender equality.

NEGLECTED WOMEN IN WESTERN POLITICAL THOUGHT

Sarah Grimké (1792–1873) was one of the first American feminists to work squarely within the domain of legal theory. At a time when legal education was said to be beyond the intellectual reach of women, Grimké made a careful study of civil law, both of England and of the United States. Grimké's most famous essay is "Legal Disabilities of Women," in which she developed a comparative analysis of the legal status of women and slaves.[7]

Under Anglo-American law of the time, the legal existence of a married woman was entirely subsumed under that of her husband. Grimké, basing her argument on Blackstone's exposition of this point, draws the parallel: "The very being of [a]

---

7. Grimké's essay first appeared as a letter to the Boston Female Anti-Slavery Society. It is reprinted in McElroy, *Freedom, Feminism, and the State*, 107–113.

woman, like that of a slave, is absorbed in her master. All contracts made by her, like those made with slaves by their owners, are a mere nullity."[8] As a direct consequence of this first point, married women have no independent standing before courts (Grimké quotes Blackstone: "'If the wife be injured in her person or property, she can bring no action for redress without her husband's concurrence, and his name as well as her own: neither can she be sued, without making her husband a defendant'" (ibid., 109). "This law that 'a wife can bring no action,' &c., is similar to the law respecting slaves. 'A slave cannot bring a suit against his master, or any other person, for an injury—his master must bring it'" (ibid.). If damages are recovered for injury to a wife, as with a slave, it is the husband, or master, who receives it. Married men, like slaveholders, are given powers to impose discipline on their wives, or slaves, as they see fit. (Grimké quotes Gladstone: "The husband, by the old law, might give his wife moderate correction, as he is to answer for her misbehavior. The law thought it reasonable to entrust him with this power of restraining her by domestic chastisement. The courts of law will still permit a husband to restrain a wife of her liberty, in case of gross misbehavior'" [ibid., 110].) Grimké points out that this law places the woman "completely in the hands of a being subject like herself to the outbursts of passion, and thus unworthy to be trusted with power." She continues: "The slaveholder does kill his slave by moderate correction, as the law allows; and many a husband, among the poor, exercises the right given him by the law, of degrading a woman by personal chastisement. And among the higher ranks, if actual imprisonment is not resorted to, women are not infrequently restrained of the liberty of going to places of worship by irreligious husbands, and of doing many other things about which, as moral and responsible beings, they should be the sole judges" (ibid.). So too regarding property, all that a woman might inherit, and indeed any income she may earn, whether before or during her marriage, is ultimately her husband's. (Quoting Blackstone: "A woman's personal property by marriage becomes absolutely her husband's, which, at his death, he may leave entirely away from her." And "By the marriage, the husband is absolutely master of the profits of the woman's land during the coverture" [ibid., 110, 111].) Grimké finds a parallel in the slave laws of Louisiana: "All that a slave possesses belongs to his master; he possesses nothing of his own, except what his master chooses he should possess" (ibid., 111).

In combination, Grimké argued, these laws gave married women only slightly more legal power than slaves. To rectify this injustice, Grimké argued that all humans of age should be recognized as having full formal equality before the law. This advocacy of equal legal standing was in part motivated by Grimké's keen awareness of the wider psychological and social ramifications of people's legal self-understandings. People who are affirmed as holding equal legal status as individuals—whether they be women or men, "slaves" or "masters"—will by dint of that fact think of themselves

---

8. Ibid., 108. Grimké quotes Blackstone: "'By marriage, the husband and wife are one person in law; that is the very being, or legal existence of the woman is suspended during the marriage, or at least is incorporated and consolidated into that of the husband under whose wing, protection and cover she performs everything. 'Therefore it is also generally true, that all compacts made between husband and wife, when single, are voided by the intermarriage'" (ibid., 108).

as individuals, equally free and equally responsible across the whole of their life experiences. For example, regarding the Blackstonian provision that excused a married woman from prosecution if she could show that she was acting under the command of her husband, Grimké wrote: "It would be difficult to frame a law better calculated to destroy the responsibility of woman as a moral being, or a free agent" (ibid., 109). Grimké, writing with remarkable prescience of later feminist concerns, warns against the "bootstrapping" effects of unequal laws. Legal disabilities beget psychological disabilities that make women unlikely, or unwilling, to question their legal status as nonequals. This process in turn generates further distortions in the relationships between men and women. Regarding the effects on women in particular, Grimké wrote:

> The laws which deprive married women of their rights and privileges, have a tendency to lessen them in their own estimation as moral and responsible beings, and that their being made by civil law inferior to their husbands, has a debasing and mischievous effect upon them, teaching them practically the fatal lesson to look to man for protection and indulgence. (ibid., 113)

Angela Fiducia Tilton Heywood was born to a poor farm family in Deerfield, New Hampshire. Forced to leave home at age ten to work as a domestic servant, she was responsible for earning her own money throughout her life—working in a dress-making factory, milking cows, cleaning stables, and shelving books and cleaning at a library. Even later, when she became active as a writer and convention speaker, she supported her family and the magazine which her husband edited, *The Word,* by skillfully running a series of boardinghouses. She became one of the first advocates of labor reform for women—in particular insisting on the commercial value of domestic work. Couples, as a matter of propriety and morality, ought to recognize domestic work as an enabling condition for the man to earn whatever salary he brings to the family from work outside the home. She argued that even married women should be allowed to keep bank accounts of their own, in which they might deposit some part of their own earnings outside the home and into which their husbands might contribute some part of their salary.

In 1865, Angela Tilton married the social radical Ezra Heywood. The Heywoods advocated open discussion about sexual issues and, especially in a pamphlet called *Cupid's Yokes,* education about birth control. In 1866, Ezra was arrested under the Comstock Laws (which prohibited the mailing of "obscene" materials) for sending copies of that pamphlet through the mail. During her husband's imprisonment, Angela Heywood took up the editorship of *The Word.* Under her direction, that paper intensified its "plain-speech policy" by which sexual organs were named without euphemism. In a line of essays under the title "The Woman's View of It," Angela Heywood described the social distortions caused by people's—both men's and women's—lack of understanding of themselves as sexual beings. "It is so strange that human life could have throbbed on thousands, if not millions of years without intelligent, serious consideration of our body-sexed selves, of the pregnant issues involved in personal, blended Being."[9] Heywood asked: "Why not make voyages of discovery into our body-selves,

---

9. "The Woman's View of It—No. 1," January 1883, in McElroy, *Individualist Feminism of the Nineteenth Century,* 43.

study attractive, fruitful lessons of Moral, Sexual Physiology?" (ibid., 46). Men as much as women are capable of loving relationships, and as needful of relationships of honest intimacy. Sexual knowledge is a precondition of such relationships. Thus: "In nothing is the devilish stupidity of men more apparent than in decreeing sexual knowledge 'obscene'" (ibid.).

If the freedom to distribute and to receive sexually explicit materials that others regard as obscene is one precondition of human agency, another is that people's liberty to love as they choose not be restricted by other people through state agencies. Patterns and durations of love relationships are not fixed or universal. Angela Heywood advocated free love and was harshly critical of any state-sanctioned attempts to force one pattern of love on all members of society. Her target was state-licensed marriage. "The ceremony of legal marriage by a third person—a clergyman or magistrate—who represents society, debars us from personal responsibility, invades personal liberty, and exhibits the weakness of accepting conventional force rather than essential right as the arbiter of love relations."[10]

Like Grimké, Heywood was keenly aware of the wider educative effects of legal statutes. Divergent legal statuses for men and women generate divergent curricula that shape the character and attitudes of members of each gender. "Men have been learning from opportunity, and women from *in*opportunity; their lessons have therefore been different."[11] The goal is not just equality, but an equal capacity for autonomy and an equal acceptance of responsibility: "We want a social order which will bespeak the welfare of both, that we may, in candor, face each other eye to eye and ask 'Who are you, what are you, and how do you earn your living?' These questions are all potent and significant of genuine or false character, and, in true society, must be of imperative importance" (ibid., 34).

Lillian Harman entered into an "autonomistic" marriage with Edwin Cox Walker on September 19, 1886. The couple was jailed on September 21 on charges of violating the Kansas Marriage Act of 1867, which forbade any couple to present themselves as "married" without state-sanction. On October 19 the court found them guilty, sentencing Walker to 75 days in jail and Harman to 45. As a condition of their release, the couple was also ordered to pay court costs, which they refused to do. They appealed, and in January 1887 the Kansas Supreme Court heard their case, *State v. Walker and Another.*[12]

The court transcript provided details of Harman and Walker's marriage ceremony. Noting that they found all public forms of marriage ceremony objectionable—"a pandering to the morbid, vicious, and meddlesome element of human nature"—the couple explained that they were announcing the terms of their marriage publicly only as a guarantee to one another, and especially from Walker to Harman, of the true terms of their union. Walker vowed:

10. "Men's Laws and Love's Laws," September 1876, in McElroy, *Individualist Feminism of the Nineteenth Century*, 35.

11. "Women's Love: Its Relations to Man and Society," July 1876, in McElroy, *Individualist Feminism of the Nineteenth Century*, 33.

12. Supreme Court of Kansas, March 4, 1887, *Pacific Reporter* 13 (1887): 280–289, reprinted in McElroy, *Individualist Feminism of the Nineteenth Century*, 125–132.

> I abdicate in advance all the so-called "marital rights" with which this public acknowledgment of our relationship may invest me. Lillian is and will continue to be as free to repulse any and all advances of mine as she has been heretofore. In joining with me in this love and labor union, she has not alienated a single natural right. She remains sovereign of herself, as I of myself, and we severally and together repudiate all legal powers conferred upon husbands and wives.[13]

Harman's vows repeated these stipulations, and continued: "I enter into this union of my own free will and choice.…I make no promises that it may become impossible or immoral for me to fulfill; but retain the right to act, always, as my conscience, and best judgment shall dictate. I retain, also, my full maiden name, as I am sure it is my duty to do." Finally, Lillian's father, Moses Harman, while noting his personal approval of the union, stated his refusal to "give away the bride," explaining that he wished "her to be always the owner of her person, and to be free always to act according to her truest and purest impulses, and as her highest judgment may dictate" (ibid., 129).

In court, the couple affirmed that they had neither sought nor obtained any state license for their marriage and that their ceremony had not been performed by any agent of the state or state-licensed minister. They further affirmed that they had begun matrimonial cohabitation after their ceremony. Their appeal was thus denied. Still refusing to pay court costs, Harman and Walker remained in jail until April. They paid the court costs only when Moses Harman was jailed on other charges, leaving no one to run the Harman family's radical paper, *Lucifer, the Light Bearer.*

Voltairine de Cleyre (1866–1912) was an ardent feminist and accomplished scholar of the American Founding. In "Anarchism and American Traditions," de Cleyre argued that the Declaration of Independence signaled the start not of a war but of a *revolution:* a revolution not just against a particular king at a particular time, but an ongoing struggle against coercive, liberty-limiting institutions of all sorts. Because the internal dynamic of bureaucratic institutions is toward the extension of their own power, revolution above all else calls for vigilance on the part of citizens against that dynamic within governmental agencies. According to de Cleyre, the two domains in which that revolutionary attitude had most clearly faltered in her day were the areas where citizens had allowed government to become most directly and minutely involved: education and commerce.

Revolutionaries such as Thomas Jefferson had advocated a system of public education. Aware of the fragility of the spirit of liberty in the face of the dynamics of coercive centralization, Jefferson thought that a teaching of Revolutionary history should be central to such education. De Cleyre quoted Jefferson:

> The spirit of the times may alter, will alter. Our rulers will become corrupt, our people careless.…From the conclusion of this war we shall be going downhill. It will not then be necessary to resort every moment to the people for support. They will be forgotten, therefore, and their rights disregarded. They will forget themselves in the sole faculty of making money, and will never think of uniting

---

13. McElroy, *Individualist Feminism of the Nineteenth Century,* 128.

to effect a due respect for their rights. The shackles, therefore, which shall not be knocked off at the conclusion of this war, will be heavier and heavier, till our rights shall revive or expire in a convulsion.[14]

De Clyre argued, however, that Jefferson established a system of common education

not with the intent of burdening the memories of our youth with the dates of battles or the speeches of generals, not to make of the Boston Tea Party Indians the one sacrosanct mob in all history, to be revered but never on any account to be imitated, but with the intent that every American should know to what conditions the masses of people had been brought by the operation of certain institutions, by what means they had wrung out their liberties, and how those liberties had again and again been filched from them by the use of governmental force, fraud, and privilege. (ibid., 38)

State-sponsored schools had used their authority to breed among citizens a sense of "security, laudation, complacent indolence, passive acquiescence in the acts of government protected by the label 'home-made,'" rather than to instill in them "a wakeful jealousy, a never-ending watchfulness of rulers, a determination to squelch every attempt of those entrusted with power to encroach on the sphere of individual action" (ibid.).

De Cleyre's feminism tended in an anarchist direction. She saw the sin of the founders as lying in their failure to trust wholly in liberty, attempting instead to compromise between liberty and government. In my terms, the founders' Constitution was an attempt to strike a balance between indirect and direct forms of social construction. DeClyre worried that the founders misjudged the power of direct-governmentalist forms to usurp the space reserved for indirect-governmentalism. Like some antifederalists of the founding period, de Cleyre was skeptical even of the Bill of Rights. "Make no laws whatever concerning speech, and speech will be free; so soon as you make a declaration on paper that speech shall be free, you will have a hundred lawyers proving that 'freedom does not mean abuse, nor liberty license'; and they will define and define freedom out of existence" (ibid., 44). Freedom of speech, like all freedoms, is kept alive only by each individual's determination to exercise freedom in his or her own way, especially in the face of those who would invoke governmental powers to curb them or to channel their choices in some particular, preferred direction. It is this revolutionary spirit of liberty, and wariness of coercive institutions, on which the goal of individual self-determination relies: "for tyrants are active and ardent, and will devote themselves in the name of any number of gods, religious and otherwise, to put shackles on sleeping men" (ibid., 45).

Gertrude B. Kelly (1862–1934) was an Irish immigrant and medical doctor. Her main life's work concerned the plight of poor working women in the tenements of Newark, New Jersey. Despite her special interest in the needs of poor women, though, Kelly insisted that traditional gender roles, and especially the statutory decrees that

14. "Anarchism and American Traditions," in McElroy, *Individualist Feminism of the Nineteenth Century*, 36.

propped up those roles, were debilitating to both men and women of all classes. Even if men were the main perpetrators of injustice toward women, still "no wrong can be done to any class of society without part at least of the evil reverting to the wrongdoers."[15] For Kelly, therefore, "there is, properly speaking, no *woman question,* apart from the question of human rights and human liberty" (ibid., 164). At a time when many other women's advocates were demanding an increase in state-financing of medical education for women, Kelly wrote a remarkable essay—"State Aid to Science" (*Speech to Alumnae Association of Women's Medical College of the New York Infirmary for Women and Children,* June 1, 1887)—in which she attacked the idea of state aid of any kind to science. Kelly argued that direct-governmental programs, however well intentioned, were inherently incapable of contributing efficiently to scientific progress and that, even if such programs were capable, it would be morally wrong to allow it to do so.

According to Kelly, "the State, or the State-aided institutions have never been able, even with the most Chinese system of civil-service examinations, to sift the worthy from the unworthy with half the efficiency which private individuals or corporations have done."[16] This difficulty is magnified in the case of state sponsorship of science because most leaps in scientific knowledge are revolutionary. The tendency of direct-governmental programs, in every domain, is "to crystallize and fossilize any institutions or ideas on which they lay their protecting hands" (ibid., 180). Proponents of state aid to science, Kelly argued, forget that such aid cannot be given to science, but rather is given to particular doctrines and dogmas. But how, especially in light of the scientific ideal of falsifiability, are those doctrines to be selected? "Is the State, then, to reward all those who oppose a statement as well as all those who support it, or is it only to reward certain of the questioners, and, if so, who is to decide what statements have not been refuted?" (ibid., 178–179). For the government to bring scientific experts onto its payroll would only worsen the situation. By that very act, the government would structure the incentives for such people in a way that would make them resist any idea or revolution that might deprive them of their salaries: "One of my chief objections to State-aid to anything is that it tends to develop a great many big idle queens at the expense of the workers. There is no longer any direct responsibility on the part of those employed to those who employ them, as there is when private contract enters into play" (ibid., 180).

Even if targeted governmental programs were able to aid science efficiently, Kelly argued, it would be morally wrong for the state to do so: "Now, to tax a man to support something that he does not wish for is to invade his right to property, and to that extent to curtail his life, is to take away from him his power of obtaining what he desires, in order to supply him with something that he does not desire" (ibid., 182). Such schemes of aid amount to a form of paternalism: "You may say that you desire to increase his happiness, his knowledge, etc., but I maintain that you have no right to decide what is happiness or knowledge for him, any more than you have a right to decide what religion he must give adherence to" (ibid., 182).

---

15. "A Woman's Warning to Reformers," January 23, 1886, quoted in McElroy, *Individualist Feminism of the Nineteenth Century*, 174.

16. "State Aid to Science," in McElroy, *Individualist Feminism of the Nineteenth Century*, 179.

Instead, Kelly argued that progress in science—as in many other areas of human understanding—is most efficiently and justly advanced by the principles of what Hayek would later call the "spontaneous order." The diffusion of decision-making power among individuals and small groups, rather than its centralization in bureaucratic agencies, has already proven its ability to produce spectacularly complex forms of order. Kelly mentioned the development of languages of beauty and complexity, and the way market forces—once rights to property and contract are secured—supply even great cities with food while no government has yet proven itself even capable of adequately supplying its own armies. Rather than receiving state aid, science should be allowed to advance by individuals and small groups contributing their shares in a climate of freedom:

> It will advance by having no opinion protected from discussion and agitation, by having the greatest possible freedom of thought, of speech, and of the press. That the unaided efforts of a people are capable of causing advance belongs fortunately no longer to the domain of opinion, but of fact. They have already caused all the progress that has been made, not only without the aid of the State, but in opposition to the State and the Church, and all the other conservative and retrogressive elements in society. (ibid., 184)

GENDER: CONSTRUCTIVIST VS. EPISTEMIC

Susan Okin was a direct-governmental feminist. The justificatory base of Okin's direct-governmentalism was liberal egalitarianism. As a liberal egalitarian, she believed that the liberal state has an obligation, founded on justice, not only to affirm all citizens as holders of equal liberties, but also to redress inequalities in the worth of citizens' liberties that arise from traditional Western gender roles. Like many egalitarian liberal feminists, Okin focused on economic inequalities. She advocated the establishment of governmental bureaucracies designed to track and correct inequalities in the worth of women's liberties caused by the resource advantages that men hold over women.

Okin's post-Marxist critics, by contrast, affirm an ideal of gender egalitarianism that is less fettered by the traditional liberal concerns for rights held by individuals. This post-Marxist ideal of egalitarianism is more thoroughgoing than the liberal one. It encompasses cultural, sexual and even psychological relations between the sexes. As with Okin's liberal feminism, the advocacy of targeted governmental rules and regulations is basic to post-Marxist feminism. Indeed, this direct-governmentalist approach provides the deep common ground of practically all public policy programs advocated by feminists within today's academy.

Direct-governmentalist forms of feminism share a common methodological root. The root, shared alike by egalitarian liberal feminists such as Okin and post-Marxist feminists such as MacKinnon, is found in the constructivist approach they take to sexual oppression. By this, I mean that all such feminists—insofar as they intend their work to have a public policy payout—are methodologically committed to treating gender as a conceptual class, with the gender class "women" oppressed by the gender class "men." This reliance on class is clearest with post-Marxist feminists, who substitute the category "women" for the Marxist category "workers" in their analysis of domination and/or exploitation. But egalitarian liberal feminism shares this same methodological commitment. Liberal feminists differentiate "women" and "men" as the conceptually primary classes in their advocacy of specific government edicts intended to correct inequalities in the worth of citizens' liberties that result from traditional Western gender roles, roles which they see as benefiting men.

The nineteenth-century thinkers whose views I have described also sometimes discussed issues of sexual oppression in constructivist, class-based ways. This is understandable, since many of them were offering critiques of the state-backed legal disabilities of their day, disabilities that were themselves formulated atop constructivist, gender-based conceptions of citizen identity. (Like the contemporary feminists, the advocates of those legal disabilities were direct governmentalists: they advocated direct governmentalist measures as a way of realizing their ideal of patriarchy.) However, none of these early feminists' primary concerns about sexual oppression can be captured in constructivist terms. Instead, their primary concern was with individuals, whether male or female. As Kelly wrote: "The woman's cause is man's—they rise or sink/Together,—dwarfed or god-like—bond or free."[17]

Of course, many contemporary feminists express a concern for the effects of gender roles on men as well as women, and on individuals as well as on groups. Susan Okin, of course, was prominent among egalitarian liberal feminists in this regard. However, hardly any of these feminists treat the effects of gender on individual people as *conceptually primary* to their analyses in the way these nineteenth-century feminists did. For these earlier, individualist feminists, a social order is at base not a devise for realizing some goal. Society is instead a discovery procedure. The meaning of gender is to be found only in the output of the decisions and actions of individuals interacting for their own purposes on the basis of information held only by those individuals themselves. In this way, individualist feminists take an epistemic rather than a constructivist approach to gender.[18] Their impulse was to search rather than to plan.

The difference between the epistemic and constructivist approaches becomes vivid when we consider yet another contemporary constructivist approach to sexual oppression, but this time one that sees "men" as the class dominated by "women." This idea, stirred in the 1980s at mythopoetic retreats for men held by Robert Bly and others, has become a staple of the men's liberation literature.

William Farrell, for example, defines power as the ability to control one's life. By most major measures, Farrell argues, contemporary American men have less control over their lives than do women. The traditional male role as the silent protector, compared to the female role as the protected (or, in what Farrell describes as the contemporary variant of the role, as the "victim"), systematically disadvantages men. In America today, women live an average of seven years longer than men—a lifespan gap that has increased dramatically since 1920, when women lived just one year longer than men.[19]

---

17. "Proudhon and the Woman's Question," *Liberty*, March 12, 1887, quoted in McElroy, *Individualist Feminism of the Nineteenth Century*, 8.

18. For a nice account of the epistemic approach to gender roles and other social roles see Adam Tebble "What Is the Politics of Difference?" *Political Theory* 30, no. 2 (April 2002): 259–281.

19. Warren Farrell, *The Myth of Male Power* (Berkley Trade, 2001), 30.

The suicide rates among young boys and girls before puberty and socialization are nearly identical, but from ages 10 to 14, the boys' suicide rate is twice as high as girls; from 15 to 19, four times as high; from 20 to 24, six times (ibid., 31). Men are less likely than women to attend college (46 percent to 54 percent) and less likely to graduate (ibid., 39). Even in college, the two classes of young people are dramatically unequal in terms of their vulnerability to worries about their later earning responsibilities (ibid., 34). By the age of 20, young men begin to repress their personal interests in humane disciplines and begin focusing on disciplines that will put them in position to take high-paying jobs (85 percent of college students who major in engineering are male; over 80 percent of those who major in art history are female). Professional women are often said to be victims of a glass ceiling. But, Farrell argues, a great many more men—without any public recognition of their plight—are locked in "glass cellars." The *Jobs Related Almanac* used a combination of salary, stress, work environment, outlook, security, and physical demands to rank 250 jobs from best to worst. Twenty-four of the 25 worst jobs in America (including metal worker, truck driver, roofer, boilermaker, machinery operator, welder, miner, and ironworker) are performed overwhelmingly by men. What's more, Farrell says, despite the media attention paid to the challenges that working women face in juggling domestic and professional commitments, American men in fact work longer hours overall than women do. (A comprehensive University of Michigan study that included time spent on housework, childcare, yard work, commuting, etc., found that the average man works 61 hours per week, the average woman 56 [ibid., 37].)

Signs in post offices across the United States remind one class of young citizens— men—that they, but not another class of young citizens—women—must register for the draft. Young men know that their life projects may be interrupted at any time by a period of forced military training, risking psychological scarring, physical mutilation, and death in their role as protectors of family and country. Such posters read "A man's got to do what a man's got to do," and, in an ultimate perversion, men are socialized to call this gender-based vulnerability "power." While women stage marches to "take back the night," American men are almost twice as likely as women to be victims of violent crimes (including rape). Men are three times more likely to be victims of murder (ibid., 32). It is true that most of these crimes against men are committed by other men. But, Farrell argues, when it is noted that violent crimes against black males (which occur at even higher rates than for white males) are overwhelming committed by black males, we do not attribute this to their blackness but rather see it as a manifestation of black powerlessness. This approach invites us to look for deeper societal explanations of the violence experienced by blacks. The shocking incidence of violence against males in our society, their higher suicide rates, the erosion of their relative expected lifespans, and their unique position of vulnerability to military service, Farrell suggests, should spur similar questions.

The women's liberation movement has brought important improvements to the life prospects of women. But, Farrell claims, the excesses of that movement have sharpened these disadvantages of men. The few accepted domains for male expressions of intimacy—for example, love making with their partners—are condemned as "rape." The male capacity for sexual arousal at pictorial images is called "pornographic." Men who reveal their attraction to female coworkers are vulnerable to charges of "sexual harassment." While still socialized to measure their own worth in terms of earning power, policies of "affirmative action" for women have placed new disabilities on men in precisely that domain.

The statistical bases of many of Farrell's claims, like the statistical bases of many feminist claims, might well be contested. I lay out Farrell's claims merely to demonstrate that men's liberationists such as Farrell and women's liberationists such as Okin and MacKinnon share a constructivist approach to questions of sexual oppression. That is, they are methodologically committed to dividing citizens into two main classes—men and women—and ascribing a directional indicator of oppression between the two. There is a form of essentialism at work in this approach, an essentialism that makes it logically coherent for male liberationists and female liberationists to debate about which class is oppressed by the other. Because of the eagerness of each side to invoke direct forms of governmental correctives on behalf of their own preferred class, such debates become not merely intellectually coherent but politically charged as well.

The nineteenth-century feminists I have described offer public policy practitioners a different methodology for thinking about sexual oppression. For Grimké, Heywood, Harman, de Cleyre, and Kelly, the primary unit of social analysis was the individual person. They argued that each individual should be recognized as having the capacity for personal self-determination, for the creation of a life of his or her own choosing, whether that life be labeled traditionalist, progressive, or idiosyncratic by anyone else's standard. On this epistemic approach to gender, politically enforced rules and policies that would hinder individual self-determination are ipso facto suspect. So are rules and policies designed to channel patterns of choice-making to any antecedently approved pattern of understanding about the significance of gender. After all, these feminists saw clearly that inherited gender roles threaten the self-determination of men and women alike. Regarding the threat to men, for example, Angelina Grimké, sister of Sarah Grimké, wrote, "The fallacious doctrine of male and female virtues has well nigh ruined all that is morally great and lovely in his character: he has been quite as deep a sufferer by it as woman, though mostly in different respects and by other processes."[20]

Grimké, Heywood, and the others were humane individualists. Their "feminism" was epiphenomenal—an artifact of the specific pattern of gender-based legal inequalities of their day. The humane individualist approach retained an important place for questions about the patterns of oppression confronted by individuals as members of gender groups. An understanding of the role expectations that each individual is likely to face as a member of a gender group is a prerequisite to understanding the conditions of, or obstacles to, individual self-development. Thus, these thinkers would be extremely interested in the anecdotal, sociological, and statistical literatures assembled by contemporary male and female liberationists alike. But such information is significant to individualist feminists (Heywood, de Cleyre, and Kelly) and to gender feminists (Okin and her post-Marxist critics) in a very different way.

---

20. "Human Rights Not Founded on Sex," 1837 letter reprinted in McElroy, *Individualist Feminism of the Nineteenth Century*, 32.

For feminists such as Harman, de Cleyre, and Kelly, the primary locus of justice is not society as in integrated whole but rather the experiences of individual persons. Justice requires a particular type of formal equality: equal treatment under constitutionally entrenched laws that protect the natural rights of individuals. Wendy McElroy describes the natural law approach of Kelly and the others as akin to the nineteenth-century individualist Benjamin Tucker's account of rights as problem-solving devices. On this approach, rights are social devices that have been experimentally accepted as providing solutions to social problems. McElroy formulates the general question thus: "Given what we know about reality and what we know about human nature, is it possible to reason out a universal code of behavior to maximize the happiness and safety of human beings?"[21] The answer cannot be constructed in the abstract but rather must be understood as emerging through the test of real social experience.[22] Tucker, for example, argued that the moral institution of property arose as a means to solve the problem of scarcity. Given that many discrete goods cannot be used or held by more than one person at a time, and given that there are often many people who simultaneously might wish to use such discrete goods, rights to property served to solve the problem of competition and conflict regarding such goods. Abolitionist feminists such as Sarah Grimké used a similar argument to derive a natural right to self-ownership. The question that black slavery posed was: "Who has the right to the scarce resource of black labor?" The answer they derived for blacks applied to women as well: the labor and body of a human being belongs to the person who *is that* human being.

This natural rights approach provided a principle—the principle of self-ownership—by which these nineteenth-century feminists argued for rights to abortion, to contraceptive information and devices, to privacy in marriage agreements, and to strict limits on coercive governmental powers across all domains of peaceable human interaction. The slogan of individualist feminists of the nineteenth century was "a woman's body, a woman's right." But they applied their slogan to individual men as well as to individual women. Maleness, from this perspective, is a biological trait without political relevance. Traditional gender roles have social relevance, of course, since self-owning persons may need to understand the social currents they are likely individually to encounter as politically autonomous citizens. Even at that level, however, the emphasis is on each individual's own interpretation of the significance of gender. As self-owners, each citizen must be politically empowered to react to inherited gender roles however she or he sees fit.

---

21. McElroy, *Individualist Feminism of the Nineteenth Century*, 2.

22. This idea is developed well by Hayek. See particularly his *Law, Legislation, and Liberty, Volume 2: The Mirage of Social Justice* (Chicago: University of Chicago Press, 1976). Hayek says of the rules of conduct that regulate social order: "Appropriate rules of conduct are not derived from explicit knowledge of the concrete events we will encounter; rather, they are an adaptation to our environment...in so far as such rules have prevailed because the group that had adopted them was more successful, nobody need ever have known why that group was successful and why in consequence its rules became generally adopted....Although we can endeavour to find out what function a particular rule performs within a given system of rules, and to judge how well it has performed that function, and may as a result try to improve it...we can never rationally reconstruct in the same manner the whole system of rules, because we lack the knowledge of all the experiences that entered into its formation. The whole system of rules can therefore never be reduced to a purposive construction for known purposes, but must remain to us the inherited system of values guiding that society" (ibid., 5).

OKIN'S CRITIQUE OF POLITICAL INDIVIDUALISM

What would Susan Okin think of the indirect-governmentalist approach to feminist public policy? Famously, Okin was sharply critical of one contemporary formulation of indirect-governmentalism to which Sarah Grimké, Angela Heywood, Lillian Harman, Voltairine de Cleyre, and Gertrude Kelly were forbears: libertarianism. At the start of her critique of libertarianism, Okin asks: "What becomes of libertarian arguments when we apply them to all the adult members of society, women as well as men?" (1989a:75). Given that question, it is unfortunate that Okin (to my knowledge) never studied or wrote about the nineteenth-century feminists whose life work centered on that question.

Okin argues that libertarianism, on any formulation, tacitly relies upon a realm of family life beyond the reach of its principles (Okin 1989a:74–88). When that assumption is exposed, the political result is not the utopia of a minimal state but the dystopia of matriarchy and slavery. Okin focuses on Robert Nozick's Lockean defense of political individualism. Nozick's theory starts with an (undefended) claim of individual human self-ownership. If persons own themselves, they own their labor, and so may acquire property rights in previously unowned things with which they mix their labor. These rights, and the rights of just transfer they imply, are so strong that they show that the most extensive state that can be justified is the night watchman state of classical liberalism.

However, Okin argues, if we apply these same principles to the types of labor found within households, we get a different political outcome. Women are people. If women own themselves, they own the fruits of their labor, including the embryos they gestate and the children to which they give birth. Indeed, Okin argues that a mother's ownership of her children is a particularly clear case of Nozick's labor theory of property: "A human infant originates from a minute quantity of abundantly available and otherwise useless resources." The vast bulk of the value added in the production of an infant comes from the woman's reproductive input (ibid., 83). By Nozick's principles, women own their children. If people—who are all given birth by mothers—do not own themselves, Nozick's theory either collapses into incoherence, or yields a moral justification for matriarchal slavery.

Okin does not explain why she thinks it appropriate to describe a human embryo as being composed of material that is "abundantly available" and "otherwise useless." A great many politically reasonable citizens affirm worldviews that include a spiritual approach to questions about the meaning and importance of human life. Such citizens would likely find Okin's claim about the status of a human embryo to be deeply controversial. Regarding the most basic questions of human meaning, though, Okin's argument here requires that we follow her in approaching such questions in a narrowly material and mechanistic way. By insisting on this materialist approach, Okin cuts her analysis off from the background of natural law theory, a background that looks for purposes in the observed facts of human experience and seeks to ground claims of right by reference to such purposes. Her critique of natural rights to self-ownership is impoverished by this assumption.

Even taken materially, Okin's claim is puzzling. Modern genetics emphasizes not the "abundance" but the uniqueness of each human embryo. That uniqueness occurs precisely because of the *combined* contribution of male and female chromosomes. If, on the Lockean formulation, a person can mix his labor by gathering acorns, by shooting an arrow into a wild stag, by directing his servant to cut up turfs, or—on Okin's modification—even through unconscious processes of gestation, surely the male's labor in implanting his sperm would give him some claim of ownership too. Again, this observation immediately complicates Okin's simple *reductio* against Nozick's libertarian position. It invites more nuanced discussion of questions about ownership and obligation between parents and children on the natural law approach.

The nineteenth-century individualist feminists struggled to work out the implications of natural rights of self-ownership to questions of intrafamilial rights and obligations. Lillian Harman, for example, presented one of the earliest arguments in favor of abortion rights to use the slogan "a woman's body, a woman's right." Every woman's right to choose an abortion, Harman claimed, springs directly from each woman's ownership of her own body. Why does a fetus not possess a right to life? Harman (and Grimké's) view seems to be that a full natural right to self-ownership is held by adults only, by virtue of their full capacity for self-direction. Complications about child-parent relations persist on this approach, and contributors to nineteenth-century individualist publications such as *Liberty* were not shy in confronting them. At one extreme, some individualists argued, "If freedom is universal, children are sovereign from the moment of their birth."[23] Clara Dixon Davidson argued that parents had no inherent duty to support their (self-owning) children but merely a duty not to aggress against them.[24] J. Wm. Lloyd argued that the only natural duty here was an obligation on the part of the child: the child should as soon as possible repay its parents "for its life."[25]

Discussions of natural law are notoriously indeterminate. In part, this is a result of the complex way that the natural law approach asks us to seek normative principles in light of evolving streams of sociological data rather than from a relatively simple, constructivist original position. One indeterminacy with which nineteenth-century natural law feminists particularly struggled was the question of where, precisely, obligations founded on natural law ended and where obligations founded on what individuals (optionally) committed themselves to began. Harman's wedding vows with Walker are instructive. Regarding wedding vows generally, Harman wrote, "We regard intelligent choice,—untrampled voluntaryism—coupled with responsibility to natural law for our acts, as the true and only basis for morality."[26] Walker, as part of his vows to Harman, affirmed not only his responsibility to her regarding the care of their offspring, but also "*her paramount right to custody thereof,* should any unfortunate fate dissolve this union" (ibid., 128, emphasis added). Is Harman's right to custody a part of

23. A. Warren, "The Rights of Babies," *Liberty,* June 23, 1888, quoted in McElroy, *Individualist Feminism of the Nineteenth Century,* 139.

24. "Relations between Parents and Children," *Liberty,* September 29, 1888, in McElroy, *Individualist Feminism of the Nineteenth Century,* 140.

25. "The Problem Which the Child Presents," *Liberty,* May 26, 1888, in McElroy, *Individualist Feminism of the Nineteenth Century,* 139.

26. *State v. Walker and Another,* reprinted in McElroy, *Individualist Feminism of the Nineteenth Century,* 128.

natural law (generated, for example, by her unique work in carrying and birthing the child), or is it an optional feature of the marriage agreement that Harman and Walker devised for themselves? It seems to be something in between. Harman and Walker seem to treat the principles of self-ownership and the attendant principle that people own their labor as casting moral penumbra. Those penumbra, while not as clear a part of the core of natural law as Harman's right to self-ownership, nonetheless indicate to Walker the special relationship Harman will have to their children in virtue of the fact of her role in birthing and suckling them. Even here, however, the locus of decision making is recognized as belonging to the specific persons whose lives will be most directly affected by their choices.

Penumbral ambiguities aside, feminists in the individualist tradition were clear about the core concepts of natural law and the implications of those principles when applied to all adult members of society, men as well as women. The free choices of actual adult persons, constrained by the principle of self-ownership and its immediate corollaries of peaceable coexistence, must be respected. Any attempts to use the state directly to dictate the terms of married life, or to seek to impose on all couples any one preferred view about the significance of gender, would be a direct violation of the respect that self-owning individuals are owed. As Moses Harman, father of Lillian, stated at Walker and Harman's wedding, marriage is, or should be, "a distinctively personal matter, a strictly private affair" (ibid., 126). Thus, the preparation of the contracting parties for the duties of marriage must be the work of the parties immediately concerned. The role of government is at most indirect—defining property rights and enforcing laws of general applicability that citizens can then use for their own purposes. Moses Harman continued:

> Marriage being a strictly personal matter, we deny the right of society, in the form of church and state, to regulate it or interfere with the individual man and woman in this relation....To acknowledge the right of the state to dictate to us in these matters is to acknowledge ourselves as children or minor wards of the state, not capable of transacting our own business. (ibid., 127)

By contrast, Susan Okin was a direct-governmentalist. As a liberal, Okin was intensely committed to the ideal of full political autonomy for all citizens, men as well as women. But she consistently tied her ideal of "humanist justice" to public policies of direct-governmentalism. Those policies, by their very nature, regularly would require the sacrifice of individual freedom to direct-governmentalist statutes designed with the intention of bringing the social order as a whole to the particular "solution" regarding the meaning and importance of gender that Okin herself preferred.

Rather than limiting the power of government to protect and secure the choices of individuals (insofar as those choices are compatible with natural law), Okin advocates a far more ambitious role for governmental authorities. Okin advocates the use of governmental power to direct people's actions and choices, with the intention that a leveling of equalities in the worth of their liberties from an overall societal perspective might thereby be achieved. A "fair and just" solution to the problem of gender inequality "must encourage and facilitate the equal sharing by men and women of paid and unpaid work, of productive and reproductive labor." Thus, "we must work toward a future in which all will be likely to choose this mode of life." What is this way of life that Okin prefers? She tells us: "A just future would be one without gender. In its social structures and practices, one's sex would have no more relevance than one's eye color or the length of one's toes" (Okin 1989a:171).

How would Okin "encourage and facilitate" people's making choices that would yield her preferred social outcome? Along with laws designed to completely eradicate sexual discrimination in hiring and promotion and to outlaw sexual harassment in the workplace, Okin advocates a network of new laws and the creation of new governmental agencies. Paradigms of direct-governmentalism, all of these rules are designed to encourage the regulation of people's behavior in the hope that the social system as a whole will be brought to exhibit the pattern of gender relations she antecedently decided to be just.

First, as mentioned earlier, Okin thinks that marriage partners should be accorded equal legal entitlement to all earnings coming into the household, with employers therefore being required to distribute equal paychecks to their employees and their employees' partners. This, Okin tells us, would be no more an invasion of people's privacy than are laws requiring the public registration of marriages and births—the very requirements, recall, that earlier feminists endured imprisonment in order to protest (ibid., 181–182). Pregnancy and childbirth should be given legal status as temporarily disabling conditions, and thus "employers should be mandated to provide leave for all such conditions" (ibid., 176).

To encourage her ideal of equal parenting, Okin advocates laws that would require employers to make postbirth leaves available to fathers as well as mothers, leaves which could be taken sequentially or simultaneously on a half-time basis. Further, "all workers should have the right, without prejudice to their jobs, seniority, benefits, and so on, to work less than full-time during the first year of a child's life, and to work flexible or somewhat reduced hours at least until the child reaches the age of seven" (ibid., 176). Individuals who, for whatever reason, continue working at their careers while their coworkers take parental leave are therefore to be legally barred from receiving any rewards of seniority or benefit from that work. Also, longer periods of leave should be legally mandated for parents of children with health problems. Large-scale employers should be legally required to provide high-quality day care for children from infancy until they start school. Direct government subsidies should be provided to workers in lower-paying jobs, or those working for small businesses, to the point that they can afford day care of an equally high level for their children.

Schooling—which Okin thinks should be directly funded and controlled by the government—should be designed to inculcate in children Okin's ideal of a gender-free society. For example, she advocates new home economics courses "teaching girls *and boys* how to combine working and parenting" (ibid., 177, emphasis in original). Schools should also be required to conduct extensive after-hours programs, "where children can play safely, do their homework, or participate in creative activities" until their parents' workdays are finished.

Further, Okin advocates a system whereby the state would genetically determine the paternity of all children of single mothers at birth (presumably by the creation of a national data bank that would gather and hold information on each citizen's genetic

identity). In this way, the state could enforce the requirement that birth fathers contribute to the support of their children, with governmental subsidies where appropriate (ibid., 178). Okin also advocates the legal imposition of a universal pattern for
the financial outcome of divorce settlements: laws should be established that would
ensure that both postdivorce households meet and maintain the same standard of living (ibid., 183). Throughout, Okin mentions that couples choosing a more traditional
gendered pattern for their family would be free to do so. So too, presumably, would
be couples who developed unique views of gender—views precious to them but by
definition "idiosyncratic" by the lights of the official gender-free attitude that Okin
wants the state to promulgate. But Okin is optimistic that, with the imposition of all of
these legal requirements, "we would arrive at a model that would absolutely minimize
gender" (ibid., 174).

Okin's plan-based approach to gender freedom would be troubling to the indirect-
governmental feminists of the nineteenth century. As we have seen, rather than constructing a theoretical ideal social outcome regarding the significance of gender, they
take an epistemic approach whereby citizens are empowered to work out diverse interpretations of the significance of gender for themselves. But it is also unclear that Okin's
form of direct-governmentalist feminism is compatible with the contemporary egalitarian approach to liberalism that she wishes to affirm.

At the core of the liberal paradigm—on both its direct and indirect-governmentalist
policy varieties—is a principle of legitimacy. According to that principle, the coercive
power of the government is justified only if it is used in light of principles that are
morally acceptable to the citizens subject to that power.[27] A society with a history of
free institutions—notably, one guaranteeing citizens the freedoms of speech, association and religious practice—is likely to be populated by many "politically reasonable"
citizens, most notably (although not only) citizens who are religious in a textual or
church-based way, who may morally reject the ideal of social genderlessness on which
Okin's argument is premised.

Okin is not the only direct-governmentalist liberal whose position as a social advocate is weakened by this principle of legitimacy. Political liberals, for example, cir-
cumvent this problem on the philosophical level by emphasizing that they are merely
setting out the conditions in which it might be *possible* that their egalitarian principles
could satisfy the legitimacy constraint. Too often, however, political liberals do not
consistently make clear how this move loosens the grip of their principles with respect
to our evaluations of the basic structure of any actual society—for example, that of the
United States of America. Okin's post-Marxist critics confront this difficulty in a more
direct way. They argue that citizens who do not share their own preferred interpretation of the moral significance of inherited gender roles, including millions of adult
American women, are suffering from false consciousness. When they say "the personal
is political," they mean that the personal is not that person's. Instead, the personal is the
collective's, a collective the nature of which they themselves claim the unique authority
to construct and define. Perhaps post-Marxist feminists are super-planners, but this
feature is common to all forms of direct-governmental feminism. Divisions among

27. See John Rawls, *Political Liberalism* (New York: Columbia University Press, 1996).

types of planners do not run as deep as the division we are considering between planners and searchers.

ANOTHER FEMINISM

I have argued that the most significant division among public policy advocates of gender equality is that between direct and indirect-governmentalist approaches to equality. Viewed in light of that distinction, the most prominent division among contemporary schools of feminism in the realm of public policy—those between liberal, post-Marxist, and new wave approaches, for example—lose much of their depth and importance.

I have also suggested that the individualists of the nineteenth century offer us a refreshing approach to problems of sexual equality. Their indirect-governmentalism provides a real contrast to the direct-governmentalism that is the moral status quo of contemporary feminist policy thinking. Unlike today's direct-governmentalists, the nineteenth-century thinkers seek to ground political principles on a small set of moral axioms, axioms that played a central role in the formulation of the political documents on which America was founded. Among those axioms is the principle of self-ownership. The logical extension of that principle is that it applies equally to each adult person, woman or man. Even while recognizing the distorting effects of the laws crafted to serve the purposes of gender constructivists of previous generations, they did not seek to seize those same coercive methods for themselves. Instead, individualist feminists attended respectfully to the voices of real women and real men. These feminists insisted on their own lack of standing, and the lack of standing of anyone else, to use the coercive power of the state to impose any single, overarching interpretation of the significance of gender on anyone else. Instead, they suggested that the government of a free society should limit itself to the protection of a small set of rights, rights that serve as platforms by which diverse forms of bridges might be built across the inherited gender divide. Citizens must be allowed to build these bridges as they think best, even though we cannot predict what social patterns will emerge, or at what rate or in what direction inherited patterns might change through time. These neglected thinkers invite contemporary feminists to make what amounts to almost a disciplinary shift: from the constructivist abstractions of philosophy (or political ideology) to a more sociological, evolutionary, microeconomic perspective of social change. For the nineteenth-century indirect-governmental feminists, the personal was indeed the personal. A just government is one with the humility to allow its adult citizens to confront that fact for themselves.

In closing this essay, I would like to note that Susan Okin, in what tragically would be the final years of her life, was becoming increasingly interested in the more sociological and evolutionary dimensions of social change I described above. Of course, Okin remained a vocal and even vehement defender of direct governmentalism. But what was always most remarkable and impressive to me about Okin's feminism was the way her strident defenses of her theoretical positions would soften when they bumped up against the life experiences of real people. She was especially open-minded about the relationships of people she called friends, even when those relationships diverged from the gender-free ideal she so passionately espoused in her written work. Once, in the course of a conversation in which I explained to Susan why I thought her proposal that employers be required to send separate paychecks to workers and spouses would be a disaster in practice, I mentioned that my partner Amy and I none-theless had adopted the practice in our household of referring to all incoming checks as "ours." Susan, aware of my skepticism of direct-governmentalism, seemed genu-inely pleased that Amy and I had adopted the moral standard she had proposed. In the end, she was concerned most about what actually worked in the world to improve the relationships of women and men as equals. Susan Okin, a planner by profession, was a searcher at heart.

PART II

GENDER AND THE FAMILY

5

Equality of Opportunity and the Family

David Miller

The family is a crucial determinant of our opportunities in life, of what we "become."...We are not born as isolated, equal individuals in our society, but into family situations: some in the social middle, some poor and homeless, and some superaffluent; some to a single or soon-to-be-separated parent, some to parents whose marriage is fraught with conflict, some to parents who will stay together in love and happiness. Any claims that equal opportunity exists are therefore completely unfounded.

Okin, Justice, Gender, and the Family, *16.*

I

One of Susan Okin's main achievements in political philosophy—perhaps her greatest achievement—was to place the institution of the family at the center of the theory of social justice. She noted that, in the history of political thought, philosophers had assumed for no good reason that family relations were to be regarded as beyond the realm of justice. And in the case of the modern political philosopher whose work she admired most—John Rawls—she detected and criticized a profound ambivalence in his treatment of the family.[1] Rawls wavered between seeing the family as a key component of the basic structure of society, by virtue of its pervasive effects on the life chances of its members, and therefore as central to the theory of justice, and viewing it as a private association on which, accordingly, principles of justice were to bear only peripherally. In Okin's eyes, this was symptomatic of the way that the liberal tradition as a whole had failed to take seriously the gendered nature of family relations and to follow through on the implications this has for social justice.

At the same time, Okin never developed a fully fledged theory of justice in the family, nor a theory of social justice that comprehensively addressed the issues raised by family membership, either for parents or for children. She assumed, realistically

An earlier draft of this chapter was presented at "Toward a Humanist Justice: A Conference Honoring and Examining the Work of Susan Moller Okin," Program in Ethics in Society, Stanford University, February 2005, and at the Political Theory Workshop, Nuffield College, Oxford, 2005. A later draft was discussed at the European Consortium for Political Research workshop on Equality of Opportunity at the Joint Sessions of Workshops in Granada, April 2005. I am very grateful to these three groups for their comments and suggestions, and particularly to Patti Lenard, Debra Satz, and Andrew Williams for sending me written comments.

1. See Okin, *Justice, Gender, and the Family* (New York: Basic, 1989), ch. 5 (hereafter *JGF*), and on Rawls' later work, see Okin, "*Political Liberalism*, Justice, and Gender," *Ethics* 105 (1994): 23–43; "Justice

enough, that children would continue to be raised in familial settings, of one kind or another; and she also assumed that, because "the pluralism of beliefs and modes of life is fundamental to our society,"[2] public policy had to cater to those who opted for traditional (gendered) family relationships, despite her own view that "families in which roles and responsibilities are equally shared regardless of sex are far more in accord with principles of justice than are typical families today."[3] The various practical proposals she supported—an equal division of earned income between husband and wife, equal living standards for both households after divorce, and so forth[4]—are therefore best seen as damage-limitation exercises, means of reducing the vulnerability of women to male exploitation and oppression, rather than as recipes for ideal justice. There is still work to do, therefore, in developing a theory of social justice which sets out more specifically what place, if any, the family should have in the basic structure of a just society, and what kind of family this should be.

My own question here is slightly, but only slightly, more limited in scope: is it possible for equality of opportunity and the family to coexist? Is there an interpretation of equality of opportunity that is both ethically appealing as a principle of social justice and yet consistent with the fact that men and women continue to live together and raise children in family settings?[5] What would family relationships have to be like for this reconciliation to occur? The quotation from Susan Okin with which I began might at first glance seem to be no more than a comment on existing family realities. But on a second look, one might well conclude that in *no* society in which the family continues to play a central role in childrearing, etc., can there be substantial—more than merely formal—equality of opportunity. This is certainly the conclusion that other authors have reached. James Fishkin, for example, argued in an influential book that "under the best conditions that might realistically be imagined for a large-scale industrial society . . . the basic liberal approach to equal opportunity does not amount to a coherent ideal once complications involving the family are systematically taken into account."[6] And even Rawls, who of course gives equality of opportunity a prominent place in his two principles of justice, betrays misgivings about whether it is, in fact, achievable given the continued existence of the family, as we shall see shortly.

and Gender: An Unfinished Debate," *Fordham Law Review* 72 (2004): 1537–1567; and "'Forty Acres and a Mule' for Women: Rawls and Feminism," *Politics, Philosophy and Economics* 4 (2005): 233–248. It is noteworthy that Okin is the first feminist critic to whom Rawls refers in his final response on this subject, "The Idea of Public Reason Revisited," in John Rawls, *Collected Papers*, edited by S. Freeman (Cambridge, MA: Harvard University Press, 1999).

2. *JGF*, 180.

3. *JGF*, 183.

4. See *JGF*, ch. 7, for these proposals.

5. I will focus on heterosexual families with children, since these are still the most common cases and are the ones that pose the greatest challenge to equality of opportunity, without suggesting that they are in any way normatively superior to other forms: single-parent families, same-sex families, etc. I leave the question of the intrinsic value of the family entirely open.

6. J. Fishkin, *Justice, Equal Opportunity, and the Family* (New Haven, CT: Yale University Press, 1983), 6.

It might seem that the first step here should be to offer a definition of equality of opportunity. Given the problem that we face, however, the definition has to emerge in the course of the inquiry; part of what we have to do is to adjudicate between competing conceptions of equality of opportunity in the light of what we discover about the causal effects of the family, in particular, on the life chances of its members. How, then, should the problem be characterized? I am interested in the principle of equality of opportunity that is influential in current political debate and not, for instance, in more purely philosophical notions, such as "equality of opportunity for welfare." Equality of opportunity applies primarily to education, jobs, and public offices and to the various benefits—income and wealth, power, social status, and so forth—that are attached to these, and it requires that the society in question be structured in such a way that every member has a fair chance of acquiring these goods. It is assumed, in other words, that for various practical reasons, jobs, offices, and places in higher education cannot be allocated equally to everyone; what matters instead is that no one should be prevented from gaining access to these goods by factors that are irrelevant to their allocation ("leveling the playing field" is the metaphor often used).

But what does "irrelevant" mean here? That is, of course, the crux of the problem we are addressing, and when we try to answer the question we find that equality of opportunity tends to bifurcate into minimal and maximal versions, both of which turn out to be deeply problematic.[7] The minimal version looks at the procedures and mechanisms that are used to allocate positions of advantage and says that the allocation must exclusively track features that are directly relevant to the position in question. Jobs must be given to those best able to perform them: skin color, gender, age, etc., are all irrelevant features and must be disregarded. Similarly, educational places must be distributed according to academic achievement and potential alone. The problem, however, is that the minimal version pays no attention to the background factors that may explain how candidates have come to have the features on the basis of which the allocation is made. What if one candidate has the advantage of better schooling and a supportive family, while another has not? Minimal equality of opportunity at best achieves a shallow kind of fairness: it requires nondiscrimination at the point at which advantaged positions are being assigned. But in a society marked by pervasive inequalities of class, race, ethnicity, and gender, it fails to address the deeper unfairness that gives some candidates a far greater chance than others to display the characteristics that are judged to be relevant to the assignment.

Maximal equality of opportunity tells us to go back and *really* level the playing field by discounting the effects of all morally arbitrary features: not only all those external forces—family background, schooling, and so forth—that have shaped individuals up to now, but also the "undeserved" natural talents that may underlie present revealed aptitudes. What then is left to count as a relevant basis for assigning advantaged positions? Only features for which individuals can genuinely be held responsible, for

---

7. Similar distinctions between less demanding and more demanding conceptions of equality of opportunity have been drawn by, among others, Andrew Mason in "Equality of Opportunity, Old and New," *Ethics* 111 (2001): 760–781; and John Roemer in *Equality of Opportunity* (Cambridge, MA: Harvard University Press, 1998), sec. 1.

example, their choices and efforts. But these, too, may be put in question by maximal equality of opportunity. For it is a familiar observation that the choices we make, and our willingness to make an effort, are themselves shaped by our natural talents and also by our social environment, for instance, living in a family in which high aspirations are encouraged and a work ethic is instilled. Once this is understood, maximal equality of opportunity appears to collapse into simple equality of outcome: the only way to give everyone an equal chance to acquire advantaged positions is to distribute them equally, i.e., to reconstitute them in such a way that no one gets a "better" job or educational place than anyone else. While some philosophers might welcome this conclusion, it constitutes a reductio ad absurdum of equality of opportunity as originally understood, namely, as a principle for ensuring the fair allocation of positions of advantage, on the assumption that some inequalities of outcome in this dimension are unavoidable.

Minimal equality of opportunity, therefore, is too thin to be ethically appealing; maximal equality of opportunity tends to collapse into equality of outcome. The challenge is to find some intermediate view that staves off the collapse, but at the same time embodies a more robust notion of fairness than the minimal version. In rising to this challenge, we will consider why the existence of the family poses an obstacle to equality of opportunity (in any more-than-minimal version) and what, if anything, might be done to surmount this.

Another distinction that will prove to be important as we proceed concerns the meaning of "opportunity" and how this relates to the idea of *equal* opportunity. What does it mean to have the opportunity to do something? It means, at least, that the something in question is physically possible and legally permitted, but it also implies that the cost of doing it is not excessive for the agent concerned. Cost in this context might be monetary or nonmonetary. Someone who earns an average salary does not have the opportunity to buy a Ferrari, given that paying the price would land him in serious long-term debt. Equally, a daughter whose father threatens to beat her if she goes out in the evening does not have that opportunity. Cost here operates as a threshold notion: a person has the opportunity to do X if the cost of doing so is reasonable for her, given the benefit that X will bring. Consider two prospective students deciding whether to take a university course. One can afford to do so comfortably, while the other can manage the fees, but with more difficulty. Yet there is an obvious sense in which both have the opportunity to attend the university, whereas someone who simply cannot raise the money to attend, or can raise the money only by putting her financial future at considerable risk, does not. In other words, when we are considering the question of whether an opportunity exists for someone or not, cost differences matter only if they would take the person over the relevant threshold.

But what about *equality* of opportunity? Do the two students in the last paragraph have an *equal* opportunity to attend the university? Or does equality of opportunity imply that the costs attached to taking up an opportunity must be the same for each person? Here, I want to distinguish between *weak* and *strong* versions of equality of opportunity. Weak equality of opportunity obtains when agents have identical or equivalent opportunity sets even though the costs attached to taking up the opportunities in the sets may be different for each; strong equality of opportunity requires that the costs must also be the same for each agent. In the strong sense, then, the two students do not have equal opportunities to attend the university, since one is required to make a greater financial sacrifice than the other; in the weak sense, they do, because in neither case is the cost so great that the opportunity is closed.

Which of these two principles should guide our thinking in choosing equal opportunity policies? The strong principle is very demanding, indeed perhaps impossibly demanding, because it implies, for example, that any background differences in income and wealth are likely to translate into inequalities of opportunity. We are not, I think, concerned by the fact that the children of moderately rich families face slightly greater financial costs in attending a university than the children of very rich families; if we call this an inequality of opportunity, then the idea loses the force that it has when we apply it to the case of children from poor families, who cannot attend at all unless they are given financial support. Since the principle is meant to regulate access to positions of advantage on the assumption that flat equality of outcome cannot be achieved, it would be paradoxical to interpret it in such a way that equality of opportunity can only exist in a society that achieves flat equality. On the other hand, there are contexts in which the strong principle comes into play, for instance, in cases where a government is providing some benefit and can choose a form of provision that equalizes costs as far as possible (in an earlier discussion, I gave the example of siting a national sports stadium in a place that is equally accessible from different parts of the country).[8] In these contexts, a willful disregard for relative costs would rightly be seen as failing to equalize opportunities. So we cannot simply jettison either principle: depending on the problem we are addressing, either weak or strong equality of opportunity may be the relevant principle to invoke. When we look at the family and ask whether its existence is compatible with equal opportunity, we need to be clear whether it is the weak or the strong version of that principle we are talking about.

To complete the road map, it is worth distinguishing two different ways in which the family as an institution may block equality of opportunity. It may do so, first, because relationships *within* the family—especially between men and women, boys and girls—may deny opportunities to some members that it makes available to others. To take obvious cases, if women are not permitted to work by their husbands, or if girls are denied the education that boys enjoy, equality of opportunity in two very important domains cannot exist. But second, relationships *between* families may also violate equal opportunity, as when one family buys its members privileged education or gives them access to jobs through nepotism, and another does not. We are most likely to think about interfamilial cases when debating equality of opportunity, but it was one of Okin's major contributions to highlight the ways in which intrafamilial practices could deny equal opportunity to women and girls. The two dimensions are clearly separable: we can envisage a world in which relations within the family are

8. See David Miller, "Liberalism, Equal Opportunities, and Cultural Commitments," in P. Kelly, ed., *Multiculturalism Reconsidered* (Cambridge: Polity, 2002). In that paper, I defined opportunity in the same way as here, but identified equality of opportunity with the strong principle without qualification. I now think this was a mistake and that, in many cases, justice is satisfied so long as weak equality of opportunity is achieved.

egalitarian—men and women contribute equally to paid work, parenting, etc.—but relations between families continue to be marked by inequalities of income and social class; and an alternative (perhaps less likely) world in which an otherwise egalitarian society is still made up of traditionally gendered families. There may be reasons to think that progress toward equality along one dimension would normally be accompanied by progress toward equality on the other, but this is far from certain, and my judgment is that the recent past has brought us a significant increase in equality within families, but no increase—even, in some cases, a decrease—in equality between them. Whatever the truth about this, there are clearly two separate issues that need our attention when we ask whether equality of opportunity and the family can be reconciled.

II

Like many others in political theory, this question has both normative and empirical aspects. As I have indicated, we need to consider how equality of opportunity should be interpreted, given the underlying notion of fairness it is meant to express; and we also need to consider just how the family might block equality of opportunity so interpreted. I want to make a start on the first question by considering the work of Rawls and Okin's critique of that work. For Rawls, as is well known, it is a primary requirement of social justice that, if social and economic inequalities are to be justified, they must be "attached to positions and offices open to all under conditions of fair equality of opportunity."[9] What, then, does "fair equality of opportunity" require? According to Rawls, it means:

> [T]hose who are at the same level of talent and ability, and have the same willingness to use them, should have the same prospects of success regardless of their initial place in the social system, that is, irrespective of the income class into which they are born. In all sectors of society there should be roughly equal prospects of culture and achievement for everyone similarly motivated and endowed.[10]

What is immediately noticeable about this definition is that it interprets equality of opportunity quite narrowly, specifically in relation to the income class into which someone is born. Equality of opportunity is violated only when Smith, born into a wealthy family, has better life prospects than Jones, whose motivation and endowment are similar but whose parents are poor. Consistent with this definition, Rawls identifies the practical requirements of equal opportunity as providing equally good education for children of all classes, ensuring that jobs and offices remain "open to all on the basis of qualities and efforts reasonably related to the relevant duties and tasks," and limiting the unequal inheritance of wealth.[11] It would not be difficult to broaden this definition so that it embraced other sources of social inequality, for instance, ethnic or racial background, and Rawls, if pressed, might well have been willing to accept this— effectively widening the idea of a "sector of society" so as to include not only income

9. J. Rawls, *A Theory of Justice* (Cambridge, MA: Harvard University Press, 1971), 302.
10. Rawls, *Theory of Justice*, 73.
11. See Rawls, *Theory of Justice*, sec. 43.

classes but also racial or ethnic groups. But family membership poses a much more difficult question, one that Rawls sees but is unable to resolve satisfactorily. Indeed, he appears to contradict himself. Compare the following two passages:

> [T]he principle of fair equality of opportunity can be only imperfectly carried out, at least as long as the institution of the family exists. The extent to which natural capacities develop and reach fruition is affected by all kinds of social conditions and class attitudes. Even the willingness to make an effort, to try, and so to be deserving in the ordinary sense is itself dependent on happy family and social circumstances. It is impossible in practice to secure equal chances of achievement and culture for those similarly endowed, and therefore we may want to adopt a principle which recognizes this fact and also mitigates the arbitrary effect of the natural lottery itself.[12]
>
> [A]lthough the internal life and culture of the family influence, perhaps as much as anything else, a child's motivation and his capacity to gain from education, and so in turn his life prospects, these effects are not necessarily inconsistent with fair equality of opportunity. Even in a well-ordered society that satisfies the two principles of justice, the family may be a barrier to equal chances between individuals. For as I have defined it, the second principle only requires equal life prospects in all sectors of society for those similarly endowed and motivated. If there are variations among families in the same sector in how they shape the child's aspirations, then while fair equality of opportunity may obtain between sectors, equal chances between individuals will not.[13]

The first passage says that fair equality of opportunity can't be fully achieved so long as the family exists; the second says that it can be achieved, but something else—"equal chances between individuals"—cannot. What is going on here? The apparent contradiction between the two passages reveals that there is an ambiguity in what it means for two individuals to be "similarly motivated and endowed." This might refer to "native" motivation and endowment, that is, people's original genetic capacities, including their disposition to exert themselves in various ways; or it might refer to "developed" motivation and endowment, that is, the capacity and motivation displayed after the process of socialization is complete, say, at the point at which a person enters the labor market. If we take the first reading, then given what Rawls says about the causal effects of the family, there cannot be equality of opportunity in a society where children are raised in families.[14] Families will determine how natural talents are developed and how innate dispositions become converted into "the willingness to make an effort," and so two babies who at birth had equal potential but are reared in different families will in practice have unequal opportunities. If we take the second reading, by contrast, then

---

12. Rawls, *Theory of Justice*, 74.
13. Rawls, *Theory of Justice*, 301.
14. It might be said that there can still be equality of opportunity between social sectors, in Rawls' sense. However, this would assume that variations between families are random across income classes and so forth, and this is surely implausible. Although upper-class families, say, differ in many ways, they will still in general give their offspring more cognitive skills, higher aspirations, and so forth than lower-class families will be able to do.

the causal effects of the family are bracketed off, and we simply look at whether the economic and political system affords equal opportunities to those with similar developed capacities.

It might appear that Rawls could have escaped his difficulties by plumping for one or the other of these readings of "similarly motivated and endowed," but in fact neither provides him with a congenial position. On the second reading, equality of opportunity becomes a thin concept, and it becomes difficult to maintain his distinction between "careers open to talents" and "fair equality of opportunity," given that the latter is intended to incorporate concern for the conditions under which talents are developed, most notably the education system. If all we are concerned about is that people who are similarly endowed and motivated *as they enter adulthood* should have equal opportunities in the job market, etc., why should we be concerned that, at an earlier stage, some had greater opportunities to develop their talents than others? Put another way, if we are prepared to ignore what families do for children directly by way of equipping them with linguistic and cultural skills, a work ethic, and so forth, why should we worry about what they can do indirectly by opening the door to a superior education? But Rawls clearly does want to go further in leveling the playing field than this reading permits. If, on the other hand, he were to adopt a strong conception of equal opportunity as "equality of life chances," then it seems there would be a straightforward collision between this principle and the continued existence of the family as we know it. But Rawls does not contemplate abolishing the family; he allows that it can, and maybe should, take forms different from that of the traditional (gendered) heterosexual family, but he assumes that children will continue to be raised in small family units and, therefore, as a matter of fact, to enjoy the very significant advantages and disadvantages that result from this.[15] His principles of justice have to be tailored to accommodate this fact, and he achieves this by weakening the definition of equality of opportunity and offering the difference principle by way of compensation:

> The acknowledgement of the difference principle redefines the grounds for social inequalities as conceived in the system of liberal equality; and when the principles of fraternity and redress are allowed their appropriate weight, the natural distribution of assets and the contingencies of social circumstances can more easily be accepted. We are more ready to dwell upon our good fortune now that these differences are made to work to our advantage, rather than to be downcast by how much better off we might have been had we had an equal chance along with others if only all social barriers had been removed.[16]

These words of comfort fail to disguise the fact that Rawls really has given us no coherent account of equality of opportunity.[17]

---

15. See J. Rawls, *Justice as Fairness* (Cambridge, MA: Harvard University Press, 2001), sec. 50; and Rawls, "The Idea of Public Reason Revisited," sec. 5.

16. Rawls, *Theory of Justice*, 511–512.

17. I mean here that allowing the operation of the difference principle to reconcile us to inequalities of opportunity does not resolve the question of how the latter principle is to be understood. There are indications in Rawls that he would permit inequalities of opportunity that worked to the benefit of the least advantaged (see, e.g., *Theory of Justice*, 303), and it may also be that he would regard the family as

What does Okin have to say about Rawls' understanding of equal opportunity? She does not directly address the question I have been raising about how the impact of the family is to be taken into account when the principle is formulated. She does, though, argue with some force that "the principles of justice that Rawls arrives at are inconsistent with a gender-structured society and with traditional family roles."[18] She develops this theme in several directions, two of which have particular relevance to our problem. First, "the assumption and customary expectation, central to our gender system, that women take far greater responsibility for housework and child care, whether or not they also work outside the home" denies them the opportunity to pursue a career on equal terms with men.[19] Second, the experience of being raised in a gendered family influences women's psychological and moral perspectives and encourages them to adopt subordinate roles: "Only children who are equally mothered and fathered can develop fully the psychological and moral capacities that currently seem to be unevenly distributed between the sexes."[20] Although she does not pursue this point at length, the implication appears to be that early family experience forms women in such a way that they are deterred from taking on the full range of occupational, political, etc., roles that are available to men.

How telling are these points as criticisms of Rawls? In both cases, women are being denied opportunities that they might otherwise have had by their adherence to a norm which defines how women are expected to behave—as homemakers, in the one case, as subordinate to men, in the other. But since Rawls defines fair equality of opportunity as "equal life prospects for those similarly endowed and motivated," might he not reply here that women are just differently motivated? If they aspired to become political leaders or captains of industry, they would have an equal chance of achieving this, under institutions complying with the two principles. This brings us back to the question of what it means to have an opportunity. If we say that, for a person to have the opportunity to achieve X, it must be possible for her to pursue X without incurring unreasonable costs, what should we say about someone who is subject to a social norm that deters her from pursuing X? The questions that Okin raises about gender here clearly connect to our earlier questions about the impact of the family, since among the things that families do is to imbue children with norms that influence aspirations and career choices. How far, then, do we want to go in allowing our assessment of someone's opportunities to be affected by the norms to which she adheres?

Rawls is a liberal. He believes that each of us has the moral power to form, revise, and pursue a conception of the good, and he accordingly believes that the demands of justice must be kept separate from any such conception. Okin follows him in this

---

having rights that are protected by the first principle of justice, which takes priority over the second. I have not addressed the question of whether Rawls is able produce a plausible justification of equality of opportunity, given his general theory; I have simply pointed to ambiguities in his formulation of the principle when the influence of the family is being considered. For a wide-ranging critique of Rawls on this issue, see R. Arneson, "Against Equality of Opportunity," *Philosophical Studies* 93 (1999): 77–112.

18. *JGF*, 103.
19. *JGF*, 103.
20. *JGF*, 107.

respect.[21] As we have seen, she believes that "the pluralism of beliefs and modes of life is fundamental to our society," and she cannot therefore believe that opportunities are denied by the mere fact that people adhere to contrary norms. Vegetarians have the opportunity to eat meat, but choose not to. Religious believers have the opportunity to lie in bed on Sunday mornings, but think that they ought to go to church.[22] In what way, then, are gender (or social class) norms different, such that their perpetuation can be said to deny equality of opportunity? We have identified the question, but not yet found an adequate way of answering it.

III

At this point, I want to leave the conceptual and normative issues about equality of opportunity behind for a moment, and ask what we know empirically about the sources of opportunity. In particular, what do families do to their children that is relevant for their future opportunities to gain access to relatively advantaged positions? Obviously, if the influence of the family turns out to be close to zero, then the question with which we have been grappling loses its interest. Unfortunately, as so often happens when political philosophers turn to social scientists for enlightenment on some broad empirical question, this one turns out to be hotly disputed. Rival camps, using different general methodologies, argue that the family is a crucial transmitter of advantage, on the one hand, or, on the other, hardly matters at all. And the same is true when we consider the impact of the family on the gender system.

What is not disputed is that there is a consistent and rather stable correlation between how parents fare in life and how their children fare. As a survey by Bowles and Gintis concludes, "recent evidence points to a much higher level of intergenerational transmission of economic position than was previously thought to be the case. America may still be the land of opportunity by some measures, but parental income and wealth are strong predictors of the likely economic status of the next generation."[23] In the case of income bands, for example, "a son born to the top decile has a 22.9 percent chance of attaining the top decile…and a 40.7 percent chance of attaining the top quintile," whereas "the son of the poorest decile has a 1.3 percent chance of attaining the top decile and a 3.7 percent chance of attaining the top quintile."[24] What is very much disputed, on the other hand (as Bowles and Gintis readily admit), is the means whereby such advantages are transmitted. For, as a moment's reflection reveals, there are many different causal mechanisms that may be involved, whose normative status (from the point of view of equality of opportunity) is quite

    21. For a discussion highlighting Okin's liberalism and its implications, see J. Cohen, "Okin on Justice, Gender, and the Family," *Canadian Journal of Philosophy* 22 (1992): 263–286.

    22. For a fuller argument to the effect that embracing a norm that prohibits you from following a course of action does not in general remove the opportunity to pursue that course of action, see Miller, "Liberalism, Equal Opportunities, and Cultural Commitments," sec. 2.

    23. S. Bowles and H. Gintis, "The Inheritance of Inequality," *Journal of Economic Perspectives* 16 (2002): 21–22.

    24. Bowles and Gintis, "The Inheritance of Inequality," 7.

different. At one extreme, the mechanism might simply be genetic: parents pass on to their children genes which determine cognitive skills, personality traits (such as extraversion), good health, good looks, and so forth, all of which together determine which ladder of opportunity the child will climb, and how far up it she will rise.[25] At the other extreme, the mechanism might be the passing on of external resources, principally inherited wealth, which would allow the children to start up businesses, train for the professions, etc. The second mechanism would amount to a violation of equal opportunity on any reasonable interpretation of that ideal. The first mechanism would be consistent with any but the most maximal form which excludes native endowment as a legitimate source of advantage. On any other view, the parents' genes make the child the person that she is, and it is actual persons, not hypothetical ones, whose opportunities must be equalized. (I shall return to the underlying issue here later in the chapter.)

In between these two extremes, there are a number of other plausible ways in which parents might equip their children for access to advantage in later life.[26] They might, for instance, develop their skills: endow them with a larger or smaller vocabulary (more on this in a moment), teach them to read and to handle numbers, think in abstract terms, and so forth. They might also shape their personalities by their style of parenting, making their children more or less cooperative, more or less authoritarian, and so on. And they might pass on a wide range of cultural attitudes and norms, ranging from religious and political values, through gender norms, to basic traits such as self-discipline and independence of mind. If indeed parents are able to influence their children's development in one or more of these ways—at this stage, I am simply presenting possibilities, not making empirical claims—then it is easy to see how professional or middle-class parents whose own skills, attitudes, and norms are congruent with their advantaged social positions would tend to produce children who would become advantaged themselves.

We might call these the parents' *direct effects* on the formation of their children. There are also potentially important *indirect effects*. School choice is the most obvious mechanism, if we assume that the quality of schooling is an important determinant of later access to jobs and higher education. A bit less obvious, but potentially significant, is the wider social environment: whom the child meets in the neighborhood, whom gets invited home, which clubs he joins, and so forth. This will be significant if one thinks (see below) that a child's peer group is a very important source of beliefs and norms that may determine later life prospects. Parents determine that environment to some extent inadvertently (by choosing where to live, for example) but also to a considerable extent deliberately by encouraging the child to involve herself with certain groups of peers and to avoid others.

25. I will not discuss the difficult issues that will arise when it becomes possible deliberately to influence the genetic makeup of one's children.

26. For a more systematic attempt to explore different mechanisms that might explain the intergenerational transmission of advantage, see, for example, G. Duncan et al., "The Apple Does Not Fall Far from the Tree," in S. Bowles, H. Gintis, and M. Osborne Groves, eds., *Unequal Chances: Family Background and Economic Success* (Princeton, NJ: Princeton University Press, 2005).

On the surface, all of this is pretty obvious. What is more surprising is the depth of disagreement about how the causal mechanisms internal to the family actually work and which of them is most significant. In the literature I have surveyed, this mainly takes the form of conflict between socialization theorists, who stress the direct causal efficacy of the family, and behavioral geneticists, who as their name implies stress the child's genetic makeup and the effect this has on the way she is treated by others, including her parents. Let me cite two sources, one from either side of this divide.

An influential text from the socialization school is Hart and Risley's *Meaningful Differences in the Everyday Experience of Young American Children* (1995), which studies the development of children in the first three years of life and comes up with some striking findings. The research involved a close study of how parents in professional, working-class, and welfare families interacted with their children and especially how they talked to each other: what range of vocabulary was used, which kinds of utterances (questions, commands, etc.) predominated, etc. The upshot is that, at age three, children from professional families had an average recorded vocabulary of 1,116 words, children from working-class families 749 words, and children from welfare families 525 words; their average IQ scores were 117, 107, and 79, respectively. There was also a qualitative difference, captured in the following contrast:

> We could see in the professional families the American dream: parents adding to and handing on to their children the advantages their families had given to them. We saw the daily efforts of these parents to transmit an educationally advantaged culture to their children through the display of enriched language; through the amount of talking they did and how informative they were; and through the frequency of gentle guidance, affirmative interactions, and responsiveness to their children's talk.[27]

Conversely:

> The frequency and tone of the interactions in the welfare families limited the words and meanings the children heard. Because the welfare parents talked less often to their children, they talked in less varied contexts about less varied aspects of the children's experience. Because they spent less time interacting with their children, they had fewer opportunities to learn about their children's skill levels and the topics the children were interested in talking and hearing about. Perhaps as a result, proportionately more of their talk contained prohibitions and simple directives.[28]

Hart and Risley point out that the differences in outcome they discovered continue to have significant effects after the first three years. A retest six years later of the children studied found significant correlations between vocabulary use at age three and measures of linguistic competence at age nine (though not with general academic test scores). They also point out that programs intended to compensate for the inequalities they discovered—Head Start and the like—would not do so unless they were to involve massive, and therefore extremely expensive, interventions into the family itself.

---

27. B. Hart and T. R. Risley, *Meaningful Differences in the Everyday Experience of Young American Children* (Baltimore, MD: Brookes, 1995), 179.
28. Hart and Risley, *Meaningful Differences*, 178.

In complete contrast to the assumptions underlying Hart and Risley's study, consider works influenced by behavioral genetics, such as Judith Rich Harris's *The Nurture Assumption: Why Children Turn Out the Way They Do* (1998) or David Rowe's *The Limits of Family Influence: Genes, Experience and Behaviour* (1994). These works do not deny that personal characteristics of many different kinds are transmitted from parents to children, nor that life prospects are similarly correlated, but they explain these correlations primarily in terms of direct genetic similarities, which also have an indirect effect via the way that parents treat their (genetically related) children. Thus, behavioral geneticists study identical and non-identical twins, including twins reared in separate families, and they compare biological children with adopted children, in an attempt to isolate what effect the common family environment has on the way that children turn out. Their general conclusion is that, except in the case of severely dysfunctional families, the family environment in which a child is raised matters very little. As Harris puts it:

> [C]hildren raised by the same parents do not turn out alike, once you skim off the similarities due to shared genes. Two adopted children reared in the same home are no more similar in personality than two adopted children reared in separate homes. A pair of identical twins reared in the same home are no more alike than a pair reared in separate homes. Whatever the home is doing to the children who grow up in it, it is not making them more conscientious, or less sociable, or more aggressive, or less anxious, or more likely to have a happy marriage.[29]

Although neither of the sources I have consulted directly discusses the Hart and Risley study, it is easy to predict what they would say about it. First, we would expect to find a direct correlation between the intellectual capacities of parents and children, and therefore between their IQ scores and between more specific features, such as the range of vocabulary they use. Second, we should expect to find different styles of parent-child interactions in different families, these being a joint product of the genetic makeup of parents and children (though for the same reason we should also expect to find parents adopting a somewhat different style for each child). Third, even if the common family environment has some small independent effect on children's capacities, this will usually dwindle away still further as the child's most salient environment becomes the peer group rather than the family—thus Harris underlines the way in which immigrant children become fluent speakers of the language of their adopted country despite not having been exposed to that language in the parental home.[30]

This third point does, however, reveal that even on the behavioral genetics side of the debate, the transmission of advantage between parents and children involves more than just the transmission of genes. Peer groups may matter much more than parents for the acquisition of vocabulary, culture, role models, etc., but as noted above parents may influence which peer group becomes salient for a child. And although writers like Harris emphasize that, within peer groups, cultural norms are mainly handed down from older to younger children, they don't deny that children do bring something of

---

29. J. R. Harris, *The Nurture Assumption: Why Children Turn Out the Way They Do* (London: Bloomsbury, 1998), 353.

30. Harris, *The Nurture Assumption*, 188–192, 253–257.

the culture of the home with them when they move into their new social environment. So the debate is mainly about the significance of the *direct* influence that parents have on those features of their children that will advantage them in later life, once genetic effects have been filtered out.

I cannot hope to resolve that debate here, although any parent of children with contrasting personalities and abilities is unlikely to find any strong version of the socialization theory plausible (of course, the same evidence shows that there is a good deal of randomness in the way that genes are transmitted from parents to child). What matters is that we should have some understanding of which family-related mechanisms clearly do play a role in the transmission of advantage, and which are more debatable.

If we ask what role the family plays in the transmission of gender norms, once again we need to tread carefully. Okin argued consistently for the thesis that the family is a school of moral development and that unjust families are unlikely to produce children with an adequate sense of justice. She argued specifically for the moral benefits of co-parenting:

> [S]ince co-parenting would eliminate the gendered division of roles in heterosexual households that tends to result in different patterns of identity formation and attachment to others in girls and boys, such differences of this type that currently exist would diminish dramatically. It could reasonably be predicted that girls would develop a stronger sense of self while retaining a healthy capacity for empathy, and that boys would develop more capacity for empathy and attachment. This in turn should make the children likely to be better (and the boys more willing) co-parents if and when they have their own children.[31]

This prediction *sounds* plausible, but it needs to be backed up with hard evidence.[32] More skeptical authors influenced by behavioral genetics argue that gender differences are not the result of parents treating their male and female children differently, nor of children imitating the gender-differentiated behavior of their parents, but are almost entirely a product of genetic differences together with peer-group socialization.[33] Parents who themselves practice an unconventional division of labor in the home find that their children generally ignore these potential role models and learn from their peer groups how to behave in traditionally gender-defined ways.[34] Indeed, the piece

---

31. S. M. Okin and R. Reich, "Families and Schools as Compensating Agents in Moral Development for a Multicultural Society," *Journal of Moral Education* 28 (1999): 289.

32. Okin conceded in a footnote to one of her essays that the general thesis that "persons need to be raised in just families in order to develop a strong sense of justice" was not self-evidently true. See Okin, "*Political Liberalism*, Justice, and Gender," 38n32. To the best of my knowledge, however, she did not investigate the kind of comparative evidence that would be needed to settle the question.

33. D. C. Rowe, *The Limits of Family Influence: Genes, Experience and Behaviour* (New York: Guilford, 1994), ch. 6; Harris, *The Nurture Assumption*, ch. 10.

34. A study of children brought up in self-consciously egalitarian families showed that while the beliefs they expressed about the roles of men and women followed those of their parents, their own gender identities—the ways they characterized themselves as boys and girls—were mostly conventional and were learned from their peers. See B. Risman, *Gender Vertigo: American Families in Transition* (New Haven, CT: Yale University Press, 1998), ch. 6. As Risman observes, "[W]hen family experiences collided with experiences with peers, the family influences were dwarfed" (140). She also speculates, however, that "the identities and selves they adopt to negotiate their sexist and gendered childhood worlds" may not determine the selves they adopt later in life (149).

of evidence that Okin herself cites on this question seems ambivalent.[35] A study of household work done by girls and boys in families of different types—those with a male breadwinner and those where both parents worked outside the home—showed that girls performed a far greater share of the housework in families of the second kind. In traditional families, the chores were evenly divided. We could explain the unequal division of labor in families with two working parents by arguing that the girls were copying their mothers (who were also taking on the majority of the housework). But why should traditional families produce an equal division of domestic labor between their children if the socialization theory holds true?

Earlier in this chapter, I distinguished two strands within Okin's critique of the gendered family as an obstacle to equality of opportunity. One strand had to do with the impact of the domestic division of labor on women's opportunities outside of the home. We have still to investigate this argument, insofar as it relies on the prevalence of norms that prescribe a "proper" domestic role for women. The other strand had to do with the consequences of being raised in an unjust family for the conceptions of justice developed by children—in particular, their beliefs about equality or inequality between the sexes. What we have discovered is that there is significant disagreement among social scientists over just how much influence families have on the way children develop, and the uncertainty extends to such things as the sense of justice they acquire. So, if we are looking for mechanisms whereby gender norms are reproduced across the generations, it seems that we should first look to cultural norms transmitted through peer groups, and then to labor market and other institutions that have been shaped by these norms, rather than to the family itself. And we need to examine more closely how, if at all, norms of any kind, including gender norms, can be shown to limit the opportunities of those who embrace them.

IV

After this brief foray into social science, let us now return to the question of how we should understand equality of opportunity. One possible approach would be to stick to the maximal definition—individuals should have equal life chances, i.e., their access to advantage should depend only on their own choices and efforts—and freely concede that the family stands as a barrier to equal opportunity so defined. The next step would be to look at the family as it currently exists and decide which aspects of that complex institution are essential to it—in the sense that family relations would be drained of value without them—and which are not. Then, we would propose getting rid of those nonessential elements that infringe on equality of opportunity.[36] Thus, we might argue that parents should not have the right to choose privileged schools

---

35. Okin, "*Political Liberalism*, Justice, and Gender," 35–36. The original source is M. H. Benin and D. A. Edwards, "Adolescents' Chores: The Difference between Dual- and Single-Earner Families," *Journal of Marriage and the Family* 12 (1990): 361–373.

36. More radically, we might ask whether the family itself has any place in a just society, or whether some alternative institution for childrearing should be adopted. On this, see V. Munoz-Dardé, "Is the Family to Be Abolished Then?" *Proceedings of the Aristotelian Society* 99 (1998–1999): 37–56.

for their children—it is not essential to family life as such that they should—but that they should have the right to decide where to take their children on holiday. In the second case, there would be a minor infringement of equality of opportunity, but this would be justified by the inherent value of the activity. The hope is that those aspects of the family that seriously compromise equality of opportunity will also turn out to be nonessential, and this would depend on resolving the empirical questions raised in the previous section of the chapter.[37]

The problem with this approach, as I have already hinted, is that maximal equality of opportunity collapses into incoherence once one examines it with some precision.[38] Consider first the issue of genetically based capacities and talents. The maximal view requires that the less talented should not be disadvantaged by their lack of talent. But the efforts and choices that people make will inevitably be conditioned by their perception of their own capacities and the likely results of applying them. Thus, if people who are, say, mathematically untalented put little effort into a project requiring mathematical skills and get a poor result, should we compensate them only for their lack of ability, or also for their lack of effort, on the grounds that they made little effort *because* they knew they were untalented? Put another way, we cannot in general say what people would do or be if their genetic makeup were different—if they had capacities that they do not in fact have. To make this point, we do not need to decide whether "willingness to make an effort" is itself a genetically determined feature or remains subject to choice; all we need to do is to make the realistic assumption that people's choices and efforts in any area of life are conditioned by their perceptions of how likely they are to succeed.

This means that a viable notion of equality of opportunity has to begin with a thicker notion of the person than the maximal view. The idea is to draw a line between the person and her circumstances, and say that equal opportunity obtains when the circumstances are the same for everyone along relevant dimensions. But the person here has to be understood as already laden with tastes, character, capacities, and so forth.[39] It is these features together with the choices that such a person makes that should determine where she ends up on the several ladders of advantage. We cannot

---

37. An approach of this kind is taken by Adam Swift in "Justice, Luck, and the Family: The Intergenerational Transmission of Economic Advantage from a Normative Perspective," in S. Bowles, H. Gintis, and M. Osborne Groves, eds., *Unequal Chances: Family Background and Economic Success* (Princeton, NJ: Princeton University Press, 2005).

38. I am by no means the first to notice this. See, for example, B. Williams, "The Idea of Equality," in P. Laslett and W. G. Runciman, eds., *Philosophy, Politics and Society*, 2nd ser. (Oxford: Blackwell, 1964); B. Barry, "Equal Opportunity and Moral Arbitrariness," in N. E. Bowie, ed., *Equal Opportunity* (Boulder, CO: Westview, 1988).

39. As Barry puts it:

> [T]he fundamental attitudes, values, behavioural traits and so on that make up people's characters would (uncontroversially) have been different had they (i.e., the identical collection of cells) been placed in different conditions, but that does not entail the conclusion that they are not *theirs* in a way that is morally relevant. ("Equal Opportunity and Moral Arbitrariness," 41)

speculate about what choices she might have made had she been differently formed—she would then simply be a different person.[40]

So far, I have been looking at how genetic differences should figure in our understanding of equality of opportunity. But now we must ask where we should place the family in relation to the line between person and circumstances. Should we assimilate family influence to genetic makeup, as simply another causal factor making us the persons who we are? Or should we regard the family as a set of circumstances providing greater or lesser opportunities to a particular (young) person?

Neither answer is obviously right as it stands. Although we have seen that the personality-shaping effect of the family can easily be exaggerated, clearly families do play some part in transmitting cultural values—languages, religions, moral outlooks—to their children. And they also help to develop, or fail to develop, their offspring's innate talents. A family with many books on its shelves encourages a child with bookish tastes to become an avid reader, while equally a family that plays a lot of sports together is likely to foster any sporting talents that its younger members possess. Since these are among the capacities that will determine the use made of opportunities later in life, they will become important elements of personality.

On the other side of the line, many things that families do for their children are rightly seen as affecting their circumstances. If I inherit money from my family while others do not, that is clearly an inequality of circumstance. I would be the same person whether I received this money or not, and we could roughly plot the difference the money makes in terms of the advantages it brings. The same goes for educational opportunities insofar as they are determined by family income or choice of residence. In this aspect, families with unequal endowments are indeed an obstacle to equality of opportunity, and it is a legitimate objective of social policy to counteract this inequality by measures such as inheritance taxes and higher levels of educational spending on schools in deprived areas.

Among the more difficult cases to categorize in terms of the person-circumstances distinction are those involving the transmission of norms through the family. These would include gender norms, class norms, and religious norms; in each case, the recipient is being told that certain forms of behavior are "right" and others "wrong." The point about such norms is that they are very often internally embraced by the agent while at the same time being externally enforced by social sanctions, such as expressions of disapproval or exclusion from the group. Women who refuse to marry, working-class boys who want to stay in education after age 18, or the children of religious families who no longer want to attend church or mosque may be sanctioned in these ways. What bearing does this have on their opportunities? Are norms to be

40. Personality is not, of course, formed in a single moment. The set of circumstances one enjoys at T may influence one's personality at T1. This does not matter provided that equal opportunities obtain at T, but where they do not, and where we can show that one's capacities at T1 are less developed than they would otherwise be because of inferior circumstances at T, then equality of opportunity at T1 requires us to take this into account (for instance, it may require some form of positive discrimination in education or job selection policies).

seen as external constraints that may limit opportunities, or, assuming they become internalized, are they better seen as aspects of the person that will determine what use is made of any given opportunity set?

Our answer to this question should depend on two factors: how easy or difficult it is for someone who adheres to a particular norm to change her behavior and break the norm, and how far adhering to the norm systematically disadvantages the person who does so. Let me take each of these in turn. Since the norms are being enforced, breaking them must incur certain costs, for instance, the woman who refuses to marry might be repeatedly questioned by her family about why she hasn't been able to find a partner, a process that she finds more than a little irritating. Does this mean that her opportunity set—in this case, to remain single and, as a result, to enjoy certain other freedoms, such as choice of career path—has been restricted? As I argued in section I, an opportunity exists so long as it is possible to pursue the course of action in question without incurring unreasonable costs. Norms, then, will restrict opportunities only when breaking them would impose costs that it would not be reasonable for the person to bear. The woman whose family is nagging her to get married still has the opportunity to remain single unless the nagging becomes intolerable. On the other hand, if a churchgoing family refuses to have any contact with a child who no longer attends church, then the norm is being enforced in a way that clearly does restrict the child's opportunity to pursue other paths.

The other factor to consider is the extent of the disadvantage that conformity to the norm carries with it. Families no doubt always pass on to their children beliefs about which ways of life, which careers, etc., are more valuable than others, and this may affect the choices the children make, but in general this does not breach equality of opportunity. If one family transmits its belief in the importance of education and another its belief in material success, and as a result the offspring of the first family end up teaching in a college while those of the second become entrepreneurs, it is not inconsistent with equality of opportunity that one set of children is finally richer than the other. This is because advantage is multidimensional and there can be legitimate disagreement about which set of children is eventually better off, all things considered. Contrast with this case one where a family transmits a norm that strongly discourages its children from continuing into postsecondary education. Insofar as the lack of a college education means taking up a manual job that is less well paid, more dangerous, less stimulating, etc., etc.—i.e., worse across virtually all relevant dimensions—than nonmanual jobs, this would potentially amount to a limitation of opportunity, depending on how the norm is enforced.

If we apply this analysis to the case of gender norms, there is good reason to think that a family that succeeds in imposing such norms on its female children is systematically disadvantaging them. Okin mounts a powerful argument to this effect in her diagnosis of why women who accept the traditional division of labor within marriage become vulnerable and dependent on their partners.[41] However, to demonstrate an inequality of opportunity, we would also need to show that daughters cannot depart from the norm without incurring unreasonable costs. For some women, this will be

---

41. *JGF*, ch. 7.

true but, in liberal societies at least, for most it will not. They may embrace the norm and be disadvantaged as a result, but they have the opportunity to do otherwise: we cannot infer opportunities, or the lack of them, backward from outcomes. Of course, if we were to follow the strong principle that I identified in section I, *any* costs that are attached to deviation from gender norms would amount to a denial of equal opportunity. But this raises the bar very high, too high in my view if we want equality of opportunity to serve as a guide to practice.

I have been asking in this part of the chapter whether the influence of the family is best understood as shaping the personalities of the children or as affecting their circumstances. The conclusion is that if we focus on what families do *directly* for their children (to use the distinction introduced in section III), most of it falls on the personality side of the fence. Families may encourage their children to pursue one career path rather than another, to follow a particular faith or become fanatical about a particular sport, but in normal cases this does not diminish their *opportunities* to choose differently. By contrast, what families do *indirectly* may indeed affect the opportunity set. By sending their children to schools where they are better taught, better motivated, and will make social contacts that will be useful to them later in life, they also provide them with greater opportunities.

V

This discussion has been exploratory and in places tentative, so it may be helpful to sum up the main points I have made. First, it is difficult to hold a clear line on the question of whether equality of opportunity and the family can be reconciled; Rawls in particular illustrates this difficulty. Second, it is easy to conclude that reconciliation is impossible by combining an excessively demanding version of equality of opportunity with an overestimate of the importance of the family as a socializing agent. (I am not certain that Susan Okin was guilty of this in the quotation that heads the chapter, but I believe she may have been.) Third, we need therefore to work out a view of equality of opportunity that hinges on the distinction between people and their circumstances, with the person seen not just as a bare chooser but as constituted by capacities and traits of character, some genetic and others shaped by the family environment. Fourth, we also need to look more closely at the different mechanisms by which families may influence the life prospects of their children, in order to decide which of these are consistent with equal opportunity and which are not.

Following these recommendations would have certain practical implications. First, we would give up what we might call the "two hospital babies" test for equality of opportunity that has often proved popular with politicians and others. As Fishkin expresses this idea, "According to this notion, I should not be able to enter a hospital ward of healthy newborn babies and, on the basis of class, race, sex, or other arbitrary native characteristics, predict the eventual positions in society of those children."[42] This doesn't work because there are some native characteristics—genetically based intelligence, for example—that will be correlated to some extent with social destinations without infringing on

42. Fishkin, *Justice, Equal Opportunity, and the Family*, 4.

equality of opportunity as I have argued it must be understood; nor should we expect that a society of equal opportunity will show no correlation at all between people's class or ethnic origin and their destination. Of course, when we find such correlations, we need to look hard to discover the mechanisms that are producing them.

On a more positive note, instead of regarding the family as simply a blanket obstacle to equal opportunity, we would try to discover which of the many things that families do to their children poses the greatest threat to equality of opportunity, properly understood, and then whether the best response is to try to reform the family or to create external mechanisms that can counter its effects. I have raised some doubts about how far the family serves as a direct transmitter either of cultural advantages or of gender norms, and I have also questioned whether, even if such transmission does occur, this should necessarily be seen as infringing on equality of *opportunity*. If this skepticism is justified, then we should be focusing our attention on the indirect effects of the family via the educational system and so forth, effects that are best counteracted by external means. (Okin reached a similar conclusion by a different route: she *did* think that the traditional family was a powerful vehicle for the transmission of cultural and gender norms, but for liberal reasons favored tackling the problem by external means, through changes in marriage and divorce laws, work practices, and so forth.)

Finally, we should not expect too much of equality of opportunity: we should not expect that an equal opportunity society will necessarily be a classless or statusless society. Indeed, there is something in the worry often heard that such a society might be socially more unequal, because the people who would reach positions of advantage would know that they had done so through merit rather than privilege or luck. There are two complementary ways of responding to this worry. The first is to try to preserve or create multiple ladders of opportunity, on the assumption that a person's success in climbing one ladder will not in general be mirrored by similar success on the others— for instance, that educational achievement will not automatically translate into higher income.[43] The second is to develop and apply an idea of social justice which is pluralist, in the sense that equality of opportunity, and its associated principle of distribution according to desert or merit, is counterbalanced by principles of equality and need, so that people's overall life chances are not determined entirely by their success or failure in climbing the opportunity ladders. Theories such as those of Rawls and Walzer, as well as my own, have this pluralist character.[44] So, although policies to increase equal opportunity are an important component of the pursuit of social justice, they should not be the only component. The difficulties we have unearthed in the course of trying to make the idea of equal opportunity more precise underline the wisdom of this view.

---

43. In earlier discussions, I have emphasized the importance of having multiple spheres of recognized achievement in a society, with no single dimension of advantage being seen as dominant. See D. Miller, *Principles of Social Justice* (Cambridge, MA: Harvard University Press, 1999), ch. 9, and "Complex Equality," in D. Miller and M. Walzer, eds., *Pluralism, Justice, and Equality* (Oxford: Oxford University Press, 1995).

44. Rawls, *Theory of Justice*; M. Walzer, *Spheres of Justice* (Oxford: Robertson, 1983); Miller, *Principles of Social Justice*.

6

"No More Relevance than One's Eye Color"

Justice and a Society without Gender

Mary Lyndon Shanley

Near the end of Susan Moller Okin's book *Justice, Gender, and the Family*, she asserts, "A just future would be one without gender. In its social structures and practices, one's sex would have no more relevance than one's eye color or the length of one's toes."[1] These sentences have long given me pause. What exactly did Okin envision when she suggested the possibility of a society without gender; why did she declare that, under just conditions, sex would have so little relevance; and what measures did she think were justified to move toward the goal of a genderless society? Okin defined gender as "the deeply entrenched social institutionalization of sexual difference," which is reflected in the sharp distinction between men's and women's roles in society.[2] She claimed that the social meaning attached to biological sex was malleable, and so gender roles could be altered or even eliminated. Changing those roles, in turn, would affect people's experiences and understandings of sexual embodiment. But while the claim that "sex would have no more relevance than eye color" was untenable—sex is linked to the experience of sexual pleasure, sex is the means by which individuals procreate, and sex is the means by which society continues—Okin was not simply engaging in hyperbole. She was challenging her reader to join with her in imagining the possibility that in a society "without gender," social institutions, human relationships, and human characteristics might be quite different from what we know at present.

In what follows, I take Okin's suggestion seriously and make the case that her preferred future would be one in which gender as we know it or traditional gender roles would not exist. This interpretation is somewhat at odds with—or, I prefer to think, in dialogue with—Nancy Rosenblum's contention in this volume that "Okin did not insist that all gendered attributes or roles should be eliminated" because her point was "not to avoid the [traditional gender] roles, per se, but to avoid ascriptive roles."[3]

Thanks to Oona Ceder, Joshua Cohen, Linda McClain, Hayden Nelson-Major, and Debra Satz for conversations about this chapter in its early stages. Of course, responsibility for the argument is mine alone.

1. Susan Moller Okin, *Justice, Gender, and the Family* (New York: Basic, 1989), 171 (hereafter *JGF*); see also "Humanist Liberalism," in Nancy L. Rosenblum, ed., *Liberalism and the Moral Life* (Cambridge, MA: Harvard University Press, 1998), 39.

2. Susan Moller Okin, "Justice and Gender: An Unfinished Debate," *Fordham Law Review* 72 (2004): 1539.

3. See the chapter by Rosenblum in this volume.

Rosenblum is, I think, right to say that Okin's commitment to liberalism meant that a just society could neither dictate nor proscribe traditional gender roles, but only ensure that these not be ascriptive; indeed, how could I hold a different view when at the end of her essay "Humanist Liberalism," Okin writes, "Since the liberal state must, in Larmore's words, 'remain neutral toward disputed and controversial ideals of the good life,' it cannot simply dictate and enforce the abolition of gender."[4] But I also think that Okin *aspired to* or hoped for a society in which traditional gender roles did not exist. I find a persistent tension in her thought between her commitment to individual freedom and the neutrality of the state with respect to gender, and her belief that the world would be a better place if we could eliminate gender roles and bring a genderless society into being. The elimination of gender would serve justice in two ways. It would end male domination and give women equal liberty with men, and it would contribute to the emergence of human potentialities. Okin believed that a society without gender would allow the development of human capacities in ways we cannot anticipate at present, just as John Stuart Mill believed that "mankind" was "a progressive being" whose sensibilities and capabilities might well change in response to different social arrangements.[5]

Okin's dual concern to end the oppression that stems from ascriptive gender roles and to undermine gender itself is apparent in the two kinds of proposals she puts forward to end the male domination that defines the gender system. The first group of proposals is to ensure that the effects of sexual difference would not carry with them the disabilities and privileges that they do at present. These include not only antidiscrimination laws to achieve women's equality in the workplace, but also measures like income sharing within marriage, which would ameliorate or eliminate wives' economic vulnerability and dependence on their husbands. A second group of proposals is aimed at eliminating gender itself. Okin, along with theorists like Catharine MacKinnon, believed that gender was a reflection not of biological sex difference, but of power.[6] But their antiessentialism on this point was all they shared. Where MacKinnon argued that patriarchal social practices and institutions stemmed from domination in sexual relations, Okin believed that both gender inequality and sexual domination were rooted in the mutually reinforcing relationships among the "division of labor between the sexes (particularly regarding child care and care of the sick and elderly), the effects on children's development of being mothered rather than cared for equally by both parents, [and] the sex stratification of the labor market."[7] Her strategy to eliminate gender therefore entails doing away with the gender division of labor first between workplace

4. Susan Moller Okin, "Humanist Liberalism," in Nancy L. Rosenblum, ed., *Liberalism and the Moral Life* (Cambridge, MA: Harvard University Press, 1998), 53.

5. John Stuart Mill, *On Liberty*, edited by Elizabeth Rapaport (Indianapolis, IN: Hackett, 1978[1859]); Mill, *The Subjection of Women*, ed. Susan Moller Okin (Indianapolis, IN: Hackett, 1988[1869]).

6. See Catharine A. MacKinnon, "Difference and Dominance: On Sex Discrimination," in D. Kelly Weisberg, ed., *Feminist Legal Theories* (Philadelphia: Temple University Press, 1993), and *Feminism Unmodified* (Cambridge, MA: Harvard University Press, 1987).

7. Susan Moller Okin, "Feminism, the Individual, and Contract Theory," *Ethics* 100 (April 1990): 669.

and home and then within the family itself.[8] The radical shift in popular attitudes and public policy required to eliminate gender is a daunting task, but the great virtue of using changes in workplace policy to undermine gender is that it could be undertaken without impermissible violations of family privacy or dictating how individuals should structure their intimate and family lives.

Okin's project was not simply to create greater legal and economic equality for women within existing institutions, but also by abolishing gender to transform human experience. Equal rights did not guarantee liberation; extending equal rights to women in the absence of more far-reaching changes did no more than give some women access to the privileges enjoyed by some men. She agreed with Wendy Williams that male and female roles rested on a deep and sometimes nearly invisible "set of complementarities, a yin-yang of sex-role assumptions and assignments so complex and interrelated that we cannot successfully dismantle any of it without seriously exploring the possibility of dismantling it all."[9] An essentialist view of sexual difference, of "male" and "female" as defined by biological characteristics that give rise to the roles to be filled by "men" and "women," particularly in marriage and the family, is antithetical to freedom.

Okin was agnostic about exactly what human beings and social institutions might become under conditions of sex equality, but the abolition of gender is necessary to the emergence of "the kind of citizens we need if we are ever to achieve a just society."[10] Like John Stuart Mill, Okin challenged traditional liberalism's focus on the uniform and unchanging "individual," showing that what people experience as their own nature is formed in relationship to others and will change when the context in which those relationships take place alters. Her claim that "a just future would be one without gender" was more than a condemnation of systemic domination supported by social practice and law. Okin believed that ridding relations between men and women of gender domination would profoundly affect the kinds of relationships that people experienced, and the end of gender oppression would advance the possibility for moral development for both individuals and civil society.

THE INCOMPATIBILITY OF GENDER AND JUSTICE

The notion that a just society requires the elimination of gender was not a passing fancy found only in *Justice, Gender, and the Family*, but was part of Okin's work from first to last. Okin was "unambivalent about aiming for the elimination of gender."[11]

---

8. Okin also proposed educational reforms that would open children's minds to more diverse and fluid gender roles than at present. These included placing women in positions of authority as school principals and developing curricula that showed men and women engaged in both public work and caregiving (*JGF*, 177).

9. Wendy W. Williams, "The Equality Crisis: Some Reflections on Culture, Courts, and Feminism," in Katharine Bartlett and Rosanne Kennedy, eds., *Feminist Legal Theory* (Boulder, CO: Westview, 1991), 228–229.

10. *JGF*, 186.

11. Susan Moller Okin, *Women in Western Political Thought* (Princeton, NJ: Princeton University Press, 1992; originally published 1979, hereafter *WWPT*), 334 ("Afterword" to 1992 edition).

Although the word *gender* does not, as best as I can tell, appear in Okin's first book, *Women in Western Political Thought*, the idea is certainly there. The thesis of *Women in Western Political Thought* is that major works of Western political theory presume that women's capacity to bear children precludes them from participation in the public worlds of productive labor and political engagement, and that this is unjust.

> Women's significant but few and specific biological differences from men—the capacity to bear and suckle children, and lesser muscular strength—have been held to entail a whole range of "natural" differences—moral, intellectual, emotional— between the sexes. Because of the enforcement of such notions by political systems, laws, institutions and socialization processes, women have been stunted and crippled as human beings, and persons of both sexes have been unable to develop freely their own personalities and potential.[12]

Okin argued that nothing about women's other roles should follow from the fact of childbearing, that is, from sexual difference.[13]

By the time Okin published *Justice, Gender, and the Family* in 1989, gender was a term that was widely used. Okin wrote that "a society without gender [would be] one in which sexual difference carried no social significance, the sexes were equal in power and independence, and 'mothering' and 'fathering' a child meant the same thing."[14] This might mean either that men would do caregiving work, or that a woman who bore a child might have as little postbirth relationship with it as many fathers do with their offspring. What is clear is that dichotomous gender roles are unjust. Criticizing Rawls' assumption that his principles of justice are compatible with traditional family roles, Okin asserted that "[g]ender, with its ascriptive designation of positions and expectations of behavior in accordance with the inborn characteristic of sex, could no longer form a legitimate part of the social structure, whether inside or outside the family."[15]

Okin's cataloging and condemnation of the inequalities produced by gender roles was sweeping.[16] Although women are not bound by law to be the primary caregivers of young children, both they and others expect them to fill this role. As a result, full-time jobs are structured on the assumption that full-time workers have a full-time wife at home. In the minority of families that conform to this traditional division of labor, the

---

12. *WWPT*, 297.

13. *WWPT*, 303–304. This was always part of Okin's position and was memorably expressed in her essay "Philosopher Queens," where she argued that Plato's proposal that women should serve as guardians followed inevitably and inexorably once he had decided that guardians should not live in private households. With "women's work" collectivized, Plato realized that women's "true nature" was no different from men's. Allan Bloom argued strenuously against this interpretation, and even among feminists it did not win universal approval as an interpretation of Book V of Plato's *Republic*. See Arlene Saxonhouse, *Women in the History of Political Thought: Ancient Greece to Machiavelli* (New York: Praeger, 1985).

14. *JGF*, 12.

15. *JGF*, 103.

16. Iris Young (in her chapter in this volume) gives a clear and eloquent description of Okin's account of vulnerability by marriage and the applicability of this analysis to women not living in the United States or in other developed industrial countries.

wife and children are entirely dependent on the male wage-earner for their support. But even in the majority of families in which wives and mothers are in the labor force, women remain vulnerable to domination and exploitation. Whether women "enter clerical, sales, or service work, or train for one of the predominantly female professions such as teaching or nursing, they [are] heading not only for the relatively more flexible hours…but also for low pay, poor working conditions, and, above all, blocked mobility."[17] In 1987, women who worked full time year-round earned a median wage of $15,704, while men earned $22,204, an annual earnings ratio of 65.2 percent. In 2004, the median wage of women who worked full time was $31,223, while men with similar work effort earned $40,798, a ratio of 76.5 percent, a narrower but still significant gap.[18] The difference in earning potential, Okin argued, cannot help but affect personal relationships; men and women enter marriage with unequal earning potential, and this gap widens as the marriage continues and men add to their qualifications while women take part-time work or drop out of the labor force (even if temporarily) to raise children.

Okin did not simply chronicle the disparities in earnings and earning potentials but argued, "*A cycle of power relations and decisions pervades both family and workplace, and the inequalities of each reinforce those that already exist in the other.*"[19] An unequal power relationship exists in ongoing marriages, for the person who brings greater economic resources can insist on his views on leisure, sex, consumption, and so forth being given priority. (Even in the current decade, a letter to a syndicated advice columnist asserted that, when spouses disagree over whose taste in furnishing a house should prevail, "The person who brings home the dough should get a bigger piece of the pie.")[20] Moreover, disparate economic resources have a devastating effect on what Okin called the possibility of exit from a bad marriage; because they cannot earn much, and because they are likely to retain physical custody of children in the event of divorce, women are locked into relationships that they no longer desire, and that might be dangerous and abusive to themselves or their children.

By 1994, these patterns of domination led Okin to call gender a "castelike system," a system of interlocking and mutually reinforcing disadvantage.[21] Women's disabilities cannot be overturned simply by equal opportunity measures but warrant positive government programs to dismantle them. The gender-based division of labor takes morally irrelevant sex differences and turns them into social, economic, and legal disadvantages supported and perpetuated by an array of public institutions and practices. Okin would have agreed with Sally Haslanger that to dismantle a gender-caste system

17. *JGF*, 144.

18. *JGF*, 144; and Institute for Women's Policy Research, "The Gender Wage Ratio: Women's and Men's Earning," IWPR Fact Sheet No. C350, available at www.iwpr.org (accessed October 8, 2005). The IWPR points out that the ratio improved in part because while both men's and women's earnings fell from 2003 to 2004, men's dropped more than women's; hence "women's apparent progress masks worsening economic conditions for all workers."

19. *JGF*, 147 (emphasis in the original).

20. "Dear Abby," *Poughkeepsie Journal*, January 6, 2005, D2. The advice columnist countered that decisions in a marriage should be mutual.

21. Susan Moller Okin, "*Political Liberalism*, Justice, and Gender," *Ethics* 105 (October 1994): 41, 43.

would require that society "refuse to use anatomy as a primary basis for classifying individuals and [recognize] that any distinctions between kinds of sexual and reproductive bodies are importantly political and open to contest."[22] Social practice has attached all kinds of extraneous social roles to sexual difference, and then has attached various advantages and disadvantages to those roles. Okin's insistence on getting rid of the gender division of labor was based neither on the notion that less pleasant work should be shared nor on adherence to some kind of arithmetical division of the chores, but rather on the fact that the ascribed roles of caste are antithetical to liberal justice, at the core of which is a commitment to equal rights and equal liberty.

ELIMINATING THE INJUSTICES OF GENDER

Interpretations of what Okin meant by her call for a society without gender range from a society in which men and women would fill jobs in roughly equal numbers, to one in which all (or at least most) persons would do both caregiving and public work, to one in which "man" and "woman," "masculine" and "feminine," "male" and "female" were not exhaustive categories nor exclusive binaries.[23] Okin herself did not approach the question of what "without gender" might mean from an abstract discussion, but rather through specific ideas for combating the pernicious effects of gender in contemporary society. Her primary concern was to do away with subordination, and her analysis proceeded from concrete proposals to dismantle gender domination to more abstract issues.

Okin put forward two sets of proposals to deal with the injustices produced by gender. One was to protect the vulnerable here and now by eliminating the negative *consequences* of gender, particularly of the gendered division of labor; the other was to *eliminate gender itself* by dismantling the structures that perpetuate the gender division of labor. To protect women from the consequences of the gender division of labor, Okin proposed that all income of either partner in a marriage should belong equally to both, and that courts should enforce an equal standard of living for former spouses following a divorce. (Okin here wrote about heterosexual couples; couples in same-sex partnerships could not marry, and Okin believed that same-sex partners would not have the same assumptions concerning the gender division of labor or disparity in incomes as heterosexual couples.)[24] To begin dismantling the gender division of labor, Okin proposed adaptation of the workplace to the needs of parents. The structures of public work and family relations establish a mutually reinforcing relationship of gender

---

22. Sally Haslanger, "Gender and Race: (What) Are They? (What) Do We Want Them to Be?" *Nous* 34.1 (2000): 49. Okin approved of Cass Sunstein's judgment that "[d]ifferences that are irrelevant from the moral point of view ought not without good reason to be turned, by social and legal structures, into social disadvantages." Sunstein, *The Partial Constitution* (Cambridge: Cambridge University Press, 1993), 339, quoted in Okin, "*Political Liberalism*, Justice, and Gender," 40.

23. David Estlund discusses various interpretations of what Okin intended in calling for the abolition of gender in "Shaping and Sex," in David M. Estlund and Martha C. Nussbaum, eds., *Sex, Preference, and Family: Essays on Law and Nature* (New York: Oxford University Press, 1997).

24. *JGF*, 140.

inequality in public life and in the home. By eliminating the assumptions that workers have no family responsibilities that might require their time and attention and that employers have no obligation to accommodate those responsibilities, it would be possible to break the mutually reinforcing relationship between gender subordination in domestic and public life without violating family privacy.[25] I will examine each of these proposals in turn to show how they are steps in Okin's project to eliminate gender.

Protecting the Vulnerable

In order to offset the disparity in power within marriage and to give women the possibility of "exit" from oppressive (or even simply unhappy) marriages, Okin proposed equalizing the economic resources of marriage partners. In an ongoing marriage in which one partner does the bulk of the domestic work, both partners would have a "legal entitlement to all earnings coming into the household."[26] The simplest way to do this would be to have employers make out two wage checks in lieu of one—one to the worker, the other to the worker's spouse.[27] Earnings should "be recognized as equally earned by the two persons" in order "to help prevent the inequality of family members in the sphere of wage work to invade their domestic sphere." Okin pointed out that she was *not* suggesting "that the wage-working partner pay the homemaking partner for services rendered." She did not intend "to introduce the cash nexus into a personal relationship where it is inappropriate." Rather, the equal splitting of wages "would constitute public recognition of the fact that the currently unpaid labor of families is just as important as the paid labor." This wage splitting would avoid imposing mandatory "complete and equal sharing of both paid and unpaid labor"; it would recognize the value of caregiving work without restricting the right of couples to choose how to divide the labor.[28]

Okin also proposed measures to reduce the vulnerability of married women at the time of separation and divorce: "A legal system of a society that allows couples to divide the labor of families in a traditional or quasi-traditional manner must take responsibility for the vulnerable position in which marital breakdown places the partner who has completely or partially lost the capacity to be economically self-supporting." The person whose career has been unencumbered by domestic responsibility should

25. The assumption that workers do not have family responsibilities infuses global as well as national labor markets; see, for example, Rhacel Salazar Parreñas, *Servants of Globalization* (Stanford, CA: Stanford University Press, 2001).

26. *JGF*, 180.

27. While Okin talked of this as providing economic resources to a spouse who is not in the paid labor force, the principle would, it seems to me, apply to all couples whether in a marriage, civil union, or domestic partnership and to dual-earner as well as single-earner households.

28. *JGF*, 181–182. Ian Shapiro has criticized Okin's proposal for wage sharing as ineffectual in providing resources sufficient to help people married to low wage-earners and as an unjustifiable intrusion by the state into domestic arrangements. Wouldn't it be better, he asks, for the state to supply a universal social wage? Yes, it would. But that does not defeat Okin's contention that wage sharing is more just than giving the wage-earner title to all of the earnings made possible by the other partner's assumption of household and childrearing tasks. Ian Shapiro, *Democratic Justice* (New Haven, CT: Yale University Press, 1999), 120.

shoulder responsibility for the person who performed the domestic labor, and "*Both postdivorce households should enjoy the same standard of living*."[29] Okin did not endorse simply dividing marital property to facilitate a "clean break" at the time of divorce; a spouse who has built up earning capacity thanks to the unpaid labor of the other spouse would, in Okin's scheme, have ongoing obligations not just to support the ex-spouse but to contribute whatever is necessary to maintain the households at an equal economic level.[30]

To ameliorate the economic vulnerability of single mothers and their children, Okin proposed mandatory paternity testing followed by orders of support.[31] It is debatable whether this plan would help women in the way Okin intended. Will Kymlicka has pointed out that providing financial support often gives men visitation rights, and many single mothers want nothing to do with the biological fathers of their children.[32] Moreover, linking paternal rights to genetic links rather than to social bonds and children's well-being works against Okin's insistence that parental responsibility entails providing hands-on care to children. But Okin regarded this as a stopgap measure to channel much-needed money to single mothers and their children until programs to dismantle the gender-caste system could be implemented.

Most important to her vision of a just future society, Okin insisted that both housekeeping and caregiving are *work* and that the immense social value of caregiving work must be recognized and remunerated. Other feminists and some social conservatives have also acknowledged the value of caregiving work and have proposed supports to enable women to give time to caregiving rather than enter the paid labor market. Proposals for unrestricted child tax credits, public payments for care of dependents ("wages for caring"), and social insurance credits to caregivers are aimed at providing economic support for caregiving. With such supports, couples will not feel that both partners must enter the paid labor force to support the family; stay-at-home parents will not lose all of the benefits that waged labor provides. Anne Alstott has proposed protecting the primary caregivers (mainly women) of young children and recognizing the value of their labor by creating a "caretaker resource account" for all caregivers to which the government would deposit $5,000 for every year they

29. *JGF*, 183 (emphasis in original).

30. Martha Albertson Fineman, *The Illusion of Equality: The Rhetoric and Reality of Divorce Reform* (Chicago: University of Chicago Press, 1991), also provides an excellent discussion of the economic impact of divorce and argues against a once-and-for-all property division at divorce.

31. Okin adopted this proposal from David Ellwood, *Poor Support: Poverty in the American Family* (New York: Basic, 1988), 163–174. In 1985, only 18 percent of never-married fathers were ordered to pay child support, and only 11 percent actually paid any (and the figures are not much higher today). *JGF*, ch. 8, 210n13.

32. Will Kymlicka, "Rethinking the Family," *Philosophy and Public Affairs* 20.1 (Winter 1991): 77–97. Kymlicka also has contended that Okin's proposal tacitly accepted procreative bodies as gendered: "The begetting of a child requires the input of one man and one woman, but to attach social significance to that fact is surely to make gender socially significant." The only way to avoid this, he contends, is to ground parental rights and obligations in contract. The proposal for orders of support, however, was intended to offset the vulnerabilities of a gender-caste system in the present and was not part of Okin's vision of future society. For a discussion of contracts in establishing parental rights, see Mary Lyndon Shanley, *Making Babies, Making Families* (Boston: Beacon, 2001).

spend providing care, money that could only be spent on child care, education, or investment for retirement.[33]

There is, however, a tension between the provision of material aid to caregivers and the acceptance (and therefore possible reinforcement) of the gender division of labor. All of these proposals—income sharing in two-parent households, postdivorce equalization of household living standards, support obligations based on paternity testing, and caregivers' allowances—use the power of government to ameliorate women's vulnerability and to recognize the importance to society of childrearing and caregiving work. But while these measures would counteract the worst *effects* of a gender division of labor, neither singly nor combined would they do away with that division. Other measures are necessary to change the caste-based system of gender and its pervasive effects not only on individuals' economic resources, but also on their intellectual and moral capacities. In Okin's view, changing the structures that organize paid labor in the United States is a promising place to begin this transformation of gender and of human capabilities.

Dismantling the Gender-Caste System

Okin was well aware that her proposals to get rid of the disadvantageous effects of gender differences and to protect the vulnerable leave the gender-based division of labor—and thus gender itself—untouched. Measures that facilitate women's entry into the labor force, such as antidiscrimination measures, equal pay for equal work, day care centers, and strictures against sexual harassment, enable some women to escape some of the constraints of their gender, but only by adopting or being assimilated into male gender patterns. Given the equation of "male" with "human," these measures mean that some women at long last can do the work that society and traditional political theory have recognized as the most important human activities. But even those married women who work outside the home almost always shoulder much greater responsibility for the domestic life of their families than do their male partners.[34] Moreover, some women's freedom to take on public work is made possible by hiring other women (often immigrants and women of color) to do housework and child care; child care is still "women's work," still a private responsibility, and still performed by women with fewer economic and political resources than men. This is not the path to liberation for women.

But while "equal opportunity" for women to engage in activity previously reserved to men neither properly values caregiving nor alters the gender division of labor, it is hard to imagine ways of getting rid of that division of labor while respecting individual freedom and family privacy. When Okin imagined people in the original position, she pointed out that we do not know "our place in society or our particular conception

33. Anne L. Alstott, *No Exit: What Parents Owe Their Children and What Society Owes Parents* (New York: Oxford University Press, 2004), esp. 75–140. See also Alstott, "What We Owe to Parents: How Public Policy Can Support the Hard Work of Raising Children," *Boston Review* 29.2 (April–May 2004): 6–10.

34. See Arlie Russell Hochschild, *The Second Shift* (New York: Penguin, 2003[1989]). Statistics show that, as women have moved into the paid labor force, men's contributions to household work and child care have risen, but do not come close to proportional sharing.

of the good life. Particularly relevant in this context…is our lack of knowledge of our…convictions about the appropriate division of labor between the sexes." People do not share the same beliefs, and therefore "the positions we represent must include a wide variety of beliefs on these matters." Some people will find that they have a traditional conception of the good life that adheres to the conventional division of labor between the sexes: "The challenge is to arrive at and apply principles of justice having to do with the family and the division of labor between the sexes that can satisfy these vastly disparate points of view and the many that fall between."[35]

Some practices are beyond the pale of the acceptable because "they violate such fundamentals as equal basic liberty and self-respect" and are "based on the notion that women are inherently inferior beings whose function is to fulfill the needs of men." Among these are "approaches to marriage that view it as an inherently and desirably hierarchical structure of dominance and subordination.…Even if there were no other reason to refuse to admit such views, they must be excluded for the sake of children."[36] But despite her criticism of undue deference to "private" life, Okin did not want the state to dictate how people conducted their personal lives.[37]

The reluctance to interfere in people's choices precludes certain policies that could alter the gender division of labor within families. Joshua Cohen has suggested that such strategies could include a "mandatory shared-responsibility clause in marriage contracts…or domestic shirking could be defined as a form of sex discrimination…or there could be a regulatory scheme featuring an agency responsible for formulating standards for the division of labor in households…; or there could be tax benefits to couples (or couples with children) that share responsibilities."[38] But as Cohen has noted, these are meddlesome constraints on personal liberty and family privacy of the kind Okin wanted to avoid.

An approach less threatening to the liberal commitment to individual freedom and the accommodation of different modes of life is to address the allocation of power and resources in the public world. Okin insisted that the caste nature of gender lies in the reciprocal influence of domestic and public arrangements, and so dismantling gender hierarchy in the public realm would impact structures of domestic power. As Cohen observed, "[A] gender structured family is actually explained by the 'choices' of men and women given the constraints imposed by the current organization of the labor market."[39] The current organization of the labor market reflects a deeply gendered understanding of who should be engaged in productive labor, on the one hand, and reproductive labor, on the other. A different organization of work would not only affect men's and women's choices about whether, when, and how much to work, but in doing so would also undercut the conceptualization of the worker as essentially masculine. The alteration of the workplace, not direct intervention in family life, would move society in the direction of Okin's genderless society.

35. *JGF*, 174.

36. *JGF*, 174–175.

37. Okin identified four erroneous assumptions about the public-private divide in *JGF*, 128–133.

38. Joshua Cohen, "Okin on Justice, Gender, and Family," *Canadian Journal of Philosophy* 22.2 (June 1992): 265.

39. Cohen, "Okin on Justice, Gender, and Family," 283.

Okin proposed several measures affecting the workplace that would alter the context in which people exercise choice about paid labor and caregiving. The first was that "shared parental responsibility for child care would be both assumed and facilitated." Okin contended that both parents "are equally parents of their children and have equal responsibility for both the unpaid effort that goes into caring for them and their economic support."[40] This in turn means that workers must be thought of as parents who are actively engaged in child care, eliminating the by now "largely mythical assumption that every worker has 'someone else' at home to raise 'his' children" (an assumption hard on all women and on single parents). Child care centers, "subsidized so as to be equally available to all children," would supplement parental care, but the bulk of care of infants and young children would be supplied by parents.[41]

What kinds of policies would follow from the assumption that many workers are also parents of young children? There would be maternity leave for mothers that would be treated like other leaves for temporary disability, and employers would be required to provide such leave. These leaves would not be gender neutral nor available to men, but rather be aimed directly at pregnancy and parturition. Critiquing Shulamith Firestone's assertion that only by moving gestation out of the body entirely could women find liberation, Okin insisted that it was not women's biology that led to their oppression, "but rather [the fact] that reproduction has taken place within a patriarchal power structure, has been considered a private rather than a public concern, and has been perceived as dictating women's entire lives, and as defining their very nature."[42] Pregnancy and childbirth "should be regarded as temporarily disabling conditions like any others, and employers should be mandated to provide leave for all such conditions."[43]

After birth, however, "parental leaves...must be available to mothers and fathers on the same terms, to facilitate shared parenting." Parents might take sequential leaves or each might take a half-time leave. All workers, Okin asserted, "should have the right, without prejudice to their jobs, seniority, benefits, and so on, to work less than full-time during the first year of a child's life, and to work flexible or somewhat reduced

40. *JGF*, 175–176. Okin nearly always spoke of the two-parent or single-parent family and did not consider blended families or other family forms. Linda C. McClain, *The Place of Families: Capacity, Equality, and Responsibility* (Cambridge, MA: Harvard University Press, 2005), ch. 6, thoughtfully discusses whether and how public policy might recognize other caregiving relationships.

41. *JGF*, 175. When Okin refers to the need for nonparental child care, she consistently speaks of day care centers, not private nannies, providing that care. This seems consistent with her determination to end the assumption that child care is "women's work" and to give parental leave and other benefits to all workers (something that is notoriously hard to do for domestic workers).

42. *WWPT*, 296. Okin insisted that a "revolution in ideas" must

clearly separate out those aspects of reproduction which are biologically women's—necessarily, pregnancy, and if it is opted for, lactation—from all those long-term aspects of child-rearing which are not necessarily women's work, but have been made to seem so on account of the accepted structure of the family.... [S]ome feminists as well as antifeminists have fallen into the trap of perceiving child-rearing as inseparable from childbearing which means of course that as long as the latter is a female function, so must the former be. (*WWPT*, 299–300)

43. *JGF*, 176. She also used pregnancy leave as the thin edge of the wedge to get workers "leave[s] for illnesses or other disabling conditions," which she thought justice required "in a society as rich as ours" (*JGF*, 176).

hours at least until the child reaches the age of seven."[44] To accommodate the needs of parents of young children, employers of large numbers of workers would be required to provide on-site day care.[45]

Okin insisted that while workplace policies that assume that *all* workers have caregiving responsibilities would be a radical change from the present, *any* organization of work affects the options that people have as they choose how to arrange their personal and family lives, and "the very notion that the state has the option to intervene or not to intervene in the family is not only mythical but meaningless."[46] Frances Olsen had discussed the myriad ways in which the state sets background rules that influence people's interactions within families. For example, Olsen asked, would "nonintervention" in the family mean allowing or not allowing divorce? If the state permits divorce, then whatever grounds for divorce it establishes are a form of "intervention." The question is not *whether* state action affects the family, but *how* it affects the family.[47] Okin agreed: "The myth that state intervention in the family is an option allows those who support the status quo to call it 'nonintervention' and to label policies that would alter it—such as the provision of shelters for battered wives—intervention."[48] Critics might call proposals to facilitate labor force participation by those responsible for rearing children as interventionist, but in doing so they ignore the ways in which present practices profoundly influence family life.

In the same way, the current arrangements of the workplace are anything but "neutral" with regard to the gender-caste system, making it impossible for two adults (much less a single person) other than the well-to-do to both work and themselves provide

44. *JGF*, 176. Janet Gornick and Marcia Meyers suggest how parents who work less than full time might share child care. One parent of a preschooler might work from eight to four o'clock, while the other worked from ten to six o'clock, with the child in day care for six hours. If the parents worked less than an eight-hour day, one might work eight to two and the other ten to four, with the child in day care for four hours. Janet C. Gornick and Marcia K. Meyers, *Families That Work: Policies for Reconciling Parenthood and Employment* (New York: Russell Sage Foundation, 2003).

45. A number of policy analysts have explored ways in which the workplace might be altered to accommodate equal parenting. Gornick and Meyers have examined the family and work policies of 13 countries in an effort to identify policies that allow both women and men to engage in paid labor and in caregiving. Among the policies that seem effective is generous paid parental leave, the cost of which is borne by the employer and the state. To be effective in getting men to take the leave, it must be paid at close to full salary so that leaves are not more costly for the higher-paid partner and there is no financial incentive for the lower-paid partner to take the leave; it should be nontransferable. Gornick and Meyers, *Families That Work*, especially ch. 4, "Reconciling the Conflicts: Towards a Dual-Earner—Dual-Career Society." Any rearrangement of the workplace would also have to consider the needs of parents without partners. One important measure would be to reduce the disincentives to part-time work by requiring companies to provide the same benefits (prorated by hours worked) to part-time and to full-time workers. Nancy Folbre, *The Invisible Heart: Economics and Family Values* (New York: New Press, 2001), 228.

46. *JGF*, 130.

47. Frances E. Olsen, "The Myth of State Intervention in the Family," *University of Michigan Journal of Law Reform* 18.4 (1985): 837. See also Olsen, "The Family and the Market: A Study of Ideology and Legal Reform," *Harvard Law Review* 96.7 (1983).

48. *JGF*, 131.

adequate care to infants and young children. (And depending on how much child care they hire others to do, the rich deprive themselves of some of the learning and growth that adults derive from taking care of children, and may deprive those they hire of the ability to take care of their own children.) The ways in which work is organized (full time, continuous, physically distant from the place where children are being cared for, etc.) are human constructions and are an essential part of what makes gender a caste system. The way to begin dismantling the gender-caste system, Okin argued, is to assume that all human beings have direct caregiving responsibilities and to structure work and other public activities accordingly.

IMAGINING A SOCIETY WITHOUT GENDER

Okin regarded the gender division of labor and the economic and legal structures to which it gives rise, not sexual force or women's biological childbearing capacity, as the source of women's vulnerability and inequality. She utterly rejected the claim that different gender roles are the "natural" consequence of women's biological role in procreation and regarded it as a false rationalization for women's subordination. While agreeing with MacKinnon that gender might not even code as difference "were it not for its consequences for social power," Okin saw differential social power stemming from the division of labor, not from sexual domination.[49] In a review of Carole Pateman's *The Sexual Contract*, she insisted that "the entire comprehensive subject of the division of labor between the sexes" deserves fully as much attention as "the specific issue of men's rights of sexual access to women."[50] Okin attributed male domination and women's subordination to the reciprocal and socially constructed relationship between workplace and family. If society were to dismantle the privilege and power it gives to men through workplace structures, the gender division of labor would begin to break down. And since who is marked as a "woman" and who as a "man" is so profoundly a consequence of differential power, when the gender division of labor breaks down, gender categories themselves will begin to lose meaning.

Okin's belief in the possibility of dismantling gender was not simply speculative; her proposals for accommodating pregnancy and childbirth suggest ways to begin that task. Indeed, while Okin's proposal to reduce maternity leave to only what is needed for physical recovery might appear to be an effort to assimilate women into the male model of the worker, it's implication is just the opposite. In Okin's view, in a just society, "'mothering' and 'fathering' a child [would mean] the same thing."[51] Men would do hands-on caregiving: "I have yet to see—though I am much looking forward to seeing—the culture in which as much of men's time and energy as women's goes into preserving and maintaining the personal, familial, and reproductive side of life."[52] Rather than regarding men as independent and bound to others only through

---

49. MacKinnon, "Difference and Dominance," 281–282.

50. Okin, "Feminism, the Individual, and Contract Theory," 665.

51. *JGF*, 12. She noted, "An equal sharing between the sexes of family responsibilities is 'the great revolution that has not happened'" (*JGF*, 4).

52. Susan Moller Okin, "Feminism and Multiculturalism: Some Tensions," *Ethics* 108 (July 1998): 667.

agreement (the labor contract, the marriage contract, the social contract), social practices must change to embody the assumption that men are as responsible for and as attached to children as are women.

In a just society that has severed the link between biology and the gender division of labor (that is, between childbearing and childrearing), gender would lose its grounding. This does not mean that society should ignore pregnancy and childbirth. Okin's position was like that of Sally Haslanger, who has noted, "One could argue that we should work toward a society free of gender in the materialist sense—one in which sex-oppression does not exist—while still allowing that sexual and reproductive differences should be taken into account in a just society."[53] Taking account of reproductive differences and providing for persons who bear children, however, is very different from maintaining a system of "men's" and "women's" functions and social roles.

Okin regarded gender as a "preliberal relic" because it creates a hierarchy based on supposedly natural characteristics, but these supposedly "natural differences" are the result not of physiology but of the hierarchical constructions of male dominance.[54] What divides the world into "men" and "women" is an intricate and interlocking system of privilege and exclusion. When society eliminates gender hierarchy, the dichotomous view of human beings as either "male" or "female" might well disappear. This will not, Okin insisted, lead to "a world of hermaphroditic-looking beings with none of the differences among them we now tend to associate with femininity or masculinity." A world without gender would not be "monstrous and repressive" nor devoid of difference and eroticism. "The gender-free society that I envision," said Okin, "would not be boring; rather, it would be filled with diversity.... The difference between it and our present society is that the different personal characteristics, appearances and capacities would not be distributed—or be expected to be distributed—along the lines of sex."[55] It is impossible to know what people's experience of bodies that do and do not have the capacity to bear children would be under circumstances in which that capacity did not determine a vast array of social consequences both for those who bear children and for those who do not. It is similarly impossible to predict the ways in which bodily difference would influence sexual desire in a gender-free society, because part of sexual attraction is shaped by cultural notions of masculinity and femininity that incorporate notions of domination and subordination.[56]

Eliminating gender hierarchy would produce far more radical changes in social organization than would even the most stringently applied equal opportunity measures,

53. Haslanger, "Gender and Race," 49. See also Marilyn Frye, "The Necessity of Differences: Constructing a Positive Category of Women," *SIGNS* 21.4 (1996) : 991–1010; and Moira Gatens, "A Critique of the Sex-Gender Distinction," in *Imaginary Bodies* (New York: Routledge, 1996), 3–20.

54. *JGF*, 122.

55. Okin, "Sexual Orientation, Gender, and Families: Dichotomizing Differences," *Hypatia* 11.1 (Winter 1996): 32.

56. See Adrienne Rich, "Compulsory Heterosexuality and Lesbian Experience," in Ann Snitow, Christine Stansell, and Sharon Thompson, eds., *The Powers of Desire: The Politics of Sexuality* (New York: New Feminist Library, 1983).

and this would affect human psychology and the moral capacities of adults. In *Women in Western Political Thought*, Okin argued, "As both Plato and John Stuart Mill were well aware, no one knows what women's nature is like, as distinct from men's, and no one will know, until members of the two sexes are enabled to develop in the absence of differentiated treatment during the socialization process and throughout their lives."[57] Marx, too, believed that human nature is not fixed once and for all, and Okin noted approvingly that Marx was

> concerned with the historical process of humanity's freeing itself from the constraints of arduously producing its means of subsistence, and the eventual achievement of that "realm of freedom" in which all human beings will be able to create, and to live lives that are no longer animal, but truly human, because for the first time truly social.[58]

What human beings might become under very different economic and social arrangements was for all of these writers unknowable, but all projected a transformation of both individuals and their relationships with one another.

Okin's attention was directed mainly toward women, and she argued that women would achieve a fully developed human nature only when the reproduction and rearing of children were no longer taken to be women's defining activities.[59] But she recognized that men's capacities would similarly change when they engage in caregiving activity. "The experience of being a physical and psychological nurturer—whether of a child or of another adult—would increase [men's] capacity to identify with and fully comprehend the viewpoints of others."[60] These passages remind me of those in Mill's *The Subjection of Women* that express the hope that once male domination of women is brought to an end, true marital "friendship"—which requires the possibility of genuine reciprocity, "the pleasure of leading and of being led in the path of development"—will be possible, because of enlarged human capacities in both men and women.[61] It may be that I misperceive the affinities between Mill and Okin on the transformation of marital relations because of my earlier work on Mill;[62] in contrast, Rosenblum argues that Okin's agnosticism and lack of utopianism causes her to diverge from Mill at just this point.[63] But I hear an aspiration for new human relationships as well as for the end of systemic subordination in Okin's writings. It is important to rid the world of gender hierarchy because only in such a world can equal freedom exist, and also because only in such a world can women and men fully develop as human beings and, in doing so, alter and expand the kinds of interactions that give form to both intimate and public life. There is, in such a view, the embrace of the possibility of a radically different future.

57. *WWPT*, 297.
58. *WWPT*, 298.
59. *WWPT*, 299.
60. *JGF*, 17–18.
61. *Subjection*, ch. 4, 102–103.
62. Mary Lyndon Shanley, "Marital Slavery and Friendship: John Stuart Mill's *The Subjection of Women*," *Political Theory* 9 (May 1981): 229–247.
63. See Rosenblum's chapter in this volume.

CONCLUSION

The freedom of self-definition essential to a liberal society and to Okin's understanding of justice cannot be achieved under the conditions of systemic oppression produced and sustained by traditional gender roles and gender hierarchy. The first requirement of justice is, therefore, to eliminate both gender hierarchy and ascriptive gender roles. But there are also repeated suggestions in Okin's work that she viewed traditional gender roles themselves as impediments to the development of the capabilities and capacities of all human beings. Okin's proposals to restructure workplace practices, measures that could be implemented without violating family privacy or individual choice, arose, I think, from a hope that in society in the future gender as we know it might disappear.

In a just society, one without gender domination, men and women alike would develop their capacities for remunerative labor and caregiving work; the division of people into dyadic categories of male and female would not exist. Okin's further claim that, in a just society, "one's sex would have no more relevance than the color of one's eyes or the length of one's toes" was an exaggeration; sex would surely remain relevant to individuals' self-understanding and personal relationships (both erotic and procreative). But in Okin's view, sexuality, like gender, is socially constructed.[64] Okin's work contains a speculative thread that suggests that, in a society where gender is not ascriptive and does not produce relationships of domination and subordination, the ways in which people will experience sexuality might be quite different from the present.

In the face of the accusation that her world entailed monotonous androgyny, Okin insisted that far from being a world of deadening uniformity, a society without gender would be one with expanded understandings and experiences of human possibility. That vision of enlarged space for the development and exercise of human capacities, as well as her condemnation of the current structures and practices of oppression, animated all of her work. The denunciation of gender oppression and the belief in the progressive possibilities of human social life were two sides of Okin's liberal theory of justice. She urged her readers to enter upon the arduous task of dismantling gender as a system of oppression in both family and public life, believing that their efforts would reshape significant social institutions and practices and, in doing so, create the conditions for the emergence of greater human freedom.

---

64. Okin's belief that gender could and should be eliminated shares some ground with theorists like Judith Butler despite the philosophical distance between Okin's liberal theory and postmodernism. See, for example, Butler, *Undoing Gender* (New York: Routledge, 2004), esp. ch. 9, "The End of Sexual Difference?"

7

On the Tension between Sex Equality and Religious Freedom

Cass Sunstein

Susan Moller Okin was centrally concerned with the risk that cherished social institutions, including the family and voluntary organizations, could threaten both freedom and equality. Her important essay on multiculturalism emphasizes that "group rights," sought by many liberals, may compromise liberalism's deepest commitments, above all by denying both freedom and equality to women.[1] In Okin's view, "we—especially those of us who consider ourselves politically progressive and opposed to all forms of oppression—have been too quick to assume that feminism and multiculturalism are both good things which are easily reconciled."[2] In stressing the tension between the two, Okin argued that, if we care about individual liberty, group rights will often have to yield.

Okin's skepticism about group rights cuts across a wide range, but some of her most controversial applications involve religion. As Okin was aware, religious autonomy is often defended on grounds of both freedom and equality. But her argument plainly suggests that religious autonomy can compromise both of these values, especially in the context of sex. Indeed, religious autonomy can undermine fair equality of opportunity, a basic liberal value. I believe that Okin's argument is broadly correct and that it has many implications for both law and policy. In brief, conflicts between sex equality and religious institutions are pervasive, and they create severe tensions in a liberal social order. They raise the obvious question: what is the appropriate domain of secular law as government seeks to control discriminatory behavior by or within religious institutions?

In addressing this question, I aim to extend Okin's claims in a way that is, I hope, very much in the spirit of her general argument. My focus is on an insufficiently explored puzzle. In the United States and in many other nations, it is generally agreed that most ordinary law, both civil and criminal, is legitimately applied to religious

This chapter is a substantially revised and significantly expanded version of Cass R. Sunstein, "Should Sex Equality Law Apply to Religious Institutions?" in Joshua Cohen, Matthew Howard, and Martha Nussbaum, eds., *Is Multiculturalism Bad for Women?* (Princeton, NJ: Princeton University Press, 1999). I am grateful to Rob Reich and Debra Satz for valuable comments on an earlier draft.

1. See Joshua Cohen, Matthew Howard, and Martha Nussbaum, eds., *Is Multiculturalism Bad for Women?* (Princeton, NJ: Princeton University Press 1999).

2. Susan Okin, *Boston Review* (Oct./Nov. 1997): 25.

organizations. Thus, for example, a secular government may prohibit members of a religious institution from engaging in murder, kidnapping, assault, cruelty to animals, or intentional infliction of emotional distress, even if those acts are part of a religious ceremony or otherwise guided or even mandated by religious precepts. In these ways, the liberal principles that Okin champions—above all, the right to bodily integrity—are vindicated against religious organizations, at least in principle.

At the same time, it is generally agreed that there are important limits on the extent to which the law of sex discrimination is legitimately applied to religious organizations. Often those limits are respected voluntarily by governments. States do not, for example, require the Catholic church to ordain women as priests, and under existing law, religious institutions are plainly permitted to engage in acts that would be unacceptable discrimination if carried out by a secular entity.[3] Interference with religious autonomy is pervasive under the ordinary criminal and civil law. But such interference is usually absent if sex discrimination is the problem that the government is seeking to address. Indeed, such interference is sometimes thought to be unconstitutional or to be inconsistent with the most fundamental ideals—violating the defining commitment to respect for religious institutions.

An important commonplace of democratic theory and practice might therefore be deemed the *asymmetry thesis*. According to the asymmetry thesis, it is unproblematic to apply ordinary civil and criminal law to religious institutions, but problematic to apply the law forbidding sex discrimination to those institutions. Thus, it is uncontroversially acceptable to prevent priests from beating up women (or anyone else) as part of a religious ceremony, or to ban Orthodox Jews from assaulting Reform women rabbis (even if they are sincerely motivated by a religiously founded idea of a male rabbinate); but it is often thought unacceptable to ban sex segregation in religious education,[4] or to prohibit religious groups from excluding women from certain domains.

What is the source of this asymmetry? Can it be defended? I believe that Okin's arguments help to show that there is no good defense of the asymmetry thesis and that, in many contexts, neither liberal ideals nor the Constitution should be taken to forbid government from banning sex discrimination by religious institutions. To sustain this argument, it will be necessary to say something about the nature of liberal ideals.

---

3. American law makes the basic prohibitions on employment discrimination inapplicable where religion, sex, or national origin is "a bona fide occupational qualification reasonably necessary to the normal operation of that particular business or enterprise." 42 USC 2000e-2(e). The prohibition is generally inapplicable "to a religious corporation, association, educational institution, or society with respect to the employment of individuals of a particular religion to perform work connected with the carrying on by such corporation, association, educational institution, or society of its activities." 42 USC 2000e-1.

4. Of course, the American Constitution applies only to the state and not to private institutions; hence, the asymmetry thesis has its force when the government goes beyond the Constitution to apply a prohibition on sex discrimination to most private institutions but not to religion.

PUZZLES AND CONFLICTS

To anchor the discussion, consider some potential conflicts between sex equality and freedom of religion, conflicts that arise in one or another form in many nations:

1. Certain Jewish synagogues educate boys separately from girls, and certain Jewish schools refuse to admit girls. Some Jewish girls and their parents contend that this is a form of sex discrimination that contributes to sex role stereotyping, in a way that produces damaging effects on boys and especially girls and that may even compromise fair equality of opportunity.

2. A Catholic university refuses to tenure several women teachers in its Canon Law Department. A disappointed faculty member complains that this is a form of employment discrimination.[5] The university responds that courts should not be allowed to intervene in a religious matter of this kind.

3. A young man trains and studies for ordination to the priesthood of the Society of Jesus. He is repeatedly subjected to sexual harassment by two ordained priests. The harassment takes the form of unwanted sexual comments, propositions, and pornographic mailings. He brings suit for employment discrimination.[6] It is objected that the suit compromises religious liberty.

4. Mormon employers engage in various practices of sex discrimination in employment. They refuse to hire women for certain jobs; they claim that being male is an occupational qualification, imposed in good faith, for certain positions. These practices are undertaken in the private sector, in institutions that both have and do not have explicitly religious functions.

5. A Western nation allows immigrant men to bring in multiple wives. It recognizes their polygamous marriages and various discriminatory practices (including "assigning" teenage girls to older men for marriage) that accompany certain religious convictions.

Freedom of religion has a central place in the liberal tradition, and in the United States, as elsewhere, the law forbidding sex discrimination contains important exemptions for religious institutions. Federal law itself permits "bona fide occupational qualifications" based on sex, and usually the exemptions are voluntary. But courts have said that the free exercise clause of the Constitution requires courts to refrain from adjudicating sex discrimination suits by ministers against the church or religious institution employing them—even though ministers could certainly complain of assault or rape.[7]

---

5. See *EEOC v. Catholic University of America*, 856 F. Supp. 1 (DDC 1994), affirmed, 83 F.2d 455 (DC Cir. 1994).

6. *Bollard v. California Province of the Society of Jesus*, 1998 US Dist. LEXIS 7563 (May 15, 1998).

7. See, e.g., *Young v. Northern Illinois Conference of United Methodist Church*, 21 F.3d 184 (7th Cir. 1994).

In the religious context, this principle of religious immunity from secular law has been read quite broadly, to apply to lay employees of institutions (including high schools and universities) whose primary duties consist of spreading the faith or supervising religious rituals.[8]

As I have suggested, the resulting doctrine is a puzzle in light of the fact that almost no one believes that, in general, religious organizations can be exempted from most of the law forbidding civil and criminal wrongs. The puzzle is not only obvious but also important, for there is good reason to believe that some of the most pernicious forms of sex discrimination are a result of the practices of religious institutions, which can produce internalized norms of subordination.[9] Those internalized norms might undermine equality of opportunity itself, as when women scale back their aspirations to conform to those internalized norms. As Okin emphasized in many places, people's preferences, especially in the domain of sex equality, should not be taken as given nor as coming from the sky; discriminatory beliefs and role-based choices are often produced by a discriminatory society. Religious practices often contribute a great deal to such beliefs and choices, on the part of men and women alike. In such circumstances, it is not even clear whether the relevant preferences are authentically "theirs." As Okin also emphasized, the remedy of "exit"—the right of women to leave a religious group or order—is crucial, but in practice it may not be available. Indeed, exit will not be sufficient when girls have been taught in such a way as to be unable or unwilling to scrutinize the practices with which they have grown up. Here in particular, the ideal of equal opportunity is compromised.

There is a further problem. Seemingly isolated decisions of individual women may help to establish and reproduce norms of inequality that are injurious to other women. Women interested in sex equality therefore face a collective action problem; rational acts by individual women can help to sustain discriminatory norms. To say the least, it is not obvious how a liberal society should respond to this problem. But some measures prohibiting sex discrimination may make things better.

THE *SMITH* PRINCIPLE: GENERALITY AND ADMINISTRABILITY

To answer the underlying question, and to understand the asymmetry principle, it is necessary to step back a bit and offer some more general words about the relationship between constitutional law and religious institutions. In the United States, there is a sharp and continuing debate about whether a state may apply "facially neutral" laws to religious institutions.[10] A law is facially neutral if it does not specifically aim at religious practices or beliefs; thus, a law requiring the payment of taxes, or banning the burning of animals or the use of peyote is facially neutral, whereas a law banning the Lord's Prayer, or the practice of Buddhism, is facially discriminatory.

---

8. *EEOC v. Catholic University of America*, 83 F.2d 455 (DC Cir. 1994).

9. To say this is not to deny that norms of sex equality are often an outgrowth of religious beliefs as well, nor is it to offer a general view about whether the world's religions promote or deny sex equality; it is doubtful that any general view would make much sense.

10. Michael McConnell, "Free Exercise Revisionism and the Smith Decision," *University of Chicago Law Review* 57 (1990): 1109; Abner Greene, "The Political Balance of the Religion Clauses," *Yale Law Journal* 102 (1993): 1611.

Under current law in the United States, any facially neutral law is presumed to be constitutionally acceptable.[11] The validity of all facially neutral laws may be deemed the *Smith principle*, after the highly controversial Supreme Court decision that established it. Congress attempted to "overrule" *Smith* with the Religious Freedom Restoration Act, which would have required the state to provide a strong secular justification for any law that burdened religion, even if the law was neutral on its face; but the Court struck down the Religious Freedom Restoration Act as beyond legislative power.[12]

The *Smith* principle seems to be undergirded by two distinct ideas. The first involves an understanding of the relationship between liberty and the political safeguards that are expected to accompany democratic processes: a secular law that is neutral on its face is highly unlikely to interfere with religious liberty, properly conceived. The reason is that the democratic process is a sufficient safeguard against laws that are facially neutral but oppressive. The very neutrality (and hence generality) of such laws guarantees against oppressiveness, for when a number of groups are subject to oppressive laws, they are likely to mobilize against them and to prevent their enactment (unless there are very good reasons for them). But if a law is narrowly tailored so as to discriminate against a particular group—no public religious services for Catholics or Buddhists, for example—the ordinary political safeguards are not in play. By emphasizing the value of such safeguards and their relevance to constitutional law, *Smith* is connected with long-standing liberal themes, suggesting that a requirement of generality provides a political check on unjustified interferences with freedom.

The second basis for the *Smith* principle is one of judicial *administrability*: even if some facially neutral laws raise serious questions in principle, it is very hard to administer a test for constitutionality (or political legitimacy) that would require a kind of balancing of the opposing interests. Suppose, for example, that courts ruled that burdens on religious liberty are justified if and only if the secular reason for the burdens outweighs the intrusion on religion. We can imagine some easy cases here. A neutral tax law, for example, would almost certainly be upheld against the objection that it intrudes on the religious convictions of some, because a tax system would be very hard to run if religious objectors could exempt themselves. But many cases would be exceedingly hard for courts to handle, simply because of the difficulty of balancing the claims on both sides. The best defense of the *Smith* principle is that, even if it protects religious liberty too little, it comes close to protecting religious liberty enough—and it does so with the only principle that real world institutions can apply fairly and easily.

Under the *Smith* principle, facially neutral laws are legitimate, even if they interfere with religious liberty. A straightforward reading of the principle would suggest that, no less than

---

11. *Employment Division, Department of Human Services v. Smith*, 494 US 872 (1990). Technically, Smith holds that a facially neutral law will be upheld so long as it has a "rational basis," unless it is discriminatorily motivated. The Court did not overrule *Sherbert v. Verner*, 374 US 398 (1963) (holding that a state may not deny unemployment benefits to a Seventh-Day Adventist who was fired because she would not work on Saturday) nor *Wisconsin v. Yoder*, 406 US 205 (1972) (allowing Amish teenagers to be exempted from a requirement of school attendance until the age of 16); but it did read those cases extremely narrowly. It should be noted that the *Smith* decision was surprising as well as controversial, and it remains an object of continuing debate, not only in political and academic circles but also within the Supreme Court itself.

12. *City of Boerne v. Flores*, 117 S. Ct. 2157 (1997).

other neutral measures, laws forbidding discrimination can properly be applied to religious institutions. Hence, the asymmetry thesis is not at all compelled by the *Smith* principle. The strongest challenges to the principle are that many facially neutral laws do impose substantial burdens on religion; that they lack sufficient liberal justification; and that institutions, including judicial institutions, should not be deemed incapable of drawing the appropriate lines. I am not at all sure, but I would guess that in general, Okin would approve of the *Smith* principle insofar as it refuses to offer special protections for religious organizations and allows them to be subjected to the ordinary criminal and civil law that all other institutions must obey. Indeed, we might even see the *Smith* principle as an implicit recognition of the force of some of Okin's claims about the liberty-denying potential of certain groups.

LEGAL POSSIBILITIES

With this background, let us now turn to the reasons that a state might be permitted to apply ordinary civil and criminal law to religious institutions, but be proscribed from applying the law of sex discrimination to such institutions. Let us see, in short, how the asymmetry thesis might be defended. As we have seen, asymmetry is a common practice in many nations, whether or not it is constitutionally compelled: even if governments are not required to exempt religious institutions from sex discrimination law, they often elect to do so.

Ordinary Law Is Backed by a Compelling Interest, as Sex Discrimination Law Is Not

The first possibility is that, in principle, a state should interfere with religious practices only when it has an especially strong reason for doing so (sometimes described as a "compelling interest"). The ordinary criminal and civil law provides that reason; the law that forbids sex discrimination does not. On this view, it is one thing for a state to prohibit murder or assault. It is quite another thing for a state to forbid discriminatory practices. (Note here that, in describing the liberty-denying practices of groups, Okin's emphasis is partly on invasions of bodily autonomy, not merely on discrimination as such.)

There can be no doubt that an intuition of this kind helps to explain current practice; indeed, I believe that it plays a large role in establishing the conventional wisdom and the asymmetry thesis itself. And the idea would have some force if ordinary criminal and civil law always directed itself against extremely serious harms. But it does not. The ordinary law prohibits torts that are often relatively modest (intentional infliction of emotional distress, low-level libels, minor assaults that count as such even without physical contact). The state does not apply the tort law to religious organizations only when the underlying torts impose grave injuries. Under the *Smith* principle, there is no weighing of the state's interest to assess its magnitude. (Even before that case, there was little doubt that ordinary tort law could be applied to religious groups.) For example, the law against the intentional infliction of emotional distress is entirely applicable to religious institutions. Like everyone else, priests and rabbis are not permitted to tell people, falsely, that their children have just been run over by trucks, even if those people are religious enemies.

Religious organizations are thus subject to civil and criminal law prohibiting low-level harms. Why can't the law against sex discrimination be applied as well? At first glance, the interests behind that law are important rather than trivial. It is not easy to explain why the interest in being free from sex discrimination is, in principle, weaker than the interests that underlie various aspects of ordinary civil and criminal law. Often the interest in eliminating sex discrimination appears to be far stronger than the particular interest involved in ordinary law. We have seen that, under *Smith*, governments should be permitted, at least, to apply the law of sex discrimination to religious organizations. The asymmetry principle would seem to have no authority if *Smith* is right. But governments frequently exempt religious institutions from laws forbidding sex discrimination, even though they are subject to most ordinary civil and criminal law.

Now, perhaps, it will be responded that the *Smith* principle is wrong and that, in order for the state to respect liberty, the law should not apply to religious institutions unless the state has an especially strong reason for the application. This idea lay behind the 1996 Religious Freedom Restoration Act. As we have seen, that act was invalidated by the Supreme Court in 1997 as beyond Congress's power; but it did, and does, exemplify a widely shared view about the nature of religious liberty. On that view, a degree of "balancing" is necessary: the degree of the state's intrusion into religion must be measured against the strength of the state's reason for the intrusion. A balancing test of this kind also seems compatible with Okin's approach, insofar as it emphasizes that, with respect to groups, there can be legitimate interests on both sides of the equation.

For present purposes, what is important is that, even if we reject the *Smith* principle, we need not approve of the asymmetry between the law banning sex discrimination and ordinary law. There is no reason to accept the view that ordinary law is backed by a strong or compelling interest, while the law of sex discrimination is not so backed.

Ordinary Law Does Not Strike at the Heart of Religious Liberty, as Sex Discrimination Law Often Would

It might be thought that a prohibition on sex discrimination would impose a substantial burden on religious beliefs and practices, or even strike at their heart, whereas ordinary civil and criminal law does not. On this view, the *Smith* principle is wrong; some exemptions from ordinary law are necessary from the standpoint of religious liberty.[13] The reason for any religious exemption is respect for religious autonomy—respect that can usually coexist with ordinary civil and criminal law, but not with the law forbidding sex discrimination. For some religious institutions, a secular mandate of a (controversial conception of) sex equality would be intolerable, whereas applications of ordinary law fit comfortably, in general, with their own beliefs and practices. The asymmetry thesis might be squarely defended on this ground.

The argument is not entirely without force. Sometimes, ordinary civil or criminal law is entirely consistent with the norms of religious institutions; indeed, such law often grows directly or indirectly out of religious norms. The prohibition against murder is a foundation of both religious and secular law; much of standard law can claim

13. In *EEOC v. Catholic University of America*, the court held, without much explanation, that *Smith* did not undermine previous holdings that there was an exception for ministers from the general sex discrimination law.

religious roots. It is for this reason that applications of ordinary civil and criminal law cause no trouble for most religious organizations. The use of the law's prohibitions is compatible with, even in the service of, the goals of those organizations. And it is also possible to imagine requirements of sex equality that would go against the heart of certain religious convictions; imagine a ban on sex discrimination in the priesthood. Perhaps the asymmetry thesis can be defended on the view that ordinary civil and criminal law does not compromise religious practices, whereas a ban on sex equality would do exactly that.

But in its broadest form, this argument is quite fragile. Some aspects of ordinary civil and criminal law do strike against practices and beliefs that are central to some religions. Consider, for example, the laws forbidding animal sacrifice or the use of drugs, or even laws forbidding certain kinds of assault and imprisonment. And some aspects of the law of sex discrimination interfere not at all with some religious beliefs and practices. For some religions, some of the time, sex equality is permissible or even mandatory; in any case, it is practiced.

It is conceivable that, as a class, ordinary civil laws coexist easily with most religious practices and beliefs, whereas the law of sex discrimination does not. But to the extent that this is so, it is a contingent, time-bound, highly empirical fact, one that bears little on the question of basic principles or the resolution of particular cases. If, for example, it were thought that the state could interfere with religious practices only when the interference was not serious, we could not justify a sharp asymmetry between ordinary law and the law of sex discrimination. We would have to proceed in a more fine-grained way; we would not endorse the asymmetry thesis. We would have to ask more particular questions about the relationship between the practice at issue and the legal interven-tion. In the end, the asymmetry thesis cannot be plausibly defended on the ground that ordinary law is a smaller intrusion into religious autonomy than is sex equality law.

Balancing in Support of Asymmetry

It would be possible to defend the asymmetry thesis by rejecting the *Smith* principle and with the suggestion that an appropriate test depends on both the strength and nature of the state's interest and on the extent of the adverse effect on religion. Under this approach, we might reach the following simple conclusions:

- a weak state interest (in preventing, let us suppose, not very harmful libels) is insufficient to justify any intrusion on religion at all;
- an illegitimate interest (in, say, weakening a religion hostile to the political status quo) is entirely off-limits;
- an "overriding" interest (in, for example, preventing murder) would justify any intrusion no matter how severe; and
- a strong or "compelling" interest would justify most intrusions on religion, at least if the intrusions were not very severe.

Under this approach, most cases would therefore be easy. The hardest problems would arise where a strong or compelling interest was matched by a plausible claim that the interference would seriously jeopardize the continuing functioning of the relevant religion.

In principle, a standard of this sort seems a sensible one for a democratic social order to adopt. The major problem is that, to accept it, we would have to have a high degree of confidence in those who would be entrusted with its administration. Such a standard would require courts (or other institutions) to decide which aspects of civil and criminal law were sufficiently justified. Thus, we could imagine reasonable judgments in favor of application, to religious institutions, of a legal ban on killing and torturing animals, but against application of a legal ban on peyote, on the ground that the former created a risk to third parties. The legitimacy of applying principles against sex discrimination to religious institutions would depend on an assessment of two factors: (1) the strength of the interest in those principles, and (2) the extent of the interference with religious institutions. Here too I believe that an approach of this sort is broadly compatible with Okin's general analysis.

In responding to an earlier version of this chapter, however, Okin herself raised two objections.[14] First, she contended that an approach of this kind would give religious institutions an unfortunate incentive to claim that sex discrimination is central to their own practices. Second, she objected that the approach would require courts to ask difficult interpretive questions about the extent to which a nondiscrimination requirement would be burdensome or harmful to religious institutions. Objections of this kind might seem to cast *Smith* in a more favorable light, in a way that might simply permit states to apply sex discrimination law to religious institutions. Or such objections might be used in defense of the asymmetry thesis, to suggest that courts ought simply to allow religious institutions to discriminate on the basis of sex whenever they contend, plausibly, that such discrimination is central to their own practices. But the question is whether the considerations that Okin marshals are decisive; and I do not believe that they are.

Whenever an apparently neutral practice is brought to bear against a religious institution, and the institution objects, there is an incentive to claim that the practice in question is central to the religion, and that incentive cannot by itself mean that apparently neutral laws are either always unacceptable or always legitimate. Okin's second claim is more powerful. To say the least, courts are unlikely to be in the best position to know whether sex discrimination is central to a religion. But under any regime that calls for a degree of balancing, courts will have to ask some questions that they are not ideally suited to answer. In some cases, the claim of centrality will clearly be unconvincing, simply because it will not fit with the usual practices of the religion. In other cases, it will have evident force. The hardest cases will have to be solved with presumptions and burdens of proof, in a way that is hardly unfamiliar to courts dealing with difficult constitutional problems.

Some of the trickiest issues will be evidentiary. When judges are asking the relevant questions, ought they to look at poll-type responses from believers? Ought they to make their own judgments about doctrinal centrality? What criteria are they looking for? Doctrinal centrality, by their own lights? Poll-type responses of believers? Expertise of scholars? At first glance, the judgments of genuine experts would be most

14. See Okin's "Reply," in *Is Multiculturalism Bad for Women?* (Princeton: Princeton University Press, 1999).

reliable in this context, as elsewhere. Assessments by members of the relevant religion would be most informative but also self-serving. We could imagine a set of possible responses. Perhaps those who seek to apply the law should have to demonstrate that it will not, in fact, operate against the core of a religion's beliefs. Perhaps those who seek to evade the law ought to be required to show that it would, in fact, do so. Presumptions would be unavoidable in the event of reasonable contestation.

I am not sure how Okin herself would have resolved this problem. She did believe that tax-exempt status should not be extended to the Catholic church so long as it discriminates against women in hiring and in its institutional structure.[15] But her own position was sensitive to the interests of oppressed religious groups, in a way that would further complicate the analysis. Apparently, Okin would treat oppressed groups more favorably than those that have not been oppressed. I wonder about this distinction. In my view, the fact that a religious group has itself been subject to discrimination, or oppression, is an inadequate reason to permit it to treat women as less than equal or to deny them fair equality of opportunity.

Doubtless, different outcomes would be imaginable in different contexts, and I do not mean to sort out all of the conceivable dilemmas. My basic point is that, with a balancing approach of this kind, the asymmetry between most civil and criminal law and the law banning sex discrimination could not possibly be sustained. Under the standard I am proposing, some ordinary law would not legitimately be applied to religious institutions, and some of the law banning sex discrimination could be so applied. The legal standard would force a candid assessment of the nature of the intrusion and the strength of the underlying interest—and not rest content with homilies (by no means followed with most civil and criminal law) about the legitimate autonomy of religious institutions. Indeed, the perniciousness of those homilies, for religious as for other organizations, is what Okin was concerned to expose; and if I am right, the exposure has important implications for law.

CONCLUSIONS

I offer three simple conclusions:

1. There is a plausible rationale for the view that a democratic social order should accept all laws that do not discriminate on their face against religious institutions and practices. This principle would authorize the application to those institutions of most civil and criminal law and also of laws forbidding sex discrimination. Though plausible, this principle is not in the end acceptable, because it would allow the state to subject religious institutions to laws that substantially burden those institutions, or even strike at their heart, without at the same time serving a sufficiently important governmental purpose.

---

15. Susan Okin, "Multiculturalism and Feminism: No Simple Question, No Simple Answers," in Avigail Eisenberg and Jeff Spinner-Halev, eds., *Minorities within Minorities* (Cambridge: Cambridge University Press, 2005).

2. It is not only plausible but also correct to say that a liberal social order should disallow facially neutral laws if they (a) interfere in a significant way with religious practices or impose a substantial burden on religious institutions, and (b) are not supported by a legitimate and sufficiently strong justification. But this idea does not support a categorical distinction between ordinary civil and criminal law and laws forbidding sex discrimination. In many cases, the idea would allow religious institutions to immunize themselves from ordinary law, but forbid them from immunizing themselves from the law prohibiting discrimination on the basis of sex.

3. There is no plausible rationale for the view, embodied in the practice of many democratic nations, that it is unproblematic to apply ordinary civil and criminal law to religious institutions, but that it is problematic to apply, to those institutions, laws forbidding sex discrimination.

These conclusions mean that there is no *general* barrier to applying such laws to religious institutions. Whether it is legitimate to do so depends on the extent of the interference with religious convictions and the strength of the state's justification. Reasonable people can reach different conclusions about particular cases. There is a constant question about judicial administration. But it would follow that, in at least some of the cases traced above, the religious practice would have to yield. In the long run, acceptance of this conclusion, and rejection of the asymmetry thesis, would be likely, I think, to have significant implications for democratic theory and practice.

PART III

FEMINISM AND CULTURAL DIVERSITY

8

What We Owe Women

The View from Multicultural Feminism

Ayelet Shachar

In her seminal essay "Is Multiculturalism Bad for Women?" Susan Moller Okin made two main arguments: first, she charged that advocates of group rights paid little or no attention to the private sphere—especially the realm of domestic or family life.[1] This was a grave mistake, she argued, because many of the *gendered* aspects of culture and religion become visible once we focus on the regulation of marriage, divorce, and other aspects of family life. Second, she claimed, "most cultures have as one of their principal aims the control of women by men." As some of you will know, I absolutely agree with Okin's observation about the importance of studying the family as a crucial site for illustrating (and understanding) the potential tensions between religious accommodation and gender equality, or what I have elsewhere called the *paradox of multicultural vulnerability*.[2] However, I equally passionately disagree with her second claim, namely, that "'culture' and 'tradition' are so closely linked with the control of women that they are virtually equated."[3] I believe Okin's appraisal here is both erroneous as a matter of fact and interpretation. This wedge between us leads to a substantive divergence in our judgment calls. Okin has famously contended that "*no* argument can be made on the basis of self-respect or freedom that the female members of the culture have a clear interest in its preservation."[4] I respectfully disagree. So long as women's citizenship guarantees remain firmly in place, there are circumstances under which a degree of regulated interaction between secular and religious sources of law and identity may contribute to (rather than inhibit) the improvement of women's equality and dignity under both systems, affording them an opportunity to express their commitment to both.

To press the distinctions between these positions, I will explore the acrimonious debate that recently broke out in Canada following a proposal to establish a "Private Islamic Court of Justice" (*darul-qada*) to resolve family law disputes among consenting adults according to Shari'a principles. This proposal did not

---

1. Susan Moller Okin, "Is Multiculturalism Bad for Women?" *Boston Review* (1997), reprinted in Joshua Cohen, Matthew Howard, and Martha C. Nussbaum, eds., *Is Multiculturalism Bad for Women?* (Princeton, NJ: Princeton University Press, 1999) (hereafter *IMBFW*), 12.

2. I devote considerable attention to these themes in Shachar, *Multicultural Jurisdictions: Cultural Differences and Women's Rights* (Cambridge: Cambridge University Press, 2001).

3. *IMBFW*, 14.

4. *IMBFW*, 22.

come to the fore in the usual way, through democratic deliberation, constitutional amendment, or a standard law-reform process. Instead, a small and relatively conservative nongovernmental organization, called the Canadian Society of Muslims, declared in a series of press releases its intention to establish the said *darul-qada*, or Shari'a tribunal, as this proposal came to be known in the ensuing debate.[5] In a nutshell, their idea was to rely upon a *preexisting* legal framework, the Arbitration Act, which (at the time) permitted a wide array of family-law disputes to be resolved under its considerably open-ended terms. The envisioned tribunal would have permitted consenting parties not only to enter a less adversarial, out-of-court dispute-resolution process, but also to use the Act's *choice of law* provisions to apply religious norms to resolve family disputes, according to the "laws (*fiqh*) of any [Islamic] school, e.g., Shiah or Sunni (Hanafi, Shafi'i, Hambali, or Maliki)."[6]

My point of departure in assessing this proposal is a grounded commitment toward respecting women's identity and membership interests *as well as* their dignity and equality. I then ask what is owed to those women whose legal dilemmas (at least in the family arena) often arise from the fact that their lives are *already* affected by the interplay between overlapping systems of identification, authority, and belief. Ignoring this multiplicity of affiliations may be compatible with a model of strict separation between state and religion, but it misses the mark for these embedded individuals. In the following pages, I offer an alternative to the conventional view that a clear line can (and should) be drawn between public and private, official and unofficial, secular and religious, or positive law and traditional practice. Counter-intuitively, I argue that the prospect of *regulated interaction* (rather than mere adherence to strict separation) may provide a better response to the real-life dilemmas that arise from the complex relationship among women, religion/culture, and the state. In this richer conception of law and identity, individuals and families should be afforded greater options to express both their citizenship and group membership, rather than be forced to sacrifice one for the sake of the other.

The discussion proceeds in two main parts. It opens with a typology of three different approaches to the "claims of culture" (to borrow from Seyla Benhabib's terminology).[7] These schools of thought I label, for the sake of clarity and simplicity, as liberal feminism, postcolonial feminism, and multicultural feminism. I highlight Susan Moller Okin's path-breaking contribution to the first school of thought (liberal feminism), as well as her influence on the two other approaches identified here: postcolonial and multicultural feminism. The second part moves from theory to practice. It interrogates the Shari'a tribunal debate in order to raise a slew of important questions for our conception of citizenship in contemporary societies in the context of a wider trend toward the privatization of justice in the realm of family law. Consider the following examples: should a court be permitted to enforce a civil divorce contract that also has a religious aspect, namely, a promise by a Jewish husband to remove all barriers to remarriage by

---

5. See Syed Mumtaz Ali, "Establishing an Institute for Islamic Justice (Darul Qada)," *Canadian Society of Muslims News Bulletin,* October 2002.

6. Ali, "Establishing an Institute for Islamic Justice (Darul Qada)."

7. See Seyla Benhabib, *The Claims of Culture: Equality and Diversity in the Global Era* (Princeton, NJ: Princeton University Press, 2002).

granting his wife the religious *get* (Jewish divorce decree)? Is it legitimate to establish private religious tribunals—as alternative dispute resolution forums—in which consenting adults arbitrate family-law disputes according to the parties' religious personal laws in lieu of the state's secular family laws? And, is there room for considerations of culture, religion, national origin, or linguistic identity in determining a child's best interests in cases of custody, visitation, education, and so on? None of these examples are hypothetical. They represent actual legal challenges raised in recent years by individuals and families who are seeking to redefine the place of culture and religion in their own private ordering and, indirectly, in the larger polity as well.

In exploring these sensitive issues, I place at center stage the challenges faced by religious women who may wish—or feel bound—to follow the requirements of divorce according to their community of faith, in addition to the rules of the state, in order to remove barriers to remarriage. Without the removal of such barriers, their ability to build new families, if not their very membership status (or that of their children), may be adversely affected. This is particularly true for Muslim and Jewish women living in secular societies who have entered into the marital relationship through a religious ceremony—as permitted by law in many jurisdictions. For them, a civil divorce is merely part of the story; it does not, and cannot, dissolve the religious aspect of the relationship. Failure to recognize their split-status position—namely, that of being legally divorced according to state law, though still married according to their faith tradition—may leave these women prey to abuse by recalcitrant husbands who are well aware of the adverse effect this situation has on their wives, as they fall between the cracks of the civil and religious jurisdictions. In what follows, I elucidate the core arguments of each theoretical approach and then explain how they differ from one another in their treatment of such real-life dilemmas.[8]

RECENT DEVELOPMENTS: THREE VARIANTS OF THE FEMINIST CRITIQUE OF MULTICULTURALISM

In mapping the terrain of the feminist critique of multiculturalism, it is helpful to begin our journey with one of the most well-established schools of thought in feminist theory: liberal feminism.

Liberal Feminism

The overarching goal of liberal feminism always has been, as Alison Jaggar puts it, "the application of liberal principles to women as well as men. Most obviously, this means that laws should not grant to women fewer rights than they allow to men."[9] The claim that women deserve equal rights as free and equal beings who are capable

---

8. The following section draws upon Ayelet Shachar, "Feminism and Multiculturalism: Mapping the Terrain," in Anthony Simon Laden and David Owen, eds., *Multiculturalism and Political Theory* (Cambridge: Cambridge University Press, 2007), 115–147.

9. Alison M. Jaggar, *Feminist Politics and Human Nature* (Lanham, MD: Rowman and Littlefield, 1988), 35.

of self-determination and a sense of justice is far from trivial. It becomes truly radical, though, when it calls for the complete erasure of gender-biased norms and practices, especially in situations where women were never given a chance to define these norms and practices in the first place.[10] In the debate over feminism and multiculturalism, the latter variant of the liberal feminist position is most effectively articulated in Susan Moller Okin's writings. Her work will therefore serve as a representative of the liberal feminist approach in general.

I believe that Okin's most significant contribution to the debate concerning the relationship between feminism and multiculturalism has been to provoke an extremely important and lively debate; like a true trailblazer, she put herself on the line in challenging what she viewed as an emerging orthodoxy of support for multiculturalism. To counter this view, Okin called our attention to the potentially gendered impacts of respecting cultural or religious diversity. She emphasized in particular the need to be vigilant to extant patterns of discrimination against women and girls in the so-called private domain of family life. More provocatively, she asked whether group rights are part of the solution, or rather, as she saw it, an exacerbation of the problem of gender inequality within minority communities. The core themes advanced by Okin (perhaps excluding the latter point) appear to fit squarely within the canons of liberal feminist theory. Why, then, have so many people responded so critically to the claims made by Okin in "Is Multiculturalism Bad for Women?"[11] Three main reasons may help to explain this response. The first deals with the oversimplified conception of culture and religion found in Okin's writings, which, when challenged, also sheds doubt on her conclusions regarding the incompatibility of multiculturalism and feminism. The second focuses on the perception of female group members as ultimately co-opted, if not downright "brainwashed," individuals who cannot reasonably and genuinely wish to preserve their cultural or religious identity.[12] Within this perspective, it becomes normatively undesirable to even strive to promote *both* the value of gender equality *and* cultural/religious diversity. The third reason for the strong reaction to Okin's "verbal grenade," as she herself put it,[13] concerns the pattern of binary oppositions that underpins her analytical framework: these oppositions can be crudely summarized as a dichotomy between "us" (western freedom-and-equality lovers) versus "them" (barbaric "others" who have no respect for women's rights or dignity).[14] This leaves

10. See Rosenblum's chapter in this volume.

11. Susan Moller Okin, "Is Multiculturalism Bad for Women?" *Boston Review* (1997), reprinted in Joshua Cohen, Matthew Howard, and Martha C. Nussbaum, eds., *Is Multiculturalism Bad for Women?* (Princeton, NJ: Princeton University Press, 1999) (hereafter *IMBFW*).

12. *IMBFW*, 24.

13. See Susan Moller Okin, "Is Multiculturalism Bad for Women? Continuing the Conversation," in Deen Chatterjee, ed., *Feminism, Multiculturalism, and Group Rights* (Oxford: Oxford University Press, forthcoming).

14. See *IMBFW*, 15. This dichotomy takes many forms, "liberals" in contrast to "nonliberals," "those who consider ourselves politically progressive" versus "those who look to the past," "feminists" versus "multiculturalists." The contrast also appears to be between the "West and the Rest," as Homi Bhabha succinctly put it. See Bhabha, "Liberalism's Sacred Cow," in Cohen, Howard, and Nussbaum, eds., *Is Multiculturalism Bad for Women?* 82.

Okin's framework of analysis open to the charge (made by postcolonial feminists) that she misguidedly places the blame for cross-cultural patterns of sexism and patriarchy on the already belligerent and marginalized "foreigner." Each of these ideas merits more detailed discussion.

In her original essay on this topic, Okin argued forcefully that "group rights are potentially, and in many cases actually, antifeminist."[15] She asserted that "most cultures have as one of their principal aims the control of women by men."[16] In support of this, Okin provided an eclectic collection of examples, drawn primarily from secondary sources, to reach the following ultimate conclusion:

> It is by no means clear, then, from a feminist point of view, that minority group rights are "part of the solution." They may well exacerbate the problem. In the case of a more patriarchal minority culture in the context of a less patriarchal majority culture, no argument can be made on the basis of self-respect and freedom that the female members of the culture have a clear interest in its preservation. Indeed, they *might* be much better off if the culture into which they were born were either to become extinct (so that its members would become integrated into the less sexist surrounding culture)…[17]

While I admire Okin's unflagging commitment to promoting women's rights, my main disagreement here concerns her secularist outsider-looking-in portrayal of culture and religion: this portrayal is characterized by a deep suspicion of the value of religion and culture for human flourishing.[18] Okin makes sweeping generalizations in this vein, such as the following: "much of most cultures is about controlling women."[19] She further contends that "virtually all cultures, past and present," display as one of their *principal* aims the control of women and the restriction of their freedom.[20] Such statements make the argument both descriptively inaccurate and normatively hard to swallow for anyone who attaches value to cultural membership and religious identity.

Equally important, this distorted conception leads to an overly simplistic allocation of blame. Tellingly, Okin attributes imbalances between men and women to "certain aspects of the *content* of the [minority] cultures,"[21] rather surprisingly neglecting context, history, and processes of internal contestation and cross-communal interaction. Similarly, she pays little attention to the macro-level factors, such as the division of powers between the state and the group, access to justice, and the structure of deliberation processes which may have dramatic impact on the type and scope of

---

15. *IMBFW*, 10. See also Susan Moller Okin, "Feminism and Multiculturalism: Some Tensions," *Ethics* 108 (1998): 661–684.

16. *IMBFW*, 13.

17. *IMBFW*, 22.

18. Okin is not alone in reaching this conclusion. See, for example, Frances Raday, "Culture, Religion, and Gender," *International Journal of Constitutional Law* 1 (2003): 663–715; Courtney W. Howland, ed., *Religious Fundamentalism and the Human Rights of Women* (New York: St. Martin's, 1999).

19. Okin, "Feminism and Multiculturalism," 667.

20. Okin, "Feminism and Multiculturalism," 678.

21. Okin, "Feminism and Multiculturalism," 664 (emphasis in original).

rights, protections, and opportunities that women can enjoy in practice.[22] Finally, Okin apparently believes that, while significant changes in the gender norms of the majority culture in Western societies have occurred as a result of human agency and resistance, no comparable potential for substantive egalitarian reform exists for minority cultures.[23]

But this assessment is not fully supported by the facts. There are numerous examples of female members of the more conservative branches of "reactive" religious communities, such as Orthodox Judaism or revivalist Islam, who challenge their own traditions from within. This has been achieved by offering more gender-egalitarian reinterpretations of sacred texts in Jewish orthodox law (halakha), or by appealing to general principles of shari'a (such as compassion and justice) in lieu of a technical reading of the tenets of Islamic law.[24] Indeed, most religious communities do recognize that at least part of their tradition is a construct of human, legal origin. It is this aspect of a religious tradition that women and other agents of reform can find conducive to amendment and reinterpretation.

Clearly, feminist activists within conservative religious communities face towering obstacles. For instance, they must gain access to the tradition's centers of study and convince other group members that their voice is both valid and "authentic." Furthermore, in order to gain full legitimacy, they must garner support from at least some respected authorities in the religious establishment. This is the case because internal reforms must by definition derive from revisionist readings and innovative methods of reinterpretation of the tradition.[25] Proposals for such alternative readings are often made in the face of resistance by representatives of the more established strands of interpretation, who, under extreme circumstances, may seek to define any innovation

22. Much has been written on discursive and deliberative democracy in this context. See, for example, Seyla Benhabib, *The Claims of Culture: Equality and Diversity in the Global Era* (Princeton, NJ: Princeton University Press, 2002); Monique Deveaux, "A Deliberative Approach to Conflicts of Culture," *Political Theory* 31 (2003): 780–807; John S. Dryzek, "Deliberative Democracy in Divided Societies: Alternatives to Agonism and Analgesia," *Political Theory* 33 (2005): 218–242.

23. Although Okin seems to acknowledge the possibility for change in the power balance within the minority community, she does not take seriously this possibility in her substantive analysis of the relations between feminism and multiculturalism. Instead, women who participate in minority group traditions appear as victims of such extreme socialization that they are represented as having little or no agency in Okin's account. As she puts it: women living in minority cultures are "socializ[ed] into inferior roles, resulting in lack of self-esteem or a sense of entitlement." Okin, "Feminism and Multiculturalism," 675. She further contends that "older women often become co-opted into reinforcing gender inequality." "Feminism and Multiculturalism," 680.

24. For more on this rich body of literature, see, e.g., Susannah Heschel, ed., *On Being a Jewish Feminist*, 2nd ed. (New York: Schocken, 1995); Amina Wadud, *Qur'an and Women: Rereading the Sacred Text from a Woman's Perspective* (New York: Oxford University Press, 1999; first published in Kuala Lumpur, Malaysia: Penerbit Bakati Sdn. Bhd., 1992); A. Barlas, *Believing Women in Islam: Unreading Patriarchal Interpretations of the Qur'an* (Austin: University of Texas Press, 2002).

25. For instance, there is an ongoing debate in Islamic jurisprudence over the methods of reinterpretation, which focuses on the question of whether the "gates of *ijtihad*" have remained open. If this interpretive method is available (i.e., if *ijtihad* still permits the human endeavor of reaching conclusions about the shari'a, the divine law), then internal change and reinterpretation, including feminist reinterpretation, more readily becomes a possibility.

as "corruptive." These hard-liners may genuinely fear the corruption of the identity, if not the very dissolution, of the minority culture. But reformers may also face opposition from established leaders within the group for more prosaic reasons: for instance, this may occur in situations where the call to adopt a more egalitarian interpretation of the tradition is seen as a threat to the existing structure of authority.

These are daunting challenges, which cannot be underestimated. Yet I mention them here because they clearly illustrate that the assertion that, no argument can be made on the basis of self-respect and freedom that the female members of the culture have a clear interest in its preservation, fails to persuade unless one assumes that women who uphold their communal membership are by definition without choice and agency.[26] When this is echoed by Okin's suggestion that cultural extinction might be a relevant "solution," it becomes clear that her view of the relations between culture and equality cannot account for the potential value and meaning that women may attach to membership in a cultural or religious community. Such value may exist even in communities that systematically impose unfair moral and legal costs upon women, which ultimately make them more vulnerable.

Based on this analysis, the liberal feminist tradition maintains that minority women must be freed from the "shackles" of tradition, culture, and communal identity in order to flourish. This leads to a misguided conclusion: by valuing their communal membership, women have somehow implicitly lost the ability to understand the gendered power inequalities that they face, or have surrendered the will to fight against such injustices. Neither of these claims is tenable, however, if we reject the notion that culture and equality stand in inherent opposition to one another. Unfortunately, this binary opposition seems to inform much of the liberal feminist critique of multiculturalism. Taken to its ultimate logical conclusion, this position represents a *tout court* rejection of the very rationale for accommodating cultural diversity.

Postcolonial Feminism

The second variation on the theme of feminism and multiculturalism draws upon the academic inquiry of postcolonial discourse, sociolegal scholarship, and critical race theory. The postcolonial feminist critique is generally associated with a rejection of simplistic and uncritical understandings of culture, providing instead a critical reading of mainstream depictions of racialized minority identities and practices.[27] But this critique goes deeper. Authors such as Uma Narayan argue that group leaders also contribute to the problem: although they claim to speak for the entire edifice of "our culture," these leaders actually actively exclude "the voices, concerns, and contributions of many who are members of the national and political community."[28] Postcolonial discourse also brings a number of unique elements to the contemporary debate about

26. A similar line of argument is advanced by Martha Nussbaum, "A Plea for Difficulty," in Cohen, Howard, and Nussbaum, eds., *Is Multiculturalism Bad for Women?*

27. See Leti Volpp, "Blaming Culture for Bad Behavior," *Yale Journal of Law and the Humanities* 12 (2000): 89–116.

28. Uma Narayan, *Dislocating Cultures: Identities, Traditions, and Third World Women* (New York: Routledge, 1997), 10.

feminism and multiculturalism. One key element is that it challenges the juxtaposition of the "enlightened" West against the "barbaric" other. This juxtaposition, it is argued, reflects an orientalist perspective, with its degrading and stereotyped perception of nonwhite, nonwestern cultures and peoples.[29]

The tendency to frame multicultural discussion in this way is particularly evident in the legal system. As one scholar notes, "When faced with cultural questions, the legal system often produces distorted and questionable versions of the content of non-mainstream cultures. At the same time, it paints an equally distorted, but often more flattering picture, of the mainstream."[30] Scholars like Lama Abu-Odeh have criticized this distorting tendency by comparing, for example, the legal treatment of "crimes of honor" in the Arab world with "crimes of passion" in the United States (both involve the killing of women by male partners or family members). For Abu-Odeh, there are deep similarities "between the internal tensions within each legal system as to what constitutes a killing of women is legally tolerated (either fully or partially)."[31] The argument here is that we cannot simply assume, in Abu-Odeh's words, "the superiority of the American judicial system" in comparison to other parts of the world in addressing "the problem everywhere [of] men kill[ing] their wives."[32]

Other authors have similarly argued that the most successful claims for accommodation in the criminal law context—where defendants have invoked the traditions of their culture to explain or mitigate their actions—have been those that have employed gendered stereotypes that are familiar to judges, precisely because they are prevalent in the majority society.[33] In other words, they claim that courts are willing to recognize "cultural" factors for minority defendants only when they resonate with mainstream gendered norms. Anne Phillips eloquently summarizes the point: "in the end, it is the sameness not the difference that matters."[34]

The general lesson to be drawn from this observation is that those who are engaged in the feminism and multiculturalism debate must be cautious in their assessment of

29. By the term "orientalist," I am referring here to the charge that "Western power, especially the power to enter or examine other countries at will, enables the production of knowledge about other cultures." This production of knowledge, on balance, tends be negative: it is "stereotyping, Othering, dominatory." See Laura Chrisman and Patrick Williams, "Colonial Discourse and Post-Colonial Theory: An Introduction," in Laura Chrisman and Patrick Williams, eds., *Colonial Discourse and Post-Colonial Theory* (New York: Columbia University Press, 1994), 8.

30. Sonia N. Lawrence, "Cultural (In)Sensitivity: The Dangers of a Simplistic Approach to Culture in the Courtroom," *Canadian Journal of Women and the Law* 13 (2001): 111.

31. Lama Abu-Odeh, "Comparatively Speaking: The 'Honor' of the 'East' and the 'Passion' of the 'West,'" *Utah Law Review* 2 (1997): 290.

32. Abu-Odeh, "Comparatively Speaking," 307.

33. See, for example, Daina C. Chiu, "The Cultural Defense: Beyond Exclusion, Assimilation, and Guilty Liberalism," *California Law Review* 82 (1994): 1053–1125; Leti Volpp, "(Mis)identifying Culture: Asian Women and the 'Cultural Defense,'" *Harvard Women's Law Journal* 17 (1994): 54–101; Sarah Song, "Majority Norms and Minority Practices: Reexamining the 'Cultural Defense' in American Criminal Law," paper presented at the American Political Science Association Annual Meeting, 2002.

34. Anne Phillips, "When Culture Means Gender: Issues of Cultural Defense in the English Courts," *Modern Law Review* 66 (2003): 529. A similar theme is advanced by Austin Sarat and Roger Berkowitz, "Disorderly Differences: Recognition, Accommodation, and American Law," *Yale Journal of Law and the Humanities* 6 (1994): 285–316.

the violations of women's rights within minority communities, lest they contribute to the broader cultural processes that tend to marginalize, judge, and relegate minority practices to the realm of the exotic, irrational, and "passionate." This line of argument leads the postcolonial feminist to policy conclusions that are not dissimilar from those of liberal feminists (this is perhaps surprising, considering that the latter are a favorite target for the former's sharp pens). This convergence occurs because the postcolonial feminist is ultimately hard-pressed to find any good reason to support the accommodation of cultural and religious diversity—the hallmark of multiculturalism—given her fear that such accommodation may turn into a double-edged sword, reconstituting anyone who is "different" as less than equal.

The irony is that, by focusing almost exclusively on sexual violence, abuse, and murder committed by members of minority groups, postcolonial feminists are themselves unwitting participants in the production of an impoverished, not to mention pejorative, notion of cultural and legal pluralism. This leads to another issue: clearly, these scholars see the legal system as implicated in the abuse of culture. The opportunistic defense lawyer, for example, who will use every maneuver that is permissible within the bounds of zealous advocacy to get her client off the hook will often be complicit in reifying a damaging, degrading, and inaccurate description of minority cultures.

In this, the postcolonial theorists surely do have a point. However, no card-holding multicultural theorist (think of Will Kymlicka's work, for example) would defend a policy of accommodation if it failed to address the underlying causes of injustice that give rise to the claims of group-differentiated rights in the first place. What is more, anyone who has ever read Catharine MacKinnon's work would balk at the simplistic suggestion that, by merely adopting formal gender-equality laws, any liberal-democratic (or other) country will miraculously see the deeply entrenched power hierarchies of gender subordination evaporate into thin air. In other words, it is unlikely that most multiculturalists would defend the "abuses of culture" that postcolonial feminists rightly criticize. Furthermore, adamant feminists such as Okin hardly need a reminder that the majority of women have not yet achieved full equality in most, if not all, countries in the world; she and others of her generation have in fact devoted almost their entire professional lives to establishing this very claim.

Despite these critical observations, I believe that the postcolonial feminist critique of multiculturalism offers illuminating insights insofar as it flags the danger of overgeneralizing about the inevitably complex relations of culture and gender. However, given this critique's almost exclusive focus on crimes of sexual violence, spousal abuse, and so-called honor or passion killings (in which the accused seeks individual exemption on the basis of culture), it remains to be seen how its core arguments hold up when applied to a broader range of requests for group-based accommodation in social arenas such as education, linguistic diversity, resource development, or religious arbitration.

Multicultural Feminism

The third perspective, multicultural feminism, is a more recent development. It has evolved as a response to the surge of pro-identity-group literature since the 1990s and the liberal feminist critique thereof. While rejecting the strong versions of both of these discourses, it develops elements of each. Unlike the overemphasis on group identity manifested by first-wave multiculturalism, or the liberal feminist tendency to fail to recognize the value of identity and community for the religiously devout, multicultural feminism treats women as *both* culture-bearers and rights-bearers.

Also learning from the postcolonial critique, multicultural feminists reject simplistic definitions of "culture" that assume that minority communities offer unified, uncontested narratives of tradition, which are "pure," "authentic," or unaffected by their social context. Instead, they argue that identity groups, which today petition the state for special accommodation, have already been touched by the operation of that same state. Indeed, some of the most strict and so-called traditionalist or fundamentalist readings of religious texts can be interpreted as modern, revivalist responses to ongoing intercommunal interactions, which often occur under conditions that are unfavorable to the minority community.[35]

By adopting this more explicitly political conception of culture and identity, multicultural feminists dismantle the liberal feminist notion that the only way to promote women's rights in a diverse society is to minimize the effect of religion (or other sources of communal identity) on their lives. Differently put, multicultural feminists do not believe in an ideal of a culture-blind society as the preferred solution. They do share liberal feminist concerns about unequal power relations within minority communities and the potential for encroaching on women's hard-won citizenship entitlements that may occur if a state adopts strong accommodation measures.[36] But this leads them to different conclusions. For instance, the multicultural feminist believes that greater promise is found in freeing up a space for internal diversity to flourish within minority communities. This may be done, for example, by generating legal/institutional conditions that promote such openness, or by allowing women (and other historically at-risk members) access to, and a secure voice in, decision-making processes that involve their cultural and religious communities.[37] Indeed, part of the optimism encapsulated in the multicultural feminist approach relies on granting more credence to minority women's agency, as well as a voice in navigating the complex intersection of gender and culture in their lived experience.[38] This perspective also delves deeper into the relationship between gender/sexuality and the construction of collective group (and national) identity.[39]

---

35. For further discussion, see Marie Aimee Hélie-Lucas, "The Preferential Symbol for Islamic Identity: Women in Muslim Personal Laws," in Valentine M. Moghadam, ed., *Identity Politics and Women: Cultural Reassertions and Feminisms in International Perspective* (Boulder, CO: Westview, 1994), 391–407.

36. See Ayelet Shachar, "Group Identity and Women's Rights in Family Law: The Perils of Multicultural Accommodation," *Journal of Political Philosophy* 6 (1998): 285–305.

37. See Deveaux, "A Deliberative Approach to Conflicts of Culture"; Madhavi Sunder, "Piercing the Veil," *Yale Law Journal* 112 (2003): 1399–1472.

38. This theme is also developed in the work of authors such as Narayan, *Dislocating Cultures;* and Patricia Jeffery and Amrita Basu, *Appropriating Gender: Women's Activism and Politicized Religion in South Asia* (New York: Routledge, 1997).

39. For more on this growing body of literature, see the influential contributions of Nira Yuval-Davis and Floya Anthias, eds., *Woman-Nation-State* (London: Macmillan, 1989); and Anne McClintock, *Imperial Leather: Race, Gender and Sexuality in the Colonial Context* (New York: Routledge, 1995). See also Deniz Kandiyoti, ed., *Women, Islam and the State* (London: Macmillan, 1991); Moghadam, ed., *Identity Politics and Women.*

Because of their sensitivity to the political context in which the claims of culture are manifested, defenders of multicultural feminism treat with suspicion the liberal feminist view of religion or tradition as internally static or irredeemably patriarchal. At the same time, they also reject the almost wholesale dismissal of culture by some postcolonial critics, who ultimately appear to believe that religion is no more than "the opiate of the people," as Karl Marx memorably put it. This conclusion will likely ring hollow, however, for a devout woman who may wish to engage in her own religious tradition at the same time as she may be struggling to reform its more hierarchical and gender-biased interpretations.

While having faith in the long-term promise of internal processes of contestation and reinterpretation, multicultural feminists also face an equally urgent task of investigating and highlighting the importance of state action (or inaction) in shaping, through law and institutional design, the context in which women can achieve their claims for equality vis-à-vis the group or the state.[40] For example, if the secular state relegates any expression of minority cultural identity to the private realm, minority women may be asked to remove any markers of identity that publicly signify their cultural or religious difference. The 2004 legislation in France that restricts the display of overt religious symbols in the public schools, which is widely interpreted as "interdicting" the *hijab* (the headscarf worn by some Muslim women), epitomizes this strict secular-absolutist approach.[41] Other polities have chosen an opposite path: granting public and binding authority to religious codes, often at the expense of curbing preexisting protections for women's rights to equality and full citizenship.[42] A dramatic example of this pattern at work is found in the recent Islamicization of family law and criminal codes in the northern states of Nigeria.[43] Neither of these institutional strategies is neutral in its effects on the status of women, a point to which I will return in the following section, which explores the controversy that unfolded in Canada over the legal standing of religious arbitration tribunals in family law disputes.

In the debate over group-differentiated rights, multicultural feminists are deeply concerned about the possibility that various measures of accommodation, especially those involving policies that devolve legal authority to the established group leaders (many of whom are older men), may expose women to risk by twisting the logic of respect-for-difference into a license for intragroup subordination.[44] Militating against this unjust resolution, multicultural feminists are searching for new terms of engagement among the group, the state, and the individual—searching for ways that will

40. See Lisa Hajjar, "Religion, State Power, and Domestic Violence in Muslim Societies: A Framework for Comparative Analysis," *Law and Social Inquiry* 29 (2004): 1–38.

41. Ayelet Shachar, "Religion, State, and the Problem of Gender: New Modes of Governance and Citizenship in Diverse Societies," *McGill Law Journal* 50 (2005): 49–88.

42. I discuss these two poles, which I label "secular absolutism" and "religious particularism," on a continuum of state-religion relations in *Multicultural Jurisdictions*, ch. 4.

43. For a concise overview, see Nigeria Report.

44. This problem I have labeled "the paradox of multicultural vulnerability." See Shachar, "On Citizenship and Multicultural Vulnerability," *Political Theory* 28 (2000): 64–89, and *Multicultural Jurisdictions*.

acknowledge and benefit women as members of these intersecting (and potentially conflicting) identity- and law-creating jurisdictions.[45]

What multicultural feminists advocate, in short, is a shift in the focus on analysis from endless debates about culture (as in the disagreements between liberal and post-colonial feminists) toward a more critical understanding of the political and juridical dimensions of multicultural accommodation that may dramatically shape women's conditions. In this way, they propose that justice can be done to the multidimensional aspiration of achieving both equality and recognition as women, as citizens, and as minority group members.

These core claims of multicultural feminism can be usefully examined by look-ing at the three major flaws that we identified earlier: (1) an apolitical understanding of culture; (2) a conception of women as almost entirely without agency in terms of transforming their own community's tradition; and (3) a general disregard for the sig-nificance of macro-level legal/institutional conditions that shape the relations among the group, the state, and the individual. Each of these conceptions has been challenged by the work of multicultural feminists.

Unveiling the Political Uses of Culture

We have already discussed the rejection of a static vision of culture and identity. In recent years, multicultural feminists have identified not just the social invention of so-called authentic fundamentalism, but also the political use of culture by leaders who face opposition from within or without as a way to legitimize their hold on power. Furthermore, it is argued that respect-for-difference policies may also serve the inter-ests of the accommodating state, particularly if it is seen as a less costly way to gain the support of those who hold the power in minority communities.

India provides an interesting example. In her detailed study of the history of Mus-lim personal law, Vrinda Narain shows that the introduction of British (colonial) legal structures facilitated an institutional framework that allowed cooperation between elite members of the Hindu and Muslim communities and the colonial administra-tion; this was done in part by setting up internally diverse religious communities as distinct, "unified," and separate juridical entities. Shaped by this history, personal law in India has assumed a crucial role as a marker of communal autonomy and as a legitimate route for the *ulama* (religious scholars, literally "those who know") to stake a claim to political power. Although the autonomy granted to religious per-sonal law in regulating the family was the result of legal/institutional choices made by the colonizers, "[i]n the imagination of the Ulama, the sphere of family and fam-ily law was recast as autonomous and uncolonized."[46] As such, gender and the family became the grounds on which culture and tradition were discursively created by both the colonizers (and, later, the Indian state) and the Muslim community. Within the community itself, the religious leaders in particular used their jurisdictional power under the Muslim Personal Law (Shari'a) Application Act and the Dissolution of

45. For a detailed analysis, see Shachar, *Multicultural Jurisdictions*, ch. 6 and appendix.

46. Vrinda Narain, *Gender and Community: Muslim Women's Rights in India* (Toronto: University of Toronto Press, 2001), 18.

Muslim Marriages Act to "strengthen their control over women of the community by subjecting them to narrow interpretations of women's rights under high culture Islamic rules."[47] Such control, in turn, served to assert and galvanize the *ulama*'s own authority within the group and to establish their status as the sole legitimate representatives of the Muslim community in its various engagements with the Indian state and the Hindu majority.[48] It is precisely this astute *political* understanding of culture that is sorely lacking from the liberal feminist analysis of the relations between gender and culture. Such an understanding is also attentive to the manner in which gender inequality and claims for authenticity intersect under specific legal/institutional structures.

Entering the Temple: Feminist Theological Study

In addition to these efforts to deessentialize religion and culture, feminist scholars have taken a further step. They have now entered the temple of religion by undertaking the most revered of its internal mechanisms of cultural reproduction: theological study. Their strategy has been to highlight the potential within constitutive religious texts for alternate readings that are better able to mesh with women's freedom and equality. Feminist scholarship in Judaism, for example, is engaged with an extensive reexamination of the main halakhic (Jewish law) sources: scholars are interpreting the Torah through a critical perspective that seeks to unmask hidden interests in traditional interpretations of religious texts and to expose countertraditions of resistance to patriarchy in biblical and rabbinical literature. As Susannah Heschel puts it, the former is important because "[w]e don't simply ask what the text seems to be saying, but whose interests are being served. We examine what the text reveals, but also explore what the text conceals."[49] The latter is significant because it demonstrates that rigid and inegalitarian interpretations, even if they gained authoritative power during particular historical periods, were always contested, representing "but only one element in a multitude of conflicting voices."[50] By infusing religious study with feminist perspectives, women are asserting not only their membership in the community, but also their contributions to it as full participants.[51]

This rejuvenation of tradition through textual interpretation also manifests itself in various Islamic schools of thought. For instance, women and other reformists have offered revisionist readings of the Qur'an, readings which are inclusive of women and which treat women and men as equals before Allah. This "quiet revolution" has involved not only scriptural learning, but also prayer leading and marriage officiating by Muslim women.[52] These are controversial, yet increasingly negotiated, practices of

---

47. Narain, *Gender and Community,* 19.

48. For an illuminating discussion, see Zoya Hasan, *Forging Identities: Gender, Communities and the State in India* (Boulder, CO: Westview, 1994).

49. Heschel, *On Being a Jewish Feminist,* xii.

50. Heschel, *On Being a Jewish Feminist,* xxiii.

51. Rachel Biale, *Women and Jewish Law: An Exploration of Women's Issues in Halakhic Sources* (New York: Schocken, 1984), 9.

52. For a first-person account, see Kecia Ali, "Acting on the Frontier of Religious Ceremony: With Questions and Quiet Resolve, a Woman Officiates a Muslim Wedding."

updating the tradition to reflect contemporary realities.[53] These dramatic transfor-mations are often nonlinear: they may lead some to pursue more gender-egalitarian interpretations, while pushing others to more jealously guard a strict and rigid read-ing of the tradition as it applies to the rights of women, especially in the family.[54] Most important for the purpose of our discussion is the recognition that by entering the charged field of theological study and knowledge production, minority women have demonstrated the importance of agency and political shrewdness in the creation of more egalitarian cultural/religious practices. Contrary to the pessimistic outlook proposed by many critics, women who wish to uphold their religious membership in minority or orthodox communities can be active participants in shaping their own identities and social roles.

Turning to Democratic Deliberation and Institutional Design

Having highlighted the political uses of culture and having considered how feminist theological study and revisionism is tackling tensions between religious accommoda-tion and gender equality, multicultural feminists are now reexamining how law and governance—the pillars of institutional authority in the modern era—are engaged in shaping intercommunal and intragroup power relations. In this, they are following a well-regarded tradition of scholarship that treats institutional structures as variables which have a crucial effect on how behavior is shaped: it observes how individual and collective actions are always influenced by the unique structures of authority under which they operate. Altering the "payoffs" that a given institutional design generates holds the potential of motivating the core players to revisit once-unquestioned pat-terns of inequality. For multicultural feminists, this observation opens up a space for innovation and creativity—as does the rich comparative evidence showing the wide variations in religious-code interpretation in different jurisdictions.

A number of ideal type responses present themselves, of which I will only point to two of the more promising venues: highlighting the importance of more inclusive democratic deliberative processes in civil society and envisioning new juridical and governance procedures that would permit the historically marginalized to negotiate their manifold affiliations as women, citizens, and group members. I will elaborate briefly on each of these developments.

Advocates of deliberative procedures call for discursive processes designed specifi-cally to enhance the voices of historically vulnerable segments of the group popula-

---

53. For more on these debates, see Kecia Ali, "Progressive Muslims and Islamic Jurisprudence: The Necessity for Critical Engagement with Marriage and Divorce Law," in Omid Safi, ed., *Progressive Muslims on Justice, Gender, and Pluralism* (Oxford: Oneworld, 2003); Aziza Al-Hibri, "Islam, Law and Custom: Redefining Muslim Women's Rights," *American University Journal of International Law and Policy* 12 (1997): 1–44; Ziba Mir-Hosseini, *Islam and Gender: The Religious Debate in Contemporary Iran* (Princeton, NJ: Princeton University Press, 1999); Wadud, *Qur'an and Women.*

54. This is not the place to thoroughly analyze these tectonic reverberations. Suffice it to say that women's growing participation in the reinterpretation of their own religious traditions clearly contra-dicts the picture of a singular and simplistic narrative of identity formation for Muslim women that is portrayed, ironically, by both Western popular media and Islamic resurgence movements. I discuss these mirror-image representations and their often troubling implications for the debate over women's rights and religious accommodation in Shachar, "Religion, State, and the Problem of Gender."

tion by facilitating secure conditions for dialogue within the minority community, within the wider society, and between the two.[55] Theorists such as Seyla Benhabib and Monique Deveaux take as their starting point the need to acknowledge intragroup inequalities rather than trust in the representation and dialogue conducted through groups' official spokesmen. One example of such inclusive processes is described by Deveaux in her account of the prelegislative consultation processes that took place in South Africa before the adoption of the Recognition of Customary Marriage Act of 1998. For Benhabib, cross-cultural dialogue and intragroup contestation are seen as important methods through which the very identity formation and resignification of culture occurs.[56] She emphasizes the importance of resolving multicultural struggles in the informal (or civil society) sphere, where "political and moral learning and value transformation occur."[57] These are crucially important observations that attempt to diffuse the tension between multiculturalism and feminism by suggesting that the former is open to change by the latter. As an empirical matter, however, some hard cases will nevertheless proceed to the stage of formal (juridical) resolution. In most diverse societies, various individual-group-state conflicts—especially those in which issues of gender equality are entangled with the exercise of legal or jurisdictional authority by the minority community (or some of its representatives)—eventually find their way to the courthouse or the legislature. Here, the institutional function is to provide principled guidelines for implementing resolutions to the conflicts raised by the specific parties before them. In deciding cases or setting public policy, courts and legislatures must often go beyond granting mere permission for cultural dynamism to continue to flourish in the public sphere. After all, if such conflicts could have been resolved justly in civil society, they would not have reached the formal realm of a legal dispute or legislative amendment. The main reason for a conflict to enter this arena is that the parties seek a remedy that will change the background rules against which they operate, precisely because they were unable to come to what they see as a fair resolution under the current conditions of unequal power and voice allocation.

It is here that the legal/institutional approach comes into play. This approach locates the multicultural feminist critique at the heart of the classic field of inquiry into political life: institutional design and the allocation of power. This is the realm of constitutionality, governance, and the law; it is here that official power resides in modern states. Focusing on institutional design permits supplementing the insights drawn from the work of democratic, dialogical, and deliberative theorists with a legal/juridical framework that directly tackles the hurdles that cultural and gender conflicts must eventually overcome. These obstacles pertain to the division of power in a complex society and the authority to codify and enforce a legal order within it. In *Multicultural*

55. On the deliberative approach, see Benhabib, *Claims of Culture;* on the dialogical approach, see Bhikhu Parekh, *Rethinking Multiculturalism: Cultural Diversity and Political Theory* (Cambridge, MA: Harvard University Press, 2000). See also Duncan Ivison, *Postcolonial Liberalism* (Cambridge: Cambridge University Press, 2002).

56. Benhabib devotes much of her book to defending a social constructivist vision of culture. See, for example, *Claims of Culture,* ch. 1.

57. Benhabib, *Claims of Culture,* 106.

Jurisdictions (2001), I have outlined the contours of "joint governance" as an example of the legal/institutional approach to resolving the very real tensions that may arise out of the effort to respect women's rights alongside an accommodation of their cultural identity. I treat it here as an example of this approach.

Based on the idea of shared jurisdictional authority, joint governance seeks to evade situations in which women either lose any legitimate public assertion of their communal identity in exchange for state protection of their equality rights or see the erosion of their basic protections in exchange for cultural recognition. Instead, this approach encourages the creation of cooperative mechanisms that engage the state and the non-territorial minority group in an ongoing dialogue to improve the status of the most vulnerable. This pursuit begins by rejecting the standard position—that the authority to govern must be allocated *either* to the state *or* to the group. Indeed, women have good reason to suspect the exclusivity of power exercised at the hands of either entity: from the perspective of the historically subordinated group member, the state may seem a particularly untrustworthy partner. Conversely, putting their faith in the hands of established group leaders, many of whom strategically use the claim of religious or cultural difference as a way to build their own authority base, is a risky enterprise at best for minority women. This begs the question of institutional design: to whom should they turn if and when they seek to improve their gender status without giving up their group identity?

Instead of forcing an either-or type of choice, joint governance requires the creation of overlapping or shared jurisdictions, whereby individuals are never subject solely to the authority of either the group or the state. This allows vulnerable group members greater flexibility and room for negotiation within both entities, in that failure to perform by one entity may lead to a loss of jurisdiction over members. Such a structure of sharing and dividing authority rests on three core principles. The first is the *submatter allocation of authority*. This involves identifying the unique interrelated functions found in the specific social arena in which accommodation is sought. The second is the *no-monopoly rule*, which draws on the rich tradition of modern democratic theory to defend a separation-of-powers principle, holding that neither the group nor the state can acquire exclusive control over a contested social arena that affects individuals as group members and citizens. Third is the *establishment of clearly delineated reversal options*, which entails delegating to the individual the authority to discipline the relevant jurisdictional power-holder by utilizing predefined reversal points to turn to the competing jurisdiction when the original power-holder has failed to provide adequate remedy.[58]

This final requirement of joint governance, the reversal point, is designed to ensure that if the interests of the vulnerable party are systemically ignored or left unmet by the relevant jurisdiction, the competing authority gains the right to provide her remedy: for instance, this might be done by acquiring the authority to overturn the initial decision made by the original power-holder. Rather than risk losing authority over members altogether, astute religious leaders might be encouraged to find an internal

58. For a detailed description of these requirements, their justification, and their implementation, see *Multicultural Jurisdictions*, ch. 6 and the appendix.

solution that maintains fidelity to the tradition while also corresponding to contemporary realities and dissenting voices in the group. In this way, joint governance seeks to tackle the major problem of providing incentives for leaders and power-holders to change course by listening to the voices and concerns of those who have long been silenced and marginalized, and to find within the tradition itself resources for more equitable reinterpretation. Islamic jurisprudence in particular is replete with creative methodologies of reinterpretation that can serve as rich sources for more gender-egalitarian readings of the religious texts.[59]

FROM THEORY TO PRACTICE: THE SHARI'A TRIBUNAL AND RELATED DILEMMAS

Debates about whether and how precisely to draw the boundaries between state and religion in regulating the family have again come to the fore, leading to intensified political and legal controversies the world over. The controversy that broke out in Canada following the Shari'a tribunal proposal offers a concrete illustration of this pattern at work, as did the unwieldy storm that followed a lecture delivered by none other than the Archbishop of Canterbury, in which the Archbishop contemplated the option of allowing non-Christian tribunals the ability to formally determine certain aspects of civil disputes. Add to the mix two inflammatory components in today's political environment—religion and gender—and the stirrings of disagreement, likely followed by polarization, will soon be heard.[60] This Canadian tale will serve as the basis for my analysis of how each of the three feminist approaches discussed above may differ from one another in their treatment of this real-life dilemma.

From a liberal feminist perspective, the Shari'a tribunal proposal can be seen as challenging the normative and juridical authority, not to mention legitimacy, of the secular state's asserted mandate to represent and regulate the interests and rights of *all* its citizens in their family-law affairs, irrespective of communal affiliation. It was therefore seen by some as a foundational debate about some of the most basic questions concerning hierarchy and lexical order in the contexts of law and citizenship: which norms *should* prevail, and who, or which entity, ought to have the final word in resolving value conflicts between equality and diversity, if they arise. The vision of privatized diversity, in its full-fledged "unregulated islands of jurisdiction" variant, thus poses a challenge to the superiority of secular family law by its old adversary: religion.

Indeed, the prospect of tension, if not a direct clash, between religious and secular norms governing the family—and the fear that women's hard-won equal rights would be the main casualties of such a showdown—largely informed the opposition to the Shari'a tribunal. Add to that the charged political environment surrounding Muslim minorities in North America and Europe in the post–9/11 era, and we can easily understand why this tribunal initiative became a lightning-rod for the much

---

59. See El Fadl. See also S. S. Ali, *Gender and Human Rights in Islam and International Law: Equal before Allah, Unequal before Man?* (The Hague: Kluwer Law International, 1999). There is also a great deal of diversity in the application of shari'a norms in family law disputes in different Muslim countries.

60. For further discussion, see Ayelet Shachar, "Privatizing Diversity: A Cautionary Tale from Religious Arbitration in Family Law," *Theoretical Inquiries in Law* 9 (2008): 573–607.

larger debate about what unites us as citizens and what may divide us. And were this not enough to create an explosive situation on its own, we must take account of the fact that once these charged gender and religious questions caught the attention of the mass media, they quickly fell prey to reified notions of the inherent contrast between (idealized) secular norms and (vilified) religious traditions. In this war of images, secular family laws were automatically presented as unqualified protectors of equality as well as the deterrents to destitution or dependency (though they may leave women and children in a far poorer state than divorced husbands, for example); by contrast, religious principles, especially those associated with Islam, were uncritically defined as inherently reinforcing inequality and as the source of disempowerment for women (although certain interpretations could lead to results that are equitable and respectful to the divorcing spouses). Eventually, the Shari'a tribunal came to represent a polarized oppositional dichotomy that allowed *either* protecting women's rights *or* promoting religious extremism. Under these conditions, it is not surprising that the government chose the former over the latter. The chosen policy response was to *bar* any type of family arbitration by faith-based principles. This resolution effectively shuts down— rather than encourages—coordination or dialogue between civil and religious juris- dictions. But were there other, less oppositional, alternatives that were missed in this politicized debate, alternatives that might better have responded to devout women's multiple affiliations and identities as group members and citizens of the larger polity? I return to this question in the final section of my discussion.

The postcolonial feminist may raise another line of objection to the tribunal, asking whether religion and culture—or gender inequality *simpliciter*—are at issue. Consider, for example, the 2004 *Hartshore* decision, in which the Supreme Court of Canada upheld the use of *secular* contractual mechanisms to evade the basic equity provisions that pro- tect women's entitlements in divorce, as encoded in various provincial and federal stat- utes governing the breakdown of family relations.[61] In that decision, a woman entered a marriage agreement that was evaluated by independent legal advice as "grossly unfair": pursuant to the agreement, the wife was entitled to property valued at $280,000 on sep- aration, while the husband was entitled to property worth $1.2 million. Such "domestic contracts" are permitted by the governing secular law, but they must operate fairly at the time of distribution. If they do not, these contracts become subject to the judicial reapportionment of the property.[62] Here, it was clear that the wife received far less than what she would have been entitled to under the default statutory regime. The trial judge therefore concluded that the agreement was unfair and ordered reapportionment on a 60–40 basis in favor of the husband. This decision was approved by the Court of Appeal but ultimately reached the Supreme Court, which overturned the ruling of the trial judge. Instead of aiding the wife, the country's top justices ruled that "courts should be reluctant to second-guess the arrangements on which [private parties, in this case,

---

61. See *Hartshore v. Hartshore* (2004), 1 S.C.R. 550.

62. See *Family Law Act,* R.S.B.C. (1996), c. 128, part 5, ss. 56, 58, 59, 61, 65, 68, 89. See also *Divorce Act,* R.S.C. 1985, c.3 (2nd Supp), ss. 15.2 (amended 1997, c.1, s.2), 15.2(4) (formerly s. 15[5]). The Family Law Act permits such "domestic contracts," but they are subject to judicial reapportionment of property.

the husband and wife] reasonably expected to rely. Individuals may choose to structure their affairs in a number of ways, and it is their prerogative to do so."[63]

The *Hartshore* case represents a classic example of a court deciding to privilege notions of contractual freedom over the statutory default rules of gender equality. But because there was no "culture" or threatening minority to blame, the Court's controversial decision has not raised the same ire in the popular media and in activist circles as has the ultimately rejected idea of using religious-based arbitration procedures.[64]

A postcolonial feminist would militate against this different response, labeling it as a double standard. Indeed, she could challenge the very representation of secular and religious family law norms as posing dramatically different alternatives for women in terms of protection of their interests. The argument might proceed as follows: it is true that religious tribunals may (ab)use tradition to curb the promise of gender equality. Still, what matters—according to this line of argument—is that the secular system too has failed women. As we have just seen in the *Hartshore* decision, this is indeed a valid critique. It shows that, even without adding the complexities of a religious tribunal into the mix, the current regulation of the family is not as uniform as it may, at first blush, appear. This is a powerful argument. However, the postcolonial feminist is arguably overextending the logic of her claim: it surely requires a great deal of conviction to suggest that religious pressures are no different in kind than the secular set of pressures imposed on women in our society, although both may unfortunately lead to the same result of limiting women's freedom. This slippage occurs in part because, by making an equation between the secular and the religious, the postcolonial theorist is drastically discounting the communal pressures that may be imposed on a devout believer to comply with what is presented as a religious duty. In other words, a woman's freedom is restricted not only by familiar factors such as economic or informational asymmetry, but also by distinctive communal pressures, or what some might label "religious blackmail."[65]

Paradoxically, then, it appears that the postcolonial feminist's zeal to demystify culture and identity has led her to turn a blind eye to what makes religion and its exercise in concert with others both important and distinct for its adherents. Despite adopting a highly critical position with respect to cultural and gender essentialism, the postcolonial feminist appears trapped in a rigid framework of old orientalist hierarchies. This leaves little room, in John Strawson's words, for "both sides of the former imperial

---

63. *Hartshore,* par. 36.

64. It is hard to assume that intercommunal tensions in the post–9/11 era have had no influence on the heightened concern with which the quest for private religious arbitration, which is being specifically raised by Muslim clerics, have been met. This observation fits with the broader themes of postcolonial feminism.

65. These considerations may restrict the choices of any group member, but are likely to have a disproportionate impact on women. Think here of the debate in France over the *hijab* (the headscarf donned by some Muslim women and girls), where the veiled female body has come to represent the repository of authentic group identity (in the eyes of the group) and a threat to republican citizenship (in the eyes of the state). In both narratives, it is the power to regulate women's bodies that has come to serve as a symbol for much larger social and political debates over the meaning of citizenship and the future of intercommunal relations in that country.

divide … [to] construct a new jurisprudential discourse on an inclusive basis."[66] Without the prospect of such new jurisprudential discourse, we risk having little to offer minority women but despair.

What troubles me most with the liberal feminist and postcolonial feminist responses is not so much the bottom-line conclusion that the proposed arbitration tribunals ought to be treated with suspicion, but rather the justification process. Neither position allows for any serious discussion of whether there are any valid reasons for devout women to turn to a religious arbitration tribunal in the first place. This search for nuance, which is coupled with a critical analysis of the motivations of both state and group representatives in their struggles over jurisdictional authority, is at the core of multicultural feminist analysis. We saw earlier that this approach is informed by an explicitly political conception of culture and identity, while at the same time granting more credence than standard accounts to women's agency and voice in navigating the complex intersection of gender and religion in their lived experience. This perspective also delves deeper into the relationship between the regulation of the family and the construction of collective identity. While holding faith in deliberative processes of contestation and reinterpretation, multicultural feminists also face the urgent task of investigating and highlighting the importance of *state action* (or *in*action) in shaping, through law and institutional design, the context in which women can achieve their claims for equality vis-à-vis the group or fellow citizens outside their community. Viewed from this angle, the Shari'a tribunal proposal should rightly be perceived with a healthy dose of skepticism; one wonders whether this development represents a whole new and convenient way for the state (and its public institutions) to avoid taking responsibility for protecting the rights of more vulnerable parties precisely in those areas of social life that are most crucial for realizing *both* gender equality *and* collective identity, such as the regulation of the family. Militating against such a result, multicultural feminists are searching for new terms of engagement between the major players that have a stake in finding a viable path to accommodating diversity *with* equality, including the group, the state, and the individual—in ways that will acknowledge and benefit women as members of these intersecting (and partly overlapping) identity- and law-creating jurisdictions.

This requires envisioning creative remedies that respond to the emerging concern that the erosion of women's equality rights is increasingly the "collateral" of charged state-religious showdowns. To avert this disturbing result, I will briefly explore how, despite the fact that the strict separation approach still remains the standard or default response, courts and legislatures have recently been breaking new ground by adopting what we might refer to as intersectionist or joint governance remedies. One such example is found in the Supreme Court of Canada's 2007 decision in *Bruker v. Marcovitz*, which explicitly rejected the simplistic "privatizing identities" formula. Instead, it ruled in favor of "[r]ecognizing the enforceability by civil courts of agreements to discourage *religious* barriers to remarriage, addressing the gender

---

66. John Strawson, "Islamic Law and English Texts," in Eve Darian-Smith and Peter Fitzpatrick, eds., *Laws of the Postcolonial* (Ann Arbor: University of Michigan Press, 1999), 123.

discrimination those barriers may represent and alleviating the effects they may have on extracting unfair concessions in a civil divorce."[67] In the *Marcovitz* case, a Jewish husband made a contractual promise to remove barriers to religious remarriage in a negotiated, settled agreement, which was incorporated into the final divorce decree between the parties. This contractual obligation thus became part of the terms that enabled the *civil* divorce by a public, state entity. Once the husband had the secular divorce in hand, however, he failed to honor the agreement he signed to remove religious barriers to his wife's remarriage. The Supreme Court was not in a position to order specific performance ("forcing" the husband to implement his promise). Instead, it imposed monetary damages on the husband for the *breach* of the contractual promise in ways that harmed the wife personally and affected the public interest generally. What *Marcovitz* demonstrates is the possibility of employing a standard legal recourse (damages for breach of contract, in this example) in response to specifically gendered harms that arise out of the *intersection* between multiple sources of authority and identity in the actual lives of women who are members of religious minority communities and larger, secular states as well.

The significance of the *Marcovitz* decision for our discussion lies in its recognition that *both* the secular *and* the religious aspects of divorce matter greatly to observant women if they are to enjoy gender equality, articulate their religious identity, enter new families after divorce, or rely on contractual ordering just like any other citizen. This joint-governance framework offers us a vision in which the secular system may be called upon to provide remedies in order to protect religious women from husbands who might otherwise cherry-pick their religious and secular obligations as they see fit. This is a clear rejection of the simplistic "your-culture-or-your-rights" approach, offering instead a more nuanced and context-sensitive analysis that begins from the ground up. This requires identifying who is harmed, and why, and then proceeding to find a remedy that matches, as much as possible, the need to recognize the (indirect) intersection of law and religion that contributed in the first place to the creation of the harm for which legal recourse is now sought.

We are still left, however, with the thorny challenge of tackling the potential *conflict* between secular and religious norms governing family disputes. Recall that a significant part of the anxiety that surrounded the Shari'a tribunal debate was the fact that its advocates never fully clarified what would happen if their interpretation of customary or religious personal laws provided women with less equitable divorce settlements than those that could have been obtained under the state's secular family laws. According to the tribunal's opponents, nothing less than an attempt to use a technique of privatized diversity to redefine the relationship between state and religion in regulating the family was underway. This is an existential threat that no secular state authority is likely to accept with indifference (not even in multicultural Canada). And so, after much contemplation, the response chosen to the challenge presented by the proposed tribunal was to quash it with all the legal force the authorities could muster. This took the shape of an absolutist solution: prohibiting by decree the operation of *any* religious arbitra-

67. *Bruker v. Marcovitz*, 2007 SCC 54, para. 3; 92 (Canada).

tion process in the family law arena. Such a response, which relies on imposition by state fiat, sends a strong symbolic message of unity, albeit a unity that is manufactured by ensuring compliance with a single monopolistic jurisdictional power-holder.

A less heavy-handed approach might have been worth exploring; for instance, by delegating to religious arbitrators themselves an opportunity to determine, through their actions and deeds, whether to enjoy the benefits of binding arbitration—including the boon they were seeking of public enforcement of their awards—if they *voluntarily* agreed to comply with statutory thresholds and default rules defined in general family legislation. These "floor" safeguards typically establish a minimal baseline of protection, above which significant room for variation is permitted. These protections were designed, in the first place, to address concerns about power and gender inequities in family relations, concerns that are not typically absent from religious communities, either. If anything, they probably apply with at least equal force in the communal context as in the individualized, secular case. Under this "self-restraint" scenario—which offers an alternative to the top-down prohibition model that was eventually chosen by the government—if a resolution by a religious tribunal falls within the reasonable margin of discretion that any secular family-law judge or arbitrator would have been permitted to employ, there is no reason to discriminate against that tribunal solely for the reason that the decision maker used a different tradition to reach a permissible resolution. The operative assumption here is that, in a diverse society, we can safely assume that at least some individuals might prefer to turn to their "communal" institutions, knowing that their basic state-backed rights are protected by these alternative forums. Against this backdrop, permitting community members to turn to a nonstate tribunal may, perhaps paradoxically, nourish the motivating conditions for promoting a more dynamic, context-sensitive, and potentially moderate interpretation of the tradition that is acceptable to the faithful, as authorized by religious arbitrators themselves. The prospect for such "change from within"—or what I have elsewhere labeled *transformative accommodation*[68]—in this context may translate into a recognition by the tribunal's arbitrators themselves that if they wish to issue final and binding decisions (which permit parties to turn to the civil system for enforcement where needed), they cannot breach the basic protections to which each woman is entitled by virtue of her equal citizenship status. To ignore these entitlements is to lose the ability to provide relevant legal services to members of the community.[69] In this fashion, a qualified recognition of the religious tribunal by the state may generate conditions that permit an effective, noncoercive encouragement of more egalitarian and reformist changes from within the said tradition itself. The state system, too, is transformed from strict separation to regulated interaction. This approach also discourages an underworld of unregulated religious tribunals and offers a path to transcend the either/or choice between culture and rights, family and state, citizenship and islands of "privatized diversity."

---

68. Shachar, *Multicultural Jurisdictions*.

69. Such a result would be unattractive for a nonstate tribunal, which strives to provide distinct legal services that no other agency can offer, as well as for the individual who has turned to this specialized forum in order to bring closure to a charged marital or family dispute that bears a religious aspect that simply cannot be fully addressed by the secular court system.

Despite persistent and at times oppressive attempts by the modern state to monopolize an exclusive power to regulate the family, other relations and values have retained a hefty influence in this significant realm of life. These issues touch a raw nerve, as the public outcry that followed the actual attempt to establish a Shari'a tribunal in Canada dramatically revealed. Alas, the almost knee-jerk response of further insisting on the *dis*entanglement of state and church (or mosque, synagogue, and so forth) in regulating the family may not always work to the benefit of female religious citizens who are deeply attached to, and influenced by, both systems of law and identity. Counterintuitively, a qualified yet dynamic *entanglement* between these old rivalries may present the best hope for expanding recognition of equal citizenship for once-marginalized and voiceless religious women. Susan Moller Okin, too, would have surely embraced this as a moral and political achievement worth celebrating.

9

Okin and the Challenge of Essentialism

Alison M. Jaggar

INTRODUCTION

As a powerful wave of feminist scholarship surged through North American universities in the last three decades of the twentieth century, Susan Moller Okin rode its crest. Her careful studies of the classic texts of Western political theory helped to legitimate the project of rereading the canon through a feminist lens and her reinterpretations of liberal political principles supported bold recommendations for what she called a truly humanist justice.

Few feminist scholars can avoid controversy but Okin made little effort to do so. Her uncompromising work challenged both the fathers of Western political theory and also their twentieth-century sons. (At least one famous philosopher would not attend her talks when she visited his campus.) More unexpectedly, Okin also found herself engaged in frequent conflict with other feminists, conflicts that revolved around the issue of essentialism.

The charge of essentialism was brought against the work of many so-called second wave feminists in the 1980s and 1990s, and in my view it was often justified. Like most people, Okin sometimes reacted defensively to criticism, but here I want to argue that her response to antiessentialist challenges was not simply to dig deeper; she also responded constructively. For this reason, Okin's scholarship is not just something that present-day scholars should transcend, and her most recent work is once again on the cutting edge of feminist political philosophy. Certainly, we can learn from Okin's mistakes, as we should learn from our own, but we can also learn from the ways in which Okin developed her ideas in sometimes painful dialogue with other feminists.

OKIN'S CONTRIBUTIONS: BY DECADE AND THEME

The body of work that Okin left to us can be divided roughly into decades, each distinguished by a significant contribution. Here, I indicate those contributions with slightly tongue-in-cheek slogans.

The Decade of the 1970s: "Abandon Functionalism!"

The 1979 publication of *Women in Western Political Thought* established Okin as a leader in feminist political philosophy. In a series of powerful chapters (some published earlier as articles), Okin revealed the biases against women that were built into the work of Plato, Aristotle, Rousseau, and Mill. She believed that these biases were rooted in "functionalism," which she explained as the "tendency to regard men as complete persons with potentials and rights, but to define women by the functions they serve in relation to men" (Okin 1979:304).[1] The main functions that classical Western philosophy assigned to women were bearing and caring for children and day-to-day housework. Okin regarded these assignments as incompatible with equality and asserted that, in a truly equal society, women would "be set free from assumptions about the kind of work they are best suited for, and enabled to attain equal status with men in the work force and in all other parts of the economic and political realm. Women cannot become equal citizens, workers, or human beings—let alone philosopher queens—until the functionalist perception of their sex is dead" (Okin 1979:304).

A few feminist scholars in addition to Okin were engaged in rereading the Western political canon in the 1970s, but the clarity and rigor of Okin's work set a standard that was hard to match (Clark and Lange 1979). Okin made it clear that the biases against women revealed in the great works of Western political theory were more than the masters' idiosyncratic prejudices; instead, they were central themes in the Western political tradition. After the publication of *Women in Western Political Thought*, it was much more difficult to ignore these biases.

The Decade of the 1980s: "Justice in the Family!"

As a follow-up to *Women in Western Political Thought*, Okin had originally planned to write a parallel critique of gender bias in the socialist tradition (Okin 1979b:7–9), but instead she turned her attention to contemporary political philosophy. In 1989, she published *Justice, Gender, and the Family*, in which she discussed the work of such theorists as Robert Nozick, Allan Bloom, Alasdair MacIntyre, John Rawls, and Michael Walzer. Okin's discussions made it clear that gender bias in political theory was not limited to the classic texts.

Just as Okin's critiques of the classical political theorists were connected by a continuous strand of argument, namely, the evils of functionalism, so her critiques of contemporary theorists were also connected by a distinct line of reasoning. Specifically, Okin challenged contemporary political philosophy's assignment of family relations to the private sphere, an assignment that excluded these relations from assessment by principles of justice. In Okin's view, "the traditional, gender-structured family" is unjust, and "gender-structured marriage is an institution that makes women economically and socially vulnerable" (Okin 1989a:24). A staunch liberal feminist, Okin did not dissolve the personal into the political, as the work of some other feminist theorists at the time threatened to do; instead, she respected the need for a private realm in which individuals could make their own choices.[2] Thus, she did not advocate that the division of labor in the family should be surveilled by what Rob Reich calls the "kitchen police," and she even asserted that the option of the traditional "gender-structured marriage"

1. In her landmark book, *The Feminine Mystique*, published in 1963, Betty Friedan had diagnosed a similar "functionalism" in the work of other authors, such as Freud.

2. Alternative models, at this time, were provided by liberal feminist Alix Kates Schulman's feminist marriage contract, which stipulated the domestic tasks to be performed by each partner, and the Cuban Family Code, which included a legal requirement that both marriage partners participate in housework. In the theoretical background was Catharine MacKinnon's characterization of the private realm as a masculine construction that allows men to abuse women.

should remain available for those who chose it (Reich 2005; Okin 1989a:180). Instead, Okin sought to influence family relations indirectly though a series of policy changes that would reduce homemakers' (typically wives') economic dependence on their spouses.[3] She thought this would reduce the likelihood of women's being trapped in a gendered cycle of vulnerability and increase women's ability to build genderless families, "combining love with justice" (1989a:185). Okin regarded such reforms as crucial because she regarded the traditional family as "the linchpin of gender," and she believed that a "just future would be one without gender" (1989a:171, 170).

The Decade of the 1990s: "Oppose Patriarchal Cultures!"

In the 1990s, Okin published several articles on gender and culture. These included "Gender Inequality and Cultural Differences" (published in *Political Theory* in 1994) and a response to Jane Flax's criticism of this article (published in *Political Theory* in 1995). In 1998, Okin published an article in *Hypatia* entitled "Feminism, Women's Human Rights, and Cultural Differences" and an article in *Ethics* entitled "Feminism and Multiculturalism: Some Tensions." A slightly more popular version of the second article was published the previous year (1997) in the *Boston Review* under the provocative title "Is Multiculturalism Bad for Women?" There, it was followed by commentaries from other feminists and Third World scholars, and in 1999 this set of discussions was republished as a book with the same title. Okin's discussions of gender and culture were among the most controversial parts of her work; in correspondence with me, she said they had been misrepresented more than anything she had ever written. However, even if one finds this part of her work flawed in some ways, as I do, it still made an extremely important contribution in drawing academic attention to the gendered aspects of so-called multiculturalism.

Okin's gender and culture articles no longer focused primarily on the situation of women belonging to the majority culture in Western liberal societies; instead, Okin turned her attention to women who belong to minority cultures in these societies and on "poor women in poor countries." Okin was concerned that such women were oppressed by their cultures, and she sharply criticized Western feminists for ignoring or even justifying this oppression in the name of "respect for difference." She argued

---

3. Okin recommends that, as long as gender-structured marriage continues, both partners should be regarded as having equal legal entitlement to all earnings coming into the house, perhaps by making wage checks payable half to the earner and half to the partner who provides all or most of the unpaid domestic services (*JGF*, 180–181). She also suggests that single mothers should identify the fathers of their children at birth, so that they can be forced to provide economic support for their children. These proposals are controversial. The proposal that women identify the fathers of their children at birth has been disputed already by single mothers in the United Kingdom who do not want an ongoing economic relationship with men who may have been exploitative or abusive, particularly if, as seems likely, such a relationship would bring demands for paternal involvement in the raising of their children. Okin's proposal that homemakers be legally entitled to half their partners' wage is also problematic, since it fails to address the continuing imbalance of power that, as Okin notes, typically accompanies economic independence; if such a policy were adopted, it seems likely that the homemaking partner (most likely the wife) would be expected to spend her half of the wage on maintaining the household while her husband would feel entitled to use his half for personal enjoyment.

that many Western feminists had become obsessed with a dogmatic antiessentialism, fed by a fashionable postmodernism, two approaches that, in her view, combined to rationalize cultural relativism and to allow feminist and liberal proponents of multiculturalism to ignore the fact that "[m]ost cultures have as one of their principal aims the control of women by men" (Okin 1999:13).

The First Decade of the Twenty-First Century: Addressing Women's Global Poverty

Okin's premature death, in March 2004, prevented her from completing the work that she had planned for the present decade. Before her work was abruptly and sadly halted, however, it had begun to move in exciting new directions, turning away from the preoccupation with culture and back to political economy, this time to the global political economy. In 2003, she published an important article, "Poverty, Well-Being and Gender: What Counts, Who's Heard?" in which she challenged several assumptions of development economics and discussed three feminist books on development. Okin told me that the article was intended as a prologue to a short book that would discuss women's rights in the context of colonialism and imperialism.

THE CHARGES OF ESSENTIALISM

Background of the Charges

Groundbreaking scholarship is inevitably controversial, but it is ironic that Okin's work probably received more criticism from feminists than from anyone else. This may be due partly to the fact that mainstream scholars have often dealt with feminist work by the simple expedient of ignoring it. As Okin observed in the "Afterword" to the second edition of *Justice, Gender, and the Family*, "[Although it] is increasingly difficult to *teach* as if feminist theory does not exist...much of current mainstream scholarship proceeds regardless" (1992:318). However, the feminist controversy about Okin's work resulted not only from the fact that those who paid most attention to this work were feminists; the controversy was also stimulated by broad changes in the intellectual atmosphere of Western academies in the 1980s and 1990s. Among these changes were:

- First, the new influence of postcolonial studies, especially after the publication of Edward Said's landmark *Orientalism* in 1978.
- Second, the reaction against large-scale, "grand," or universalizing theories. In the 1980s, the emergence of new social movements, such as the environmental and queer movements, undermined Marxist aspirations for working-class unity and encouraged many political theorists to refocus their attention on the diverse organizations of civil society. At the same time, communitarianism challenged liberalism's belief in a universal moral agent and universal principles of justice.
- Third and most fundamentally, postmodernism disputed the idea that knowledge could ever be objective in the sense of neutral among competing social interests. Postmodernist theorists argued that unmarked standpoints

presented as objective typically masked the partial perceptions and specific interests of historically and socially situated subjects. On the postmodernist view, all systems of knowledge are infused with power, both reflecting and reinforcing specific power relations

These currents of thought interacted with each other in the last two decades of the twentieth century, encouraging scholars in many disciplines to investigate the power relations inherent in constructions of knowledge, in the genesis and assumptions of key categories, and in the social positions of the agents of knowledge. Within the still-new discipline of feminist studies, the conclusions of these investigations were frequently expressed in the language of essentialism.

The Challenges of Feminist Antiessentialism

The term "essentialism" has a long history in philosophy, where it has been used in many ways; it has even been suggested that "essentialism" has no essence (Fuss 1989). In the context of contemporary feminist debate, however, Charlotte Witt usefully characterizes essentialism as a claim that certain of an object's properties are necessary to it, because they explain or cause its characteristic behavior, provide the basis for classifying it as a certain kind of thing, or provide the basis of the object's identity (Witt 1995). Thus, feminist essentialism begins with large or universal generalizations by feminists about some phenomenon, such as women, men, gender, work, or sexuality. Like all generalizations, these are liable to overlook exceptions and so to be inaccurate or incomplete; for instance, to say that women are trapped in the home ignores women who work outside the home; to say that women are sexually objectified disregards women whose sexuality is socially unacknowledged, such as disabled or old women; to represent women as mothers neglects women without children.

The main problem with essentialism, however, is not empirical inaccuracy. Essentialist generalizations may well acknowledge exceptions but still be problematic precisely because they treat those cases *as exceptions*, thereby refocusing attention on cases that they take to be normative, central, or paradigmatic. Implicitly if not explicitly, essentialist generalizations purport to identify the real nature, or essence, of women, men, gender, work, sexuality, or whatever. For example, essentialist generalizations might well acknowledge that some women have no children and that some sexual activity is not heterosexual but still suggest that "real" women are mothers and that "real" sex is heterosexual intercourse. Essentialism often lurks in phrases such as "women and blacks" or "women and lesbians," which imply that one group of women is nonnormative or not "truly" women. Thus, the claims made by essentialist generalizations are not simply empirical; they also include overt or covert normative assumptions, and these assumptions require careful scrutiny.

Essentialist claims frequently express the norms of dominant populations. Often, they represent already disadvantaged populations as deviant and so contribute to their further marginalization. As many critics have pointed out, the supposedly universal woman who is the main protagonist in much of Western feminist theory has often been privileged along a number of dimensions; for instance, many Western theorists have imagined her as white, middle-class, heterosexual, able-bodied, and so on. When the situation of privileged women is taken as the model for understanding the situation of all women, those who are less privileged either become invisible or they are othered, that is, treated as exceptions to the norm. Political strategies recommended on the basis of these models are then likely to disregard the interests of women seen as other. For instance, no-fault divorce may be liberating for professional women but may condemn to poverty women with fewer employment credentials. Outlawing prostitution or even surrogate mothering may "protect" some women from exploitation but deprive others of a possible livelihood.

In the 1980s, many Western feminists began to use "essentialist" as a pejorative term, employed to criticize feminist theories of the previous decade. The critics interpreted the theoretical debates of the 1970s as rival accounts of the Platonic essence of womanhood, or the necessary and sufficient conditions of gender subordination or sexuality, family, mothering, work, or whatever. Essentialist work was said to be friendly to biological determinism and unfriendly to social constructionism, to obscure important differences and inequalities among women, and to mask social privileges. It was quickly associated with racism, classism, ethnocentrism, and neocolonialism (Carby 1984; Fuss 1989; Spelman 1988; Spivak 1988). Okin's large-scale liberal feminist theorizing became a prime target for these charges.

Applying Essentialist Criticisms to Okin

In her classic book, *Inessential Woman: Problems of Exclusion in Feminist Thought* (1988), Elizabeth V. Spelman argued that Okin's 1979 discussion of Aristotle's treatment of women exemplified essentialist thinking. Specifically, she contended that Okin's focus on Aristotle's functionalist treatment of "free" women and her neglect of Aristotle's treatment of women slaves suggested that real women were free women, an assumption clearly revealed, in Spelman's view, by Okin's use of the terminology "women" and "slaves." Spelman wrote, "When we attend to the fact that by 'women' Aristotle means free women, then Okin's concern amounts to saying that one of the objectionable aspects of Aristotle's treatment of citizen-class women was that he didn't always respect the distinction he drew between them and those men and women who were slaves" (Spelman 1988:48). Spelman regarded Okin's discussion as an illustration of her central claim that "the works and lives of middle-class women have occupied center stage in dominant Western feminist thought" and often underwrote other forms of hierarchy, such as those based on race and class (Spelman 1988:book jacket).

Similar charges were laid against Okin's treatment of families in *Justice, Gender, and the Family*. There, Okin argued strongly for the injustice of the so-called traditional family, which she took to consist of a married (heterosexual) couple and their biological offspring, with the husband being the primary economic provider and the wife the primary homemaker. However, many historians have noted that, in the United States, the family described by Okin is a nineteenth-century invention, practiced primarily by the middle and upper classes, but also emulated in the early twentieth century by privileged sectors of the working class who were able to attain a "family wage." For other large sectors of North American society, however, this model of the family is neither traditional nor paradigmatic. Most poor and working-class women have always worked for pay—in factories, in fields, in the homes of others, or doing piecework on consignment in their own homes—and they continue to be brought up with this expectation, particularly in African American, Latino, and Asian American communities (Amott and Matthaei 1991).[4] Thus, it is far from clear that the so-called traditional family is the linchpin of gender for lesbian or working-class women or women of color; for them, the linchpin may be compulsory heterosexuality or workplace discrimination or racialized violence.

Okin recognized that families varied and even that the "traditional" family had become an exception (1989a:18). She observed that homosexual families tended to be more egalitarian than heterosexual ones (1989a:140) and encouraged the formation of "nontraditional groupings" (1989a:125). Nevertheless, Will Kymlicka's 1991 review of her book charged Okin with privileging the heterosexual nuclear family, an impression supported by the fact that Okin often treated as synonymous such expressions as "adult members of the family," "parents," "both parents," "couple," and "mother and father" (Kymlicka 1991:84). Thus, an antiessentialist critic might point out that, although Okin criticized Rawls because "the" family was barely visible in his theory, nontraditional families were barely visible in her own theory; she mentioned them only in passing and never explored their potential for justice. Instead, Okin focused primarily on the traditional family, even though it was unclear how this was relevant to women of color, working-class women, or lesbians, who did not live in traditional families or for whom such families were not even an ideal. In Kymlicka's view, most of Okin's work suggested that the ideal family consisted in a heterosexual couple and their biological offspring, a social unit in which both parents would share equally the burdens of economic support, domestic work, and child care.

The accusations of essentialism reached a crescendo in the 1990s with the publication of Okin's work on culture and gender. In her reply to Okin's 1994 article "Gender Inequality and Cultural Differences," Jane Flax argued that Okin obscured differences and inequalities among women by defending "an internally undifferentiated and conflict-free concept of gender" (Flax 1995:500). She wrote, "[Okin's] exclusive focus on [women's] shared oppression obscures the equally important relations of domination between women.... [This] enable[s] white women to ignore their complicity in, and privileges obtained from their situatedness within relations of race, sexuality (if straight) and geographic locations" (1995:503). In Flax's view, "Until there are fundamental redistributions of power among races, genders, and sexualities, the cry of 'too much difference' must remain suspect. Justice is undermined by domination, not difference" (1995:508).

Some of the contributors to *Is Multiculturalism Bad for Women?* also accused Okin of cultural essentialism. According to Bonnie Honig, Okin wrongly portrayed many "foreign" cultures as "univocally patriarchal," ignoring the complicated and ambiguous nature of the unfamiliar practices that she labels sexist (Honig 1999:37). She also assumed "that Western liberal regimes are simply and plainly 'less patriarchal' than

---

4. Patricia Hill Collins, along with many other black feminists, denies that African American girls confront a choice between "either domesticity and motherhood or career" (*JGF*, 143; Collins, *Black Feminist Thought*, 124).

other regimes, rather than differently so, perhaps worse in some respects and better in others" (Honig 1999:38). Honig observed:

> [Okin's] faith that Western liberal regimes have advanced furthest along a progressive trajectory of unfolding liberal equality prevents her from engaging in a more selective and comparative analysis of particular practices, powers, and contexts that could well enlighten us about ourselves and heighten our critical awareness of some of the limits, as well as the benefits, of liberal ways of life. (1999:38–39)

SOME PRIVATE CORRESPONDENCE

Behind the scenes of the public debate, Okin and I corresponded intermittently. I first met Susan in 1980, when I invited her to a conference in Cincinnati. Susan's and my first meeting established a friendship between us that was never close but which continued over decades. Our correspondence focused largely on methodological issues, but I mention it here because it has influenced my reading of her work and my assessment of the charge of essentialism.

In one of her first gestures of friendship, Susan sent me a prepublication copy of her review of my 1983 book, *Feminist Politics and Human Nature*. Although her review was mostly favorable, it criticized my use of the idea of the feminist standpoint, and we had some correspondence about it. Ultimately, Susan modified her views on this topic and indeed seemed to utilize a similar idea in *Justice, Gender, and the Family*, where she invokes the cartoon of three elderly judges whose views on abortion are transformed when they find themselves pregnant (1989a:102). Citing studies of differences between the psychological and moral perspectives of men and women, she wrote:

> What seems already to be indicated by these studies...is that *in a gender-structured society* there is such a thing as the distinct standpoint of women, and that this standpoint cannot be adequately taken into account by male philosophers doing the theoretical equivalent of the elderly male justices depicted in the cartoon....a fully human moral or political theory can be developed only with the full participation of both sexes. (1989a:106–107; italics in original)

Our next discussion of this question occurred in 1994, when I sent her a draft of a chapter for a book I was writing on moral reasoning. My book challenged several popular models of moral reasoning, including the Rawlsian method of hypothetical reasoning in the original position. I contended that impartiality is promoted better by actual dialogue than by imagining a hypothetical original position and, in the draft chapter I sent to her, I argued that her attempt to combine the original position with the standpoint of women did not remedy the weakness of original position thinking. Okin's way of combining original position and standpoint thinking was to insist that women as well as men philosophers should participate in discussions about what would be accepted in the original position. Of course, I agreed that women should be included in discussions about justice, but I noted that women were not a homogeneous category and that differences among women were often as significant as differences between women and men. For this reason, I thought it no more likely that privileged women theorists would be able to think from the standpoint of the "least advantaged representative woman" than that male theorists would be able to think as women (1989b:245). I also noted some ways in which Susan's own theorizing seemed to reflect the insights and limits of her own life experiences. She was unhappy with my challenge, both because she expected me to be more sympathetic than I was to the idea of the standpoint of women and also because she thought it was inappropriate to link an author's substantive claims with her life circumstances. Our correspondence became quite intense, though it ended cordially. I promised that I would not publish the chapter without revising it, and in the end I have never published it.

Susan and I had more correspondence about methodology in the late 1990s, and we continued to focus on the question of actual versus hypothetical dialogue. Our final flurry of correspondence occurred early in 2004, in the weeks preceding Susan's death. At this time, I sent her a draft of an article in which I suggested that the multiculturalism debate should be framed more broadly than the way in which it appeared in her work in the 1990s (Jaggar 2005). Susan responded kindly to my comments, noting that her most recent work had already moved in some of the directions I advocated.

I found Susan's and my philosophical correspondence over the years to be very rewarding, and I fancy that I see echoes of it in her work as well as my own. Even though the correspondence focused primarily on methodology, it has helped me to see how Susan responded positively, though not always explicitly, to the charges of essentialism.

OKIN'S RESPONSES TO THE CHARGES OF ESSENTIALISM

Okin's Responses in Theory and Practice

Okin was understandably sensitive to charges that her feminist work was racist, classist, heterosexist, and so on, even if unintentionally, and she took several opportunities to address these charges. Her most direct responses appeared in her 1992 "Afterword" to the second edition of *Women in Western Political Thought* and in her 1994 article "Gender Inequality and Cultural Differences." In both places, Okin paid special attention to Spelman's criticism of her work.

Okin recognized that Spelman's "main point … is important: one should not, in the very act of critiquing a theory for excluding women, render many women invisible, because they do not fit some unstated class, race, sexual orientation, or other criterion for inclusion" (Okin 1992:327). However, she suggested that Spelman's critique of feminist analyses such as her own was unfair because it seemed to criticize such analyses "for not being as focused on class, or slave status, or race, as on gender—but [Okin says] this is not what they set out to do" (1992:327). Okin found two related flaws in Spelman's antiessentialist argument. First, she disputed what she took to be Spelman's claim that theorists who focus primarily on gender implicitly view race or class oppression as insignificant. Second, she asserted that antiessentialist feminists bear the burden of proof for showing empirically that the differences they emphasize among women in fact make a difference; Spelman's work, in her view, "is rather long on theory and very short on evidence" (1992:328). Despite these alleged flaws, Okin reported learning two positive lessons from antiessentialism: "One is to be very careful not to make false generalizations, and to take account of such differences of class, race, sexual orientation, religion, and so on, as are relevant to the argument one is making" (1992:328–329). The second lesson, she said, was "not from but in reaction to anti-essentialist claims." She asserted that feminists should *not* "jump to the conclusion that gender is simply one among many equally important differences, that differences among women are as or even more important than similarities, and that to generalize about women is always, and necessarily, misleading and/or oppressive to some." In Okin's view, "a certain skepticism about antiessentialism will help to preserve the political potential of feminism from unnecessary fragmentation" (1992:329).

Okin's 1994 article "Gender Inequality and Cultured Differences" repeated the criticism that Spelman is "long on theory and very short on empirical evidence" and then took up "the gauntlet Spelman throws down" by investigating how Western feminist ideas about justice and inequality "stand up in the face of considerable cultural and socioeconomic difference" (1994:7–9). Comparing the situation of women in rich countries to the situation of women in poor ones, Okin found that, in many instances, "the situation of poor women in poor countries is not qualitatively *different* from that of most women in rich countries but, rather, 'similar but worse,'" often so much worse that it is "like the situation of [most Western women] in the nineteenth century" (1994:11, 15). From her investigations, Okin concluded that "gender itself is an extremely important category of analysis and that we ought not to be paralyzed by the fact that there are differences among women" (1994:20).

Okin's direct answers to her antiessentialist critics were refreshing at a time when many other scholars were responding simply with rhetorical denunciations of anti-essentialism and postmodernism. Okin is certainly correct to remind us that gender is a vital category of analysis, whose fruitfulness has been revealed in a vast body of feminist scholarship, and she is also right to insist that commonalities and differences among women must be investigated empirically. Iris Young provided an impressive model of how this can be done as she deployed Okin's idea of the cycle of gendered poverty in the developing world (Young essay, this volume). Despite these strengths, I find that the theoretical responses that Okin made to her antiessentialist critics in the early 1990s failed to acknowledge the full force of their criticisms.

One problem is that Okin tended to interpret the criticisms primarily as empirical challenges, capable of resolution simply by adducing evidence about the real world conditions of women's lives. However, possible claims of commonality and difference are in principle endless, and so particular claims always rest on value judgments about which commonalities and differences are significant. Moreover, people in different social situations are likely to assess commonalities and differences differently. If faced directly with these points, it is unlikely that Okin would have denied them, but she did not take them into account when reflecting on feminist theory in general and her own work in particular. Thus, her talk about burdens of proof and the need for evidence failed to acknowledge that, in contexts of inequality, disagreements about women's commonalities and differences are likely to be only partially disagreements about matters of fact; more fundamentally, they are likely to reflect divergent assessments about what matters, especially what matters politically. In treating antiessentialist challenges as concerned primarily with empirical accuracy, Okin disregarded their normative and indeed political core.

A second problem in Okin's 1990s responses is a tendency to minimize the importance of antiessentialist criticisms. For instance, she wrote:

> It should not be difficult to be aware that black women have hardly been oppressed
> by being put on pedestals, that lesbian women are oppressed in ways other than by
> being subordinates in traditional families, and that poor single mothers or single,
> childless career women experience different forms of inequality from those expe-
> rienced by middle-class women in traditional marriages. (1992:329)

The tone of this sentence suggests that concerns about difference are mere matters of detail, easily remedied, a suggestion that is problematic in at least two ways. First, even recognizing difference often is not as easy as Okin seemed to suggest. It is true that Okin observed, "unfortunately, most people have a tendency to write partly, even if unconsciously, from their own experiences," but this observation treated the question of positionality only as a matter of individual rather than systematic differences (1992:329). Okin did not acknowledge that differences are usually both more visible to those who are disadvantaged by them and also more important. Thus, disadvantaged women are more likely than privileged women to be aware of systems of privilege and disadvantage that affect both groups. They are also more likely to think that these systems matter. Second and even more important, taking full account of differences is likely to involve far more than simply tidying up details. As Okin herself noted in her first book, when previously minor characters are transformed into major ones, "the entire cast and the play in which it is acting look very different" (1979b:12). Informing a feminist theory by difference might well mean radically transforming it.

A third problem in Okin's theoretical response to antiessentialism is her failure to appreciate the significance of Flax's concerns abut the power inherent in writing theory. Because she interpreted the question of difference primarily as an empirical challenge, raising questions that could be addressed by any careful theorist, Okin not only disregarded the special difficulties faced by relatively privileged theorists in becoming aware of some differences; she also acknowledged no problem with determinations of such differences' salience being made by people who are not disadvantaged by them and may even benefit from them. Thus, Okin dismissed Flax's point that theorizing about the less privileged was one way in which more privileged women exercised power over them. She still saw the question only as one concerning "the political significance of difference," rather than recognizing it as also a question about the political recognition, evaluation, and even construction of difference.

In sum, I find that Okin's theoretical responses in the early 1990s to antiessentialist challenges were unsatisfactory because she tended to treat these challenges as hypercritical carping, which threatened to dissolve the category of gender into endless individual differences (1992:328). Okin resisted acknowledging that differences among women are often more than manifestations of diversity and even more than disparities that make some women better off than others; they are also relationships of inequality that give some women power over others, including the power to deny the existence of the inequalities.

Despite these shortcomings in her earlier theoretical responses to antiessentialist challenges, I find that Okin's practical responses were much more impressive. In the 1990s, Okin dramatically shifted the focus of her work away from "free" Athenian women and middle-class American women and toward disadvantaged women: "minorities," immigrants, and the global poor. Her 2003 article in *Philosophy and Public Affairs* explicitly stated her concern with "the economically poorest quarter of the world's population, especially the women who are disproportionately represented among them," and she planned a new book on the same topic. Thus, in her philosophical work, Okin increasingly followed her own Rawlsian advice to address the concerns of the "least advantaged representative woman" (Okin 1989b:245).

Okin's Methodological Responses to the Charge of Essentialism

Women in Western Political Theory was unself-conscious about its methodology. Okin presented straightforwardly her "analysis of the arguments and conclusions of Plato, Aristotle, Rousseau and Mill, concerning women and their proper social and political role" (Okin 1979b:9). Although she noted that taking a new focus presents a new perspective on social and political theory, she did not explicitly situate herself as a reader/critic nor reflect on how her situation might influence her focus or her reading (1979b:12).

A decade later, this unself-consciousness was beginning to be replaced by a new awareness that people's thinking is influenced by their life situations. *Justice, Gender, and the Family* defended Rawlsian hypothetical reasoning in the original position, but we have seen that Okin's commitment to this approach was already qualified by her talk about a "standpoint of women." In her 1989 *Ethics* article, "Reason and Feeling in Thinking about Justice," Okin rejected the "rational choice" interpretation of the original position, according to which "there might as well be just one person behind the veil of ignorance since the deliberations of all are identical" (Okin 1989b:242). Instead, she proposed a more "caring" interpretation, in which reasoners are asked to think from the point of view of each person in turn, a feat that requires "both strong empathy and a preparedness to listen carefully to the very different points of view of others" (1989b:245). Hypothetical dialogue was now presented as presupposing actual dialogue.

Okin's *Political Theory* articles included considerable methodological reflection. In the first, Okin expressed doubt about the reliability of actual dialogue:

> [S]ome of us discern problems with going in the direction of formulating a theory of justice entirely by listening to every concrete individual's or group's point of view and expression of its needs....Is it a reliable route, given the possibility of "false consciousness"?...how can all the different voices express themselves and be heard and still yield a coherent and workable theory of justice? (1994a:5)

Her concern about possible false consciousness led Okin to oppose the "interactive" or "dialogic" feminism that she attributed to Ruth Anna Putnam and that I also advocated. She rejected dialogic feminism because she believed:

> [W]e are not always enlightened about what is just by asking persons who seem to be suffering injustices what they want. Oppressed people have often internalized their oppression so well that they have *no* sense of what they are justly entitled to as human beings. This is certainly the case with gender inequalities....

> This is why a concept such as the original position, which aims to approximate
> an Archimedean point, is so valuable, *at least in addition to some form of dialogue.*
> (1994a:19; italics added)

In the mid-1990s, Okin was still clearly reluctant to abandon original position
thinking completely, but now she seemed to recommend it only as a supplement to
empirical dialogue (1994:18). After this time, indeed, her published work included few
if any recommendations to original position reasoning. Nevertheless, Okin remained
resistant at this point to postmodern insights about the relation between knowledge
and power. When Jane Flax expressed concern about "enlisting poor women from
other countries as evidence in a dispute among women in the First World" (1995:502),
Okin caricatured this concern as an "apparent underlying conviction that each person's situatedness renders her incapable of saying, and somehow reprehensible for trying to say, anything about anyone in a situation different from her own" (1995:513). In
Okin's view, the main question was: "Do the theories devised by First World feminists,
particularly our critiques of nonfeminist theories of justice, have anything to say, in
particular, to the poorest women in poor countries, or to those policymakers with the
potential to affect their lives for better or for worse?" (1994:9). By reducing the issue to
a question of the truth or otherwise of Western feminist theorizing, Okin evaded Flax's
point about the authority of theorists and their theories. Although Okin had conceded
in 1992 that we must recognize differences when they are relevant to our arguments,
she failed to consider that who "we" are affects the arguments we make. She did not
acknowledge Flax's concern not only with empirical truth but also with which truths
are stated and which left unstated, with who produces theory and who is its object.

Within the decade, however, Okin had begun to take these concerns more seriously.
In her concluding "Reply" to the published discussions in "Is Multiculturalism Bad for
Women?" she not only asserted that "the multiple voices of members of a group" must
be heard but identified young women as a group whose voices were especially important
and especially likely to be inaudible (1999:118, 126). And Okin's 2003 article recommended that proposed lists of capabilities should be assessed by the method of listening
to the "silent voices," which Brooke Ackerly attributed to described Third World feminists (Okin 2003:280). Okin sought to put this methodological precept into practice by
listening to the silent voices of poor women speaking in the pages of the Beijing Platform
for Action and the first two volumes of the World Bank publication *Voices of the Poor*
(Beijing Declaration 1996; Narayan, Chambers, et al. 2000; Narayan, Patel, et al. 2000).

In my view, Okin achieved only limited success in practicing the method of Third
World feminist social criticism. For instance, she did not reflect on the fact that the
voices of the poor were already interpreted and represented in the volumes she read,
nor did she consider that the *Voices of the Poor* volumes are so long and complex that,
like the Bible, they contain endless quotations capable of supporting multiple readings. Moreover, Okin's method remained nondeliberative. Nevertheless, it seems to me
extremely significant that, in the last years of her life, Okin's reflections on methodology came to center on concern for the marginalized. Okin stopped talking about the
original position, she began advocating a method of inquiry that "does not presume
either equality or complete knowledge" (2003:298), and she came to recognize explicitly the value of developing less top-down approaches to conceptualizing well-being.

The limitations of Okin's last work only point up the difficulty of doing theory in a way that takes these recommendations seriously.

Okin and Essentialism

Okin's increasing self-consciousness about methodology and her changing foci and methods seem to me to reflect a progressive, though never explicit, acceptance of anti-essentialist and postmodernist ideas. Moreover, I think that this evolution in Okin's work demonstrates the benefits of the essentialism debate for feminist studies, despite its frequent sharpness and painfulness. The debate revealed the biases lurking in much Western feminist theory and the need for more inclusive and power-aware methods of theorizing. Okin's work became even stronger as she came increasingly to recognize the validity of these concerns.

Why did Okin resist these ideas for so long? To answer this question, we must remember that she came of age politically and philosophically in the 1960s and 1970s, when extreme hostility and ridicule were directed against the idea of "women's liberation," and feminism was vilified as weakening and diverting attention away from more important struggles for racial/ethnic and class justice. In her first book, Okin asserted that she was focusing on sex equality not because she considered other types of inequality unimportant but rather "because the unequal treatment of women has remained for too long shamefully neglected by students of political thought. Other types of inequality—class inequality in particular, but also inequalities based on race, religion, caste, or ethnicity, have not been so consistently ignored" (1992:11–12).

In the 1970s, Okin and her generation of feminists—which is also my generation—were in something like the position of Kuhnian "revolutionary" scientists; we were struggling to overthrow established paradigms by establishing the theoretical and political importance of the categories of sex and gender. Okin knew how hard fought these theoretical and political gains had been, she knew that they were still precarious in philosophy, at least, and she was concerned that their critical edge not be blunted and that feminism be asked once again to subordinate concerns about gender. Okin's critics, by contrast, occupied positions more like those of Kuhnian "normal" scientists. They had the luxury of being able to take gender for granted as a category of theoretical and political analysis and so could focus on refining this category and making it more sophisticated. The antiessentialists deserved their victory in the "essentialism wars," but their achievement depended on earlier victories in earlier battles by feminists such as Susan Okin.

CONCLUSION: THE PROFESSIONAL AND THE PERSONAL

Susan Okin produced an impressive body of work over the course of a long career that nevertheless ended too soon. Her focus changed and her views evolved over the years, but some continuing themes are evident throughout her work. They include a passionate concern for the equality of all women, across history and across the world; an increasing concern for the least advantaged women; and a concern for the ways in which the Western tradition of political theory, including political economy, has rationalized structures and cultures of domination.

Okin's valiant scholarship demonstrates that liberal feminism, like the liberal tradition more generally, is "a fighting creed" (Taylor 1992). Drawing on the core liberal principles of autonomy and equality, Okin reached extremely radical conclusions, most notably the need to abolish gender. At the same time, she was rightly proud of producing specific recommendations for public policy rather than limiting herself to vague hand waving. She hoped that expanding the opportunities for individual choice by reducing economic and cultural coercion would create a more humanist justice.

I wish I had known Susan Okin better but, in my limited acquaintance with her, it seemed to me that the same virtues marked both her professional and personal lives. Prominent among these virtues were compassion and kindness. Okin cared passionately about equality and freedom for women across the world, and she worked hard to promote it, both in her scholarship and later in her support of the Global Fund for Women. She was also kind to colleagues and friends, in my own case providing not only valuable philosophical feedback on my ideas but also advising me on dealing with a wayward teenager: one of her suggestions was to encourage participation in amateur dramatics.

Okin's life and work were also marked by courage. She challenged the giants of Western political philosophy with bold and unrelenting arguments and also engaged directly with her feminist critics. As well as being courageous, Okin was a person of great integrity, which was evident both in the rigor of her scholarship and in the way in which she lived her life. This integrity was manifest in her intellectual and ethical responsiveness, which allowed her to grow and develop throughout her career and in her personal life.

To end with more slogans, this time not used tongue-in-cheek, Susan Moller Okin recognized that the personal *is* political, she struggled to live with contradictions, and she worked hard for a better world, which she believed to be possible.

10

The Dilemma of a Dutiful Daughter

Love and Freedom in the Thought of Kartini

Chandran Kukathas

I was told that I should not forget that I was a Javanese, not a European woman. I could adopt European values as long as these did not conflict with our *adat*.

I have learned three things from Europeans—love, sympathy, and the concept of justice, and I want to live according to these.

—Kartini, November 20, 1901

Europe will teach us truly to be free.

—Kartini, June 10, 1902

Reform is the product of the times!—it is not brought into being by the will of a single person.

—Kartini, May 18, 1903

RADEN ADJENG KARTINI

Kartini (April 21, 1879–September 17, 1904) was a woman of noble birth who lived nearly all of her short life in the Japara administrative district of Java, where her father, a Javanese aristocrat, worked for the Dutch colonial administration as governor.[1] As a daughter of the regent, she was given the opportunity to attend a Dutch school, but only until her 12th birthday. Thereafter, as was the custom for Javanese girls of her station, she was confined to her home until her marriage—in November 1903. The length of this confinement was due in part to Kartini's determination not to accept any arranged marriage and to devote her energies to furthering both her own education and the prospects for education of Javanese women generally. Born Raden Adjeng

---

1. The quotes from Kartini above all appear in *Letters from Kartini: An Indonesian Feminist 1900–1904*, translated by Joost Coté (Melbourne: Hyland House and Monash University, 1992), 131, 234, and 406, respectively. (All subsequent references to this volume are abbreviated *LFK*, with date of the letter and page number of the volume following). The title Raden Adjeng in the subheading indicates that Kartini was an unmarried woman born into the Javanese aristocracy. Kartini was her only name. Upon marriage, a Javanese noblewoman would take the title Raden Ayu. Though she was an aristocrat, Kartini was not a princess, as the title of one collection of her letters misleadingly suggests. See Raden Adjeng Kartini, *Letters of a Javanese Princess*, translated from the Dutch by Agnes Louise Symmers, edited by Hildred Geertz (Lanham, MD: University Presses of America, 1985 [1920]).

Kartini, she did not crave the title of Raden Ayu, to the astonishment of relatives who wondered why a woman would not want to marry. The answer to this puzzle is found in the hundreds of pages of letters Kartini wrote to her Dutch friends, expressing, among other things, her wish to travel and to see Europe, her hopes for improvement in the circumstances of the Javanese people and of Javanese women in particular, and her desire for a freedom she felt was denied to her by her role as a woman raised under Javanese traditions. These letters, which reveal to us the mind and spirit of Kartini, are also the source of her fame and stature in modern Indonesia. Her birthday is a public holiday, and she is honored as a feminist and nationalist whose writings contributed to the movement for Indonesian independence. In spite of her vigorous criticisms of polygamy and arranged marriage, however, she succumbed to family pressure and became the fiancée of the regent of Rembang, a widower some 16 years her senior, with seven children and three wives. Kartini died as the result of complications following the birth of her son, a little more than ten months after her wedding. A person of some notoriety in her own community, largely for the unconventional attitudes she shared with two of her sisters, Roekmini and Kardinah, she became a figure of wider significance when students in the nascent Indonesian independence movement began to draw inspiration from her writings in the decade following her death. The translation of her letters into Indonesian and their publication in 1922 extended her influence more widely still. In her own life, however, her most cherished ideals remained unfulfilled.

My purpose in this chapter is to offer an account of Kartini's life and thought and an assessment of its significance. More particularly, I hope to draw out and reconsider her analysis of the difficulties that confront women in modernizing societies, pulled as they are in different directions by the demands of loyalty and custom, on the one hand, and the desire for independence, on the other. Kartini's life and writings reveal to us a social critic grappling with the problem of reconciling tradition with values that transcend time and place. Such a critic confronts two hostile audiences: a local one that views what is not native as simply foreign and sees in the critic's pleadings only betrayal; and an outside one that sees the local critic as merely an apologist for questionable customs. Kartini tackled both audiences, in her life as well as in her thought, and a consideration of her efforts will be instructive.

There is, however, a more particular reason for considering Kartini's life and thought here. The issues with which Kartini grappled as an individual and a feminist were precisely those issues that preoccupied Susan Okin in her exploration of the tension between feminism and multiculturalism. In a series of powerful essays, Okin argued that feminist principles and some multicultural ideals come unavoidably into conflict because, to the extent that multiculturalism advocates the toleration or protection of all minority cultures, it is simply incompatible with feminism's insistence that women everywhere should be recognized as entitled to treatment as equal citizens and to live lives as free as those of men. Protecting or tolerating some minority cultures could only mean condoning, in the name of culture, women's inequality and lack of freedom. In this regard, Okin was especially critical of those who argued for a significant degree of tolerance of minority cultures that are inhospitable to or oppressive of women on the grounds that women in such cultures are free to the extent that they have the right to exit their communities and traditions. In Okin's view, the right of exit, important though it is, can only do its work if women are not already socialized in such a way as to make this right merely a formal entitlement and, thus, quite valueless. If women are to enjoy realistic rights of exit, she insisted, they need more than promises: they need, at the very least, an education that will enable them to make informed choices.[2]

However, two questions present themselves. What steps might reasonably be taken to ensure that women receive a particular kind of education if this goes against the wishes of their communities or traditions? And how much difference can education really make in the face of the power exerted by the forces of custom and culture? These are questions that Kartini confronted both in her writings and in her personal life. An examination of her life and thought should therefore throw valuable light on the problem of women and multiculturalism, illuminating both the insights and the difficulties in Susan Okin's analyses of this question.

KARTINI AND HER MILIEU

Kartini was born on April 21, 1879, the daughter of Raden Mas Adipati Ario Sosroningrat, the regent (and so, the highest-ranking native official) of Japara. She was the natural daughter of Ngasirah, the regent's second wife—his *selir* rather than his *padmi*, or principal wife, the Raden Ayu. Kartini was the fourth born, and eldest daughter, of Ngasirah's eight children. Raden Ayu Moerjam, the younger, principal wife, had three children with Kartini's father.

Such blended families were scarcely unusual in nineteenth-century Java, at least among the *priyayi*, or nobility, though wives and daughters had little say in their composition. Marriages were arranged by parents, and husbands were at liberty to acquire additional wives at their own discretion. It was not uncommon for the nobility to live in families of two, three, or four wives and ten or more children, though polygyny was rare in Javanese peasant society. *Priyayi* households were often larger still, particularly if the husband was a high-ranking official, such as a *bupati* (regent) or *patih* (a native official below regent). Younger relatives, including nieces and nephews, often lived in the household under the *ngenger* custom, by which poorer relatives had their children raised by their well-to-do relations, who would assume all of the responsibilities of foster parents, though without legal adoption. Because the custom conferred great prestige on the foster parents, some ambitious *priyayi* were tempted to take in as many children as possible and sometimes ended up exploiting them as servants. Widowed sisters and children were also often taken into the household under the *ngenger*

2. See in particular Okin's "'Mistresses of Their Own Destiny': Group Rights, Gender, and Realistic Rights of Exit," *Ethics* 112.2 (2002): 205–30; "Multiculturalism and Feminism: No Simple Question, No Simple Answers," in Avigail Eisenberg and Jeff Spinner-Halev, eds., *Minorities within Minorities: Equality, Rights and Diversity* (Cambridge: Cambridge University Press, 2005), 67–89; "Is Multiculturalism Bad for Women: Continuing the Conversation," in Deen Chatterjee, ed., *Feminism, Multiculturalism, and Group Rights* (Oxford: Oxford University Press, forthcoming). I offer critiques of Okin's views in my "Is Feminism Bad for Multiculturalism," *Public Affairs Quarterly* 5.2 (2001): 83–98; and "Exit and Gender," in Chatterjee, *Feminism, Multiculturalism and Group Rights*.

custom. Though sometimes treated as servants, *ngenger* relatives held a higher status. They were, for example, allowed to sit on chairs and eat with the family, which servants never were. The family also assumed the financial burden of providing for their education and the duty of making arrangements for the weddings of nieces when they came of age. Interestingly, after the 1920s, as more and more women acquired a school education and were able to enjoy greater independence, the *ngenger* custom came to be regarded as humiliating for widows.[3]

A *priyayi* household, such as that in which Kartini was raised, was exclusively the domain of the principal wife. The husband was expected to take little interest in household matters. The position of the principal wife was higher than that of second, third, and other wives. The social status of *selir*, who were often lower-class or peasant women, was generally very low, though their children had the same entitlements as children of the *padmi*. Marriage to a *selir* seldom involved an elaborate wedding ceremony (though it might still look elaborate when compared with modern Christian ceremonies), and a *priyayi* man married to several *selir* was still considered to be a *jaka*, or unmarried man, until he took a *padmi* and underwent the more complex ceremonies and rituals to do so. The *padmi* would live in the main building of the *dalem*, or residence, of the *priyayi* and would generally share the social life of the husband, while the *selir* would live in an apartment within the *dalem* grounds, where she would cook her own meals and raise her own children, assisted by female servants, and usually enter the main building only when called by her husband. In Kartini's household, the woman to whom she refers in her letters as "Mama" was her father's principal wife, who entered the residence after Kartini's mother had already borne her husband two children as his *selir*.

The relationship among the different members of the *priyayi* household was a complex one. Even though the children of *selir* had the same privileges within the household and the same rights of inheritance as their step-siblings, they did not have the same rank as this was expressed in Javanese linguistic etiquette. That etiquette was complex indeed. A husband wishing to refer to his *padmi* or *selir* had "to choose between nine different designations for spouse, which conform to sixteen distinctly conceptualized situations."[4] Such was the complexity of Javanese etiquette generally that Kartini herself observed, in one of her early letters to her correspondents in Holland, that Europeans who had been in the Indies for years still had difficulty making sense of it. "Often I have had to explain everything to my friends, but then, after talking for an hour till my throat was dry, they would know just as much about conventions as a newborn baby."[5]

To these layers of complexity, however, were added the complications that were the consequence of Dutch colonial rule. Although the Dutch rulers were relatively

---

3. In this and the following paragraphs on Javanese culture, I have drawn substantially on Koentjaraningrat, *Javanese Culture* (Singapore: Oxford University Press, 1985), esp. 259–64.

4. Koentjaraningrat, *Javanese Culture*, 263.

5. Letter August 18, 1899, in Kartini, *On Feminism and Nationalism: Kartini's Letters to Stella Zeehandelaar 1899–1903*, translated with an introduction by Joost Coté (Clayton: Monash Asia Institute, 1995), 12. All further references to this volume are abbreviated *SZ*, followed by date of the letter quoted and page number of the volume.

tolerant of Eurasians and sometimes of others of mixed descent, it nonetheless remained true that "racial classification was the cornerstone of colonial administration."[6] In Kartini's time, Dutch law in the Indies distinguished three different groups: Europeans, inlanders ("natives"), and foreign Orientals (mostly Chinese). Though the racial ideology and doctrines of white or European superiority were notable developments in nineteenth-century Western thought, the origin of the system of racial classification in the Indies had just as much to do with the practical problem of establishing a colonial administration as with the currency of ethical ideas. In the early days of the United Dutch East India Company, in the seventeenth and eighteenth centuries, religion rather than race was the basis upon which peoples were distinguished. Christian natives were treated more or less as equals under Dutch law and, in the end, even non-Christians in the towns, such as Batavia, could expect some legal recognition. This posed little problem as long as the Dutch influence extended only along the coastal towns and as long as those towns remained substantially Christian. But as the Dutch extended their reach into the interior, and as natives came to be more closely tied to the cities, the practice of leaving the pagan or non-Christian natives to their own, somewhat obscure and unwritten, law made it necessary to make new distinctions between Europeans and natives. The establishment in the 1830s of the "cultivation system," which provided that only natives could own land, while others were forced to rent, gave further impetus to the system of racial classification, as did the conscious policy of maintaining dual jurisdictions, with separate Dutch courts for Europeans and native courts for natives. The presence of large numbers of Chinese and smaller numbers of Japanese further complicated matters, as qualifications and exceptions were made to deal with the inconsistencies and anomalies generated by the system. And of course, intermarriage and the birth of children of mixed descent complicated things further still since it became important to try to determine exactly who was a European.[7]

Kartini was born into this world—a world governed by Dutch administrative law overseeing a system of native law run in part by native officials, none of whom had training in Dutch law. It was a world in which natives did not enjoy the equal protection of the law and in which educated natives also had little prospect of advancement in the colonial hierarchy. (In this respect, Dutch colonial practice was very different from that of the British in India after 1858, when governmental authority was transferred from the East India Company to the Crown, which opened administrative offices up to all of its subjects, at least in principle.) Most important, Dutch policy discriminated against natives by neglecting to provide them with the educational facilities made

6. C. Fasseur, "Cornerstone and Stumbling Block: Racial Classification and the Late Colonial State in Indonesia," in Robert Cribb, ed., *The Late Colonial State in Indonesia: Political and Economic Foundations of the Netherlands Indies 1880–1942* (Leiden: KITLV Press, 1994), 31–56, at 31.

7. The impact of this system on the lives of the many kinds of people living under it—natives, Europeans, "foreign orientals," and people of mixed race—is explored with great insight by Pramoedya Ananta Toer in the first novel of his tetralogy, *The Buru Quartet: This Earth of Mankind*. Kartini's letters and ideas are the subject of discussion among characters in the second novel, *Child of All Nations*, though the chronology is inaccurate.

available to Europeans.[8] One significant consequence of this was that the opportunity to learn Dutch was very limited. In many circumstances, natives who were proficient were denied the privilege of conversing or dealing with Europeans in Dutch. Kartini was thus unusual because she was not only given the opportunity to learn the language but also was able to master it in spite of a formal education that went no further than elementary school, and she was able to use and refine it in an extensive correspondence with Dutch women who befriended and mentored her.

KARTINI'S PERSONAL IDEALS AND POLITICAL IDEAS

It seems unlikely that a young woman growing up in the *kebupaten* (official residence) of a regent in nineteenth-century Java could become a rebel, whether philosophically or in some more practical way. In Kartini's case, rebellion looked unlikely because her opportunities for learning about or interacting with the world outside the boundaries of the household were so limited. After she completed her elementary schooling, she was confined to the compound of the official residence in accordance with the requirements of *adat,* or customary law. She later described her circumstances to Stella Zeehandelaar:

> I was locked up in the house, totally separated from the outside world to which I could not return unless it was at the side of a husband, a complete stranger chosen for us by our parents....European friends—I only learnt this later—had tried everything possible to change my parents' views, to change what for this young and life-loving child was such a cruel decision; but they could achieve nothing. My parents were immovable—I entered my prison. Four long years I served behind four thick walls without ever seeing anything of the outside world.[9]

Kartini was not, however, denied books or correspondence with Dutch friends, and through these sources, as she later implied, "the spirit of the age, my helper and protector,"[10] entered. After 4 years, aged 15, she saw the outside world again for the first time—an experience she enjoyed once more six months later. Then, in 1898, her parents scandalized the local Javanese community by allowing Kartini and her sisters to travel to Batavia to participate in the festivities celebrating the coronation of the new queen. By this time, Kartini had become thoroughly convinced that Javanese traditions were far too confining not only for her but also for Javanese women more generally. Within a year, she would become a firm defender of more radical principles of freedom and equality and a dedicated advocate of practical reform to change the situation of women in Javanese society.

---

8. In the last two decades of the nineteenth century, the colonial government did expand primary education substantially. In 1882 there were 300 primary schools for Indonesians in Java and the outer islands, with 40,000 students, only 44 of whom were girls. The total number of students doubled by 1897. However, the greatest expansion of schooling was due not to government effort but private initiative, most importantly by Christian missions from 1890 onward. On this see Colin Brown, *A Short History of Indonesia: The Unlikely Nation* (Crow's Nest, New South Wales: Allen and Unwin, 2003), 103.

9. *SZ,* May 25, 1899, 3.

10. *SZ,* May 25, 1899, 4.

The sources of Kartini's thinking included not only the books and letters she read. In 1895, she made the acquaintance of Mrs. Ovink-Westenenk, the widowed sister-in-law of the assistant resident of Japara, and of his wife, Mrs. Ovink-Soer. Through Mrs. Ovink-Soer in particular, Kartini came to know of the leading Dutch feminist journals of the time, notably *De Hollandsche Lelie*, *De Echo*, and *Nederlandsche Taal*. By the time Assistant Resident Ovink was transferred from Japara in 1899, Kartini had developed an independent life of the mind even within the confines of her circumstances as an unmarried Javanese noblewoman. On March 15, 1899, at Kartini's request, *De Hollandsche Lelie* published a notice:

> A young lady in Java who has received an extended and enlightened education… would be very pleased if a cultivated fellow subscriber in Holland would enter into correspondence in order to engage in an exchange of views with an educated young girl.[11]

The result was a four-year correspondence with Stella Zeehandelaar, a Dutch feminist working as a clerk in the office of the Post and Telegraph Department in Amsterdam. (Zeehandelaar was unusual among "progressive" women of that time for taking an interest in the condition of native women in the colonies.) It was through this correspondence that much of Kartini's thought found expression.

Even more important, however, was her meeting in 1900 with Rosa Abendanon-Madri, and her husband, Jacques Henry Abendanon, the director of education, religion, and industry in the Dutch colonial administration. Both were reformers who hoped to see not only the expansion of native education but also the establishment of schools for Javanese women. One result of their first visit to the regent of Japara was the initiation of a deep friendship between Kartini and Rosa Abendanon-Madri, and an even more extensive correspondence over the ensuing four years. In her letters to Rosa, whom she came to call Mother, Kartini attempted to articulate her personal beliefs and revealed her hopes for herself and for the realization of what she came to regard as her mission to help the advancement and liberation of Javanese women.

What then were Kartini's beliefs and ideals? In answering this question, it is important to bear in mind that we are not considering the thought of a philosopher or a systematic thinker but the reflections of an intelligent, largely self-educated, young woman communicating with an older woman whom she regarded as a mother figure and with a Dutch penpal she would never meet. We do not find in these writings a new theory of freedom nor a distinctive conception of equality. But we find a consistent view of the world and a degree of insight born of the writer's appreciation of what it meant for a person in her position in her times in her part of the world to hold such views.

Two ideals above all inform Kartini's thinking: love and freedom. In her writings and in her life, she was preoccupied with the problem of how to secure freedom, both for herself and for others. Love, however, she regarded as "the highest commandment"[12] and "the most elevated religion."[13] Reconciling the pursuit of freedom with

---

11. Quoted in Joost Coté, "Introduction," *On Feminism and Nationalism*, iv.
12. *LFK*, July 14, 1903, 429.
13. *LFK*, December 14, 1902, 346.

faithfulness to the principle of love was the issue that most exercised her imagination. To grasp the nature of the problem for Kartini, we will look more closely at her understanding of freedom.

Kartini sought freedom for herself, but also freedom for the Javanese—and for Javanese women in particular, since, in her estimation, they enjoyed very little of it. Freedom meant two things: self-development and liberation from the confining power of custom and tradition. One could not be had without the other. The obstacles to the achievement of freedom were the lack of education, the uncritical acceptance of tradition, and the inequality of status fostered by Javanese custom and reinforced by Dutch law and rule. These obstacles, she thought, hampered not only her own liberation but also the liberation of Javanese women, and Javanese people more generally. They key to freedom for all Javanese, men and women alike, she suggested, lay in bringing European values into Javanese society.

It is remarkable that Kartini was so forthright in her insistence that European ideas would be the source of her own and Javanese liberation. To be sure, these sentiments were expressed in letters to European women who were not merely correspondents but mentors and sources of practical help. (Rosa Abendanon-Madri made strenuous efforts to secure for Kartini a scholarship to study in Holland, and Stella Zeehandelaar introduced her to influential figures in the Dutch colonial administration.) But Kartini was scarcely sycophantic in her discussions of the European impact on the Indies. She was quite clear about the attitudes of most Europeans:

> Father said to me once: "Ni, do not think there are many Europeans who are *really* fond of you. There are only very few."
> Father really did not have to say this, we know this *very well* ourselves; we can count on our fingers those who have a *sincere* regard for us, and we do not even need 2 hands for that. *Most* effect sympathy in order *to pose* or as a calculated *ploy.*[14]

She was also highly critical of the Dutch administration of the colonies and took a skeptical view of various efforts made to alleviate the condition of natives. Reading the Dutch Commission on the Decline of Welfare report that asked why natives were still poor, she scornfully observed that hitting grass cutters, who earned 10 to 20 cents a day, with a business tax and instituting a tax on bat manure to extract revenue from the poorest farmers surely had something to do with it.[15] She was similarly dismissive of Dutch motives in establishing a government monopoly on the sale of opium, which it claimed was aimed at discouraging the use of opium among natives. The fact was that the government derived significant revenues from its sale and had rejected a proposal from the regent of Rembang which would have ended opium use in the district. "So you see, it is not the Native population but the *Government* which cannot do without the opium."[16]

14. Letter from Kartini and Roekmini to Rosa Abendanon, *LFK*, October 27, 1902, 311.

15. *LFK*, August 10, 1904, 518.

16. *LFK*, August 10, 1904, 519. See also *SZ*, May 25, 1899, 6, where Kartini comments on how the sale of opium "fills the purse of the Neth. Indies government" and notes that the government had prohibited the sale of morphine because it would lessen the sale of opium.

Nonetheless, Kartini insisted that the coming of Western civilization to Java was a good thing and that the best of the Europeans were the models for all to imitate.[17] Europe and Europeans would bring freedom to the Indies. What Europe promised to bring to Java, in Kartini's mind, was a change in outlook and the possibility of education. It promised Kartini herself the opportunity to develop intellectually and morally, but also held out the prospect of a more fundamental transformation of Javanese traditions and attitudes. Of central importance would be the transformation of marriage.

For Kartini, marriage more than any other institution was the obstacle standing in the way of women's development and freedom in Java. Marriage in the Javanese tradition was, according to Kartini, a defective institution in a number of respects: it was a relationship not of equals but of master and subordinate(s); it was not a voluntary association but the product of coercion; it denied women the opportunity to be independent; it hampered the intellectual and moral development of women, who were brought up to think that being a wife and serving a man was all that they should aspire to; and, quite simply, it left many Javanese women miserable yet "so accustomed to their mistreatment, they no longer see any injustice in it, regard their subjugation with complete stoicism as the entitlement of men, as the inheritance of suffering of every woman."[18]

In her letters, Kartini expressed disdain for marriage as a condition which could mean only the end of her freedom and which would deny her the opportunity to love. She shared this attitude with her sisters Kardinah and Roekmini[19] and attempted, unsuccessfully, to persuade her stepmother that requiring her daughters to marry was harming them and that there was nothing wrong in remaining unmarried—though Mama could not see that a woman who did not wish to marry could have any motive other than vanity.[20]

Ironically, it was the situation of her own mothers that had first prompted Kartini's unfavorable reaction to marriage. Her natural mother, Ngasirah, had married in the knowledge that one day her husband would take a principal wife—"that she would some day get a mistress."[21] Yet, it seemed to Kartini that this was an intolerable burden for any woman to bear: to wait powerlessly for the arrival of a rival or a superior and then to accept the position of second wife. Moreover, she saw that it poisoned her own relationship with her natural mother. When her stepmother arrived, she had no love for her husband's children and could not love Kartini when she was born to her husband's *selir*—though she did her duty by all her children.[22] The young Kartini, sensing Mama's distance, did all she could to secure her approval and affection, but at a price:

17. "The urge to imitate is inherent in human beings I believe. The masses imitate the habits of their betters, who in turn follow those of the higher classes and ultimately these imitate the very best—the Europeans." *SZ*, May 25, 1899, 5.

18. *LFK*, August 1900, 26.

19. Roekmini was the daughter of Raden Ayu Moerjam and so, strictly speaking, Kartini's step-sister.

20. *LFK*, November 20, 1901, 130. The occasion for this exchange with her step-mother was Mama's request that she use her influence to persuade Kardinah to accept the marriage arranged for her, since Kardinah had become depressed at the prospect of becoming a wife.

21. *LFK*, December 21, 1900, 58.

22. Raden Ayu Moerjam had herself been a step-daughter and "knew the suffering of a child of a *heartless* mother." *LFK*, December 21, 1900, 58.

Let me pass over that sad period, when my best intentions were misunderstood—explained to my disadvantage—when I experienced nothing but hatred when I offered only love. My own mother turned against me as a result of misunderstanding—she, especially she, for whose sake I humiliated myself, crawled on the ground, for a little affection—put up with everything, everything.[23]

Polygamy was the aspect of Javanese marriage for which Kartini reserved her sternest criticisms, and her contempt for the practice was the source of her unwillingness ever to marry. "To be able to love, there must be respect, in my opinion," she wrote, "and I cannot [have] respect for Javanese men."[24] How could she, Kartini argued, when a man, already a husband and father, could ask another woman into his house because he has had enough of the mother of his children. Of course, there was no reason why he shouldn't, since Islamic law viewed it as neither a crime nor a scandal. Yet, even "if a thousand times over it was not a crime in terms of Islamic law and learning," Kartini insisted, she "would forever call it a sin."[25] Though Javanese women took this situation for granted, even in the principalities, such as Surabaya and Yogyakarta, where it was not uncommon for aristocrat men to have as many as 26 wives, "almost every woman I know here curses this right that men have. But wishes achieve nothing: something must be done."[26]

One reason that Kartini looked to Europe as a source of Javanese liberation was that she viewed Europeans as modern and progressive when it came to marriage, whereas "[w]e here in Java have only just arrived at the eve of the new day."[27] Yet the importance of Europe ran deeper. It held out the opportunity for Kartini herself to cleanse her person of her own Javanese attachments and liberate herself from attitudes she was unable to shake. She wanted desperately to go to Holland to study and to return to Java as an educated woman who was properly prepared to open a school for young women. But even apart from the attractions of study, she saw a stint in Holland as providing a form of moral therapy:

I want to breathe in the European air to rid myself completely of the residue of prejudice which still clings to me—there is not much that still holds me back. Holland must and shall make me in reality a free woman. Your air, your cold, must dislodge all the prejudices which still cling to me. Only then shall I be free![28]

---

23. *LFK*, December 21, 1900, 59.

24. *SZ*, November 6, 1899, 15.

25. *SZ*, November 6, 1899, 15. Kartini continues: "I regard as a sin all deeds which cause one's fellow human beings to suffer. To sin is to hurt another human being, human or animal. And can you imagine what hellish pain a woman must experience when her husband comes home with another whom she has to recognize as his lawful wife, her rival. He can torment her to death, mistreat her as much as he likes; as long as he does not choose to give her freedom again, she can whistle to the wind for her rights."

26. *SZ*, August 23, 1900, 46.

27. *SZ*, August 23, 1900, 47.

28. *SZ*, May 17, 1902, 94. Kartini illustrates this point in the following passage on p. 95: "So you see, despite my strong sense of freedom, I have not been able to avoid my native upbringing which keeps young girls strictly apart from male strangers. If you are constantly told that it is unseemly to allow yourself as a young girl to be revealed to the gaze of strange men, and if you must stay out of the presence of men then eventually it must make you nervous to meet such creatures. This must not continue, that prejudice must be removed." She makes a similar point in *LFK*, June 10, 1902, 234.

Kartini thought that a little education was not enough, either for her or for other Javanese women. It was important not only to acquire knowledge and become cultured but also to change one's thinking. Women in the Prianger region, for example, though educated in Dutch, were "despite their European education, their nice, pleasant little manners,... *really, really* Native in thought and attitudes," and they could "see no problem in marrying a man who is married—who has a wife, often wives and children."[29]

The key to bringing about change in the Indies, in Kartini's mind, was to change the consciousness of particular individuals, those who would set an example for others to imitate. Individual liberation was the path to liberation for society. And in this she saw herself as about to play a substantial role. By educating herself and ridding herself of her prejudices, her Javanese ways, she would put herself in a position to influence others, first directly as a teacher of children, and second, less directly, by showing by example what was possible.[30] This, she was certain, would be an important struggle, though a painful one.

The reason it would be painful was that the pursuit of freedom necessarily meant going against Javanese tradition. Indeed, freedom meant, in part, the repudiation of *adat*. The overturning of marriage customs was not an end in itself, nor could it be achieved without taking on native customs more generally. In particular, this meant questioning the preoccupation of the Javanese with distinctions of status or rank and asserting the ideal of equality—an ideal that had very little resonance among the people in Kartini's social circle, natives and colonizers alike. To be sure, Kartini insisted that she had no wish to turn her people into "half Europeans" or "European Javanese."[31] Observing the fashion of replacing the *sirih* in its golden case with "garish artificial flowers from which gaudy ribbons were trailing" in some modern Javanese weddings, she noted: "I am not sure whether I should be pleased that some of the traditional customs have been lost when I see what they have been replaced with. The imitation European!"[32] This did not, however, change her view that tradition needed to be confronted.

Particularly galling to her was the fate of the government's plan to train the daughters of regents when "*most of the* Regents whose advice was sought declared themselves against the plan as it went against the *adat* which prohibits young girls from receiving instruction outside the home."[33] But it was not only the traditions that bore directly

29. *LFK*, October 1, 1901, 121.

30. *LFK*, November 29, 1901, 151: "'We must embark on a royal route—that is—go to Holland, study in Holland. Our people are not very susceptible to high ideals or noble principles,' Kartono [the youngest of Kartini's three older brothers] says justly. 'We must surprise them with an example which *speaks* to them and which *persuades imitation*.'"

31. *LFK*, June 10, 1902, 232. Kartini continues: "with this education we aim above all to make of the Javanese, real Javanese, Javanese *inspired* by a *love* and a *passion* for their land and people, with an *eye* and *heart* for their beautiful qualities—and needs! We want to give them the finer things of the European civilization, not to force out or replace the finer things of their own, but to *enrich* it."

32. *LFK*, December 14, 1902, 349.

33. *SZ*, January 9, 1901, 65. Kartini continued: "Oh! *Those Conservatives.* If they only knew what they had repudiated, *but what else could be expected from our stuffy land—*...But silence now, we should not be unfair in attacking those who cannot feel anything for the progressive plans of the government

on her own aspirations that she criticized. She had little regard, and perhaps even a measure of contempt, for the idea of aristocracy. Asked by Stella Zeehandelaar if she was a princess, Kartini replied: "No more than you." She admitted that her father was the distant descendant of a prince and that Mama was closely related to the royal house of Madura: "But we do not give a hoot for this. For me there are only two types of aristocracy: the aristocracy of the spirit and moral aristocracy. I think nothing is so ridiculous, nothing more silly than people who allow themselves to be honored on the basis of their so-called 'high birth.'"[34] This disdain for aristocracy extended to its rules of etiquette: "You cannot imagine how that old mother 'etiquette' rules in the circles of the Javanese nobility. You cannot move a muscle or that awful woman stares grimly at you!"[35] Kartini herself refused to have anything to do with conventional forms with her younger siblings, in spite of criticism of their free and easy relationship: "Liberty, equality and fraternity! The younger sisters and brothers with me and amongst themselves conduct themselves as free and equal friends."[36]

Kartini was no less troubled by the inequality between the aristocracy and the common people, though she had been raised in a society in which difference in status was unquestioned.[37] Unsurprisingly, then, she was highly critical of the unequal status of natives and Europeans. On the one hand, the aristocracy enlisted the help of the government to maintain their own privileges, for example, by attempting to further restrict Javanese access to European schools and by preventing ordinary people from

---

and the interests of their daughters. In order to appreciate something one first needs to understand it and how can *these narrow minded people* understand the desires of our young modern generation, these people who *still live in complete darkness*, who have never thought differently. Where in enlightened Europe, the centre of civilization, the source of light, the struggle for justice is still being waged fiercely and furiously, can we expect that *in* the…Indies, which has been in deep slumber for centuries, and which is still asleep, it would be accepted, even permitted that the women, who for centuries had been regarded and treated as an inferior being, could be regarded as a person who is entitled to a freedom of conscience."

34. *SZ*, August 18, 1899, 10.

35. *SZ*, August 18, 1899, 11. In passages that follow (pp. 11–12), Kartini gives Stella a number of examples of the requirements of etiquette. "A young sister or brother of mine may not pass by me without crawling over the ground. Should a sister be sitting on a stool and I pass her, then she must immediately slide to the ground and stay there with bowed head until I am completely out of view. My younger brothers and sisters may not say 'jij' or 'je' [informal you] to me and may only address me in high Javanese; and, after each complete sentence which falls from their lips they must make me a sembah, that is, put both hands together and bring them up just under the nose."

36. *SZ*, August 18, 1899, 13

37. Kartini recounts her shame when she thoughtlessly treated a wood-carver as an inferior. "Once, when we stood enraptured by his craft, we asked him: 'Hey fellow, where do you get this beauty from?' For a moment the downcast eyes were focused on us, a shy smile played around his mouth and he answered simply: 'From my heart, Bendoro'—And I became annoyed with myself that I had a higher social position than he—I on the stair—and he beside us on the ground, in a humble position, making himself insignificant because…we happened to be the children of a father to whom power and prestige had been granted. What right did we have to accept that token of respect from someone whom we regarded as a *hundred* times our superior? I hated myself. And this is how a member of the 'aristocrat brood' thinks; no wonder that it is coming to bed down with the social democrats!" *LFK*, August 24, 1902, 266.

being educated in Dutch.[38] On the other hand, Javanese officials bowed before Europeans with an obsequiousness that reflected the great inequality of power: "The most minor European official has the right to sit on a chair while native officials below the rank of regent of whatever age, origin or expertise, [are] directed to sit on the floor when Europeans are present."[39] Kartini herself, though respectful, seemed unintimidated by her Dutch "superiors." When the resident of Semarang, Mr. Sijthoff, ridiculed her and her sisters for their vegetarianism, saying that no one should know or no one would want to marry them, Kartini bowed briefly and said that everyone could know of it. When he suggested that he might issue a decree that everyone should eat meat, she responded: "Do so,…and then the government can begin by providing the people with cattle."[40]

Kartini was unusual. Women did not usually entertain such views, nor were they so outspoken. Despite her mild manner and gentle nature, her conviction that she was a free person and that she was right to have ambitions other than marriage made her a notorious figure in the Javanese community. Unlike most of her compatriots, she wanted to live in a society in which she did not have to bow her head before others, particularly men: "It is required that I politely (hypocritically) lower my eyes—that I will not do. I want to look them *in* the eyes not lower my eyes before them, nor look *at* their eyes."[41] The cost of this attitude was gossip that called her coquettish—the news of which pained her because she could not bear to be associated with anything frivolous.[42]

As someone who believed in her own freedom and who had worked to educate herself, Kartini was committed to the goal of bringing education to Javanese women in greater numbers. Aside from writing letters, she made plans, with J. H. Abendanon, to head a school for daughters of regents (thwarted in the end by the regents themselves) and made strenuous efforts to obtain a scholarship to study in Holland, with the help of Abendanon and, later, more successfully, of H. H. Van Kol, a Dutch MP and leader of the Dutch Social Democratic Party. Kol's visit to Japara in April 1902 brought her notoriety and was the source of gossip accusing her of coquettish behavior, sexual promiscuity, and desire for a Dutch husband. But the meeting eventually brought the result she wanted: in November, she was offered a government grant to study in Holland, and her father granted her permission to accept.

Yet, within two months, these plans lay abandoned. She turned down the scholarship she had coveted, and six months later, on June 9, 1903, she was promised to the regent of Rembang. She asked her parents to be permitted to continue her studies, take her

---

38. *SZ*, January 13, 1900, 30. Kartini, like many Javanese, thought it was imperative that people in the Indies be taught Dutch. Her brother, Kartono, in an address to the XXV Congress of Netherlands Language and Literature, presented an argument for the spreading of Dutch language use throughout Java, claiming that, in a population of 26 million, Dutch speakers numbered only in the hundreds. See *SZ*, appendix 2, 116–24.

39. *SZ*, August 23, 1900, 51.

40. *LFK*, December 14, 1902, 345.

41. *LFK*, October 11, 1902, 305.

42. *LFK*, 11 October 11, 1902, 305.

exams, and open the school she had planned to establish and also that she be "allowed to continue for one more year of my dream of freedom and self-development, to still be allowed to go to Batavia to participate in one year of a course and to try to complete it in that year."[43] Her parents found her request "reasonable and natural," and they agreed subject to the approval of the regent of Rembang. But her plans to study in Batavia were also abandoned, and, that November, she married a man she did not know.

No one took the news of Kartini's marriage harder than Stella Zeehandelaar. By marrying, she wrote Nellie Van Kol, "Kartini gave the lie to her whole being....thereby she sacrificed one of her greatest ideals."[44] Why did an exceptionally independent-minded young woman abandon a lifelong dream of "her own free will"[45] and decide to remain in the Indies? And why did she also agree to wed when she had always insisted that she would only marry, if at all, for love?

KARTINI'S DILEMMA

Accounting for Kartini's decisions is not a simple matter. Stella Zeehandelaar died convinced that her marriage to the regent of Rembang was a part of a wider conspiracy (that included the colonial government) to deny her the opportunity to study in Holland. A "beautiful and promising life was sacrificed to selfish interests."[46] But a satisfactory explanation of Kartini's decisions may be more complex. We need to consider a number of other matters, including the influence of Javanese traditions, the relationship Kartini had with her family, and Kartini's beliefs themselves—though distinguishing Kartini's beliefs from her relationships and from her traditions may not be easy.

The immediate cause of Kartini's rejection of her scholarship to Holland was J. H. Abendanon, who persuaded her that she should not leave Java. Abandenon had himself failed to persuade the authorities to give Kartini a study grant, just as he had failed in his efforts to expand public education in the Indies and to make Dutch language education more widely available to native schoolteachers, leaders, and the daughters of native administrators. When Kol succeeded in securing the grant, Abandenon advised Kartini not to take it. His reason, which Kartini accepted, was that going abroad would jeopardize her ultimate goal. As she explained to Stella Zeehandelaar: "the public whom we wish to serve has yet to get to know us. If we should leave now, then we would estrange ourselves from it. And when we returned in several years['] time we would be regarded as European women."[47] People simply would not entrust their daughters to Europeans, much less to a Europeanized Javanese woman. Better to postpone Holland, and study in Batavia first.

Though Kartini suggested some other advantages of study in Batavia—it would be a chance for her parents to get used to her absence without her being a long way

---

43. *LFK*, June 1903, 432.

44. Letter dated September 26, 1904, quoted in Joost Coté, "Introduction," *SZ*, ix. Stella Zeehandelaar was, at the time of writing, unaware that Kartini had died nine days earlier.

45. *SZ*, April 25, 1903, 108.

46. Letter to Henry van Kol, October 26, 1904, quoted in Joost Coté, "Introduction," *SZ*, x.

47. *SZ*, April 25, 1903, 109.

away, and she would be able to adjust to being away from home without being in a foreign land—these were beside the point. The fact was that she had to take notice of public opinion. Mrs. Van Kol had written to her, "To achieve an ideal, one has to renounce many, many dreams." Kartini concurred: "The first dream we have to set aside is to present ourselves to the public as we are."[48] Though she would have preferred that "people...get to know us as we are, and then from conviction, give us their children," this was impossible.[49] The combination of Kartini's own ideals and the pressure exerted by Javanese traditions worked against the fulfillment of her immediate hopes for travel. Had her ambition been purely to develop her own talents and person, public opinion might not have mattered so much. Had Javanese traditions been less hostile to women's education or independence, travel abroad might never have been an issue. But given that things were the way they were, she had to work surreptitiously, though dissembling was not in her nature.

Yet the influence of tradition on Kartini's decision may have run deeper still. To accept the grant or, for that matter, to study in Batavia, Kartini needed her father's permission. Sosroningrat was an educated and cultivated man—one of the very few regents who were fluent in Dutch—and unusual for having been willing to have his children, including his daughters, schooled and taught a foreign language. He granted his permission for Kartini to travel, study, and teach. By Kartini's own account, he would not have forced her to do anything. Nonetheless, his own wish was that his daughter *not* travel abroad but remain at home—and marry. On receiving his permission to seek the scholarship, Kartini immediately sensed his grief and "suffered with him"—and felt no jubilation.[50]

It was not only her sensibilities but also her convictions that gave rise to this reaction: "There is a duty, called gratitude, there is a high and holy duty called the love of a child, and there is a low, cursed evil, called egotism."[51] Was her pursuit of her ideals nothing more than egotism—an egotism that was leading her to forsake a higher duty? There were in the world far too many ungrateful children—even more than there were insensitive parents—and she did not wish to be one of them.[52] Kartini's letters are full of acknowledgments of her parents' devotion and sacrifice and her father's great love for her.[53] She also recounts in detail her anxiety about her father's illness and his fragility after he was diagnosed with a heart condition.[54] Her first duty, surely, was to her parents, and especially to her ailing father. Beside that duty, traveling to further her education seemed like an indulgence, an expression of the egotism she despised.

48. *SZ*, April 25, 1903, 110.

49. *SZ*, April 25, 1903, 110. "We must not do this, the public must never know what we are fighting against. The name of the enemy against which we are going into battle must never, never be heard: polygamy."

50. *LFK*, July 15, 1902, 246–47.

51. *SZ*, May 20, 1901, 65.

52. *LFK*, August 13, 1900, 23.

53. In recounting her anguish when her natural mother turned against her, she writes: "only Father's great love kept me going, prevented me from doing myself in." *LFK*, December 21, 1900, 59.

54. *SZ*, May 20, 1901, 64; *SZ*, October 24, 1901, 80.

Here was the dilemma. Duty seemed to call upon her to overcome her wishes and desires, to remain at home to support and care for her parents rather than subject them to further stress by her absence. To do otherwise would be to fail in a fundamental duty. Yet to go and "work at the realization of [her] ideals, work for the future—work for the well-being of thousands who are bent under the unrighteous laws, under the false understanding of good and evil"—this seemed no less a duty, even if it also coincided with the ego's longings.[55] In the end, for all of Abendanon's reasoning about the tactical merit of postponing study abroad, it was Kartini's convictions about her duty to those she loved that may really have been decisive.

All of that said, however, it may not have been her convictions alone that were the decisive factor in leading Kartini to forsake her ideals. The convictions themselves were ideas shaped by the very forces against which she had struggled. In her very first letter to Stella Zeehandelaar, she had written:

> Day and night I ponder on the means by which it might yet be possible to escape the strict moral code and customs of my country yet....The old Eastern traditions are firm and strong but I could shake them from me, break them, if it were not for that other bond, even more securely and strongly fixed than any centuries old tradition, which binds me to my world: the love I have for those who gave me life, to whom I owe everything, everything. May I, do I have the right, to break the heart of those who throughout my life have shown me nothing but love and goodness and who have surrounded me with such tender care? I would break their hearts if I indulged my desires and did what my whole being yearns for with every heartbeat, with every breath I take.[56]

According to her Eastern, Javanese, traditions, she had no right to break any hearts. But her sense of this came from the strength of her Javanese upbringing. Love did not just bind her to her parents and siblings but, as she put it, love bound her to her world—to her customs and traditions.

This may account not only for Kartini's decision not to pursue her studies abroad but also for her meek acceptance of the proposal of marriage. She did not have the resources to refuse, for she was still encumbered with the attitudes and prejudices that she thought only European air would wash away.

SOME CONCLUDING OBSERVATIONS

Kartini's life tells a story of an individual's struggle to secure her own freedom and also to make a difference in the world. Though it ended before she had the chance to effect her plans, she was determined to make a difference. "I want my writing to have a lasting impact,"[57] she told Stella Zeehandelaar, although on several occasions she declined

---

55. *LFK*, September 4, 1901, 108. "What is the greater duty—the first or the second? Egotism I have always regarded as the worst sin which exists, and deeply, deeply despised it—similarly ingratitude—and that other, our ideal, has become part of our existence; we cannot live without it, no less than we can live without the love of those who are dear to us."

56. *SZ*, May 25, 1899, 1–2.

57. *SZ*, October 11, 1902, 107.

requests to write for magazines when she suspected that she was sought only for her novelty value—a source of amusement and wonder for the curious in Holland.[58] This is not the place to attempt a full assessment of the impact of Kartini's work, but I do want to ask what we can take away from an encounter with Kartini's life and writings. Here are some thoughts, offered not so much as lessons one might extract and formulate in a few glib generalizations but as reflections to be engaged with and subjected to further scrutiny.

One topic that Kartini's life and writings clearly illuminate is the complex nature of social criticism and the difficulties faced by the critic—particularly if she is a Third World feminist, but perhaps even if she is not. The difficulty is in part simply practical: how is she to find the means to bring about the changes—in thinking, in social structures, in opportunities for people—that are the point of social criticism? But the difficulty is also personal: how is she to reconcile her critical stance with her identity? The practical and personal issues are interrelated. Kartini was aware, and became ever more conscious, of the fact that her success as a social critic and, therefore, as a reformer, depended crucially on her capacity to establish her identity in her social world. Her credibility in her own society rested on her ability to relate to her social world. It would not have been enough simply to try to show Javanese people that the values she wanted to promote were universal, or even that they resonated with Javanese traditions. The interpretation, as well as the reception, of the message was always going to be tied closely to the identity of the messenger. Adopting an identity too distant from the society might lead to alienation and ineffectiveness, while adopting an identity that was too close might lead to incapacitation, as the critic would become unable to criticize and repudiate.[59] Equally important, the reformer cannot act successfully if she acts alone. Social criticism and social reform must, to some degree, be collective endeavors. As Kartini noted, reform is the product of the times.

Kartini's life and thought also bring out the extent to which the pursuit of individual freedom, or liberation, does indeed depend on successful social criticism and reform, for freedom is not something that can easily be enjoyed alone. Kartini came to believe that individual liberation—her liberation—was not possible without changes in society. There cannot be autonomy without a culture of autonomy. She could not become autonomous unless Javanese society became one that was at least tolerant of, and preferably hospitable to, autonomy. This also meant that there were limits to her capacity for self-transformation, limits given by her circumstances and culture—unless, of course, she was willing to pay the price of abandoning her community and culture altogether.

This brings me to a further issue: the extent to which one's freedom depends upon one's capacity to dissociate altogether from the people, the community, the group, the traditions that restrict, confine, oppress, and make life go badly. One option available to Kartini was simply to go to Europe, with the knowledge that this would give her

---

58. "A Dutch-writing Javanese woman is considered interesting, that is the secret of easy success." *SZ*, March 14, 1902, 89.

59. On this subject more generally, see Brooke A. Ackerly, *Political Theory and Feminist Social Criticism* (Cambridge: Cambridge University Press, 2000), esp. chs. 5 and 6.

the opportunity not only to study and fulfill her dreams of self-realization but also to make a new life for herself, perhaps never to return to Java. It might have enabled her to marry for love, or to become an independent writer, or simply to pursue unknown possibilities. There were no financial obstacles in her way, permission to go had been granted, and friends and admirers awaited her in Holland. The problem, however, was that to go she had to be a different person, one who was more indifferent to what others thought, more concerned about her own life and happiness than about her family's, more of an egotist—or at least someone who cared more about her personal freedom than she did about what she had been raised to see as her duty.

In a revealing passage in a letter to Rosa Abandenon on the anniversary of their meeting, Kartini described her situation in the third person:

> Her brother, hearing of her determined longing for freedom, for independence and emancipation, laughed mockingly: "Of course you can stand on your own two feet, when you walk in front of a gamelan." This cruel expression cut her to the quick. She did not think about the insult which was thrown at her, she saw only the raw truth which stood starkly before her eyes: "There were only *two* paths open to a young Native girl to survive this life—either marriage or…shame!" It groaned and moaned: "Either Raden Ayu or dancing girl!" Oh God! Oh God! On the one hand delivered over to the whim of a man, on the other, to shame. Could she learn resignation? Her young head was in a turmoil of hundreds of thoughts—in her heart a spirit of opposition against the existing conditions was developing. She would not, she did not want to submit to it. She wanted, she must, find a new way.[60]

The life of a dancer before a gamelan orchestra was an option, and it would have allowed her to remain unmarried. But in the eyes of Kartini's family, and indeed in her own eyes, this kind of life would have been shameful. Yet one could surely say that, as an egalitarian who thought we should not look down on any human being, however humble, Kartini should not have seen the life of a dancer as shameful. Indeed, it was only shameful to *priyayi* families, but not in the eyes of others. But Kartini could no more shake off this sense of the shamefulness of one of her options than she could take on the part of an egotist, indifferent to the attitudes of her world.

It might also be worth noting that often exit is easier when circumstances are harsh than when oppression is gentle. Of course, when conditions are violent and extremely restrictive, exit may be impossible. But when conditions are milder, exit may be difficult for another reason: the opportunity costs of leaving are simply too high. Giving up the love that one has enjoyed may be simply too great a price to pay. Exit may be possible only when the price is right.

There is, however, another conclusion we might draw from the Kartini story, which is not far in spirit from the conclusion that Stella Zeehandelaar drew. The decision that Kartini took was not authentically hers. What Kartini's decision and the reflections that preceded them reveal is not so much her dilemma as her moral confusion. In spite of her education and her longing for freedom, she had acquired so little of an authentic self that she could not grasp that not every self-interested act is reducible to mere "egotism," and that however appropriate it might be that she show some gratitude to

---

60. *LFK*, August 1900, 35.

her parents, she could not owe them "everything." After all, would it not be self-interest bordering on egotism for her parents to ask everything of her, leaving nothing for herself? Perhaps what the Kartini story reveals is the power of tradition and its capacity to overwhelm the individual, perhaps to the point of forcing her to betray the values that otherwise define her. Culture is not a conspiracy, but it might as well be. Some cultures might nourish authenticity; others starve or suffocate it. Kartini's story is a tale of a dilemma but also a lesson in the power of cultural suppression.[61]

There is much to be said for this point of view. Perhaps it is true, as Eamonn Callan suggests, that for Kartini, it would have required an authenticity of godly proportions to win against the powerful adults who settled her fate. Yet it has also to be asked what we are to make of a level of authenticity that enables its subject to reason with depth and sophistication—and yet not win. What recognition do we grant those women, and their choices, if they are much more than uneducated, unreflective followers of tradition, who see a dilemma where others see none? The danger in divorcing freedom entirely from rationality is that it leads us to describe as free even those who are duped or manipulated into acting against their interests. The danger of tying freedom to rationality, and rationality to particular outcomes, is that this leads us to describe as unfree even those who have chosen thoughtfully and carefully but badly.

Kartini, for all of her intelligence and learning, was as confused about many matters as she was insightful about others. In the end, however, she *was* free, despite her tendency to overstate the depth of her duties and to underappreciate the virtue of selfishness. She was as free, that is, as any person who might exhibit the opposite failing.

For anyone who asks the question "is multiculturalism bad for women?" or who reflects more generally on the tension between feminism and multiculturalism, Kartini's case is an interesting one, for it brings out very clearly the powerful hold that culture exerts on individuals and on individual women in particular. Susan Okin, in her critique of multiculturalism, pointed out that women especially tend to carry the burden of their parents' expectations that they will transmit their culture to the next generation, and the Kartini story bears this out.[62] It also makes clear that having a formal freedom to exit does not suffice to ensure that individuals will be able to fulfill their desires to pursue ambitions beyond those set by their families. Yet Kartini's dilemma also tells against Okin's own proffered solution to the liberation of women from constricting cultures: state intervention to provide education and, if necessary, punishment of cultural communities,[63] to create more "realistic" rights of exit. This is because it is difficult to see how Kartini's right of exit could have been made any more realistic. She had an education, she had a desire to pursue her own goals, she had the resources to do so, and she had parental approval. What she did not have was the social milieu that would allow her to pursue those ambitions and still enjoy both the approval of the community and a clear conscience. For women to enjoy the kind of freedom that Kartini longed to exercise may require a cultural transformation—of the

61. In making these observations, I have drawn on Eamonn Callan's critical response presented at the conference honoring Susan Okin.

62. See Okin, "Mistresses of their Own Destiny," 222.

63. Okin, "Feminism and Multiculturalism: Some Tensions," 676.

kind that Kartini saw herself as trying to foster. Education backed by state power may be simply too clumsy a method for bringing such change about, even while a formal right of exit is also insufficient to do so.

EPILOGUE

The case of Kartini has, at least to my mind, a strange ending. So let me finish with a few notes about the last year of her life, and leave it to the reader to determine what to make of them.

Kartini dreaded the prospect of marriage to the regent of Rembang. She described her wedding garment as her "costume of disguise," and Roekmini called it her "burial cloth."[64] Marriage meant the shattering of her hopes and entry into a new cage.

Within a few months, however her feelings were very different. She quickly came to admire the regent who, as it turned out, shared many of her ideals. The reason he had sought out her parents and proposed marriage was that she was, by reputation, an independent-minded and interesting woman with a passion for social reform. The regent was a highly educated man who had traveled to Holland and Europe and had read widely. He therefore encouraged Kartini's intellectual interests and helped her prepare to open the school she wanted to found. He admired her learning and encouraged her to write a book on Javanese myths and legends, on which he proposed they work together. He shared her disdain for frivolity, as well as her criticisms of the Dutch administration and her sense of the injustice of the conditions of natives in the Indies. According to Kartini, he enlarged her perspective on the world. Of the things she came to admire about him, one was his unwillingness to subordinate himself: "my husband dares to look everyone in the eye." Tell my sisters, she said, "my husband is worthy of my love and respect, totally."[65]

The regent's letter to J. H. Abandenon, thanking him for his good wishes after learning of Kartini's death, suggests that her feelings for her husband were returned. Of her final moments, he wrote:

> Dr Revenstijn returned 4 days later, he said that the discomfiture was the consequence of the lesions caused by the birth and thus quite normal. He gave the Raden Ayu medicine but half an hour later the discomfiture increased and shortly afterwards, quietly and calmly, while lying in my arms and in the presence of the doctor, she passed away. Five minutes before her death she was totally alert and until the last moment remained conscious. I cannot express in words how deeply shocked I felt at that moment. I had been so happy with her during those ten months. In all that she had thought and strived for she was the personification of love, and her perspective was so broad that there is no one among her Native sisters who is her equal.[66]

64. *LFK*, July 24, 1903, 447.
65. *LFK*, August 10, 1904, 519.
66. *LFK*, Letter from the Regent of Rembang, September 25, 1904, 527.

IV

DEVELOPMENT AND GENDER

11

Discordant Cooperation

Reinventing Globalization to Reduce Gender Inequality

Robert O. Keohane

Susan Moller Okin was outraged about gender inequality. It engaged her intellectually and deeply moved her emotionally. During the last phase of her career, she shifted her attention from gender inequality in the rich countries to the even greater injustices inflicted on women as a result of gender inequality in poor countries. As she did everywhere, she questioned orthodoxy, both the orthodoxy of neoliberal economics and the orthodoxy of multiculturalism. My emphasis in this chapter will be on her engagement with the political economy of gender and development and with the effects of globalization on women.

In January 2004, Okin spent two weeks in India with the Global Fund for Women and attended the World Social Forum. In her published writings and in private correspondence, she emphasized a number of ways in which economic globalization and policies of neoliberalism have been bad for women in developing countries.[1] But she also recognized the other side of the coin: that social globalization—the diffusion of ideas and the operation of social movements on a global basis—can promote feminist social criticism and gender equality. In a paper published in 1999, she said, "There are some aspects of globalization that, far from endangering democracy, present new opportunities for democratic participation and popular influence to emerge and to affect international law-making."[2] She and her coauthor, Brooke Ackerly, mentioned

This chapter is dedicated to the memory of Susan Moller Okin, who was my colleague at Brandeis University in the early 1980s and a dear friend for over 22 years; it was originally written for a conference in her honor in February 2005. I am particularly indebted to Brooke Ackerly and Tamar Gutner for their extensive and detailed critical comments on earlier versions of this chapter. I am also grateful to Ruth Grant, Jane Jaquette, Mary Fainsod Katzenstein, Nan Keohane, Jane J. Mansbridge, and the editors of this volume for helpful comments on later versions. Unfortunately, I have not been able to update my analysis with research on the directions taken by the World Bank during the presidency of Paul Wolfowitz (2005–2007).

1. Even successful economic development, as conventionally defined, can have negative effects on the work burdens and autonomy of women, and it can have different effects on different sets of women. See Boserup 1990.

2. Brooke Ackerly and Susan Moller Okin, "Feminist Social Criticism and the International Movement for Women's Rights as Human Rights," in Ian Shapiro and Casiano Hacker-Cordón, eds., *Democracy's Edges* (New York: Cambridge University Press, 1999), 134.

population mobility, improved means of long-distance communication, global media, the transnational spread of ideas, and the activities of nongovernmental organizations (NGOs).

In this chapter, I seek to honor Susan Okin's deep commitment to gender equality and her contribution to thinking about these issues by asking whether globalization could be "reinvented" in a way that would help to promote gender equality in developing countries. At the most general level, my argument is that feminist social movements would be wise not to reject globalization but to use the opportunities provided by it to promote gender equality. These opportunities will require institutional involvement: institutional leadership and institutional change will be necessary for significant progress on this set of issues to be made.

More specifically, feminists will need to engage with the World Bank, since the bank is the only large global multilateral institution with the capacity to provide such leadership. Under the presidency of James Wolfensohn, who left office in 2005, the bank showed itself to be more open to change than some other global institutions. The argument of this chapter is that feminist social movements and NGOs should engage with the World Bank while maintaining a healthy critical distance from it. As of mid-2008, the Bank was recovering, under the presidency of Robert Zoellick, from a period of controversy and disarray during the presidency of Paul Wolfowitz. It is possible that the next few years will be an auspicious time for feminist activists to press their agenda on a new Bank leadership that is anxious to rebuild constituencies for its work.

In using the term, "gender," I follow Susan Okin's definition: "the deeply entrenched institutionalization of sexual difference."[3] The central problem that Okin analyzed was how the institutionalization of sexual difference led to economic and political inequality, to the disadvantage of women. Practices deeply embedded in specific organizations privilege men over women directly through discrimination and indirectly through rewarding roles traditionally performed by men or by making demands (such as time-related demands to work) that cannot be met by people with responsibility for the care of small children, who are usually women. Institutions—in the broader sense of persistent social practices and norms—also perpetuate gendered stereotypes. Studies of institutions involved in rural development in poor countries demonstrate that, as Anne Marie Goetz writes, "institutions do not just passively mirror gender differences in social organization; they also *produce* gender differentiation through their structures and in their everyday practices."[4]

Institutions shape behavior by structuring incentives, as well as by furnishing taken-for-granted norms, which people may accept even when they are highly disadvantageous to them. Political power is at the heart of both incentive systems and norms. Empowered people create incentive systems, typically to advantage themselves and people like them, and build normative structures that suit their own beliefs and practices. If these systems generate inequality through gender differentiation, only the

3. Susan Moller Okin, *Justice, Gender, and the Family* (New York: Basic, 1989), 6 (hereafter *JGF*).

4. Anne Marie Goetz, ed., "Introduction," in *Getting Institutions Right for Women in Development* (London: Zed, 1997), 12; see also World Bank, *Engendering Development* (Oxford: Oxford University Press, 2001).

empowerment of people with different interests and different subjective values is likely to change their systematic bias. Empowerment is therefore at the heart of any strategy to reduce gender inequality.

In choosing the phrase "reinventing globalization," I am indebted to thematic statements by Alison Symington in describing the 2002 triennial meeting of the Association for Women's Rights in Development (AWID).[5] Symington begins with a standard academic definition of globalization: "a stretching of social, political and economic activities across frontiers such that events, decisions and activities that take place in one region can have significance for people in other regions."[6] The author argues that neoliberal versions of economic globalization are harmful to women. But promoting a romantic vision of self-reliance is not the answer:

> Would we not be passing up our most strategic tools by disregarding the avenues of communication and interaction opened up by internet, satellite and transportation developments, the accountability mechanisms created by doctrines of universal jurisdiction in criminal, human rights and humanitarian law, and the new employment and education opportunities now available to so many women around the world?[7]

It will be clear from this chapter that I regard contemporary, deeply entrenched patterns of gender inequality as profoundly unjust. These unacceptable inequalities constitute a major reason that globalization needs to be reinvented, rather than merely redirected in incremental ways. But the reinvention of globalization does not necessarily mean insisting on radical changes in the structure of global capitalism. We can all imagine a more equitable system than the current one, in which access to capital and markets is controlled by relatively small elites, heavily male and mostly based in rich countries. In that sense, many of us find ourselves profoundly unsympathetic to global capitalism, as Susan Okin certainly did. However, it would only be worthwhile to insist on radical changes—rejecting reformism—if a better alternative system seemed feasible.

State socialism has failed to generate either sustained economic growth or freedom, and other potential political-economic systems have not been tried on a large scale. Furthermore, the fact that China and India have renounced socialism and have embraced their own forms of capitalism removes any major point of opposition to capitalism in the world system. Even if a radically transformed system of global production and exchange were feasible, it is hard for me to imagine that it could be implemented within our lifetimes.

---

5. The Association for Women's Rights in Development is a 5,000-member transnational network of activists, supported by funding from the Ford Foundation and the Open Society Institute (www.awid.org). All documents and all budgetary figures cited in this chapter can be found on the Web sites of the relevant organizations, which are listed in the bibliography.

6. Quoted from David Held and Anthony McGrew, *The Global Transformation Reader: An Introduction to the Globalization Debate* (Cambridge: Polity, 2000), 54.

7. Alison Symington, "Re-Inventing Globalization for Women's Rights and Development," in *Reinventing Globalization: Highlights of AWID's 9th International Forum on Women's Rights in Development* (2002). Available at www.awid.org (accessed October 11, 2004).

One does not, therefore, need to be "for global capitalism" to view reformist projects of reinventing globalization as more attractive than simply protesting against the ills generated by capitalism. Reformist projects keep their focus on the plight of poor women who are suffering injustice today. Advocates of such projects accept trade-offs, some of which may be morally ambiguous, since they involve working with relatively sympathetic institutions and groups *within* the system of global capitalism, whose values are unlikely fully to match those of the advocates. Reformists emphasize the consequences of their actions as much as the purity of their intentions. They eschew adopting a lofty moral purity, which is ethically problematic when the putatively pure individuals are sheltered from the effects of failure by their own situations of privilege.

However, to merit the phrase "reinventing globalization," reformist projects cannot merely be palliatives, which help particular individuals or groups while leaving unjust structures of oppression intact. Reinventing globalization to reduce gender inequality requires the *empowerment* of women as a key aspect of any genuine reform. Merely using women instrumentally as a means of economic development, or even poverty reduction, is not reformist but conservative. That is, emphasis must be placed on women's agency—giving women at all levels, from public policy making to household—the ability to participate in and to make important decisions.[8]

The World Bank, like other large organizations in contemporary society, is deeply implicated in the institutionalization of gender differentiation, and it has a mixed record of effectively promoting development. Its ambitions, and sometimes its claims, have been so great that it has been the object of much severe criticism.[9] Nevertheless, under Wolfensohn, the bank reached a higher level of organizational awareness of issues of gender and development than that of most governments. Problems of global inequality and failed development are too deep to expect sudden and dramatic improvements; and in any case, large public bureaucracies such as the bank move slowly. But in my view, the World Bank is a potential resource that feminists should take seriously.

This chapter therefore takes global capitalism as a given and the World Bank as a potentially progressive force. It asks: how can the strategies of NGOs and social movements toward the World Bank help to reinvent globalization in ways that would empower women and reduce gender inequalities? As a student of world politics, I do not expect such strategies to generate harmony on major issues with serious distributional implications. On the contrary, discord is the prevalent condition of world politics: never-ending contention among advocates of different values and interests, competing in a realm that lacks authoritative governmental institutions. Yet, sometimes, cooperation emerges out of discord.[10] I am looking in this chapter for the potential sources

    8. Brooke Ackerly, "What's in a Design? The Effects of NGO Programme Delivery Choices on Women's Empowerment in Bangladesh," in Goetz, ed., *Getting Institutions Right for Women*, 140–158.

    9. Jonathan R. Pincus and Jeffrey A. Winters, eds., *Reinventing the World Bank* (Ithaca, NY: Cornell University Press, 2002).

    10. Robert O. Keohane, *After Hegemony: Cooperation and Discord in the World Political Economy* (Princeton, NJ: Princeton University Press, 1984).

of cooperation between feminist social movements and the World Bank that could emerge from the prevalent patterns of discord.[11]

THE MORAL UNACCEPTABILITY OF CONTEMPORARY POVERTY AND INEQUALITY

I am not a political philosopher, so I do not pretend to be engaging in the sort of applied moral philosophy that Susan Okin pursued so effectively. On the contrary, for the sake of my argument here, I take as given her moral philosophy as a grounding for the more positive empirical exercise of this chapter. She accepted much of the egalitarian liberalism expressed in the works of John Rawls, but with two major qualifications. First, she demonstrated in her work over 15 years that major contemporary formulations of such philosophies, such as those of Rawls, have failed to extend their principles of distributive justice to the family.[12] Second, she was unwilling to limit the application of liberal principles of justice, especially as they apply to women, to Western democracies.[13] To her, gender inequality was unacceptable anywhere, and particularly onerous in poor countries since it affects poor women who lack well-being in the most fundamental sense: they are unable to feed, clothe, and provide shelter for themselves and their children.[14]

Okin read widely and deeply in the empirical literature on development and inequality in poor countries. She emphasized the failures of overall growth and argued that income inequality has been increasing. Without engaging in detailed analyses of empirical patterns of growth and inequality, or necessarily agreeing with all of her interpretations of trends, I will try here to sketch a picture that demonstrates that her moral concern about these issues was justified.

Aggregate economic growth in gross domestic product (GDP) per head worldwide has been extraordinary during the postwar period. In constant dollars, calculated on the basis of purchasing power parity, global GDP rose over seven times between 1950 and 2000, and per capita income tripled during that time. But growth has been very uneven: in the 1973–1998 period, annual per capita growth was estimated at 3.54

11. These arguments are obviously contestable. Susan Okin had more sympathy than I do for projects of radical change, although she was certainly aware of the pitfalls. If she were still alive, she would surely subject my arguments to her critical scrutiny.

12. Susan Okin, "Justice and Gender: An Unfinished Debate," *Fordham Law Review* 72 (2004): 1537–1567; *JGF*.

13. Susan Okin, "Is Multiculturalism Bad for Women?" in Joshua Cohen, Matthew Howard, and Martha Nussbaum, eds., *Is Multiculturalism Bad for Women?* (Princeton, NJ: Princeton University Press, 1999); compare John Rawls, *The Law of Peoples* (Cambridge, MA: Harvard University Press, 1999).

14. Susan Okin, "Poverty, Well-Being and Gender: What Counts, Who's Heard?" *Philosophy and Public Affairs* 31.3 (Summer 2003): 280–316. This article was critical of Martha Nussbaum's argument in her *Women and Human Development* (2000), but Okin and Nussbaum both believed in the universal applicability of liberal democratic values, and both emphasized that institutional practices need to be fundamentally changed so that women can exercise more autonomy in their lives. To a nonphilosopher, therefore, their positions seem relatively similar to one another despite their differences over such issues as whether to emphasize rights or capabilities.

percent in the developing countries of Asia, but effectively zero (0.01 percent) in Africa. As the Growth Commission of the World Bank recently reported:

> This accelerating growth has created new challenges. The first is a clear divergence in incomes within and between countries. Of the roughly 6 billion people on the planet, about 65 percent live in high-income or high-growth economies, up from less than a fifth 30 years ago. The remaining 2 billion people live in countries with stagnating, or even declining, incomes. The world population is projected to increase by 3 billion people by 2050. Unfortunately, 2 billion of this extra population will live in countries that are currently enjoying little or no growth. Thus, if these trends persist, the proportion of the world population living in low-growth environments might increase.[15]

Poverty has fallen since 1970. Using a poverty standard of $1 per day, the World Bank argues that poverty rates fell from 29 percent in 1990 to 24 percent in 1998.[16] Most of this progress was due to great advances in India and China; poverty in Africa may have increased, and extreme poverty (income of less than $1 per day) afflicts 46 percent of its population. By World Bank estimates, 1.2 billion people still lived in poverty in 1998. With respect to inequality, all estimates are controversial, and conclusions depend heavily on technical measurement decisions, for instance, whether to use exchange rates or purchasing power parity measurements of income, whether to count each country equally or weight countries by population, and whether to rely on aggregate national accounts or population surveys. Prudent conclusions would be that inequality is enormous in the world; that during the period since decolonization it has not been falling rapidly; and that both inequality and changes in inequality vary enormously by country and region.[17]

Battles still rage about the impact of neoliberal development strategies and about the role of the World Bank in promoting growth.[18] Our knowledge of the complex combinations of conditions that promote or retard sustained economic development remains seriously deficient. There are notable success stories, especially in Asia, and clear failures, notably in Africa. Unfortunately, it is clear that countries with extensive International Monetary Fund (IMF) and World Bank (WB) programs have not done well: as Okin pointed out, "for the twelve countries that received fifteen or more WB or

---

15. Commission on Growth and Development of the World Bank, "The Growth Report," by Michael Spence et al., 2008. Available at www.growthcommission.org. See also Martin Wolf, *Why Globalization Works* (New Haven, CT: Yale University Press, 2004), 107.

16. World Bank, *World Development Report* (New York: Oxford University Press, 2000–2001), 23.

17. "The big story here is not change, but lack of it. The distribution of income across nations remained remarkably stable over a period of substantial income growth in the world [1960–1989]." Glenn Firebaugh, "Empirics of World Income Inequality," *American Journal of Sociology* 104.6 (May 1999): 1597–1630. See also Xavier Sala-i-Martin, "The Disturbing 'Rise' of Global Income Inequality," NBER Working Paper 8904, April 2002.

18. William Easterly, *The Elusive Quest for Growth: Economists' Adventures and Misadventures in the Tropics* (Cambridge, MA: MIT Press, 2001); Jeffry Sachs, *The End of Poverty: Economic Possibilities for Our Time* (New York: Penguin, 2005); Paul Collier, *The Bottom Billion* (Oxford: Oxford University Press, 2007); Dani Rodrik, *One Economics, Many Recipes* (Princeton: Princeton University Press, 2007); "The Growth Report" (see n. 15).

IMF adjustment loans between 1980 and 1994, the median per capita growth rate was zero."[19] Of course, it could easily be that the worst-governed countries with the worst prospects were precisely those that received more than one adjustment loan per year; those that did well did not apply for loans, and where the loans were successful, they would tend to stop. Nevertheless, Okin was correct that, especially in Africa, development efforts have been disturbingly unsuccessful. The World Bank certainly cannot be considered a resounding success. Global poverty and inequality are morally unacceptable by any universalistic cosmopolitan standard.

These conclusions hold irrespective of gender differences. But, as Okin consistently argued, gender inequality is severe. Even if there were no global inequality by household—a utopian thought—there would be tremendous individual-level inequality as long as gender issues are not addressed. The major factors affecting income—education, work experience, and job characteristics—are affected by pervasive discrimination against women. Girls in South Asia, sub-Saharan Africa, and the Middle East receive fewer than two years of schooling, on average, for every three received by boys.[20] Women are consistently employed in lower-level positions than men.[21] In developing countries, women receive only 73 percent of what men earn—80 percent of which cannot be explained by differences in education, work experience, or job characteristics.[22] Furthermore, there is pervasive discrimination within the household: "In many cultures, when any scarcity exists women and girls tend to get less to eat and less health care than men and boys in the same household."[23] Indeed, as Okin consistently emphasized, no clear line can be drawn between the public and the private sphere: some of the worst violations of women's rights take place within the home, manifested in unequal access to basic goods such as food, in domestic violence, and in control (or lack of control) over sexuality. Informal practices of gender inequality are at the core of the problem.

AIDS: A GENDERED CATASTROPHE

The AIDS epidemic illustrates the significance of informal practices of gender inequality for economic development, institutions, and the lives of women, children, and, indeed, men.

More than 20 million people have died from AIDS, 3 million in 2003 alone.[24] Heterosexual intercourse is now the principal means of transmission. Although only 11 percent of the world's people live in Africa, two-thirds of those with HIV/AIDS live in Africa, disproportionately in southern Africa. The probability of a

---

19. Okin, "Poverty, Well-Being and Gender," 283.

20. World Bank, *Engendering Development*, 43.

21. Ester Boserup, "Economic Change and the Roles of Women," in Irene Tinker, ed., *Persistent Inequalities: Women and World Development* (New York: Oxford University Press, 1990), 14–24.

22. World Bank, *Engendering Development*, 55.

23. Okin, "Poverty, Well-Being and Gender," 284.

24. All figures in this paragraph are from the World Health Organization's *Annual Report, 2004*, ch. 1. Available at http://www.who.int/whr/2004/en/03_chap1_en.pdf.

15-year-old in Kenya dying before reaching 60 years of age rose from 18 percent in the early 1990s to 48 percent by 2002. In Malawi, the comparable probability rose to 63 percent and in Zimbabwe to 80 percent. Overall life expectancy fell in Botswana between 1985–1990 and 2000–2005 from 65 to 40 years, and in South Africa, it is estimated to have dropped during the same period of time from 60 to 50 years. As a World Health Organization (WHO) report states, "Overall, life expectancy at birth in the African Region was 48 years in 2002; it would have been 54 years in the absence of AIDS."

AIDS in Africa has spread so much largely because of male promiscuity, abetted by migration patterns. Despite the fact that men are largely responsible for the spread of AIDS in Africa, 58 percent of HIV/AIDS sufferers in Africa are women, and they are infected, on average, 6–8 years earlier in their lives than are men. About three-quarters of people aged 15–24 in sub-Saharan Africa who are infected by HIV/AIDS are women, for whom the risk of becoming infected during unprotected vaginal inter-course is greater than it is for men.[25] A 2004 report by UNAIDS shows that only about one-third of young women aged 15–24 were aware, at the turn of the millennium, of three basic HIV-prevention methods.[26] Even if women were better informed, social and economic inequalities would make it difficult or impossible for them to prevent their infection. In southern Africa, in particular, "migrant labour systems have aggra-vated women's economic dependence on their male partners to a much greater extent than in other parts of the continent where women are more prominent in market trad-ing and other forms of commercial activity."[27] Furthermore, violence against women is widespread worldwide, and violence increases vulnerability to AIDS infection. As one researcher states: "The high prevalence of HIV/AIDS which has occurred in southern Africa over the last 15 years is importantly a result of the breakdown of family life of black South Africans and most particularly the inability of South African women to negotiate or control their sex lives."[28]

When Okin declared that informal practices of gender inequality are crucial bar-riers to development, she may or may not have been thinking of AIDS. Regardless, her statement most assuredly applies to the AIDS problem in southern Africa. The effects of these practices have been compounded by the unwillingness of a number of governments to take measures to deal with the epidemic. One-third of the world's governments do not yet have policies to ensure that women have access to resources for the prevention and care of AIDS, and many policies that exist on paper are not implemented.[29]

25. UNAIDS, *AIDS Epidemic Update 2004*. Available at http://www.unaids.org, 7, 11.

26. UNAIDS, *AIDS Epidemic Update*, 9. The three methods are avoiding penetrative sex, using condoms, and having sex with only one, faithful, partner.

27. UNAIDS, *AIDS Epidemic Update*, 10.

28. Gwyn Prins, "AIDS, Power, Culture and Multilateralism: A Case Study," paper presented at a Social Science Research Council conference on "Multilateralism under Challenge," Washington, DC, November 29–30, 2004, 18.

29. Kofi Annan, Address to XV International AIDS Conference in Bangkok, July 11, 2004. UN Press Release SG/SM/9418.AIDS/77. Available at http://www.unaids.org.

President Thabo Mbeki of South Africa was particularly resistant to recognizing the AIDS epidemic and to taking measures to deal with it. When he was asked in the South African National Assembly in October 2004 about how male sexual behavior and the apparent pervasiveness of rape might account in part for the spread of HIV in South Africa, he accused the questioner of ignoring the central issue of racism. Refusing to discuss the link between HIV and AIDS, Mbeki said he would not keep quiet while "others whose minds have been corrupted by the disease of racism, accuse us, the black people of South Africa…as being, by virtue of our Africanness and skin colour, lazy, liars, foul-smelling, diseased, corrupt, violent, amoral, sexually depraved, animalistic, savage—and rapist."[30]

During his tenure in office, United Nations secretary general Kofi Annan was much more thoughtful, declaring that AIDS requires the education of girls and the empowerment of women and girls: a "change that will transform relations between women and men at all levels of society."[31]

Throughout the AIDS crisis, rich countries such as the United States and multilateral institutions were slow to react. Since 2001, however, both the United States under the Bush administration and institutions such as the United Nations and the World Bank have sought, along with private foundations such as the Bill and Melinda Gates Foundation, to take vigorous action.[32] Tragically, the worst offenders have been the governments of countries, such as those of South Africa and Zimbabwe, whose people are most adversely affected by AIDS. When the World Bank undertook a relatively small AIDS program in Zimbabwe in 1993, it did not even attempt to change patterns of sexual behavior, since when bank officials tried to discuss the issue, Zimbabweans responded "with jokes about people having too much sex." Even after the bank made AIDS a priority in 1999 with an allocation of $1 billion, it met resistance from recipient governments. By April 2003, less than 10 percent of those funds had been allocated.[33]

If one ever doubts how central gender inequalities are to development, one need only look at AIDS. Even if development were defined in purely economic, material terms, the impact of AIDS is devastating. It has reduced economic growth rates by 2–4 percent in Africa—to negative levels—and could, according to WHO, "result in complete economic collapse in some high-burden countries," as the most active, energetic, and productive segments of the population are hit disproportionately hard.[34]

30. *Cape Times* (South Africa), October 22, 2004. Available at http://www.capetimes.co.za/index .php?fSectionId=271&fArticleId=2270410 (accessed December 14, 2004).

31. Annan, Address to XV International AIDS Conference in Bangkok.

32. The global health program of the Gates Foundation awarded almost $4 billion in grants during 2004, according to its Web site. The Gates Foundation accounted for about 5 percent of the funds received by the Global Fund to Fight AIDS, Tuberculosis, and Malaria, more than any other country or international organization except for France, Italy, Japan, the United Kingdom, and the European Commission. See http://www.theglobalfund.org (accessed December 14, 2004).

33. Sebastian Mallaby, *The World's Banker: A Story of Failed States, Financial Crises, and the Wealth and Poverty of Nations* (New York: Penguin, 2004), 317, 330.

34. World Health Organization, *Annual Report, 2004*, available at http://www.who.int/whr/2004/ en/03_chap1_en.pdf, 2.

GLOBALIZATION AND GENDER INEQUALITY: THE ACKERLY-OKIN CATALYTIC MODEL

Susan Okin approached issues of globalization and gender from the perspective of feminist social criticism. As I understand the Ackerly-Okin version of feminist social criticism, it has three central elements: (1) deliberative inquiry, involving discussion and social criticism that include members and nonmembers of a society; (2) skeptical scrutiny of prevailing values, focusing on exploitable inequalities; and (3) criteria for judgment, based on a belief in gender equality as an essential moral principle and on the specification of minimum standards for achieving it.[35] Ackerly and Okin describe the activities of NGOs devoted to women's rights and argue that these NGOs "made constructive use of globalization."[36] Feminist social criticism is facilitated by what Ackerly calls "multi-sited critics," who are knowledgeable both about local practices and about critical standpoints from outside.[37]

The AIDS epidemic dramatically supports four propositions about gender and development that were developed by Susan Okin on the basis of feminist social criticism:

1. It is not sufficient to guarantee women equality in the public sphere, even if policies for formal gender equality are fully implemented. Many of the most crushing inequalities and burdens on women's capacities to lead good lives result from relationships conventionally considered outside the public sphere, including inequality and violence inside the family and the devaluation of women's work in the home.

2. Traditional practices, including religiously sanctioned practices, often oppress women by denying them opportunities for education, health, sustenance, freedom from violence, and meaningful activities outside the home.

3. These practices are so strongly upheld by prevailing beliefs in the localities involved that they are unlikely to change without the participation of outsiders, who can reinforce the political voice of people inside the societies who are critical of prevailing practices.

4. A necessary condition, therefore, for a great reduction in gender inequality is a vigorous indigenous movement of feminist social criticism, able to point out the inequities of traditional practices in terms understandable in the society concerned.[38]

It seems to follow from these four propositions that a fully *nonglobalized* world—in which each country is fully insulated from events outside of it—would, in many parts of the world, be bad for gender equality. The concept of human rights, and the related concept of women's rights as human rights, has some of its strongest advocates in

35. Ackerly and Okin, "Feminist Social Criticism," 138–139.

36. Ackerly and Okin, "Feminist Social Criticism," 143.

37. Brooke Ackerly, *Political Theory and Feminist Social Criticism* (New York: Cambridge University Press, 2000).

38. Ackerly and Okin, "Feminist Social Criticism."

wealthy liberal democracies. Indeed, there is new empirical evidence that the Convention on the Elimination of All Forms of Discrimination against Women (CEDAW) has had a positive impact on women's rights. Controlling for other factors, two separate studies have shown that CEDAW ratification is associated with educational opportunities for women.[39] There is also evidence that CEDAW is associated with access to modern forms of birth control and with higher female life expectancy, participation in the economy, and representation in national legislatures.[40]

Okin and Ackerly sketch what I call a "catalytic" model of change. As Okin points out, too much pressure, or too much domination, from Western liberals undercuts local activists and could give rise to charges of imperialism.[41] But too little involvement can help to perpetuate an oppressive status quo. The outside critic, and the multi-sited critic, can stimulate a process of feminist social criticism by raising questions that problematize what is otherwise taken for granted and that validate similar concerns expressed by people within the society. However, to accomplish their goals, insiders must take the lead.

If this analysis is correct, it clarifies the issue of what multilateral institutions and NGOs can and cannot do. They cannot directly achieve gender equalization, since they do not exert direct effects on local communities, much less within the home, and they carry neither the coercive capacity of coherent, tightly organized states nor the emotionally laden appeal that sometimes accompanies nationalism. If they are to make a difference, they will have to facilitate or promote feminist social criticism—to help provide a safe space for such criticism, to stimulate it, and to legitimate it, in some combination. Is there any reason to believe that multilateral institutions or NGOs can do this effectively?

MULTILATERAL ORGANIZATIONS, NGOS, AND GENDER INEQUALITY

Both multilateral organizations and NGOs profess interest in reducing or eliminating gender inequality. Since multilateral organizations are more politically constrained than NGOs in what they can say, one might be tempted to rely on NGOs and what has come to be known as "global civil society" to take the lead. However, discussions of the vitality of global civil society should not be allowed to obscure the fact that NGOs are tiny compared even to multilateral organizations, much less to states. What NGOs can accomplish by themselves is therefore quite limited.

Consider first the most important international financial institutions: the World Bank, the IMF, and the Global Fund to Fight AIDS, Tuberculosis, and Malaria. In

39. Mark Gray, Miki Caul Kittilson, and Wayne Sandholtz, "Women and Globalization: A Study of Quality of Life and Equality Indicators in 180 Nations, 1975–2000," unpublished manuscript, Department of Political Science, University of California, Irvine (2005), 48; Beth Simmons, "Women's Equality: Education, Work and Reproduction," in Simmons, *International Human Rights: Law, Politics, and Accountability* (forthcoming).

40. Gray et al., "Women and Globalization"; Simmons, "Women's Equality."

41. Okin, "Poverty, Well-Being and Gender."

fiscal 2003, the two major arms of the World Bank group—the International Bank for Reconstruction and Development (IBRD) and the International Development Association (IDA)—together loaned $20 billion.[42] The IMF's lending for the Poverty Reduction and Growth Facility, the main development effort of the IMF, amounted to about $1.4 billion in 2004.[43] Pledges to the Global Fund, for periods of time running from one to eight years, total $5.5 billion.[44] These numbers are reasonably large, although even World Bank lending was only about 1 percent of the U.S. government's budget.

The resources available to UN agencies are much less than those at the disposal of the IMF and World Bank. Even relatively large UN agencies, those not focused on women, have budgets that are only about 2 percent of World Bank lending. UNICEF's budget is less than $350 million per year, and that of the World Health Organization is less than $450 million. The political explanation for these disparities is simple: voting at the IMF and World Bank is weighted by contributions, whereas at the United Nations, one state has one vote. Donors are reluctant to give huge amounts of money to organizations over which they exert little formal control. The World Bank also borrows large amounts in capital markets—an activity for which the backing of rich states is essential.

The NGOs and women-oriented arms of the UN system are another order of magnitude smaller than the general-purpose UN development agencies, such as WHO. The United Nations Development Fund for Women (UNIFEM) had a budget in 2002 of about $36 million.[45] Oxfam America had a budget in 2003 of $29.9 million.[46] The Global Fund for Women, a grant-making organization focused on the empowerment of women, had a budget of $5.1 million in 2002–2003.[47] So Oxfam America, which seeks to empower women, among other development goals, has a budget that is about as large as UNIFEM—about 10 percent of that of UNICEF and less than two-tenths of 1 percent of World Bank lending.

Even the apparently large sums allocated by the World Bank and the IMF are widely seen as insufficient to meet the millennium development goals of the United Nations: to eradicate extreme poverty and hunger, achieve universal primary education, promote gender equality, and achieve five other related goals.[48] The conclusion therefore seems inescapable that the programmatic activities of NGOs—delivering aid to people who need it—will have only a minor *direct* impact on the eradication of gender

42. World Bank, "Implementing the Bank's Gender Mainstreaming Strategy: Second Annual Monitoring Report, FY 03" (January 29, 2004). Available at www.worldbank.org (accessed October 12, 2004).

43. International Monetary Fund, *IMF Annual Report, Fiscal 2004*. Available at www.imf.org.

44. The Global Fund to Fight AIDS, Tuberculosis, and Malaria's Web site is http://www .theglobalfund.org.

45. United Nations Development Fund for Women, *UNIFEM Annual Report 2002–2003*. Available at www.unifem.org.

46. Oxfam America, *Annual Report 2003*. Available at www.oxfamamerica.org.

47. Global Fund for Women, *Annual Report 2003*. Available at www.globalfundforwomen.org.

48. United Nations, *United Nations Millennium Declaration* (2000). Available at www.un.org/ millenniumgoals; Peter Heller, "Can the IMF Contribute to the Promotion of the MDGs Relating to Gender Equality?" Speech to a meeting of High-Level Women in International Finance, Economics, and Development, Dubai, September 20, 2003. Available at www.imf.org (accessed October 11, 2004).

inequality. Grants by organizations such as Oxfam can be important because of their positive impact on specific communities and individual people and because of their potentially very important demonstration effects. In particular, community-based action can help women to organize and thereby empower them, without necessarily bringing in huge new resources. By successful innovation, NGOs can lead the way, encouraging governments and multilateral organizations to follow in their footsteps. By themselves, however, even the best NGOs cannot change large-scale gendered structures of power and privilege on a global basis. Implementing good ideas for economic advancement and empowerment so that hundreds of millions of people are affected will require substantial sums of taxpayers' money, typically channeled through multilateral institutions.

A second conclusion is that increases in knowledge and deepening of understanding are critical to reducing gender inequality. If NGOs that are committed to women's rights are to succeed, they will have to change how we think about gender issues. To do so, they will have to engage in successful pilot programs, showing what can be done to reduce gender inequality, and in effective advocacy. The accomplishments of NGOs committed to women's rights—for instance, at the Vienna UN Conference on Human Rights in 1993 and the 1995 Beijing Conference on the role of women—have not been the result of direct programmatic activity alone. Programmatic activity has been important to demonstrate that something can be done well, but the impact of what NGOs can do themselves needs to be magnified many times. To achieve this, NGOs committed to women's rights have mobilized networks of supporters to transmit a message that has resonated in multilateral institutions and the global media. The mobilization process for Vienna involved networks of women working in NGOs, in multilateral organizations, and in national governments, both northern and southern.[49] The NGO Forum of the 1995 Beijing Conference featured a computer center that facilitated networking and political mobilization worldwide.[50]

Demonstration and advocacy by NGOs can catalyze demonstration and advocacy by multilateral organizations, thus magnifying the direct effects of NGOs. With respect to this point, it is important to understand that multilateral organizations have increasingly become what have been called "international knowledge institutions," which seek "to authoritatively define the knowledge base for global policymaking."[51] No single NGO or government has sufficient legitimacy to define the nature of global problems. Multilateral organizations have many deficiencies with respect to their legitimacy and accountability, but neither states nor NGOs are more credible with a general audience, especially in developing countries themselves, than agencies such as UNAIDS, WHO,

49. Charlotte Bunch and Niamh Reilly, *Demanding Accountability: The Global Campaign and Vienna Tribunal for Women's Human Rights* (Rutgers, NJ: Center for Women's Global Leadership, and New York: United Nations Development Fund for Women, 1994), 7 and ch. 10.

50. Lois West, "The United Nations Women's Conference and Feminist Politics," in Mary Meyer and Elizabeth Prugl, eds., *Gender Politics in Global Governance* (Lanham, MD: Rowman and Littlefield, 1999), 192.

51. Clark Miller, "Knowledge, Reason and the Constitution of Democratic Order in International Governance," unpublished paper, Lafollette School of Public Affairs, University of Wisconsin, Madison (2004), no pagination.

and the World Bank. Only by catalyzing the epistemic activities of multilateral organizations can NGOs magnify their own efforts.

My third proposition may be more controversial. I believe that, if effective programmatic action is to be taken in the near future on a global basis to reduce global gender inequality, the World Bank will have to be deeply involved. As we have seen, multilateral organizations such as the World Bank and the IMF have much greater resources available to them than do NGOs. Among the multilateral organizations, the bank not only does much more poverty-related lending than the International Monetary Fund; it is far ahead of the IMF in its attention to gender issues. In the next section, I will discuss the bank's recent activities in more detail, but perusal of the two organizations' Web sites is telling. A 2005 search of the bank's Web site for "gender inequality" yielded over 800 items, which from their titles all seem directly to focus on this set of issues. A similar search on the IMF Web site turned up 201 items, the overwhelming majority of which referred to poverty reduction strategy papers, which are prepared by the countries involved with the aid of staff from the bank and the fund. Furthermore, the bank has a page on its Web site devoted to gender, which features work by its Gender and Development Group and links to a number of in-depth reports. Searching the IMF site for gender yielded a list of hundreds of documents without thematic organization. The first such document was a speech by Peter S. Heller, deputy director of the Fiscal Affairs Department, to a meeting of High-Level Women in International Finance, Economics, and Development in Dubai on September 20, 2003.[52] Heller argued that the IMF could contribute to the promotion of the millennium development goals related to gender equality, but his speech made it clear that he was appealing for action and that very little had in fact been done.

THE CONVERSION OF THE WORLD BANK TO FEMINIST CRITICISM

Susan Okin concluded one of her last published articles as follows: "Until what women do counts as much as what men do, until women's capabilities are fostered as much as men's, until women's voices are heard as strongly as men's…, the development of the LDCs is doomed. The project simply cannot succeed until gender, as well as poverty, is central to it."[53]

This statement may seem radical, but it is paralleled, in less stirring prose, by official bank statements, approved by the board of directors or uttered by the president. In the preface to a major World Bank report, *Engendering Development* (2001), President James Wolfensohn declared that "large gender disparities…are inextricably linked to poverty."[54] *Engendering Development* led to *Integrating Gender into the World Bank's Work: A Strategy for Action*, which was approved by the board of directors in September 2001 and published in January 2002.[55] The first lines of chapter 1 of that document read:

52. Heller, "Can the IMF Contribute?"
53. Okin, "Poverty, Well-Being and Gender," 316.
54. World Bank, *Engendering Development*, xi.
55. World Bank, *Integrating Gender into the World Bank's Work: A Strategy for Action* (Washington, DC: World Bank, January 2002).

> Gender equality is an issue of development effectiveness, not just a matter of political correctness or kindness to women. New evidence demonstrates that when women and men are relatively equal, economies tend to grow faster, the poor move more quickly out of poverty, and the well-being of men, women and children is enhanced.[56]

The next ten pages of *Integrating Gender* document these claims on the basis of a variety of studies, most done by the World Bank itself—by far the leading source of systematic information on development. A key point of *Integrating Gender* is that gender equality is not at odds with economic development but, on the contrary, is a key tool for achieving meaningful development—as well as being valuable in its own right.

Since the mid-1990s, a number of World Bank studies have shown that educating women generates higher marginal returns than educating men: it lowers birth rates, and it increases agricultural productivity.[57]

Integrating Gender goes on to echo another complaint made by Okin and others about philosophical and economic studies that take the male-headed household as an unproblematic unit of analysis:

> In standard neoclassical economic theory, households are usually regarded as sharing a single utility function and an equitable distribution of resources and well-being. Recent studies, however, suggest that this view is often invalid. Unequal gender relations—which are found in most countries of the world—tend to bias the extent to which male versus female household members enjoy the benefits of the household's assets and resources.[58]

To read *Integrating Gender* is to understand that, during James Wolfensohn's tenure as president of the World Bank, feminist critics won the *intellectual* battle at the bank. As Okin argued, this battle was won through a combination of intellectual accomplishments, such as Amartya Sen's research on development and poverty, and political action, including relentless organizing and lobbying at UN meetings, such as the 1993 World Conference on Human Rights in Vienna and the Fourth World Conference on Women in Beijing in 1995.[59] The UN General Assembly adopted an even more extensive statement on gender issues in 2000.[60] All of these statements have nominally been accepted by all states that belong to the United Nations.

Integrating Gender was meant to be an operational document. Most of it was devoted to outlining changes in the policies and practices of the bank, which were designed to make country-level operations more sensitive to gender issues. The plan for "mainstreaming gender" focused on a "country gender assessment" (CGA), to be carried out for each country in which there are bank projects, to identify "the gender-responsive

56. World Bank, *Integrating Gender*, 1.

57. Isobel Coleman, "The Payoff from Women's Rights," *Foreign Affairs* (May–June 2004). Available at http://www.foreignaffairs.org (accessed May 23, 2005).

58. World Bank, *Integrating Gender*, 10.

59. See also Emilie Hafner-Burton and Mark A. Pollack, "Mainstreaming Gender in Global Governance," *European Journal of International Relations* 8.3 (2002): 339–373.

60. United Nations General Assembly, *Report of the Ad Hoc Committee of the Whole of the Twenty-Third Special Session of the General Assembly* (2000). Document No. A/S-23/10/Rev. 1.

actions that are important for poverty reduction, economic growth, human well-being, and development effectiveness."[61] The CGA was then to be used to identify policy and operational actions that the government may decide to take. An example, from Vietnam, is an analysis of the effect of layoffs as a result of reform of state-owned enterprises. A study found that women who were laid off benefited from lump-sum payments, while men benefited more from compensation packages defined as a multiple of earnings. Taking the situation of women into account, the proposed bank action involved a compensation package with a substantial lump-sum component.[62] The third step in the process involved incorporating a gender dimension into the criteria used to assess the quality of the poverty reduction strategy paper (PRSP) for each country. The PRSP was to be prepared by stakeholders in the country—so that they would have "ownership" of the process. It was then supposed to be the key analytic tool to be used by both the bank and the fund to guide their activities. Each PRSP was to be evaluated jointly by bank and fund analysts in what is called a joint staff assessment (JSA). The gender-mainstreaming strategy called for gender issues to be integrated into the JSAs.

In organizations, strategies are only as good as their implementation, and someone more qualified than I, and more focused professionally on the activities of the World Bank, would have to evaluate the implementation of *Integrating Gender*. It is not clear that enhanced attention from bank staff necessarily has translated into effective action by governments. Indeed, the bank's own implementation report in 2004 said: "The Bank *and some of our clients* are learning to recognize the importance of gender equality for poverty reduction and sustained economic growth" (italics added).[63] The italicized phrase implies the key problem faced by the bank. The "hard-loan," or IBRD, side of the bank makes a profit on its lending activities, which is essential to maintaining the professional staff that is at the heart of its knowledge-producing activities. The "soft-loan" side of the bank—the IDA—needs willing clients to stay in business. The key tensions that the bank always needs to face are between the demands of NGOs and advocacy groups, including those pressing for the empowerment of women and gender equality, on the one hand, and resistance by governments, on the other. Structurally, there will always be resistance—from client governments—to the bank's attempts to promote policies to improve environmental quality, empower women, and devote special attention to the poor and powerless.[64]

Not surprisingly, feminist advocacy groups have often been critical. An early report from the advocacy group Gender Action documented the initially slow pace of implementation.[65] The number of gender experts within the bank had risen from 1 (in 1977) to 115, but this number still represented only about 15 percent of the number of environmental experts and less than 1 percent of bank staff. Furthermore, relatively

61. World Bank, *Integrating Gender*, 18.

62. World Bank, *Integrating Gender*, 27.

63. World Bank, "Implementing the Bank's Gender Mainstreaming Strategy," 17.

64. Bruce Rich, "The World Bank under James Wolfensohn," in Pincus and Winters, eds., *Reinventing the World Bank*, 26–53.

65. Elaine Zuckerman and Wu Qing, "Reforming the World Bank: Will the New Gender Strategy Make a Difference?" (Heinrich Boll Foundation, 2003). Available at http://www.genderaction.org.

few bank staff apart from the gender experts seemed to know about the gender-mainstreaming strategy or to have strong incentives to implement it. Nevertheless, the Gender Action researchers found that gender issues were being increasingly included in country assistance strategies through the country gender assessments: progress was slow, but some progress was being made.

It comes as no surprise to anyone who has studied gender-related inequalities that resistance to change is tenacious. It is easier for the bank to reform its nominal policies than its actual practices and much easier to reform its own practices than to persuade governments to change their ways. If the bank is to promote women's equality, this will require not only incremental work from bank staff but also agitation from outside. In this regard, Brooke Ackerly's concept of "multi-sited critics" may be useful in thinking about the role of operational staff members of the World Bank who are committed to gender equity. Since they are affiliated with the World Bank, they cannot be freewheeling critics who point to all of the contradictions between nominal policies and real practices. But they do need relentlessly to point out key contradictions at the operational level. They can use egalitarian policies to discredit antiegalitarian practices. And if the strategy of focusing on the bank is to succeed, they need to be held accountable for their advice, although this is difficult because they do not control the outcomes themselves. The bank should encourage their multisited policy entrepreneurs not only to maintain good working relationships with their governmental counterparts, but to keep working, diplomatically but effectively, for change. The cogent research findings from groups such as Gender Action are valuable resources for people inside and outside the bank who are pressing for more effective implementation of the gender-mainstreaming strategy.

BANK-FOCUSED STRATEGIES FOR NGOS

It is evident that the adoption of UN resolutions, often hypocritically, by the highly gendered governments of highly gendered societies does not mean that feminist critics have won the operational battle. Nor does the enunciation of progressive World Bank policies in officially sponsored reports mean that the battle is over or that activism is no longer needed. The bank did not move in the 1990s toward its more progressive position under its own power. On the contrary, it was pushed and prodded by the criticism of observers, such as Susan Okin, and by the example and criticism of NGOs, such as Gender Action and the Global Fund for Women. Without such outside pressure on a continuing basis, there is every reason to believe that bank policies would again be dominated by two sets of interests: those of shareholder governments and of recipient governments. Neither of these interests—without internal and external pressure on them—can be trusted to give priority to issues of gender equity.

However, official statements at UN conferences, by the World Bank, and in the 1979 CEDAW do provide a point of leverage, since hypocrisy is not a position anyone can publicly defend in an international meeting. As Prugl and Meyer state, "[T]he significance of international documents is not that governments will automatically implement them but that national and local groups can use them to hold their governments accountable."[66] As noted earlier, there is empirical evidence now that the Convention on the Elimination of All Forms of Discrimination against Women has made a significant impact on women's lives.[67]

Since the World Bank is by far the largest multilateral development agency, reinventing globalization for gender equality requires successful engagement with the bank. For the bank to intensify its work to promote gender equality, there will have to be continuing pressure from outside, amplifying the voices of those pushing for change from within. For implementation of the new nominal practices to occur, and for the further extension of principles of gender equality, the women's rights as human rights movement will have to maintain an organized and mobilized political presence. Both commitment and resources are important.

For the necessary combination of commitment and resources to be mobilized, social movements concerned with global poverty and gender inequality will have to organize in rich democracies as well as in less developed countries. The political and organizational base in rich countries for effective influence on issues of gender and development is narrow. Even more than most politics, this process of reinventing globalization will be Weber's "slow boring of hard boards," although the means will be the contemporary techniques of networking and instant communication. To be effective in reinventing globalization, these social movements will have to be focused. A natural negative focus is the AIDS epidemic in southern Africa, whose dimensions are shocking and whose human implications are easily dramatized. Efforts to reinvent globalization to promote gender equality need to include constructive engagement with the World Bank leadership, insofar as such leadership is willing to press for genuine progress on these issues.

In my view, the most promising strategy for the promotion of progressive change would combine support for the World Bank's leadership when it actively promotes gender equality with attempts to accelerate lagging policies and implementation. In her 2003 *Philosophy and Public Affairs* article, Okin recognized the bank's centrality and its moves toward incorporating gender issues into its practices, and she criticized the slowness and inadequacy of its work so far. In my judgment, feminist social movements and NGOs should, as Okin did, neither demonize the bank nor glorify it, but subject it to criticism within the context of support for what the bank claims to be doing.

My argument is certainly not that NGOs should cease innovation and criticism. On the contrary, NGO innovation and criticism have been crucial in making progress so far. It is imperative that NGOs continue to maintain critical distance from the bank and to demand deeds rather than just words from its new leadership. Nor do I advocate abandoning the language of human rights, which is the intellectual basis on which improved policies and practices can be built. What I do suggest is that focused efforts to work with the World Bank on issues of gender inequality may have higher payoffs for women, and for development, than broad general claims.

---

66. Elizabeth Prugl and Mary Meyer, "Gender Politics in Global Governance," in Mary Meyer and Elizabeth Prugl, eds., *Gender Politics in Global Governance* (Lanham, MD: Rowman and Littlefield, 1999), 13.

67. Simmons, "Women's Equality."

Where are the resources going to come from to make a major impact on gender inequality, if not from the World Bank? We have seen how small NGO resources are compared to the bank's. No major rich country can be relied upon to give priority to development, much less to gender equity in development. The World Bank is surely a flawed organization, but of the organizations with the financial and organizational potential to make a huge difference, it is among the most promising.

I recognize that any such strategy involves trade-offs. As the history of environmental NGOs indicates, unrelieved outrage is often a more effective fundraising strategy than the explication of a nuanced, well-considered strategy for effective reform. Indeed, there is plenty of room for outrage. The depth and extent of world poverty remains a scandal. Capitalism continues to generate inequality, as it always has. The World Bank in its structural adjustment phase managed both to aggravate those inequalities and to be, on the whole, ineffective in disciplining governments. The AIDS crisis has exposed the male-dominated practices and the policies of governments which have both created and exacerbated the virulent epidemic. The World Bank, despite its mixed record, has sometimes been an ally against terrible abuses. It has the potential, if pressed sufficiently vigorously, to do more. It should be engaged, not demonized.

CONCLUSION

The AIDS epidemic demonstrates how crucial gender issues are to development. Focusing on gender is not a fashionable northern fad, exporting political correctness to poor countries that cannot afford it. On the contrary, without focusing on gender, real development will not occur and human suffering will be much greater than it needs to be. If this point ever needed demonstration, the AIDS epidemic tragically does so.

As Susan Okin emphasized, the most effective pressure for change in pervasive gender inequalities will come from people who live in the countries in which action needs to be taken. But if these potential activists are isolated from their natural allies in the wealthy democracies, they will have difficulty finding safe spaces for criticism, or the ability to be heard, even locally. Hence, feminist social activism will continue to try to reinvent globalization, to use globalism as a tool for change.

Some of this activism will continue to be entirely at the transnational level, creating and maintaining networks. Conferences such as Beijing in 1995 have been enormously successful in establishing such networks where they formerly did not exist. The results, at least in terms of policy declarations by governments, have been impressive. But these networks necessarily remain at the elite level, linking activists in rich democracies with those relatively few women who can travel, or at least have access to modern means of communication, in developing countries. They are coordinated by small organizations. For example, as of 2005, the Association for Women's Rights in Development (AWID) had a staff of 18 people, mostly young, as indicated on its Web site (www.awid.org). As noted above, it stretches credulity to believe that their impact on gender inequality, at a global level, would be very large.

In the awareness-raising stage of the struggle for gender equality, feminist movements used major UN conferences to get attention from the media and to put across their powerful message about the connections between gender equality and development. The problem now is to deepen our knowledge base about the consequences of gender inequality and how it can be radically transformed and to ensure that programmatic action, carried out by governments on the ground, reflects this new awareness. Although its effectiveness is quite uneven and its practices need serious reform, the World Bank is the principal point of access for feminists to affect the policies of governments in less developed countries.

The continuation of tensions within the bank and between NGOs and client governments should not surprise us. Nor should a high level of criticism and dissatisfaction fool us into believing that nothing is being accomplished. As indicated at the beginning of this chapter, cooperation on issues that involve competing values builds more on discord than on harmony. It comes as a process of mutual adjustment between people or groups whose independent perspectives differ. Women's capabilities will only be valued on a global basis if there is sustained international cooperation to realize it. In this decade, such cooperation will be most effective if the World Bank takes a leadership role in the struggle. The frequent discord that accompanies this process should be regarded as a perfectly normal aspect of contentious cooperation.

The background conditions exist for dramatic progress to be made. Our understanding of the gender dimensions of international development and antipoverty efforts has expanded greatly since the mid-1990s. There is a vibrant NGO community, part of which is specifically focused on gender equality. The World Bank during the Wolfensohn presidency became publicly committed to the empowerment of women and to the reduction and eventual elimination of gender discrimination. UNAIDS has spoken forthrightly about how gender inequality contributes to the epidemic. Feminist social movements are now linked together, in a complex variety of networks, and are also connected to other groups in global civil society. But the resources available to overcome gender inequality are pitifully small. They will only increase if political movements that care about women and international development become as strong as comparable movements that emphasize women's rights in rich countries, the environment, or human rights in general.

We are seeing the emergence of a contentious process of discordant cooperation involving feminist social movements, the World Bank, and governments—in both rich democracies and less developed countries. To move toward Susan Moller Okin's vision of a world of gender equality, this process of discordant cooperation will have to follow the direction that she charted and to be accelerated and enhanced.

12

The Gendered Cycle of Vulnerability in the Less Developed World

Iris Marion Young

In *Justice, Gender, and the Family*, Susan Okin gives a powerful account of how the interaction of gender relations in the family with gendered norms of workplaces reinforces women's vulnerability in both spheres. Because most of the facts on which Okin draws in that book refer to the specific context of the United States in the 1970s and 1980s, it is not unreasonable to conclude that her account of the public-private dynamics reinforcing the subordination of women applies only within that context.

This chapter argues that the basic structural logic of the gendered cycle of vulnerability that Okin so clearly articulated well describes the relations that condition and constrain the lives of many women, particularly urban women and women who migrate from rural to urban areas, in at least some less developed countries. I will discuss how structures of paid employment in North America and Europe, moreover, have converged to a certain extent with those in these supposedly less developed contexts more than was true of the context that Okin assumed. While the gendered structure of paid employment has changed significantly in advanced industrial societies, much about the basic structure of gender relations that Okin theorized remains intact. Relations between social policy and the gendered division of labor in the family, moreover, have analogous consequences for women in both the global South and the global North.

OKIN'S ACCOUNT OF THE GENDERED CYCLE OF VULNERABILITY

Susan Okin's aim in *Justice, Gender, and the Family* was to expose the hypocrisy of the claims of philosophers, policy makers, and others in late twentieth-century American society to be committed to women's equality. While many powerful or influential people pay lip service to gender equality, at the same time they continue to assume that the private sphere of the family and public spheres of employment and policy are normatively and practically independent of one another. Operating with this implicit assumption, they are unable to see how the gender division of labor in the family interacts with and helps to structure relations in public spheres. This gendered division of labor, Okin argued, is the foundation of persistent inequalities between

This chapter was initially prepared for a conference in honor of the work of Susan Moller Okin, Stanford University, February 3–5, 2005.

women and men. Only when men truly share unpaid domestic work will public and private equality between men and women be possible. This goal requires more than the good intentions of men and women to achieve, because numerous external interests and structural processes conspire to reinforce this gendered division of labor in the family.

The ideology of separate spheres exiles family life beyond the scope of principles of justice, beyond the proper reach of state regulation, and outside the responsibility of employers. This ideology is pernicious because institutions of the state and private enterprise assume, rely on, and help to constitute relations of power and inequality in the family. Okin's central account of the situation of women in the late twentieth-century United States depicts what she calls a gendered cycle of vulnerability in which the position of women in the family restricts their opportunities to participate in paid employment and politics, and then these public inequalities turn back and reinforce gender inequality in the family. Strictly speaking, Okin's analysis was not original; she consciously drew on insights that the feminist movement and feminist research had been developing for a decade. What Okin did was express this account with more analytical clarity than any theorist before or, I would submit, since.

Despite massive changes in the norms and attitudes about the proper roles of men and women in marriage that took place in the twentieth century in advanced industrial societies, Okin asserts that gender-structured marriage remains in place. Most people still assume that housework and child care are primarily the responsibility of unpaid women in the home. While this assumption may not any longer be enforced by law, and is enforced by explicit sanctions only among some subgroups, even many people with sexually egalitarian attitudes assume and expect this gender division of labor for themselves and others. Okin argues that this gender structure is entirely contingent; married couples could do without it. She cites studies that find that same-sex couples more often than not share household tasks relatively equally.[1]

The allocation of unpaid domestic work and childrearing to women primarily, Okin argues, "involves women in a cycle of socially caused and distinctly asymmetric vulnerability. The division of labor within marriage (except in rare cases) makes wives far more likely than husbands to be exploited both within the marital relationship and in the world outside the home" (1989:138). Okin distinguishes two situations for women, each of which contains these vulnerabilities.

The partners in some marriages choose to abide by what is regarded as a traditional division of labor, in which the wife works full time at unpaid household and childrearing responsibilities, and the husband earns income from paid employment to support the entire family. In this arrangement, women along with their children are entirely dependent on the husband for their material well-being. Public institutions and husbands rarely acknowledge or reward the unpaid work that women do. Being primary wage earners makes many men feel entitled to make major family decisions, and sometimes men use their position of power to abuse their wives emotionally or physically.

---

1. *JGF*, 140–149; Okin cites Philip Blumstein and Pepper Schwartz, *American Couples* (New York: Monroe, 1983).

If the couple separates or divorces, which happen often, even in these traditional marriages, the wife and her children are very likely to end up living in poverty. Often, the wife has not acquired the marketable skills and job experience that will enable her to earn a good income, and courts rarely enforce alimony or child support even up to half of the husband's income.

In twenty-first-century America, however, as well as in other advanced industrial societies, women, even married women with children, have entered the labor force in large numbers. The basic structure of the gender division of labor in the family persists, however, along with its implications for women's disadvantage and vulnerability. More often than not, a pattern of unequal earnings remains, with men earning significantly greater income than their wives, either because of the nature of their occupations, the longer hours they work, or both. Women arrange their wage-earning activities around their housework, child care, and sometimes elder care responsibilities far more often than do men—by working part time, or close to home, or moving in and out of the workforce as their family responsibilities require. The dynamics of gendered vulnerability to domination, exploitation, and deprivation are only slightly mitigated in these relationships. Whether the context is a couple where one is the wage earner or both are, the gender division of unpaid work renders women vulnerable in four areas: (1) in the norms surrounding entry into marriage, (2) within marriage, (3) in paid work, and (4) in separation or divorce. All women, even unmarried women and even women who are not mothers, are made vulnerable to domination, exploitation, and deprivation by these structural processes, which pivot around the gendered division of labor in the family.

More lucrative and recognized paid employment tends to be gendered male, in the sense that employers act as though workers have no family responsibilities that might conflict with the demands of work. Married women with children typically take primary responsibility for household work and child care. Even when they also work outside the home, they typically depend on their husbands' earnings for their and their children's material well-being. As a result, women often work longer hours for less recognition and compensation than their husbands, and they have unequal power in the relationship. While women usually want men to do more housework and child care, Okin cites studies which show that men's contribution to household labor rises only slightly when their wives work outside the home. Women thus often work a double day, while men do not. Their tacit knowledge of women's dependence on them and the costs of exit for women from a relationship mean that men often dominate the decision making in the family. This power inequality renders women vulnerable to the physical and psychological abuse experienced by a shockingly large proportion of women in Western industrial societies.

Many men do not avail themselves of the power that the gendered structure of the division of labor affords them. Many others who do act on male privilege may not know that they are doing so. In this postfeminist era, many men and women actively try not to reproduce the gendered division of labor in the family and the power inequality it brings. Many of these egalitarian-intentioned couples find, however, that structural constraints produced by employment opportunities and lack of state attention to domestic work and child care lead them to allocate work between them in a manner against their initial intentions. They rationally choose to enhance the husband's skills rather than the wife's, for example, because doing so will lead to greater economic security.

Okin argues that the disadvantages produced by the gendered division of labor are felt by most women, not only those who are married with children. The generalization of gender inequality occurs primarily through processes of socialization and sex-typed paid employment. Parents, schools, and other socializing agents have changed significantly in the last half-century in affluent Western societies in the extent to which they socialize girls to be wives and mothers primarily. Even so, many attitudes and practices remain that encourage paying more attention to the development of lucrative skills in boys than in girls. The majority of girls and women in education and training programs continue to study in typically feminine fields, such as English teaching, social work, or cosmetology.

The gender typing of occupations itself has a major foundation in the gender division of labor in the family. Many typically female jobs are extensions of or mirror the housekeeping and care activities primarily allocated to women in the home. Other predominantly female jobs, such as retail work, take advantage of the fact that many women seek to organize their paid employment around their child care and other family responsibilities—the scheduling of hours in retail jobs may be more flexible than other jobs, and the places of employment may be shorter distances from home. As a result of these sorts of dynamics, many women tend to be crowded into a few female-dominated occupations, which allows employers to keep wages low, offer few benefits, and discourage organizing among workers. All women, not only married women with children, are affected by these patterns of gender socialization and the sex typing of jobs. The fact that the situation of many women opens them mostly to jobs with relatively poor earnings and job security turns back to condition their relationship with the family, making it necessary or desirable for them to partner with people who earn better wages in order to have a good standard of living for themselves and their children.

Okin argues that women cannot achieve equality unless social structures change to encourage men to share equally in domestic work and child care. The public world of work makes it difficult for many professional and nonprofessional employees to allocate time and attention to family needs. Employers of persons in most "good" jobs act as though employees have no responsibilities to distract their attention from their jobs, that they can and should be available to work long hours, and that they have someone who works in the home taking care of their needs for emotional support and personal care. It is to the financial and organizational advantage of employers to behave as though they have no responsibility to enable employees both to be productive workers and to devote time and attention to the needs and wants of their families. Few employers offer child care facilities, paid family leave, flex time, or other benefits that might enable fathers and mothers to combine paid work with family care. Employers' refusal to take the family lives of workers into account helps to make domestic work invisible, and this invisibility tends to contribute to the exploitation of the unpaid workers who do it. Public policy does little to take up the slack and itself ignores unpaid domestic work and thus renders it invisible.

Okin makes much of women's and children's vulnerability to poverty that follows from these gendered structures. If a mother never partners with a wage earner, or if the partnership dissolves, she often cannot obtain a job that will support her and her children at a decent level of well-being. She rarely has support available to combine full-time work with taking good care of her children. Most absent fathers contribute little or nothing to the financial needs of their children, and courts historically have demanded little of them.

To summarize, Okin's theory of gender injustice in the late twentieth-century United States exposes mutually reinforcing relationships between gender inequality in family relations and in public work relations. She argues that "a cycle of power relations and decisions pervades both family and workplace, each reinforcing the inequalities between the sexes that already exist within the other" (4). The structural relations of gender are unjust because they produce asymmetrical power and vulnerability:

> A cycle of power relations and decisions pervades both family and workplace, and the inequalities of each reinforce those that already exist in the other. Only with the recognition of this truth will we be able to begin to confront the changes that need to occur if women are to have a real opportunity to be equal participants in either sphere. (1989:147)

The ultimate goal of these changes, Okin declares, is the disappearance of gender as a set of socially constituted dispositions, norms, and expectations about the behavior of persons sexed male and female. Public institutions should take steps that will help to bring about such changes, including providing child care outside the home and accommodating the family responsibilities of workers by offering paid care leave, flex time, part-time work at good wages with job security and benefits, and the like. Until the abolition of gender in this sense occurs, all social and political institutions should take steps to compensate for gendered vulnerabilities. Okin recommends wages for housework, better divorce settlements through which newly single women and children will not be left in poverty, and similar measures.

THE STRUCTURAL LOGIC OF THE CYCLE OF VULNERABILITY

Okin locates her account of the dynamics of gendered disadvantage in the specific context of the United States in the 1970s and 1980s. In this particular society, dominant public norms paid lip service to equality between men and women, but these conflicted with the continuing norms and expectations that women have primary responsibility for unpaid work in the family. In this society, men on average had more secure, better-paying, and more prestigious jobs that made little or no allowance for the family responsibilities that workers may have had. While some married mothers chose to be homemakers full time, more tried to combine their family responsibilities with paid employment. More often than not, they worked outside the home because the family needed the money, but many married mothers also sought self-fulfillment through their paid work.

These were circumstances specific to the context in which Okin developed her analysis. Later in this chapter, I will discuss how there have been some changes in them even in the United States. Several of these specific circumstances, however, do not correspond to the situation of poor married mothers in less developed countries, to which I wish now to turn our attention. Public norms in many of the societies of Asia, Africa, Latin America, and the Middle East do not affirm women's equality with men. In them, many husbands have difficulty earning income sufficient to support a family. Most of the women who enter paid employment in many less developed contexts do not seek to develop their creative potential as individuals. They work, rather, in order to contribute to the survival of their families and to try to improve the prospects of their children by paying for their schooling.

Despite the contextual differences between the society Okin had in view when she developed her account of the gendered cycle of vulnerability and the contemporary context of many less developed societies, I believe that Okin's general analysis can reveal important aspects of gendered oppression in most societies of the world today. In order to extend her account to women's situations in some less developed societies, it is necessary to abstract it from her specific context and lay bare its general structural logic.

The main issue in the logic of the cycle is not equality or inequality. The more general issue is vulnerability to abuse, exploitation, and material deprivation. Women everywhere, especially poor women in the less developed world, are more vulnerable to physical and/or emotional domestic abuse than are men, more vulnerable to poverty, and more vulnerable to exploitation by paid employers. To be sure, many men are vulnerable to poverty and exploitation. The vulnerability of women, however, is more systematically related to gender relations and is of greater magnitude.

The foundation of women's vulnerability is the gendered division of labor in the family, which allocates to women the primary responsibility for care of the household, children, and other family members who need assistance. Women themselves may be wholly committed to and affirm their domestic role, or they may be ambivalent about it, or they may try to escape it. In cases where explicit social and legal norms do not enforce the gendered division of labor, various pressures, expectations, and incentive structures still operate systematically to enforce it. Even when women are not traditionalists who believe that women's place is at home, their gender socialization disposes them to take responsibility for unpaid care work more than most men are inclined to.

Few societies organize subsistence around household production alone. Most households interact with markets. Consequently, nearly every society today separates relations within the family and the unpaid work of the home from relations outside families and the work done through markets or organized by public institutions. Nearly every society, moreover, assumes and relies on unpaid domestic work. Despite this reliance, the public norms of nearly every society affirm a separation of public and private. They function as though the power relations, economic opportunities, and social projects of nonfamilial institutions operate independently of the family and that family relations are independent of them. In nearly every society, however, there are systematic structural relations of mutual influence between family relations and the dynamics of costs and benefits, power and domination, opportunity and obstacle, in nonfamily institutions. For example, the fact that women have the primary responsibility for care work at home often makes them dependent on husbands for the material support of themselves and their children. This dependence further renders women vulnerable to domination or abuse.

If and when women seek paid employment, they are vulnerable to exploitation because they often wish to combine paid employment with carrying out their family responsibilities. Poor and working-class women are often more willing than their male counterparts to accept low wages and poor working conditions, and they often compete with many other women for a limited number of such jobs. The gendered division of labor in the family thus produces gendered occupational structures and forms of exploitation in paid work.

Women raising children alone, either because they have never partnered or because they are separated, everywhere are particularly vulnerable to poverty. In the absence of significant social supports, it is very difficult for one adult both to care for children and a household and to earn an income in the private market sufficient to provide a decent standard of living. Many societies, moreover, stigmatize single mothers, which makes their lives even more difficult.

The gendered division of labor in the family thus produces gendered vulnerability in earning power and insufficient public recognition. These public gender dynamics in turn reinforce the gender division of labor in the family. Poor mothers and working mothers must often depend on their daughters to help with household work, which prevents the girls from attending school or being trained for secure employment. The implicit or explicit reliance of public institutions on unpaid work done in the home often enlarges the amount of unpaid work that must be done, thus enforcing women's primary responsibility to do it even when they would rather do less. Public gender dynamics assume and expect men to concentrate on public activities, which makes it difficult for them to contribute to domestic work and child care even if they want to. The cycle is reproduced in the socialization of both girls and boys. Since both state institutions and many private enterprises benefit from the gendered division of labor because they avoid internalizing the costs of social reproduction, their policies and actions help to perpetuate the cycle of gendered vulnerability. I will now argue that the structural logic of the gendered cycle of vulnerability appears in the context of less developed societies as well as in advanced industrial societies.[2]

GENDERED VULNERABILITY IN LESS DEVELOPED SOCIETIES

Three decades of contentious UN-sponsored conferences, along with many other encounters between women's advocates in the global North and in the global South, have generated an affirmation that the experiences, commitments, needs, desires, and agency of women vary enormously with local contexts and economic conditions. Feminists, and Western feminists in particular, have too often elevated their experiences and

---

2. V. Spike Peterson offers a framework for analyzing international political economy that involves interactions among productive, reproductive, and what she calls virtual economies. See Peterson, "Rewriting (Global) Political Economy as Reproductive, Productive and Virtual (Foucaultian) Economies," *International Feminist Journal of Politics* 4.1 (April 2002): 1–30.

political priorities derived from their own contexts to general imperatives for a global movement. Mindful of this history and the dangers of generalizing, I nevertheless will now suggest that the structural dynamics that Okin outlined for American society in the late twentieth century usefully exposes the operations of gender injustice in at least some contexts of economically disadvantaged societies in the early twenty-first century. Specifically, I will show that the gender division of labor in the family, which operates as a strong and enforced norm among many newly urbanized women, produces and reproduces a vulnerability to domination and exploitation in wage employment.

I will make this argument first by interpreting a specific context. Saba Gul Khattak has studied the situation of women who take work into their homes or who work in small factories in three industries—garments, carpets, and plastics—in three Pakistani cities: Karachi, Lahore, and Peshawar.[3] Khattak finds that the norms and practices of the gender division of labor that assign to women primary responsibility for the home and children make them especially vulnerable to labor exploitation. Their wage work is more an extension of the gender division of labor, which disadvantages women, than it is a liberation from male domination.

Khattak surveyed 162 women workers in the three cities. All view wage work as a burden that departs from traditional norms where women are responsible only for care of their homes and children. They have been pulled into the labor market because their families desperately need cash income: their husbands either cannot find work themselves or earn too little to support their families. These women and their neighbors and families construct a women's willingness to sell her labor under these dire conditions as an expression of motherly and wifely self-sacrifice. This set of circumstances differs significantly from the typical case that Okin assumed for American couples in the 1980s; she assumed that husbands have significant earning power.

Most of the women surveyed prefer to work from their homes, even though factory work pays significantly better. They find that wage work at home best accommodates their family responsibilities. By subcontracting at home, they can combine wage work with child care, cooking, and other household tasks. Taking work into their homes keeps up the appearance that they are not working for wages, thus preserving their modesty and the honor of the male head of the household.[4] By working at home, the women also avoid long trips to factories on public transportation during which they face the threat of sexual harassment. And sexual harassment is also a common threat within factories. In this respect, the situation of women in these Pakistani neighborhoods is very different from what Okin assumed for American women; American norms in the late twentieth century did not discourage women from going out into public to work. I will return to this issue later in this chapter.

These disincentives for women to seek factory work and their desire to combine their wage work with domestic work and child care make these women especially

---

3. Saba Gul Khattak, "Subcontracted Work and Gender Relations: The Case of Pakistan," in Radhika Balakrishnan, ed., *The Hidden Assembly Line: Gender Dynamics of Subcontracted Work in a Global Economy* (Bloomfield, CT: Kumarian, 2002), 35–62.

4. Compare the discussion of purdah norms in the context of poverty and labor markets in Naila Kabeer, *Reversed Realities: Gender Hierarchies in Development Thought* (London: Verso, 1994), 151–153.

vulnerable to exploitation. Manufacturers seek women home workers because they can ignore labor regulations and maintain labor flexibility. Knowing that these women would rather work at home than outside, they offer low wages. They need not pay overhead costs and have no responsibility for working conditions. The women work at least eight hours a day, six and a half days a week, to meet their work targets. Home workers have no medical benefits or social security rights. Home workers have even less opportunity than factory workers to discuss their working conditions with one another or to organize to bargain collectively with employers.

Khattak found that the wage-earning women she surveyed experience no reduction in their unpaid domestic work responsibilities. On the whole, the men in their households do not assume more domestic responsibilities because their wives are working. Children, especially girl children, probably spend more time on household chores. They also often help the mothers with their subcontracted wage work.

Okin developed an account of the gendered cycle of vulnerability in order to demonstrate that the structural dynamics of paid employment are not independent of gendered relations in households. The assumptions and arguments in modern political theories presume that the private world of the family is shielded from the power relations of the state and the capitalist economy, and in this way both obscure gender injustice and the way the basic structures of the whole society rely on it. Contrary to the assumptions of many feminists in American society in the 1970s and 1980s, Okin's account shows that paid employment does not necessarily undermine this injustice and may reinforce the gendered dynamics of exploitation and power inequality.

The mutual reinforcement of vulnerability in the home and in wage work is even more pronounced in the situation of women home workers in Pakistan. In some respects, it is better for them and for their families that these women earn some income. Most of these women report that they do feel entitled to spend some of these earnings on themselves as well as on their family members. In addition, being earners raises their self-esteem somewhat. Their entering the labor force is not at all a route to freedom or empowerment, however. They remain subordinate to their husbands and to senior relatives, to which the commands of a boss have been added. They exhaust themselves adding paid work to their unpaid domestic work, and they reproduce the cycle in their daughters by keeping them at home to help.

The gendered cycle of vulnerability between home and work increasingly structures the lives of poor women in the less developed world. The findings of the study I have cited on urban Pakistan are similar to those that other research in the same volume finds for women workers in the Philippines, Thailand, Sri Lanka, and India.[5] Some women who work in factories are young and unmarried, bringing income into their parents' homes. Employers often prefer them because they believe that the young women are docile and easily intimidated and will not organize and demand better

5. Radhika Balakrishnan and Asad Sayeed, "Subcontracting: The Push-Pull Factor"; Swarna Jayaweera, "Women Subcontracted Workers in Sri Lanka"; Rosalinda Pineda Ofreneo, Joseph Y. Lim, and Lourdes Abad Gula, "The View from Below: Impact of the Financial Crisis on Subcontracted Workers in the Philippines"; Jeemol Unni and Namrata Bali, "Subcontracted Women Workers in the Garment Industry in India," all in Balakrishnan, ed., *The Hidden Assembly Line.*

conditions.[6] Others are married women and mothers, who either take in home work or work fairly close to home, leaving young children in the care of neighbors, elderly relatives, or older siblings, usually girls.[7]

The preferred use of women in some of the world's most exploitative labor-intensive consumer goods production has become so prevalent a pattern that it is no exaggeration to suggest that a gendered global division of labor allocates relatively unskilled manufacturing work in highly competitive labor-intensive export industries to women. Women workers are concentrated in jobs in export-processing zones and in informal employment in low-wage subcontracting sectors. These systems rely on flexible production, temporary contracts, part-time work, and unstable working conditions. According to Lourdes Beneria, in Sri Lanka in 1991 and 1992, the proportion of female labor in export-processing zones was as high as 86.3 percent and 84.8 percent, respectively. In textiles and clothing, the proportion of women in the labor force in selected Central American and Caribbean countries has reached above 60 percent, and 95 percent in the case of Panama.[8]

Consciously or unconsciously, employers make use of women's primary commitment to domestic work and family obligations to pay women little and to escape labor regulations. Many women actively affirm this primary commitment to their domestic work, and many are pressured by husbands and other relatives not to work away from home. Many families believe that they have no choice, however, but for every member able to earn income to do so. Although some of its details are context-specific, the general form of a gendered cycle of vulnerability for women that Okin theorized appears in these contexts of the global South and the North. The norms of the gendered division of labor in the family, to which most women themselves are committed, make working at home attractive to them. They and their families often consider the husbands as heads of the household who rightly have greater decision-making power than the women in the family. Male heads of poor families in the developing world, however, are increasingly unable to support their families, partly because of high male unemployment rates and partly because employers and local states pressured by international financial institutions recognize that they can induce women to work for lower wages. The inequality of the women in the family and the allocation of domestic work

6. Leslie Salzinger documents the explicit preference for workers defined as feminine in the *maquiladoras* of Mexico as early as the 1960s. Female workers were and are constructed as docile, dexterous, willing to work for low wages, and able to tolerate boredom; see Salzinger, *Genders in Production: Making Workers in Mexico's Global Factories* (Berkeley: University of California Press, 2003). See also Kimberly Ann Elliot and Richard B. Freeman, *Can Labor Standards Improve under Globalization?* (Washington, DC: Institute for International Economics, 2003), esp. 18–19; Linda Y. C. Lim, "Capitalism, Imperialism and Patriarchy: The Dilemma of Third-World Women Workers in Multinational Factories," in Visvanathan et al., eds., *Women, Gender and Development Reader*, 216–229.

7. For a detailed and fascinating account of one set of women who work in flower-exporting facilities in Bogotá and the child care cooperatives that have succeeded in obtaining recognition from the government, see Molly Talcott, "Gendered Webs of Development and Resistance: Women, Children and Flowers in Bogotá," *SIGNS: Journal of Women in Culture and Society* 29.2 (Winter 2004): 465–490.

8. See Lourdes Beneria, *Gender, Development and Globalization: Economics as if People Mattered* (New York: Routledge, 2003), ch. 3, 79.

and child care primarily to them thus make women particularly vulnerable to exploitation in the paid workforce. To the extent that the daughters must help their mothers with their domestic work instead of going to school, this cycle of vulnerability is reproduced in the next generation. One difference from the story that Okin tells about the typical gender relations in the United States is this: in the studies cited here, the earnings of men less often bring families to a position of economic security and upward mobility. The pattern does exist in other strata of the society, however. In either case, the fact that women have the primary responsibility for unpaid domestic labor makes women and their children very vulnerable if their husbands leave or die, or if they do not have husbands.[9]

RECENT DEVELOPMENTS IN GENDER-STRUCTURED WORK AND THE FAMILY

In the 1980s, feminists in the United States had some grounds for optimism about the prospects of improving women's lives and status. Discriminatory laws had been abolished and overt policies forbade continuing practices of sex discrimination. Sexual harassment and battery were recognized as serious problems, at least in public discourse. Millions of women entered professions and trades from which women had until very recently largely been excluded.

Critiques like Okin's of the lag between these developments and changes in the gender division of labor in the family aimed to deepen and accelerate this progress. If work opportunities are really to be open to women, some of the burden of domestic responsibility must be lifted from them. If we are serious about equality for women, then the lives, activities, and status of men must converge more with that of women; it is not simply that women and their places must change, but men and their places must change as well.

When we consider the paid working lives of women and men in the United States in the twenty-first century, we do find some convergence.[10] Its nature, however, is the contrary of what feminists have hoped for. Much paid employment in the advanced industrial economies of North America and Europe has moved toward the sorts of jobs for which researchers have found that employers prefer women in the developing world: light manufacturing and service industry work. More and more people work part time, or on temporary contracts, or nonstandard hours. Jobs in retail and service occupations have proliferated, while those in professions have stagnated and those in

9. See Sylvia Chant, "Single-Parent Families: Choice or Constraint? The Formation of Female Headed Households in Mexican Shanty Towns," in Nalini Visvanathan, Lynn Duggan, Laurie Nisonoff, and Nan Wiegersman, eds., *The Women, Gender and Development Reader* (London: Zed, 1997), 155–162; compare Kabeer, *Reversed Realities*, 156–158.

10. Alison Jaggar remarks on the convergence in the situations of women in Western and non-Western societies in the context of neoliberal globalization processes. She does not deny that there are local and cultural specificities, but argues that it is important to notice structural similarities. Jaggar, "'Saving Amina': Global Justice for Women and Intercultural Dialogue," *Ethics and International Affairs* 19 (Spring 2005).

heavy manufacturing have greatly declined. Union jobs are on the decline, average hourly wages are down, and pension benefits have shrunk.

According to Harriet Presser, in the Current Population Survey in 1997, only 29.1 percent of employed persons worked what is thought of as a standard work week—30–40 daytime hours, Monday through Friday. Part-time workers are more likely than full-time workers to work at least some evenings and weekends, and an increasing proportion of workers is officially part time.[11] Jobs in North America and Europe, according to Joel Handler, are increasingly short term, especially for lower skilled workers.[12] In the United Kingdom, almost one-quarter of the jobs are part time, with varying weekly hours. Ninety percent of part-timers are permanent.[13]

There is much reason to think that these developments are gendered. Since the early 1980s, there has been a massive increase of women in the labor force in the northern advanced industrial economies and in the developing industrial economies of the South. These women have been both pushed and pulled. Many women have sought independence and the development of their skills in paid work. At the same time, a decline in traditional manufacturing employment, where many men used to be able to earn good incomes in secure jobs with guaranteed pensions, has forced many women into the workforce simply to help support themselves and their families. The mutual reinforcement of vulnerability in private and public to which Okin called attention remains. Initially, many women workers preferred part-time employment because they wanted to combine paid work with unpaid work in the home. As I have shown, however, many employers have their own reasons for utilizing workers on a part-time, temporary, or casual basis, often during nonstandard hours. Many women who now work in such jobs say that they would prefer full-time work during standard hours, but they cannot find such work. They are vulnerable to overcrowding, low pay, poor benefits, and unpredictable work schedules, which sometimes makes it difficult for them to arrange child care, a special problem for single mothers who are relatively unskilled.[14]

Leah Vosko documents that this sort of work, historically more associated with women workers, is becoming more standard across North America. Throughout much of the twentieth century in Europe and North America, public policy, union strength, and employment culture converged to produce the rise of what Vosko calls the standard employment relationship: well-paid, full-time, secure work for many with good benefits and a pension upon retirement. This standard was never universal; it was available to men primarily and tended to exclude people of color and immigrants. Increases in female employment in the late twentieth century, Vosko suggests, allowed the dismantling of this standard to such an extent that the characteristics of typically female jobs are becoming more normative for all workers: low pay, nonstandard hours, temporary

---

11. Harriet B. Presser, *Working in a 24/7 Economy: Challenges for American Families* (New York: Russell Sage Foundation, 2003), 15.

12. Joel F. Handler, *Social Citizenship and Workfare in the United States and Western Europe* (Cambridge: Cambridge University Press, 2004), 31, 104–105.

13. Handler, *Social Citizenship*, 145.

14. Presser, *Working in a 24/7 Economy*, 64.

contracts, few benefits, etc.[15] Increasingly, men's work is converging with women's in both the developed and the developing world.[16] The gap in the average incomes earned by women and men has been closing everywhere, for example, less because women's earnings have been rising than because men's have been falling. When feminists in the 1970s and 1980s called for equalization, this is not what we had in mind.

The pattern holds for most of the countries of the European Union as well. A massive entry of women into the labor force has accompanied a contraction of the manufacturing sector, where many men traditionally worked. Nearly half of women workers in the United Kingdom work part time, and in the Netherlands 63 percent of all women in the paid labor force are part-time workers. Many of these women would prefer full-time work, but the sex segregation of occupations and gender discrimination collude with employers' interests to close many opportunities for full-time work. As in North America, part-time, temporary, low-wage work at nonstandard hours is becoming increasingly common among male workers as well.[17]

One would hope that developments such as these would have brought convergence in the time that men and women spend on unpaid domestic work. Indeed, there may be some convergence, especially among married couples with explicitly egalitarian commitments. On the whole, however, the pattern of the gender division of labor that allocates primary responsibility for the care of household and children to women remains in place.[18]

Especially with more women entering the labor force across the world since the 1980s, one might have hoped that the social policies of states would make up for husbands' apparent continued inability or unwillingness to share unpaid domestic work, by offering more public care services and/or subsidizing home care and home maintenance services. However, the opposite has occurred all over the world. Governments have been reducing social spending, with the unnoticed consequence that a greater burden of care work falls on unpaid workers in the family.

In the developing world, so-called structural adjustment policies, which are often urged or forced on governments as a condition of receiving loans or grants, have included measures such as reduction of social services, increases in fees for clinics and schools, elimination of subsidies for basic foodstuffs, and devaluation of currencies. While governments have usually ignored the consequences, each of these sorts of measures has direct effects on the amount and kind of unpaid work that falls on family members. When the price of food rises, the women who are the primary food preparers usually must increase the time they devote to preparing food for their families, because they are less able to use convenience foods or to purchase already prepared food. When clinics close or raise their fees, family members take care of their sick at home as best

---

15. Leah F. Vosko, *Temporary Work: The Gendered Rise of a Precarious Employment Relationship* (Toronto: University of Toronto Press, 2000); cf. Handler, *Social Citizenship*, 31.

16. Salzinger, *Genders in Production*.

17. Handler, *Social Citizenship*, 145–171.

18. Presser reports that in dual-wage-earner marriages with children in the United States, women devote a significantly greater amount of time to housework and child care than do men. *Working in a 24/7 Economy*, 129.

they can without the help of health professionals. When the cost of education rises, families often decide to send boys but not girls to school in the upper grades.[19]

These gendered consequences of neoliberal policies in the developing world are sometimes dire: women work to exhaustion because the load of unpaid domestic work has increased at the same time that they also are trying to earn paid income. As families necessarily try to reduce their consumption of goods that require cash to acquire, women and girls often suffer because of the gender preferences that privilege men and boys. Decisions to reduce social services in the advanced industrial world, however, also have consequences for the amount of unpaid work that family members must do in the home. When a government decides to reduce the amount that it will reimburse families for the home care of frail elderly relatives, for example, the hours that family members, usually women, spend in caring for these persons usually increases. When governments fail to fund child care, they implicitly rely on unpaid family labor, typically women's.

This relationship between social policy and gender exemplifies the gendered cycle of vulnerability in a somewhat different way. Public spending and services can be targeted to ease the burden of unpaid domestic work, the bulk of which still falls to women all over the world. When social policy changes fail to respond to these needs or actually increase them, policy makers implicitly assume that such work will be done privately by family members. Indeed, public rhetoric increasingly exhorts family members to take care of their own, rather than expect the costs of such care to be spread across the society. The burden of necessary care work increases, and women usually do most of it, because someone must, and various social norms and pressures assume and enforce that it is women's work. Thus, women who might have obtained more education or more economic independence through more wage work or self-employment find their opportunities curtailed by the increased demands of domestic work. Macroeconomic policies that cut services thus reinforce women's position in the gender division of labor.

SUMMARY AND FINAL NEW QUESTION

This chapter has reviewed the structural account of the gendered cycle of vulnerability that Susan Okin articulated in her most important book. These structures render women vulnerable to gender-specific forms of violence, domination, exploitation, and poverty. The foundation of women's vulnerability is the gendered division of labor in the family, which allocates to women the primary responsibility for care of the household, children, and other family members. The public norms of nearly every society today affirm a separation of public and private, and they often ignore and obscure the contribution of unpaid household work to the well-being of members of society. In nearly every society, however, there are systematic structural relations of mutual influence between family relations and the dynamics of costs and benefits, power and

---

19. Ashfar and Dennis, *Women and Structural Adjustment in the Third World* (New York: St. Martin's, 1993).

domination, opportunity and obstacle, in nonfamily institutions. These dynamics reinforce gendered divisions in paid employment and reinforce gendered vulnerability in the family.

I have argued that, despite the large differences between the context in which Okin developed her account and the context of some less developed countries in the early twenty-first century, her framework of the basic logic of a gendered cycle of vulnerability well illuminates the situation of many women in them. Moreover, although the gendered structure of paid employment in advanced industrial economies has changed significantly since the time that Okin wrote, the general logic of a gendered cycle of vulnerability still applies.

There is an important set of issues, however, about which Okin's account is nearly silent. I alluded to this issue in my discussion of women home workers in Pakistan. These workers seek or agree to home work, as I said, at least partly because they wish to observe the norms of sexual modesty and stay close to home. For all of its breadth and power, Okin's account hardly mentions sexuality as a variable that conditions women's vulnerability. In many societies of the less developed world, norms that privilege the sexual rights of husbands in relation to wives are explicit and enforced, as are systems that enforce various signs of sexual modesty among women. If women violate these norms, even out of the need to support their families, or because individual men have forced them to, they often face serious negative consequences.

We in the liberated West should not deceive ourselves, moreover, that dynamics of desire and norms of sexuality play no part in the structures of our societies nor contribute to a gendered cycle of vulnerability. Women paid workers face threats of sexual harassment and are liable to stranger as well as acquaintance rape. Continuing feminist research about gender relations and the vulnerabilities they produce and reproduce would benefit from applying Okin's analysis of the mutually reinforcing relations between the supposed private and public spheres. To the interactions between domestic work and paid work should be added a third point, I am suggesting, sexuality. Alongside the gendered division of labor in the family and public life, heterosexual norms, desires, and expectations should be added as factors influencing the decisions and behavior of both men and women.[20] These allegedly private structures of sexuality also profoundly influence the status of women in paid employment and contribute to their vulnerability.

20. For one account of some of the implications of sexuality beyond Okin's view, see my "Reflections on Families in the Age of Murphy Brown: On Justice, Gender and Sexuality," in Iris Marion Young, *Intersecting Voices: Dilemmas of Gender, Political Philosophy and Policy* (Princeton, NJ: Princeton University Press, 1997); in two other papers, I have argued that norms of sexuality are as significant as the division of labor to constituting gender structures. See Young, "Gender as Servility: Thinking about Women as a Group," in *Intersecting Voices*. See also Young, "Lived Body vs. Gender: Reflections on Structural Inequality," in Iris Marion Young, *On Female Body Experience: Throwing Like a Girl and Other Essays* (Oxford: Oxford University Press, 2004).

Contributors

Joshua Cohen is a professor of political science, law, and philosophy at Stanford University and director of the Program in Global Justice.

Alison M. Jaggar is a professor of philosophy and women's and gender studies at the University of Colorado at Boulder.

Robert Keohane is a professor of public and international affairs in the Department of Politics at Princeton University.

Chandran Kukathas is the chair of political theory in the Government Department at the London School of Economics.

David Miller is a professor of political theory at Oxford University.

Rob Reich is an associate professor of political science at Stanford University and director of the Ethics in Society Program.

Nancy Rosenblum is Senator Joseph S. Clark Professor of Ethics in Politics and Government at Harvard University.

Debra Satz is a professor of philosophy and the director of the McCoy Family Center on Ethics in Society at Stanford University.

Ayelet Shachar is Canada Research Chair in Citizenship and Multiculturalism in the Faculty of Law at the University of Toronto.

Mary Lyndon Shanley is a professor of political science at Vassar College.

Cass Sunstein is a professor of law at Harvard University and the Harry Kalven Visiting Professor of Law at the University of Chicago.

John Tomasi is an associate professor of political science and the director of the Political Theory Project at Brown University.

Elizabeth Wingrove is an associate professor in political science at the University of Michigan.

Iris Marion Young was a professor of political science at the University of Chicago.

Bibliography

Abou El Fadl, Khaled. 2005. *The Great Theft: Wrestling Islam from the Extremists.* San Francisco, CA: HarperCollins.

———. 2001. *Speaking in God's Name: Islamic Law, Authority, and Women.* Oxford: Oneworld.

Abu-Odeh, Lama. 1997. "Comparatively Speaking: The 'Honor' of the 'East' and the 'Passion' of the 'West.'" *Utah Law Review* 2:287–307.

Ackerly, Brooke A. 2000. *Political Theory and Feminist Social Criticism.* New York: Cambridge University Press.

———. 1997. "What's in a Design? The Effects of NGO Programme Delivery Choices on Women's Empowerment in Bangladesh." In Goetz, ed., *Getting Institutions Right for Women in Development,* 140–158.

Ackerly, Brooke A., and Susan Moller Okin. 1999. "Feminist Social Criticism and the International Movement for Women's Rights as Human Rights." In Ian Shapiro and Casiano Hacker-Cordón, eds., *Democracy's Edges.* New York: Cambridge University Press.

Al-Hibri, Aziza. 1997. "Islam, Law and Custom: Redefining Muslim Women's Rights." *American University Journal of International Law and Policy* 12:1–44.

Ali, Kecia. 2003a. "Acting on the Frontier of Religious Ceremony: With Questions and Quiet Resolve, a Woman Officiates a Muslim Wedding." In Omid Safi, ed., *Progressive Muslims on Justice, Gender, and Pluralism.* Oxford: Oneworld.

———. 2003b. "Progressive Muslims and Islamic Jurisprudence: The Necessity for Critical Engagement with Marriage and Divorce Law." In Omid Safi, ed., *Progressive Muslims on Justice, Gender, and Pluralism.* Oxford: Oneworld.

Ali, S. S. 1999. *Gender and Human Rights in Islam and International Law: Equal before Allah, Unequal before Man?* The Hague: Kluwer Law International.

Ali, Syed Mumtaz. 2002. "Establishing an Institute for Islamic Justice (Darul Qada)." *Canadian Society of Muslims News Bulletin.* October.

———. 1994. *The Review of the Ontario Civil Justice System: The Reconstruction of the Canadian Constitution and the Case of Muslim Personal/Family Law.* Available at http://muslim-canada .org/submission.pdf.

Alstott, Anne. 2004. "No Exit: What Parents Owe Their Children and What Society Owes Parents." New York: Oxford University Press.

———. 2004. "What We Owe to Parents: How Public Policy Can Support the Hard Work of Raising Children." *Boston Review* 29.2:6–10.

Amod v. Multilateral Motor Vehicle Accidents Fund. 1999. 4 S. Afr. L. R. 1319 (S. Afr. S.C.).

Amott, Teresa L., and Julie Matthaei. 1991. *Race, Gender, and Work: A Multi-Cultural History of Women in the United States.* Boston: South End.

Annan, Kofi. 2004. Address to XV International AIDS Conference in Bangkok, July 11. UN Press Release SG/SM/9418. AIDS/77. Available at http://www.unaids.org.

Arbitration Act. ss. 6, 9.

Arendt, Hannah. 1958. *The Human Condition.* Chicago: University of Chicago Press.

Arneson, Richard. 1999. "Against Equality of Opportunity." *Philosophical Studies* 93:77–112.

Ashfar, Haleh, and Carolynne Dennis. 1992. *Women and Adjustment in the Third World.* London: Palgrave MacMillan.

Auden, W. H. 1970. "Justice." In *A Certain World: A Commonplace Book.* London: Faber and Faber.

Baehr, Amy R. 1996. "Toward a New Feminist Liberalism: Okin, Rawls, Habermas." *Hypatia* 11.1:49–66.

Balakrishnan, Radhika, ed. 2002. *The Hidden Assembly Line.* Bloomfield, CT: Kumarian.

Balakrishnan, Radhika, and Asad Sayeed. 2002. "Subcontracting: The Push-Pull Factor." In Balakrishnan, ed., *The Hidden Assembly Line.*

Barlas, A. 2002. *Believing Women in Islam: Unreading Patriarchal Interpretations of the Qur'an.* Austin: University of Texas Press.

Barry, B. 1988. "Equal Opportunity and Moral Arbitrariness." In N. E. Bowie, ed., *Equal Opportunity.* Boulder, CO: Westview.

Beijing Declaration. 1996. *Platform for Action, Covenant for the New Millennium.* Santa Rosa, CA: Free Hand.

Beneria, Lourdes. 2003. *Gender, Development and Globalization: Economics as if People Mattered.* New York: Routledge.

Benhabib, Seyla. 2002. *The Claims of Culture: Equality and Diversity in the Global Era.* Princeton, NJ: Princeton University Press, 2002.

Benin, M. H., and D. A. Edwards. 1990. "Adolescents' Chores: The Difference between Dual- and Single-Earner Families." *Journal of Marriage and the Family* 12:361–373.

Bhabha, Homi K. 1999. "Liberalism's Sacred Cow." In Joshua Cohen, Matthew Howard, and Martha Nussbaum, eds., *Is Multiculturalism Bad for Women?* Princeton, NJ: Princeton University Press.

Biale, Rachel. 1984. *Women and Jewish Law: An Exploration of Women's Issues in Halakhic Sources.* New York: Schocken.

Bill and Melinda Gates Foundation. http://www.gatesfoundation.org.

Blumstein, Philip, and Pepper Schwartz. 1983. *American Couples.* New York: Monroe.

Bollard v. California Province of the Society of Jesus. 1998. US Dist. LEXIS 7563 (May 15).

Boserup, Ester. 1990. "Economic Change and the Roles of Women." In Tinker, ed., *Persistent Inequalities,* 14–24.

Bowles, Samuel, and Herbert Gintis. 2002. "The Inheritance of Inequality." *Journal of Economic Perspectives* 16.3:3–30.

Boyd, Marion. 2004. *Dispute Resolution in Family Law: Protecting Choice, Promoting Inclusion.* December. Available at http://www.attorneygeneral.jus.gov.on.ca/english/about/pubs/boyd/fullreport.pdf.

Brettschneider, C. "Publicly Justifiable Privacy and Rawls' Political Liberalism: An Analysis of the Rawls/Okin Exchange." Unpublished paper.

Bunch, Charlotte, and Niamh Reilly. 1994. *Demanding Accountability: The Global Campaign and Vienna Tribunal for Women's Human Rights.* Rutgers, NJ: Center for Women's Global Leadership, and New York: United Nations Development Fund for Women.

Canadian Council on American-Islamic Relations. 2004. "Appendix to Review of Ontario's Arbitration Process and Arbitration Act: Supplementary Survey." September.

Canadian Council of Muslim Women. "Letter against the Use of Religious Laws in the Arbitration of Family Law Disputes."

Carby, Hazel. "White Women Listen! Black Feminism and the Boundaries of Sisterhood." 1997. In Rosemary Hennessy and Chrys Ingraham, eds., *Materialist Feminism*. New York and London: Routledge. (Original work 1982)

Carr, Wendell Robert. 1970. Introduction. In John Stuart Mill, *The Subjection of Women*. Cambridge, MA: MIT Press.

Chant, Sylvia. 1997. "Single-Parent Families: Choice or Constraint? The Formation of Female Headed Households in Mexican Shanty Towns." In Nalini Visvanathan, Lynn Duggan, Laurie Nisonoff, and Nan Wiegersman, eds., *The Women, Gender and Development Reader*. London: Zed.

Chiu, Daina C. 1994. "The Cultural Defense: Beyond Exclusion, Assimilation, and Guilty Liberalism." *California Law Review* 82:1053–1125.

Chrisman, Laura, and Patrick Williams. 1994. "Colonial Discourse and Post-Colonial Theory: An Introduction." In Laura Chrisman and Patrick Williams, eds., *Colonial Discourse and Post-Colonial Theory*. New York: Columbia University Press.

City of Boerne v. Flores. 1997. 117 S. Ct. 2157.

Clark, Lorenne, and Lynda Lange. 1979. *The Sexism of Social and Political Theory*. Toronto: University of Toronto Press.

Cohen, G. A. 2001. *If You're an Egalitarian, How Come You're So Rich?* Cambridge, MA: Harvard University Press.

———. 1995. *Self-Ownership, Freedom, and Equality*. Cambridge: Cambridge University Press.

Cohen, Joshua. 2002. "Taking People as They Are?" *Philosophy and Public Affairs* 30.4:363–386.

———. 1992. "Okin on Justice, Gender, and Family." *Canadian Journal of Philosophy* 22.2:263–286.

Coleman, Isobel. 2004. "The Payoff from Women's Rights." *Foreign Affairs*. May–June. Available at http://www.foreignaffairs.org. Accessed May 23, 2005.

Collins, Patricia Hill. 1990. *Black Feminist Thought: Knowledge, Consciousness, and the Politics of Empowerment*. Boston: Unwin Hyman.

Constitution of the Republic of South Africa, 1996. 1996. No. 108. Available at http://www.info.gov.za/constitution/1996/96cons.htm.

"Dear Abby." 2005. *Poughkeepsie Journal* (January 6): D2.

Deveaux, Monique. 2003. "A Deliberative Approach to Conflicts of Culture." *Political Theory* 31:780–807.

Divorce Act. 1985. R.S.C. 1985, c.3 (2nd Supp), ss. 15.2 (amended 1997, c.1, s.2), 15.2(4) (formerly s. 15[5]). (Also amended 1999).

Dryzek, John S. 2005. "Deliberative Democracy in Divided Societies: Alternatives to Agonism and Analgesia." *Political Theory* 33:218–242.

Duguay v. Thompson-Duguay. 2000. OJ, no. 1541 (Ontario Supreme Court of Justice).

Duncan, G., et al. 2005. "The Apple Does Not Fall Far from the Tree." In Samuel Bowles, Herbert Gintis, and M. Osborne Groves, eds., *Unequal Chances: Family Background and Economic Success*. Princeton, NJ: Princeton University Press.

Dworkin, Ronald. 1986. *Law's Empire*. Cambridge, MA: Harvard University Press.

Easterly, William R. 2001. *The Elusive Quest for Growth: Economists' Adventures and Misadventures in the Tropics*. Cambridge, MA: MIT Press.

EEOC v. Catholic University of America. 1994. 856 F. Supp. 1 (DDC 1994), affirmed, 83 F.2d 455 (DC Cir. 1994).

Eisenstein, Zillah. 1988. *The Female Body and the Law*. Berkeley: University of California Press.

Elliot, Kimberly Ann, and Richard B. Freeman. 2003. *Can Labor Standards Improve under Globalization?* Washington, DC: Institute for International Economics.

Ellwood, David. 1988. *Poor Support: Poverty in the American Family*. New York: Basic Books.

Employment Division, Department of Human Services v. Smith. 1990. 494 US 872.

Estlund, David. 1997. "Shaping and Sex." In David Estlund and Martha Nussbaum, eds., *Sex, Preference, and Family*. New York: Oxford University Press.

Family Law Act. 1996. R.S.B.C., c. 128, part 5, ss. 56, 58, 59, 61, 65, 68, 89.

Family Law Act. 1990. ss. 2(4)–(7), 56(5)–(7), R.S.O. ch-F-3 (Ont.)

Firebaugh, Glenn. 1999. "Empirics of World Income Inequality." *American Journal of Sociology* 104.6 (May):1597–1630.

Fishkin, J. 1983. *Justice, Equal Opportunity, and the Family*. New Haven, CT: Yale University Press.

Flax, Jane. 1995. "Race/Gender and the Ethics of Difference: A Reply to Okin's 'Gender Inequality and Cultural Differences.'" *Political Theory* 23.3:500–510.

Folbre, Nancy. 2001. *The Invisible Heart: Economics and Family Values*. New York: New Press.

Franke, Katherine. 2004. "Sexual Tensions of Post-Empire." *Studies in Law, Politics and Society* 33:65–90.

Freeman, Samuel. 2001. "Illiberal Libertarians: Why Libertarianism Is Not a Liberal View." *Philosophy and Public Affairs* 30.2:105–151.

Friedan, Betty. 1963. *The Feminine Mystique*. New York: Norton.

Friedman, Milton. 1962. *Capitalism and Freedom*. Chicago: University of Chicago Press.

Frye, Marilyn. 1996. "The Necessity of Differences: Constructing a Positive Category of Women." *SIGNS: Journal of Women in Culture and Society* 21.4:991–1010.

Fuss, Diana. 1989. *Essentially Speaking: Feminism, Nature and Difference*. New York: Routledge.

Geduldig v. Aiello. 1974. 417 US 484.

Gender Action. http://www.genderaction.org.

Global Fund to Fight AIDS, Tuberculosis, and Malaria. http://www.theglobalfund.org.

Global Fund for Women. www.globalfundforwomen.org.

Goetz, Anne Marie, ed. 1997. Introduction. In Anne Marie Goetz, ed., *Getting Institutions Right for Women in Development*. London: Zed.

Goldman, Alvin I. 1999. *Knowledge in a Social World*. Oxford: Clarendon.

Gornick, Janet C., and Marcia K. Meyers. 2003. *Families That Work: Policies for Reconciling Parenthood and Employment*. New York: Russell Sage Foundation.

Gray, John. 1991. Introduction. In John Stuart Mill, *On Liberty and Other Essays*. New York: Oxford University Press.

Gray, Mark M., Miki Caul Kittilson, and Wayne Sandholtz. 2005. "Women and Globalization: A Study of Quality of Life and Equality Indicators in 180 Nations, 1975–2000." Unpublished manuscript, Department of Political Science, University of California, Irvine.

Greene, Abner. 1993. "The Political Balance of the Religion Clauses." *Yale Law Journal* 102: 1611–1644.

Grewal, Inderpal, and Caren Kaplan, eds. 1994. *Scattered Hegemonies: Postmodernity and Transnational Feminist Practices*. Minneapolis: University of Minnesota Press.

Hafner-Burton, Emilie, and Mark A. Pollack. 2002. "Mainstreaming Gender in Global Governance." *European Journal of International Relations* 8.3:339–373.

Hajjar, Lisa. 2004. "Religion, State Power, and Domestic Violence in Muslim Societies: A Framework for Comparative Analysis." *Law and Social Inquiry* 29:1–38.

Handler, Joel F. 2004. *Social Citizenship and Warfare in the United States and Western Europe*. Cambridge: Cambridge University Press.

Harris, J. R. 1998. *The Nurture Assumption: Why Children Turn Out the Way They Do*. London: Bloomsbury.

Hart, B., and T. R. Risley. 1995. *Meaningful Differences in the Everyday Experience of Young American Children*. Baltimore, MD: Brookes.

Hartshore v. Hartshore. 2004. 1 S.C.R. 550.

Hasan, Zoya. 1994. *Forging Identities: Gender, Communities and the State in India.* Boulder, CO: Westview.

Haslanger, Sally. 2000. "Gender and Race: (What) Are They? (What) Do We Want Them to Be?" *Nous* 34.1:31–55.

Held, David, and Anthony McGrew. 2000. *The Global Transformation Reader: An Introduction to the Globalization Debate.* Cambridge: Polity.

Hélie-Lucas, Marie Aimee. 1994. "The Preferential Symbol for Islamic Identity: Women in Muslim Personal Laws." In Valentine M. Moghadam, ed., *Identity Politics and Women: Cultural Reassertions and Feminisms in International Perspective.* Boulder, CO: Westview.

Heller, Peter S. 2003. "Can the IMF Contribute to the Promotion of the MDGs Relating to Gender Equality?" Speech to a meeting of High-Level Women in International Finance, Economics, and Development, Dubai, September 20. Available at www.imf.org. Accessed October 11, 2004.

Hercus v. Hercus. 2001. OJ, no. 534 (Ontario Supreme Court of Justice).

Heschel, Susannah, ed. 1995. *On Being a Jewish Feminist.* New York: Schocken.

Himmelfarb, Gertrude. 1974. *On Liberty and Liberalism: The Case of John Stuart Mill.* New York: Knopf.

Hirschl, Ran, and Ayelet Shachar. 2004. "Constitutional Transformation, Gender Equality, and Religious/National Conflict in Israel: Tentative Progress through the Obstacle Course." In Beverly Baines and Ruth Rubio-Marin, eds., *Constituting Women: The Gender of Constitutional Jurisprudence.* Cambridge: Cambridge University Press.

Honig, Bonnie. 1999. "My Culture Made Me Do It." In Joshua Cohen, Matthew Howard, and Martha Nussbaum, eds., *Is Multiculturalism Bad for Women?* Princeton, NJ: Princeton University Press.

Howland, Courtney W., ed. 1999. *Religious Fundamentalism and the Human Rights of Women.* New York: St. Martin's.

International Monetary Fund. www.imf.org.

Isaac, Jeffrey. 1995. "The Strange Silence of Political Theory." *Political Theory* 23.4:636–652.

Ivison, Duncan. 2002. *Postcolonial Liberalism.* Cambridge: Cambridge University Press.

Jacquette, Jane S. 1990. "Gender and Justice in Economic Development." In Tinker, ed., *Persistent Inequalities*, 54–69.

Jaggar, Alison M. 2005. "'Saving Amina': Global Justice for Women and Intercultural Dialogue." *Ethics and International Affairs* 19.3:85–105.

———. 1983. *Feminist Politics and Human Nature.* Lanham, MD: Rowman and Littlefield.

Jayaweera, Swarna. 2002. "Women Subcontracted Workers in Sri Lanka." In Balakrishnan, ed., *The Hidden Assembly Line.*

Jeffery, Patricia, and Amrita Basu. 1997. *Appropriating Gender: Women's Activism and Politicized Religion in South Asia.* New York: Routledge.

Juleiga Daniels v. Robin Grieve Campbell NO and Others. 2004. CCT 40/0.

Kabeer, Naila. 1994. *Reversed Realities: Gender Hierarchies in Development Thought.* London: Verso.

Kandiyoti, Deniz, ed. 1991. *Women, Islam and the State.* London: Macmillan.

Kartini, *On Feminism and Nationalism: Kartini's Letters to Stella Zeehandelaar 1899–1903.* Translated with an introduction by Joost Coté. Clayton: Monash Asia Institute, 1995.

Kartini, *Letters from Kartini: An Indonesian Feminist 1900–1904.* Translated by Joost Coté. Melbourne: Hyland House and Monash University, 1992.

Keohane, Robert O. 1984. *After Hegemony: Cooperation and Discord in the World Political Economy.* Princeton, NJ: Princeton University Press.

Khattak, Saab Gull. 2002. "Subcontracted Work and Gender Relations: The Case of Pakistan." In Balakrishnan, ed., *The Hidden Assembly Line.*

Kittay, Eva. 2004. "Falling Short." *Boston Review* 29.2:17.

Koentjaraningrat. *Javanese Culture*. Singapore: Oxford University Press, 1985.

Kymlicka, Will. 1995. *Multicultural Citizenship: A Liberal Theory of Minority Rights*. Oxford: Oxford University Press.

———. 1991. "Rethinking the Family." *Philosophy and Public Affairs* 20.1:77–97.

Lawrence, Sonia N. 2001. "Cultural (In)Sensitivity: The Dangers of a Simplistic Approach to Culture in the Courtroom." *Canadian Journal of Women and the Law* 13:107–136.

Lim, Linda Y. C. 1997. "Capitalism, Imperialism and Patriarchy: The Dilemma of Third-World Women Workers in Multinational Factories." In Nalini Visvanathan, Lynn Duggan, Laurie Nisonoff, and Nan Wiegersman, eds., *The Women, Gender and Development Reader*. London: Zed.

Locke, John. 1988. *Second Treatise*, edited by Peter Laslett. Cambridge: Cambridge University Press.

MacKinnon, Catharine A. 1993. "Difference and Dominance: On Sex Discrimination." In *Feminist Legal Theory*, D. Kelly Weisberg, ed. Philadelphia: Temple University Press.

———. 1987. *Feminism Unmodified*. Cambridge, MA: Harvard University Press.

———. 1983. "Feminism, Marxism, Method and the State: An Agenda for Theory." *SIGNS: Journal of Women in Culture and Society* 515:7.

———. 1982. *Feminist Theory: A Critique of Ideology*, edited by Nannerl Keohane, Michelle Rosaldo, and Barbara Gelpi. Chicago: University of Chicago Press.

Mallaby, Sebastian. 2005. "Saving the World Bank." *Foreign Affairs* (May–June):75–85.

———. 2004. *The World's Banker: A Story of Failed States, Financial Crises, and the Wealth and Poverty of Nations*. New York: Penguin.

Mannheim, Karl. 1940. *Ideology and Utopia*. London: Routledge and Kegan Paul.

Mansbridge, Jane, and Susan Okin. 1993. "Feminism." In Robert E. Goodin and Philip Pettit, eds., *The Blackwell Companion to Contemporary Political Philosophy*. Oxford: Basil Blackwell.

Marital Property Act. 1980. S.N.B., c. M-1.1, s. 41.

Marx, Karl. 1978. "Critique of the Gotha Program." In Robert Tucker, ed., *Marx-Engels Reader*. New York: Norton.

Mason, Andrew. 2001. "Equality of Opportunity, Old and New." *Ethics* 111:760–781.

McClintock, Anne. 1995. *Imperial Leather: Race, Gender and Sexuality in the Colonial Context*. New York: Routledge.

McConnell, Michael. 1990. "Free Exercise Revisionism and the Smith Decision." *University of Chicago Law Review* 57:1109–1153.

Meyer, Mary K., and Elizabeth Prugl, eds. 1999. *Gender Politics in Global Governance*. Lanham, MD: Rowman and Littlefield.

Mihic, Sophia, Stephen Engelmann, and Elizabeth Wingrove. 2005. "Facts, Values, and 'Real' Numbers: Making Sense in and of Political Science." In George Steinmetz, ed., *The Politics of Method in the Human Sciences: Positivism and Its Epistemological Others*. Durham, NC: Duke University Press.

Mill, John Stuart. 1970. *The Subjection of Women*. Cambridge, MA: MIT Press.

Miller, Clark. 2004. "Knowledge, Reason and the Constitution of Democratic Order in International Governance." Unpublished paper, Lafollette School of Public Affairs, University of Wisconsin, Madison.

Miller, David. 2002. "Liberalism, Equal Opportunities, and Cultural Commitments." In P. Kelly, ed., *Multiculturalism Reconsidered*. Cambridge: Polity.

———. 1999. *Principles of Social Justice*. Cambridge, MA: Harvard University Press.

———. 1995. "Complex Equality." In D. Miller and M. Walzer, eds., *Pluralism, Justice, and Equality*. Oxford: Oxford University Press.

Mir-Hosseini, Ziba. 1999. *Islam and Gender: The Religious Debate in Contemporary Iran.* Princeton, NJ: Princeton University Press.

Munoz-Dardé, V. 1999. "Is the Family to Be Abolished Then?" *Proceedings of the Aristotelian Society* 99:37–56.

Narain, Vrinda. 2001. *Gender and Community: Muslim Women's Rights in India.* Toronto: University of Toronto Press.

Narayan, Deepa, Robert Chambers, Meera Kaul Shah, and Patti Petesch. 2000. *Voices of the Poor: Crying Out for Change.* New York: Oxford University Press.

Narayan, Deepa, with Raj Patel, Kai Schafft, Anne Rademacher, and Sarah Koch-Schulte. 2000. *Voices of the Poor: Can Anyone Hear Us?* New York: Oxford University Press.

Narayan, Uma. 1997. *Dislocating Cultures: Identities, Traditions, and Third World Women.* New York: Routledge.

New York Domestic Relations Act. ss. 253, 236B.

Nozick, Robert. 1974. *Anarchy, State, and Utopia.* New York: Basic Books.

Nussbaum, Martha. 2004. "On Hearing Women's Voices: A Reply to Susan Okin." *Philosophy and Public Affairs* 32.2:193–205.

———. 2000. *Women and Human Development: The Capabilities Approach.* Cambridge: Cambridge University Press.

———. 1999. "A Plea for Difficulty." In Joshua Cohen, Matthew Howard, and Martha C. Nussbaum, eds., *Is Multiculturalism Bad for Women?* Princeton, NJ: Princeton University Press.

———. 1992. "A Feminist Theory of Justice." *New York Review of Books* 39.16:43–48.

———. 1990. "Aristotelian Social Democracy." In R. B. Douglas et al., eds., *Liberalism and the Good.* New York: Routledge.

Ofreneo, Rosalinda Pineda, Joseph Y. Lim, and Lourdes Abad Gula. 2002. "The View from Below: Impact of the Financial Crisis on Subcontracted Workers in the Philippines." In Balakrishnan, ed., *The Hidden Assembly Line.*

Okin, Susan Moller. Forthcoming. "Is Multiculturalism Bad for Women? Continuing the Conversation." In Deen Chatterjee, ed., *Feminism, Multiculturalism, and Group Rights.* Oxford: Oxford University Press.

———. 2005. "'Forty Acres and a Mule' for Women: Rawls and Feminism." *Politics, Philosophy and Economics* 4:233–248.

———. 2004. "Justice and Gender: An Unfinished Debate." *Fordham Law Review* 72:1537–1567.

———. 2004. "Response to Martha Nussbaum." Unpublished letter in author's possession (Rosenblum).

———. 2003. "Poverty, Well-Being and Gender: What Counts, Who's Heard?" *Philosophy and Public Affairs* 31.3:280–316.

———. 1999. "Is Multiculturalism Bad for Women?" and "Reply." In Joshua Cohen, Matthew Howard, and Martha Nussbaum, eds., *Is Multiculturalism Bad for Women?* Princeton, NJ: Princeton University Press.

———. 1998a. "Feminism and Multiculturalism: Some Tensions." *Ethics* 108:661–684.

———. 1998b. "Feminism, Women's Human Rights, and Cultural Differences." *Hypatia* 13.2:32–52.

———. 1998c. "Humanist Liberalism." In Nancy L. Rosenblum, ed., *Liberalism and the Moral Life.* Cambridge, MA: Harvard University Press.

———. 1997. "Is Multiculturalism Bad for Women?" *Boston Review* (October–November):25–28.

———. 1996. "Sexual Orientation, Gender, and Families: Dichotomizing Differences," *Hypatia* 11.1:30–48.

———. 1995. "Response to Jane Flax." *Political Theory* 23.3:511–516.

———. 1994a. "Gender Inequality and Cultural Differences." *Political Theory* 22.1:5–24.

———. 1994b. "*Political Liberalism*, Justice, and Gender." *Ethics* 105:23–43.

———. 1990. "Feminism, the Individual, and Contract Theory," *Ethics* 100:658–669.

———. 1989a. *Justice, Gender, and the Family.* New York: Basic Books.

———. 1989b. "Reason and Feeling in Thinking about Justice." *Ethics* 99:229–249.

———. 1988. Editor's Introduction. In John Stuart Mill, *The Subjection of Women.* Indianapolis, IN: Hackett.

———. 1984. "Feminist Theory: A Critique of Ideology." *Ethics* 94:723–724.

———. 1979a. "John Stuart Mill, Liberal Feminist." In *Women in Western Political Thought.* Princeton, NJ: Princeton University Press.

———. 1979b. *Women in Western Political Thought.* Princeton, NJ: Princeton University Press.

———. 1977. "Philosopher Queens and Private Wives: Plato on Women and the Family." *Philosophy and Public Affairs* 6.4:345–369.

Okin, Susan Moller, and Rob Reich. 1999. "Families and Schools as Compensating Agents in Moral Development for a Multicultural Society." *Journal of Moral Education* 28:283–298.

Olsen, Frances E. 1985. "The Myth of State Intervention in the Family." *University of Michigan Journal of Law Reform* 18.4:835–864.

———. 1984. "The Politics of Family Law." *Law and Inequality* 2.1:1–19.

———. 1983. "The Family and the Market: A Study of Ideology and Legal Reform." *Harvard Law Review* 96:1497–1578.

Ontario Women's Justice Network. 2005. "URGENT: Declaration on Religious Arbitration in Family Law." June 1.

Parekh, Bhikhu. 2000. *Rethinking Multiculturalism: Cultural Diversity and Political Theory.* Cambridge, MA: Harvard University Press.

Pateman, Carole. 1988a. "The Patriarchal Welfare State." In Amy Gutman, ed., *Democracy and the Welfare State.* Princeton, NJ: Princeton University Press.

———. 1988b. *The Sexual Contract.* Stanford, CA: Stanford University Press.

Peterson, V. Spike. 2002. "Rewriting (Global) Political Economy as Reproductive, Productive and Virtual (Foucaultian) Economies." *International Feminist Journal of Politics* 4.1:1–30.

Phillips, Anne. 2003. "When Culture Means Gender: Issues of Cultural Defense in the English Courts." *Modern Law Review* 66:510–531.

Pincus, Jonathan R., and Jeffrey A. Winters, eds. 2002. *Reinventing the World Bank.* Ithaca, NY: Cornell University Press.

Presser, Harriet B. 2003. *Working in a 24/7 Economy: Challenges for American Families.* New York: Russell Sage Foundation.

Prins, Gwyn. 2004. "AIDS, Power, Culture and Multilateralism: A Case Study." Paper presented at a Social Science Research Council conference on "Multilateralism under Challenge," Washington, DC, November 29–30.

Prugl, Elizabeth, and Mary K. Meyer. 1999. "Gender Politics in Global Governance." In Meyer and Prugl, eds., *Gender Politics in Global Governance*, 3–16.

Raday, Frances. 2003. "Culture, Religion, and Gender." *International Journal of Constitutional Law* 1:663–715.

Rawls, John. 2001. *Justice as Fairness.* Cambridge, MA: Harvard University Press.

———. 1999a. "The Idea of Public Reason Revisited." In his *Collected Papers*, edited by S. Freeman. Cambridge, MA: Harvard University Press.

———. 1999b. *The Law of Peoples.* Cambridge, MA: Harvard University Press.

———. 1999c. *A Theory of Justice*, rev. ed. Cambridge, MA: Harvard University Press.

———. 1996. *Political Liberalism*, 2nd ed. New York: Columbia University Press.

———. 1971. *A Theory of Justice*, Cambridge, MA: Harvard University Press.

Reich, Rob. 2005. "Comments on Nancy Rosenblum's *Okin's Liberal Feminism as a Radical Political Theory*." Paper presented at Toward a Humanist Justice, Stanford conference, February 2005.

Rich, Bruce. 2002. "The World Bank under James Wolfensohn." In Pincus and Winters, eds., *Reinventing the World Bank*, 26–53.

Risman, B. 1998. *Gender Vertigo: American Families in Transition*. New Haven, CT: Yale University Press.

Roemer, John. 1998. *Equality of Opportunity*. Cambridge, MA: Harvard University Press.

Rosenblum, Nancy L. 2003. "Democratic Families: The 'Logic of Congruence' and Political Identity." *Hofstra Law Review* 32.1:145–170.

———. 1998. *Membership and Morals: The Personal Uses of Pluralism in America*. Princeton, NJ: Princeton University Press.

———. 1997. "Democratic Sex." In David Estlund and Martha Nussbaum, eds., *Sex, Preference, and Family*. New York: Oxford University Press.

Rowe, D. C. 1994. *The Limits of Family Influence: Genes, Experience and Behaviour*. New York: Guilford.

Rubin, Gayle. 1975. "The Traffic in Women: Notes on the 'Political Economy' of Sex." In Rayna R. Reiter, ed., *Toward an Anthropology of Women*. New York: Monthly Review Press.

Russell, J. S. 1995. "Okin's Rawlsian Feminism? Justice in the Family and Another Liberalism." *Social Theory and Practice* 21.3:397–427.

Sachs, Jeffry. 2005. *The End of Poverty: Economic Possibilities for Our Time*. New York: Penguin.

Said, Edward W. 1978. *Orientalism*. New York: Pantheon.

Sala-i-Martin, Xavier. 2002. "The Disturbing 'Rise' of Global Income Inequality." NBER Working Paper 8904, April.

Salzinger, Leslie. 2003. *Genders in Production: Making Workers in Mexico's Global Factories*. Berkeley: University of California Press.

Sandel, Michael. 1982. *Liberalism and the Limits of Justice*. Cambridge: Cambridge University Press.

Sarat, Austin, and Roger Berkowitz. 1994. "Disorderly Differences: Recognition, Accommodation, and American Law." *Yale Journal of Law and the Humanities* 6:285–316.

Saxonhouse, Arlene. 1985. *Women in the History of Political Thought: Ancient Greece to Machiavelli*. New York: Praeger.

Shachar, Ayelet. 2005. "Religion, State, and the Problem of Gender: New Modes of Governance and Citizenship in Diverse Societies." *McGill Law Journal* 50:49–88.

———. 2001. *Multicultural Jurisdictions: Cultural Differences and Women's Rights*. Cambridge: Cambridge University Press.

———. 2000a. "On Citizenship and Multicultural Vulnerability." *Political Theory* 28:64–89.

———. 2000b. "The Puzzle of Interlocking Power Hierarchies: Sharing the Pieces of Jurisdictional Authority." *Harvard Civil Rights–Civil Liberties Law Review* 35.2:385–426.

———. 1998. "Group Identity and Women's Rights in Family Law: The Perils of Multicultural Accommodation." *Journal of Political Philosophy* 6:285–305.

Shanley, Mary Lyndon. 2001. *Making Babies, Making Families*. Boston: Beacon.

———. 1995. "Unwed Fathers' Rights and the Perpetuation of Patriarchy." *Columbia Law Review* 60:60–103.

———. 1989. *Feminism, Marriage and the Law in Victorian England*. Princeton: Princeton University Press.

———. 1981. "Marital Slavery and Friendship: John Stuart Mill's *The Subjection of Women*," *Political Theory* 9:229–247.

Shapiro, Ian. 2005. *The Flight from Reality in the Human Sciences*. Princeton, NJ: Princeton University Press.

———. 1999. *Democratic Justice*. New Haven, CT: Yale University Press.

Simmons, Beth A. Forthcoming. "Women's Equality: Education, Work and Reproduction. In Simmons, *International Human Rights: Law, Politics, and Accountability*. Song, Sarah. 2002. "Majority Norms and Minority Practices: Reexamining the 'Cultural Defense' in American Criminal Law." Paper presented at the American Political Science Association Annual Meeting.

South African Law Reform Commission. 2003. *Project 59: Islamic Marriages and Related Matters*. July. Available at http://wwwserver.law.wits.ac.za/salc/report/report.html.

Spelman, Elizabeth V. 1988. *Inessential Woman: Problems of Exclusion in Feminist Thought*. Boston: Beacon.

Spivak, Gayatri Chakravorty. 1988. "Can the Subaltern Speak?" In Cary Nelson and Lawrence Grossberg, eds., *Marxism and the Interpretation of Culture*. Urbana: University of Illinois Press.

Strawson, John. 1999. "Islamic Law and English Texts." In Eve Darian-Smith and Peter Fitzpatrick, eds., *Laws of the Postcolonial*. Ann Arbor: University of Michigan Press.

Sunder, Madhavi. 2003. "Piercing the Veil." *Yale Law Journal* 112:1399–1472.

Swift, Adam. 2005. "Justice, Luck, and the Family: The Intergenerational Transmission of Economic Advantage from a Normative Perspective." In Samuel Bowles, Herbert Gintis, and M. Osborne Groves, eds., *Unequal Chances: Family Background and Economic Success*. Princeton, NJ: Princeton University Press.

Symington, Alison. 2002. "Re-Inventing Globalization for Women's Rights and Development." In *Reinventing Globalization: Highlights of AWID's 9th International Forum on Women's Rights in Development*. Available at www.awid.org. Accessed October 11, 2004.

Talcott, Molly. 2004. "Gendered Webs of Development and Resistance: Women, Children and Flowers in Bogotá." *SIGNS: Journal of Women in Culture and Society* 29.2:465–490.

Taylor, Charles. 1992. *Multiculturalism and "The Politics of Recognition."* Princeton, NJ: Princeton University Press.

Tinker, Irene, ed. 1990. *Persistent Inequalities: Women and World Development*. New York: Oxford University Press.

Tocqueville, Alexis de. 1955. *The Old Regime and the French Revolution*. New York: Anchor.

UNAIDS. *AIDS Epidemic Update 2004*. http://www.unaids.org.

United Nations. 2000. *United Nations Millennium Declaration*. Available at www.un.org/millenniumgoals.

United Nations Children's Fund. www.unicef.org.

United Nations Development Fund for Women. www.unifem.org.

United Nations General Assembly. 2000. *Report of the Ad Hoc Committee of the Whole of the Twenty-Third Special Session of the General Assembly*. Document number A/S-23/10/Rev. 1.

Unni, Jeemol, and Namrata Bali. 2002. "Subcontracted Women Workers in the Garment Industry in India." In Balakrishnan, ed., *The Hidden Assembly Line*.

Volpp, Leti. 2000. "Blaming Culture for Bad Behavior." *Yale Journal of Law and the Humanities* 12:89–116.

———. 1994. "(Mis)identifying Culture: Asian Women and the 'Cultural Defense.'" *Harvard Women's Law Journal* 17:54–101.

Vosko, Leah F. 2000. *Temporary Work: The Gendered Rise of a Precarious Employment Relationship*. Toronto: University of Toronto Press.

Wadud, Amina. 1999. *Qur'an and Women: Rereading the Sacred Text from a Woman's Perspective*. New York: Oxford University Press.

Walzer, M. 1983. *Spheres of Justice*. New York: Basic Books.

West, Lois A. 1999. "The United Nations Women's Conference and Feminist Politics." In Meyer and Prugl, eds., *Gender Politics in Global Governance*, 177–193.

Williams, B. 1964. "The Idea of Equality." In P. Laslett and W. G. Runciman, eds., *Philosophy, Politics and Society*, 2nd ser. Oxford: Blackwell.

Wingrove, Elizabeth Rose. 2000. *Rousseau's Republican Romance*. Princeton, NJ: Princeton University Press.

———. 1999. "Interpellating Sex." *SIGNS: Journal of Women in Culture and Society* 24.4:869–893.

Witt, Charlotte. 1995. "Anti-Essentialism in Feminist Theory." *Philosophical Topics: Feminist Perspectives on Language, Knowledge, and Reality* 23.2:321–344.

Wolf, Martin. 2004. *Why Globalization Works*. New Haven, CT: Yale University Press.

Wolfensohn, James. 2004. "Securing the 21st Century." James Wolfensohn's Annual Meeting Address, October 3. Available at www.worldbank.org. Accessed October 11, 2004.

World Bank. 2004. "Implementing the Bank's Gender Mainstreaming Strategy: Second Annual Monitoring Report, FY 03." January 29. Available at www.worldbank.org. Accessed October 12, 2004.

———. 2003. *Gender and Equality: The Millennium Development Goals*. Washington, DC: World Bank.

———. 2002. *Integrating Gender into the World Bank's Work: A Strategy for Action*. Washington, DC: World Bank.

———. 2001. *Engendering Development*. Oxford: Oxford University Press.

———. 2000–2001. *World Development Report*. New York: Oxford University Press.

World Health Organization. 2004. *Annual Report, 2004*. Available at http://www.who.int/whr/2004/en/03_chap1_en.pd.

Young, Iris Marion. 2004. "Lived Body vs. Gender: Reflections on Structural Inequality." In her *On Female Body Experience: Throwing Like a Girl and Other Essays*. Oxford: Oxford University Press.

———. 1997a. "Gender as Servility: Thinking about Women as a Group." In her *Intersecting Voices: Dilemmas of Gender, Political Philosophy and Policy*. Princeton, NJ: Princeton University Press.

———. 1997b. *Intersecting Voices: Dilemmas of Gender, Political Philosophy and Policy*. Princeton, NJ: Princeton University Press.

Young v. Northern Illinois Conference of United Methodist Church. 1994. 21 F.3d 184, 7th Cir.

Yuval-Davis, Nira, and Floya Anthias, eds. 1989. *Woman-Nation-State*. London: Macmillan.

Zuckerman, Elaine, and Wu Qing. 2003. "Reforming the World Bank: Will the New Gender Strategy Make a Difference?" Available at http://www.genderaction.org.

Index